HYPER / TEXT / THEORY

EDITED BY

George P. Landow

HYPER / TEXT / THEORY

THE JOHNS HOPKINS

UNIVERSITY PRESS

BALTIMORE & LONDON

I N M E M O R I A M

J A M E S H . C O O M B S

Printed in the United States of America on acid-free paper

The Johns Hopkins University Press
2715 North Charles Street
Baltimore, Maryland 21218-4319
The Johns Hopkins Press Ltd., London

ISBN 0-8018-4837-7
ISBN 0-8018-4838-5 (pbk.)

Library of Congress Cataloging-in-Publication Data will be found at the end of this book.
A catalog record for this book is available from the British Library.

HYPER / TEXT / THEORY

What's a Critic to Do?: Critical Theory in the Age of Hypertext

George P. Landow

1

After the technologists come the theoreticians.

—Friedrich A. Kittler

Convergences

Hypertext, an information technology consisting of individual blocks of text, or lexias, and the electronic links that join them, has much in common with recent literary and critical theory. For example, like much recent work by poststructuralists, such as Roland Barthes and Jacques Derrida, hypertext reconceives conventional, long-held assumptions about authors and readers and the texts they write and read. Electronic linking, which provides one of the defining features of hypertext, also embodies Julia Kristeva's notions of intertextuality, Mikhail Bakhtin's emphasis upon multivocality, Michel Foucault's conceptions of networks of power, and Gilles Deleuze and Félix Guattari's ideas of rhizomatic, "nomad thought." The very idea of hypertextuality seems to have taken form at approximately the same time that poststructuralism developed, but their points of convergence have a closer relation than that of mere contingency, for both grow out of dissatisfaction with the related phenomena of the printed book and hierarchical thought. For this reason even thinkers like Hélène Cixous, who seem resolutely opposed to technology, can call for ideas, such as *l'écriture feminine,* that appear to find their instantiation in this new information technology.

I wrote *Hypertext: The Convergence of Contemporary Critical Theory and Technology* in part to convince literary theorists and computer scientists that they have interests in common and might therefore wish to talk to one another now and then. One can take several approaches to these extremely suggestive similarities between theory and electronic computing. One can take advantage of these convergences—or rather, interrelations—to enable workers in each field to help each other, since hypertext has the potential to serve as a laboratory for theory while theory illuminates the design, use, and cultural effects of the new electronic technologies. As the essays in this volume demonstrate, one can investigate the relations of hypertext and theory in many different ways. Charles Ess uses the work of Jürgen Habermas and the Frankfurt School to examine this new information technology's potential for true democratization while Stuart Moulthrop, author of the hypertext novel *Victory Garden* and many studies of the technology's implications for culture, uses Deleuze and Guattari as the point of departure for his own skeptical ruminations on the relations of hypertext and political power.

Other essays in this volume consider the notions, crucial to hypertext, of linearity and nonlinearity. Espen Aarseth, who examines various kinds of nonlinearity, places hypertext within a framework created by other forms of electronic textuality, including that generated computationally at the reader's direct or indirect prompting. In "Socrates in the Labyrinth," David Kolb approaches the idea of nonlinear textuality by inquiring what hypertext implies for philosophy and philosophical discourse. In contrast to Kolb, who investigates the matter of hypertextual argument, J. Yellowlees Douglas, Gunnar Liestøl, and Mireille Rosello use contemporary theory to come to terms with hypertext narrative. Thus, Douglas draws upon reader-response criticism to illuminate it, whereas Liestøl applies the ideas of Gerard Genette and Ludwig Wittgenstein and Rosello those of Michel de Certeau. Terence Harpold, a hypertext programmer who has previously written on the relation of hypertext to Bakhtin, Derrida, and Jacques Lacan, continues his investigations of the medium with particular relation to the hypertextual fiction of Michael Joyce. Finally, drawing upon Derrida, Lacan, and Wittgenstein, and his own conception of teletheory and heuretics, Gregory Ulmer offers an example of the new form of writing that hypertextuality demands.

Any discussion of the cultural implications of hypertext and hypermedia requires, first of all, that one have some idea of both the general meaning of these terms and also the specific embodiments of them in actual systems. Therefore, before moving on to these more detailed discussions of the relations between hypertext and theory, I propose to examine in what ways available systems and the materials created within them fulfill the promise of this new information technology. Since most people, particularly humanists, first come upon the general idea of hypertext in the form of Apple Computer's HyperCard, the best way to begin involves a few comments on this particular system.

Although the first version of HyperCard, which came installed free on many Macintosh computers, introduced more people to the possibilities of hypertext than any other program, it does not represent true hypertext, and it therefore has had the unfortunate effect of conveying too limited an idea of what this powerful technology is or might become. A clever and extremely handy data base manager, HyperCard 1.0 relied, as its name suggests, on a card metaphor; and such reliance, although suited to electronic address books and many other valuable applications, meant that the text of each lexia had to fit within the narrow scope of a single card, which did not, unlike most word-processing programs, have scrolling fields. Furthermore, like some other early attempts to create a hypertext system, HyperCard 1.0 displayed only a single card at a time, thereby preventing author and reader from capitalizing upon the larger screens that have increasingly become available and greatly limiting the potential of hypertext. HyperCard 1.0 also relied upon unidirectional links between single cards, and so offered only primitive navigational assistance and had other limitations to testing the full capacities of the medium. In particular, it had no provision for working on networks. I point out these limitations not to criticize this program, which has done so much to attract people to the idea of hypertextuality, but to urge that we not conceive of hypertext solely in terms of HyperCard.

My colleague Paul Kahn reminds me that HyperCard 2.0 is essentially a powerful erector set from which to build hypertext systems. Examples employing it include Geoffrey Bilder's Abulafia, Keyboard, and the Voyager Company's Expanded Book. Other hypertext systems for the Macintosh include Eastgate System's Storyspace, to which all the humanities-oriented materials originally created for Intermedia have been transferred.[1] Other systems exist for UNIX and MS-DOS, including Toolbook and Linkway for IBM personal computers and their clones, and OWL's Guide, Interleaf's WorldView, Electronic Book Technologies' DynaText, Xerox's Acquanet, and SEPIA, from the Darmstadt Integrated Publication and Information Systems Institute.

Reading Leather-bound Volumes in the Bathtub; or, The Hypertext Reading Site

These remarks about the need to separate the general concept of hypertext, particularly during the early stages of its development, from its specific embodiments lead me to caution that one must also distinguish between digital textuality and the experience of reading it on a particular apparatus. A central fact about the digital word lies in its intrinsic separation of text from the physical object by means of which it is read. Friedrich A. Kittler points out that in contrasting different cultural epochs, one must distinguish "not emotional dispositions but systems. Information networks can be described only when they are contrasted with one another."[2] One must take care, however, to contrast information regimes and their related cultural effects at significant, rather than at trivial or transient, sites. I make this point because many people confronting electronic textuality confuse the experience of reading it with the particular technology on which it is read. One encounters two forms of reservations about reading electronic text: "You can't read an electronic book in the bathtub" and "How can you compare reading text on a screen with the experience of reading a leather-bound volume? Reading on a computer takes away the pleasure of encountering the physical object."

Given the computer-monitor technology most humanists have encountered, these reactions make perfect sense: reading a text on a personal computer or mainframe terminal both constrains one (by forcing one to read at a particular physical location) and, like most cheap paperback books, also removes a good deal of the physical pleasure associated with what many academics purport to hold as their ideal of the book—the luxuriously leather-bound object. Second, this entirely understandable reaction misses the central point about electronic textuality—its fundamental distinction from the object on which it is read. At present, when most humanists compare the experience of reading electronic text on a computer screen to that of reading a printed page, they concentrate, with good reason, almost entirely on the presentation mode, and they therefore point out several aspects of their experience that have to do more with current computer technology than with electronic text itself. For this reason, I emphasize the crucial distinction between electronic textuality and its display on changing technology, and I shall also suggest several ways in which the act of reading will change as the nature of the reading site or mechanism changes.

First there is the issue of portability, and then that of a reduced or denatured physicality—neither of which, as I shall show, necessarily derives from electronic textuality itself. I have little interest, I must admit, in reading books, leather-bound or otherwise, in a bathtub—particularly since that time I lent friends a prized first edition of a 1950s science fiction classic that ended up in their tub. Nonetheless, as one who has always done a good deal of reading reclining on sofas or stretched out on a bed, I certainly sympathize with those who protest that they do not like to read at a computer screen. Several technological developments, however, promise to make radical changes in the reading site of electronic text. New laptop computers, which already approach the size of a large book, have begun to change the nature and location of computer use, and I already encounter students who come to classes and seminars with Apple Powerbooks on which they consult and take notes within hypertext webs. Another innovation is the wireless modem, which permits one to move about in a particular location, holding a computer approximately the size of a printed book while remaining electronically connected to a server computer and the data bases it supports. This technology, which permits one to read in a bathtub, if that is what one really wants to do, promises a true electronic book—if by *book* one means a reading site that bears a strong physical resemblance to the objects we now use to read.

The advent of pen-based computing, which has already appeared in the hands of people who deliver packages, promises to bring the full powers of the reader-author to the miniature portable computer. Although still in its infancy, pen-based computing shows how a supposedly superseded, once-dominant information technology can blend with electronic textuality. Beginning with the recognition that for many applications handwriting proves more convenient than using a keyboard, pen-based computing permits one to use a stylus to add notes to or otherwise modify computer text. On a system I have used, one deletes a letter or word by drawing through it a line that ends with a squiggle—essentially, the conventional proofreader's delete symbol—and one indicates boldface text by writing the letter *b* over it. Although keyboarding seems far more efficient than handwriting as a means of adding large quantities of text, handwriting provides a convenient way to edit and take notes.

In the examples of pen-based computing that I have seen, the reading and writing functions take place at the same site, but changes in computer-display technology suggest that one can vary either site or use multiple ones to suit the need and occasion. Expensive fine-grained color monitors already exist that provide as aesthetically pleasing a presentation of text as most printed books. But recent developments, some already in wide use, show that in the future readers will not necessarily confront alphanumeric text and images sitting before a monitor. In many educational institutions and other organizations people already use color projection of computer information when making presentations before large groups. In my course on hypertext and literary theory my students and I make use of color projection. Ceiling-mounted projection systems, which permit one both to move about in a room without blocking the projector and to read from various vantage points, free the reader from the terminal. One can expect that eventually some form of this technology will liberate all readers of the digital word from the need to sit in front of computer screens.

Another replacement for the conventional computer monitor takes the form of headsets containing a tiny monitor no more than an inch by an inch that, reflected in a mirror, appears very large and very legible. Such extremely lightweight head-mounted devices, which SONY has developed for television, provide another possible way of replacing the computer monitor in certain situations.

Holography promises a third, more distant replacement for video display terminals. Combined with image-processing software, holographic, variable-size images could permit the art historian to place an object within a variety of settings. One could, for example, represent objects full size and within representations of their actual settings and in their actual conditions at various times in their history. In fact, one can already use powerful workstations that produce projected images to examine individual works that can be examined with varied lighting and contrast and from multiple vantage points. In the example that I saw at Princeton University in 1991, such a system projected giant images of Piero della Francesca's fresco cycle, *The Story of the True Cross,* located in the chapel of San Francesco in Arrezo, Italy.[3] The site of the church is difficult to reach, and the paintings often difficult, if not impossible, to see in detail without the scaffolding with which the photographs were made; but using digital images derived from these photographs, the viewer can move through the church, studying the work from different vantage points in relation to individual walls and from different heights above the floor. With such technology, which also permits the cultural historian to experience objects as they appear at different historical moments, one can examine works within the varying contexts provided by changing settings, condition of the object, and so on.

Mode and Genre in Hypertextuality

Many who first encounter the notion of hypertext assume that linking does it all, and in an important sense they are correct: linking is the most important fact about hypertext, particularly as it contrasts to the world of print technology. Similarly when considering the general idea of the electronic book, one correctly emphasizes that it exists as electronic codes and not as physical marks on a physical surface; it is always virtual, always a simulacrum for which no physical instantiation exists. Nonetheless, central as these points are, one can derive neither political nor literary implications from these bare, if enormously suggestive, definitions alone, for the actual instantiations of such systems in particular technologies have a major influence.

At the worst, hypertext enthusiasts endow it with such utopian promise that Norman Meyrowitz, one of the authors of the classic "Reading and Writing the Electronic Book," entitled his keynote address at a major hypertext conference "Hypertext—Does It Reduce Cholesterol, Too?"[4] In educational terms, writers who become enthralled by the notion of hypertext linking, which is, admittedly, a crucial supplement to the print text, sometimes write as if linking would do it all—whatever the "all" is that they wish to achieve. In this way they seem much like authors new to the world of print might have, believing that that once-novel information technology could do all of the writer's task, rather than simply assisting in particular ways, and that the writer no longer had to pay attention to matters of rhetoric and organization.

Similarly, those with dystopian expectations, or even just healthy skepticism, again try to extrapolate negative effects from a few facts or features of generic hypertextuality. Of course, extrapolating big effects from little bits of data is something that we in the humanities do very well—it practically defines our enterprise. Like Carlyle, Ruskin, and Arnold, who delighted in virtuoso acts of interpretation derived, ultimately, from Old Testament prophecy, contemporary critical theorists like deMan, Barthes, and Derrida establish their particular ethos by brilliantly revealing the unexpected presence of mice in molehills. It's what we do best. Anyone writing of the literary, cultural, and political implications of hypertext, however, needs first to have some practical experience with hypertext systems and with documents on those systems. One can no more usefully speak with confidence of generic hypertext than of generic print. First of all, not all printed text appears in books. An enormous amount of it comes to us as business cards and forms, order blanks, restaurant menus, advertising inserts in newspapers, posters, railroad and bus schedules, and the like. Even if one counts newspapers, magazines, and comic books as books, literature and the literary book turn out to occupy but a tiny proportion of print production: by far the greater number and proportion of books are telephone directories and other institutional and public lists, repair manuals, merchandise and component catalogues, and so on.

These kinds of divisions according to application and audience pertain to hypertexts as well. In fact, some of the greatest interest in these new information technologies arises in applications, such as aircraft repair manuals, in which the limitations of book technology have long been apparent. The repair manual for a modern airliner runs to 100,000 pages, of which very many, say 25 percent, change each year. Since FAA regulations require aircraft mechanics to consult these manuals for changes and government advisories each time they carry out any repair or maintenance procedure, they probably devote a greater portion of their work day to consulting books than does the average instructor in a department of literature, much of whose time is spent on lecturing, grading papers, advising, attending committee meetings, and carrying out other activities in which professional reading plays little or no part. Some estimates claim that aircraft mechanics spend more than half their working day performing research in the form of consulting printed text. Therefore, any improvement in the way maintenance workers can obtain information promises to save both the individual worker's time and also the enormous financial and ecological cost of producing frequently replaced paper documentation. Companies like Boeing Aircraft Corporation have therefore devoted great attention to hypertext repair manuals, which permit the maintenance worker to trace the history of a particular component or system and also to follow out its connections to other components.

That aircraft, airline, and other industries whose technicians must perform as knowledge workers have turned their attention to hypertext manuals has several implications for literary and cultural theory, the first of which is that many people not usually thought of as professional readers or knowledge workers will spend many hours of their working lives experiencing electronic text long before most scholars of literature and culture become aware that it exists. Another is that if those interested in literature and culture do not make their needs felt, the only hypertext systems available will have been shaped by the needs of those not primarily concerned with creating, studying, or disseminating cultural artifacts.

Therefore, before considering some of the problems and possibilities that hypertext raises for literary and cultural theory, I propose to examine two distinct, if related, modes or genres of hypertext—those that are system- or technology-determined and those that are not. System-determined hypertext takes three forms, each of which has radically different implications for reader and author. Although writers concerned with literary and cultural applications of this new information technology seem never to mention the fact, some forms of hypertext that are not chiefly text- or image-based concern logical and conceptual links and are meant to assist decision making. As far as I have been able to determine, some early attempts at these kinds of hypertext systems, which held the greatest appeal for workers in computer and cognitive science and in business, seem to have much in common with early structuralism—including its rigidity and its consequent difficulty of application to cultural or other actual phenomena. Even though such hypertext logic analyzers strike me as having too much in common with Shandy's abstract and always-deferred plan for educating his unfortunate son, one should at least point out that a number of workers in the field see them as a significant branch of hypertext. More recent work, like Xerox PARC's Acquanet, the Darmstadt SEPIA system, and Marc and Jocelyne Nanard's MacWeb, combines logical or categorizing link structures with other features and seems to offer a great deal of promise.[5]

More immediately relevant to those concerned with the implications of hypertext for literary and cultural studies, however, are two other principal divisions, those between networked and stand-alone systems and those between read-only hypertext, in which readers' contributions are limited to choosing their own reading paths, and hypertext in which readers can also add text, links, or both. The stand-alone implementations, like HyperCard, that constitute most people's experience of hypertext represent only a small portion of what characterizes hypertext, which offers far more than the "electronic book." Furthermore, applications that only provide large amounts of read-only memory (CD-ROMs), whether they employ the analogue technology of laser disks or the digital technology of compact disks, do not meet the full requirements of true networked hypertext technology either. In fact, if one places writing, book technology, CD-ROM, and networked digital information technology on a spectrum, in one particularly important way CD-ROM and laser disks appear closer to print than to digital technology. Although conventional floppy disks and CD-ROMs store information in digital form, they do so in a manner that, like print and writing, requires the physical transfer of the record to the reading site. True, one can place each of these digital storage media on a server, so that more than one reader can potentially make use of them, but unless the information is transferred to computer memory, it cannot take advantage of the crucial fact about digitality—that digitized text and other data can be manipulated simultaneously by many users.

Because CD-ROM technology exemplifies the ways digitized information increases the scholar's ability to access information quickly, it provides a convenient entrance to our subject. Using color images stored in the form of digital coding (or digitized), an art historian can use information in ways impossible with print technology, laser disk, or videotape. These new possibilities arise because digital technology

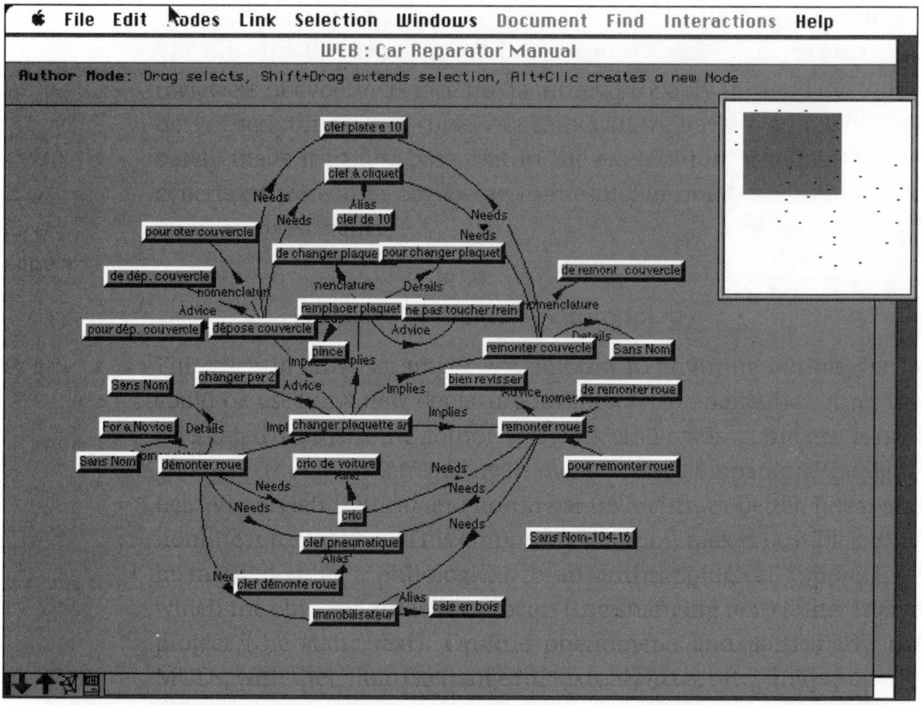

MacWeb, a concept-based hypertext with typed links. Created by Jocelyne and Marc Nanard, MacWeb permits authors to create link types. For example, this hypertext version of an automobile repair manual employs the following typed (or categorizing) links: "implies," "needs," "nomenclature," and "details." At the upper right of the Web View appears the MacWeb Skyview, which orients users by showing them both the structure of the entire hypertext document and the particular section of it at which they are currently looking. This electronic manual clearly exemplifies a hypertext with network, rather than axial, structure.

permits virtually instant retrieval of images or other data from anywhere on a disk, because a search brings one directly to the location (the address) of an image rather than requiring a sequential scan through hundreds or even thousands of images. CD-ROMs already exist for entire museum collections, and one readily envisages placing on them the entire oeuvres of single artists or entire schools. When combined with computer technology, such devices permit one to work with images much as classicists now work with texts. Putting on a single compact disk the entire Thesaurus Linguae Grecae, which contains more than 95 percent of all archaic and classical Greek texts, has permitted classicists to relate any particular word or phrase to its every occurrence in ancient Greek.[6] This capacity to create customized word lists has enabled scholars to investigate particularly thorny problems in dating, attribution, stylistic development, and translation. In this and other ways, electronic computing has dramatically amplified the range of problems scientists can tackle, and it has already begun to have the same effect on the humanistic disciplines.

CD-ROM technology, which tantalizes art historians and other students of culture by its promise of near-instant access to large bodies of visual information, nonetheless represents only a crude and costly hint of things to come, because it brings with it some of the basic problems of book technology. In particular, present disks require a separate player for each user, and they also require frequent physical changing, since any individual disk, particularly those produced as catalogues by individual institutions, contains a necessarily limited amount of information. For example, even if there existed CD-ROMs of the Tate Gallery and Manchester City Art Galleries collections, anyone working with, say, the relationship of early Netherlandish painting and nineteenth-century Pre-Raphaelitism would either have to change disks frequently —or have access to a system with several CD-ROM players working simultaneously. Furthermore, the information on these disks provides only a resource for scholarly reference, not a means for writing, because present technology does not permit users either to append notes to specific images or to incorporate them into their own texts.

The solution to many of these problems involves creating more efficient means of storing and retrieving digitized information of the kind already contained on CD-ROMs. Essentially, one must do for visual information what one already does far more easily for verbal information—store it in a central repository (data base) so that one can then share it among many readers by means of a network that joins this data base and the devices (terminals) on which readers examine verbal and graphic information. The great and defining power of digital technology lies in its capacity to store information and then provide countless virtual versions of it to readers, who then can manipulate, copy, and comment upon it without changing the material seen by others. When combined with electronic networks, digitized information technology produces a new kind of information medium in which reading, writing, and publication take on new characteristics.[7]

Networks capable of limited versions of such information exchange already exist within individual laboratories, classrooms, libraries, and throughout entire universities. Networks capable of interactive computing (as opposed to batch processing) already stretch across oceans and continents to join universities, museums, libraries, and other institutions around the world, thereby permitting readers in one location—say, Providence, Rhode Island—to consult card catalogues of institutions located in Berkeley, California, or Cambridge, Massachusetts.[8] Such a network, the Internet, already permits electronic mail and transfer of data that includes fully formatted text and text with images. In fact, many of the essays in this volume, including those by Espen Aarseth and Gunnar Liestøl, who live in Norway, traveled back and forth over the Internet using an ftp (file transfer protocol) program called Fetch developed at Dartmouth College. By clicking (mousing down) upon a few menu buttons, authors who were working on a Macintosh connected to the Internet uploaded documents written using Microsoft Word, automatically converting them to a format suited to electronic transfer, and placed them in a folder on a machine at Brown University's Institute for Research in Information and Scholarship (IRIS); when I retrieved (or downloaded) their essays, they automatically opened on my computer in Microsoft Word, with all their original formatting preserved. After reading the essays, I added comments and queries and placed them back in the same folder for the authors to retrieve them.

The combination of electronic textuality and high-speed, broadband networks, which enormously increases the rate of transferring and hence sharing of documents, promises ultimately to reconfigure all aspects of scholarly communication, particularly those involving education and publication. Three examples of my recent experiences with scholarly communication via the Internet will show what I mean. First, using a combination of electronic mail and Fetch, I direct or serve as a reader for doctoral dissertations at universities in the United States and Europe. At the most basic level of simple practicality, the new information technology changes the nature of my teaching because it enables me to carry out professional responsibilities that would otherwise prove difficult or even impossible. One indication of the importance of electronic mail and text-transfer technology is that I probably stay in closer contact with geographically distant students to whom I am linked by Internet than with some at my own institution who do not use it. In other words, the digital word reconfigures education, continuing the process begun with the invention first of writing and then of printing, and frees the student from the need to be in the physical presence of the teacher. This freedom, which comes at a certain cost, also has the compensatory advantage of sharing scarce resources among institutions and providing the foundation for what some educators call "distant learning," learning outside colleges and universities. The most important advantage of such technology lies in the way it creates new kinds of electronic communities capable of nurturing intellectual and other concerns.

An instance of such electronic community appears in my second example, which also involves Fetch and the Internet. Using this same technology, I obtained two essays from Australian sources. An Australian friend known only through extensive electronic communications placed one essay in my folder at IRIS, realizing I would find it of interest; the other I downloaded from a server at Deakin University, in Geelong, Victoria, Australia. I find several things about the way I came upon and then read these essays typical of the manner in which electronic textuality changes our relation to the institutions of scholarship: (1) I read through both essays entirely on line, in one case adding my own comments or boldfacing a few passages for easier reference at a later time; (2) one of the authors was an American teaching at a university in the Midwest, but I only read her essay and began to communicate with her via electronic mail after encountering it "in" Australia; (3) this essay was one of ten that Chris Bigum and Bill Green used as the center of their "electronic salon," based at Deakin University, "on the re-articulation of education and the new information technologies" that took place during November 1992.

As I have pointed out elsewhere in a discussion of electronic conferences, the potent combination of the digital word and the electronic network fundamentally reconceives notions of scholarly communication, creating new forms of it:

> Before networked computing, scholarly communication relied chiefly upon moving physical marks on a surface from one place to another with whatever cost in time that movement required. Networked electronic communication so drastically reduces the time scale of moving textual information that it produces new forms of textuality. Just as transforming print text to electronic coding radically changed the temporal scale involved in *manipulating* texts, so too has it changed the temporal scale of *communication*. Networked electronic communication has both dramatically speeded up scholarly communication and created new forms of it.[9]

The very speed of networked electronic communication changes our experience of publication.

My third example relates to the papers from the Deakin electronic conference in another way. One part of that conference, as we have seen, involved selecting and then in effect publishing essays by placing them on a server. Then participants from Australia, Asia, Europe, and North America used electronic mail to comment, often at length, upon the individual essays and upon other readers' responses to them. The electronic conference "produces a multiauthored textuality that the participant experiences as blending important characteristics of speech and writing. In some ways the electronic conference appears closer to speech than to written language, for it possesses the transiency and something of the immediacy of speech. Yet, though such conferences seem more distinctly occasional and therefore more ephemeral than writing, they exist in the form of alphanumeric codes and therefore have some of the fixity and potential permanence of any written record" (Landow, "Electronic Conferences," 350). Each of these three examples, I must emphasize, concerns the digital word in general but not the specific form of hypertext.

The fundamental importance of networked hypertext in fulfilling the potential of the medium only appears when one adds its last crucial element—the ability of the reader to add links, comments, or both. Vannevar Bush, Douglas Englebart, Ted Nelson, Andries van Dam, and the other authors of "Reading and Writing the Electronic Book" all emphasized that in hypertext the function of reader merges with that of author and the division between the two is blurred (Landow, *Hypertext,* 6–7). The particular importance of networked textuality—that is, textuality written, stored, and read on a computer network—appears when technology transforms readers into reader-authors or "wreaders," because any contribution, any change in the web created by one reader, quickly becomes available to other readers. This ability to write within a particular web in turn transforms comments from private notes, such as one takes in margins of one's own copy of a text, into public statements that, especially within educational settings, have powerfully democratizing effects. J. Hillis Miller claims that "the electronic book will be potentially democratic and anti-canonical not because of some ideologically motivated decision, but by virtue of its technological nature."[10] Since not all current hypertext systems include the crucial democratizing features that permit readers to contribute to the text, theorists must take care not to confuse, as Miller himself does, the effects of read-only and read-and-write systems.[11]

Author-created Hypertext Modes

In addition to such system-generated differences in the individual hypertext document, others derive from their authors, genres, and purposes. Hypertext, therefore, can appear in the form of a single work, which may in turn be a web written for reading on line, one adapted from a print work, or one adapted with such amplification as to become a hybrid; and a web can also take the form of groupings of such subsets. These distinctions derive from the limitations of current data-storage technology, which encourages configuring sets of lexias into discrete webs or electronic books. Even so, webs created in systems like Dynatext and Storyspace permit readers to follow links from one web to another, thereby immediately blurring their edges.

I confronted the strengths and weaknesses of a hypertext version of the electronic book when converting *Hypertext* first to Intermedia and then to Storyspace and Dynatext. The original book described several instances of how differently I would have written it in hypertext rather than in a standard word processor (78–87). These differences chiefly derived from two features of Intermedia that reconfigured habits of argumentation. The first was the system's ability to link a single passage in a particular text to several other lexias, and the second involved the tendency of any lexia, even a converted endnote, to become equal in importance to the block of text to which it refers. Converting the entire book led me to encounter other issues as well.

First, in creating this example of adaptive hypertext, I had to decide what such an adaptation would include and how much extra text, if any, would appear. One can take at least four different approaches to creating a hypertextual version of a printed book, the first of which—and to me the least interesting—requires little more than placing the text of the print volume in an electronic environment that, like World-View or the Voyager Expanded Book, maintains original page layout and numbering. The second approach involves replacing the page presentation with one more suitable to a monitor and then adapting the print version in minor, but interesting, ways such as converting all the notes to lexias. Even in hypertextualizing the endnotes there are several alternatives. One can simply treat the endnotes for the entire volume as a separate document and link sentences that bear note numbers to the relevant notes. Given the tendency of hypertext to atomize documents into separate lexias, a more appropriate method requires placing single notes in individual lexias and linking them to the relevant portions of the so-called main text. A minimalist hypertext conversion further retains the original sections of the published book as basic units and then links them to the table of contents and, following a linear order, to each other.

A last, more challenging and more interesting translation requires both taking greater advantage of the possibilities of hypertext and also including the kind of materials a hypertext version demands, including works by other scholars, comments by reviewers, and materials created by my students, who have used both the published book and two versions of it in hypertext. To take full advantage of the capacities of hypertext as a new form of writing, the original form of *Hypertext* had to change, becoming even less a linear argument and more one that took advantage of network organization. To this end, Gene Yu, my research assistant, and I made three basic changes in the original. First, even though I had written *Hypertext* in a manner somewhat analogous to that I used when writing in a hypertext environment and had divided each chapter into sections, these individual sections would each have to be divided into smaller lexia. Second, believing the table of contents inadequate to guide the hypertext reader, I added overviews for hypertext and critical theory. One could also add overviews for narrative, information technology, and conceptions of the self, and for individual critical theorists, particularly those who play important roles in either the original book or the materials later created by others (Bakhtin, Barthes, Baudrillard, Deleuze, Derrida, Guattari, Haraway, Lyotard, Miller, and so on), as well as for a third category, writers of fiction and poetry discussed in the original book or materials added by classes. Obvious possibilities here include Borges, Calvino, Cortàzar, and Coover.

Whereas the first three approaches involve a read-only, essentially fixed version of the text, the fourth, which more nearly matches the book's claims about hypertext, presents it in a form in which readers can add to the text and comment upon it. In both the original classroom version, which employed Intermedia, and the more recent one, which used Storyspace, readers have the right to add links, comments, and even their own subwebs.

Since I wanted to create a hypertextual translation of *Hypertext* in part for use in English 116, my Brown University course on hypertext and literary theory, I needed it to realize the potential of the medium as fully as possible. However, hypertexts do not have to take such elaborate forms. A simple, but practicable form of an amplified hypertext far simpler than my project appears in the Transparent Language presentations of French, German, and Latin texts. In essence, each of these electronic presentations, which come in versions for the IBM PC and Macintosh computers, presents a text linked to a dictionary, a grammar reference work, and grammatical, though not otherwise interpretive, commentary. Thus, to use the Transparent Language version of Franz Kafka's "Das Urteil," which Lisa Svec created using a translation by Willa and Edwin Muir, one places a disk containing the basic program, the electronic text, and supplements for a particular work into the disk drive of one's computer and either uses it there or copies it to one's hard drive. Clicking upon the icon for "Das Urteil," one starts up the Transparent Language system and then opens the story, the text of which appears in a large window at screen left. At the right of and below the text appear five smaller windows, labeled (top to bottom) "Comments," "Word Meaning," "Word Grouping" (or occasionally "Phrase Meaning"), and "Notes," and beneath the text window "Sentence or

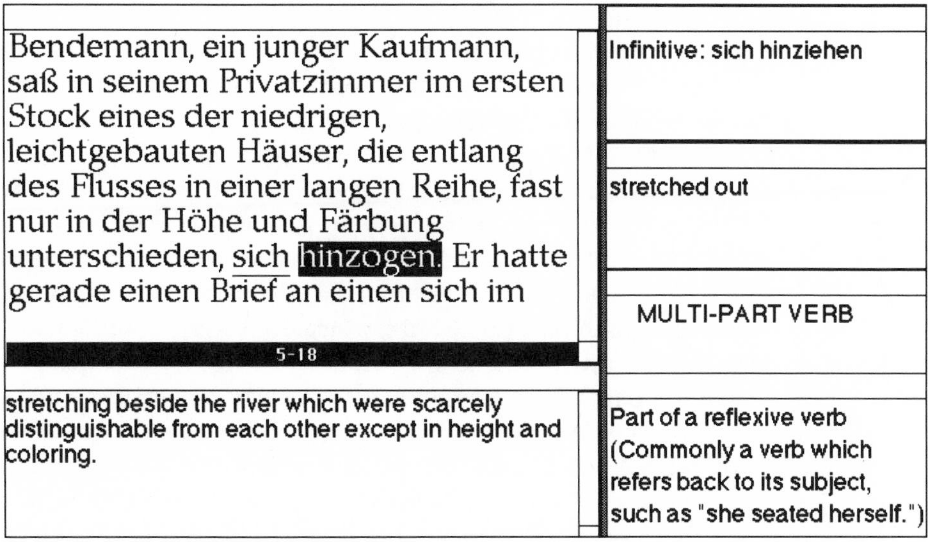
Bendemann, ein junger Kaufmann, saß in seinem Privatzimmer im ersten Stock eines der niedrigen, leichtgebauten Häuser, die entlang des Flusses in einer langen Reihe, fast nur in der Höhe und Färbung unterschieden, sich hinzogen. Er hatte gerade einen Brief an einen sich im
5-18
stretching beside the river which were scarcely distinguishable from each other except in height and coloring.
Infinitive: sich hinziehen
stretched out
MULTI-PART VERB
Part of a reflexive verb (Commonly a verb which refers back to its subject, such as "she seated herself.")

This screen is open on a version of Franz Kafka's "Das Urteil" in Transparent Language, an electronified book system with hypertext features.

Clause Meaning." Clicking upon the word *hinzogen* in the second sentence of the story makes it appear in reverse video–that is, in white letters on a black rectangle—while *sich,* the word immediately before it, appears underlined. (Clicking upon *sich* produces the opposite effect: it becomes the activated word whereas *hinzogen* appears underlined to show that it has an important grammatical relation to *sich.*) Each of the windows now contains information: The comments window states, "Infinitive: sich hinziehen," and the word-meaning window defines the verb in context as "stretched out," while the window for word grouping contains "Multi-part verb" and that for notes states, "Part of a reflexive verb (commonly a verb which refers back to its subject, such as 'she seated herself')." Finally, the window entitled "Sentence or Clause Meaning," which appears beneath the large text window, contains the following phrase: "stretching beside the river which were scarcely distinguishable from each other except in height and coloring." A glance back at the previous clause reveals that this one refers to the houses there mentioned.

Not all words provoke such abundant assistance. Clicking upon *Es,* the very first word of the story, for example, simply makes the word *it* appear in the word-meaning window while under "Sentence or Clause Meaning" is a translation of the entire sentence. Controls permit the reader to shut any or all of these windows and then open them at any time by using either the standard Windows or Macintosh menu or a key combination. In the Macintosh version of the system, for instance, holding down the apple icon ( ) and the s-key at the same time opens (or closes) the window entitled "Sentence or Clause Meaning."

This example of a simple, stand-alone hypertext represents an electronic version of printed student editions that contain glossaries and rudimentary assistance with grammar. What then has changed? In the first place, the system explains everything, no matter how simple the word or phrase. Such abundant annotation allows for a range of users from absolute beginners to readers who need only occasional assistance. Second, the electronic links, which on my system bring up requested readings instantaneously, radically change the experience of looking up a word or phrase. One effect of such instantaneous gratification of one's intellectual desire to learn or confirm the meaning of a word or phrase turns out to be, not surprisingly, that readers consult definitions far more frequently than do users of print dictionaries and other reference works. After all, if one discovers that looking up a word takes more than a minute, one pretty quickly begins to look up only those words one believes absolutely necessary to grasp the rough meaning of a sentence. Electronic linking, which blurs the borders of any informatized text, also brings with it an almost incredible acceleration of certain reference functions. This dramatic change in the temporal scale of consulting a reference text turns the reader's experience into a continuing tutorial, since the greater speed and convenience of the linked definition makes readers use it as a kind of flashcard. Even in this simple example of a linked text, the very presence of the electronic link inevitably reconfigures not only the experience of text conceived as a free-standing entity but, further, binds any such linked text into a new relation with a reference work. In other words, linking works of whatever sort—engineering manuals, physics texts, works of fiction—with a reference text blurs the once fundamental difference—fundamental in the Gutenberg world—between texts designed to be read through and those designed only for consultation.

In the Transparent Language example, a work of fiction is essentially turned into an instructional text, a textbook, by the linking of reference works to Kafka's tale. In contrast, Terence Harpold's *Microbiology Textstack,* the electronic version of John C. Sherris's *Medical Microbiology,* reconceives the very notion of a textbook by drawing upon the capacities of the linked digital word to make information accessible to the needs of each reader.[12] The Keyboard system, a customized and greatly extended version of HyperCard 2.0, offers the reader what Harpold calls a "Browser, a tool that makes it easy to view a summary of the contents of the stack [in this case, book], and to jump to any card. The

The design of the bacterial cell must thus differ fundamentally from that of other cells. As we have seen in Chapter 1, this is precisely the case, and the unique design is designated *prokaryotic*.

Prokaryotic cell design is unique
Chemical similarities to eukaryotic cells

A generalized bacterial cell is shown in Figure 2.4. The major structures of the cell belong either to the multilayered *envelope* and its *appendages* or to the interior core consisting of the *nucleoid* (or nuclear body) and the *cytosol*. In contrast to the alien nature of this body plan, the general chemical nature of the bacterial cell is more familiar to a eukaryotic cell biologist. Greater than 90% of its dry mass consists of five macromolecularlike substances similar to those found in eukaryotes: proteins (about 55% of the dry mass); RNA, consisting of the familiar mRNA, tRNA, and rRNA (about 20%); DNA (about 3%); carbohydrate (about 5%); and phospholipid (about 6%). In addition there are a few macromolecules unique to prokaryotes: a peptidoglycan called *murein* is found in all walled bacteria, and a few other unique molecules (lipopolysaccharide and teichoic acids) are found in specific groups of bacteria.

Small size and simple design facilitates rapid growth

Microbiology TextStack • Figure 2.3

Arrangement of spherical bacterial cells.

Diplococcus Tetrad Streptococcus

Staphylococcus

...sign that help explain the success of bacteria in metabolic by-products with the environment, tructures and the formation of new cells by roperty of bacteria—their ability to grow at least an ular level,

Microbiology TextStack • Figure 2.4

Relative sizes of micro...

Schematic of structures of a dividing bacterium.

Limits of resolution
50
El...
mi...
0.0

Classes of organisms

0.001

Capsule Ribosomes Cytoplasm Common pili

Flagella

Cell wall
See Fig 2.5

Cell membrane

Mesosome Plasmid Nucleoid Sex pilus

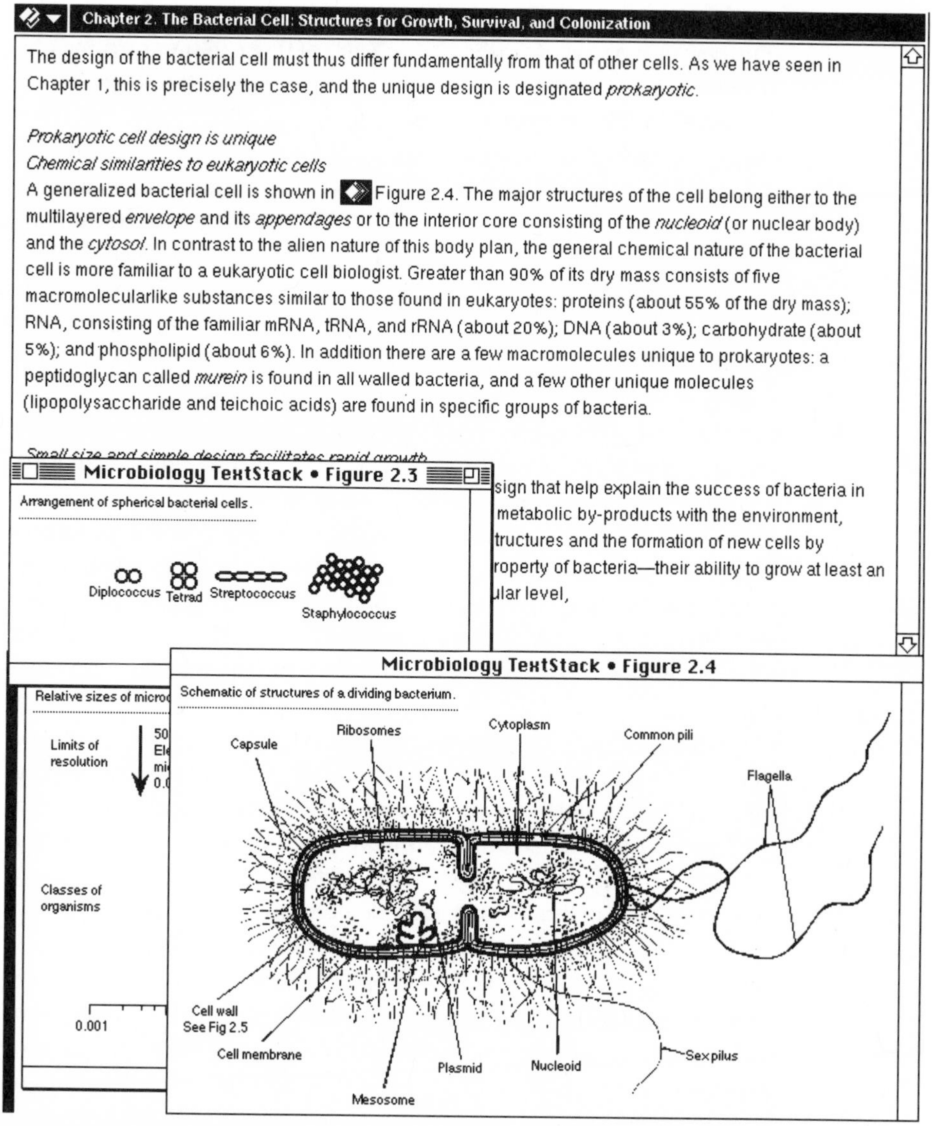

The *Microbiology Textstack* reconceives the very notion of a textbook. The Keyboard system, a customized and greatly extended version of HyperCard 2.0, permits readers to keep open numerous relevant diagrams and microphotographs according to their needs rather than the practical requirements of book design and technology.

Browser is a floating window (technically, a 'windoid'), and may remain open while you move around in the stack. . . . [A] scrolling field in the upper left corner of the Browser lists the chapters or subject areas in the stack. Clicking on a line in this list changes the contents of the scrolling 'detail' list along the bottom of the window, which displays subtopics, figures, tables, etc. within the selected chapter, as well as numbers of the pages (cards on which any of those items are found)."[13] The characteristic speed and manipulability of the digital word appears in the range of well-implemented features that distinguish the *Microbiology Textstack* from its print original. In addition to permitting readers to change the magnification of any of the many diagrams and microphotographs included, the system also allows them to search for any word or phrase; and since it also keeps track of the reader's path with a utility called the Keyboard Trail, readers can at any point return to a previously visited card.

Such a reading record represents a limited example of the way electronic technology easily adapts text to suit the reader's needs. Other features that permit annotation transform the reader into an author. Using a bookmark facility similar to that found in many electronic text-presentation systems, readers can annotate individual cards or passages in them. A specific menu lets readers "flip between successive bookmarks, or jump directly to any bookmark" (45). Finally, the Keyboard system affords not only recording and revisiting of both individual cards and reader annotations but also the fulfillment of Vannevar Bush's original vision by creating guided tours through personalized trails.[14]

Jeff Todd Titon's Voyager Expanded Books version of his chapter on Black American music in *Worlds of Music: An Introduction to the Music of the World's Peoples*, like many promising educational hypertext projects, takes the form of an amplified translation of a print work that responds directly to the shortcomings of print. In fact, the volume's jacket reveals the limitations of book technology by announcing that readers of *Worlds of Music* may purchase an accompanying audio package: "Designed as the perfect supplement to the text, the audio package—available as two cassettes or three compact discs—contains 61 recorded selections. Each selection is cross-referenced to the text, and most were made in the field by the authors."[15] As one might expect, Titon's hypermedia version reifies implicit links between individual passages of music and their discussions in the text, thereby drawing closer together the musical passages and the discussions of them.

Titon's hypermedia presentation of the hymn "Amazing Grace" well exemplifies the extension of text by electronic linking. In the original print text Titon compares the way two congregations, one white Southern Baptist and the other African American, sing this hymn, and does so by translating sound into visual information in the form of musical notation. Since his presentation also involves relating

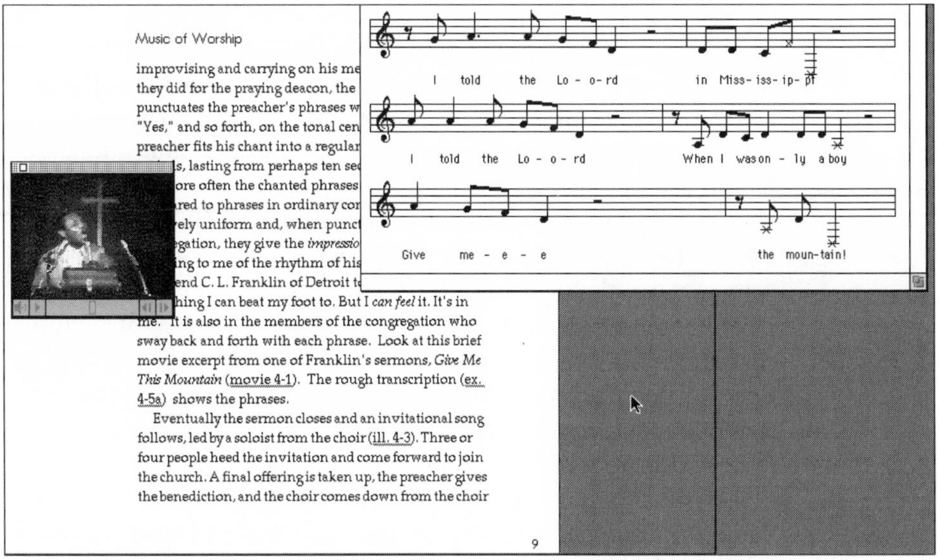

Jeff Todd Titon's Voyager Expanded Books version of his chapter on Black American music in *Worlds of Music* rearranges the experience of the text and its boundaries. Readers have the music he discusses available at any time, and they can replay portions of it or call up its musical notation. The Expanded Books version also includes animation in the form of QuickTime movies.

hymnody and contemporary music to black preaching styles, he also translates into musical notation an example of preaching by the Reverend C. L. Franklin (who happens to be Aretha Franklin's father). Students and instructors using the supplementary tape or cassette can consult the passages mentioned in *Worlds of Music.* The hypertext version rearranges the experience of the text and its boundaries with electronic links, for the reader has the music mentioned available at any time, and the reader can replay portions of it, or call up the musical notation for it, at any time.

In his hypermedia version, Titon also includes animation in the form of QuickTime movies created from videos he made of the Reverend Mr. Franklin's preaching. Since the discussion emphasizes rhythm and response, the cinematic presentation conveys a kind of information and experience difficult, if not impossible, to convey in print. To see and hear Mr. Franklin preaching, the reader becomes also a listener and a viewer, by clicking on an underlined phrase (in this case "*movie 4.1*") at which point a window one-and-a-half inches high by two inches wide containing an image appears superimposed on the text. A simplified control panel beneath the window permits users to play the image-and-sound sequence easily as many times as they wish.

The electronic textbook has here obviously evolved beyond the printed book, providing more kinds of information, some of it in the form of digital simulacra, and different kinds of experience than did the earlier version, which relied solely on alphanumeric text, photographs, and musical notation. Like the Transparent Language and Keyboard examples, Titon's project shows the kind of transformations linking characteristically produces in the electronified book, perhaps the most obvious of which lies in the fact that it inevitably opens up the text, in the process blurring the distinction between the single self-sufficient text and that new entity, the web or metatext.

In an essay written while she was updating "Reading and Writing the Electronic Book" five years after its initial publication, Nicole Yankelovich predicted a movement of attention from electronic books to groups of electronic books, or electronic libraries, such as were exemplified by *Context32* and the other Intermedia webs I described in *Hypertext.*[16] The larger webs exemplify such electronic libraries, but even much smaller ones centering on a single text, such as the *Dickens* and *In Memoriam* webs, obviously move beyond the organization and scope of the electronic books we observed in the Transparent Language and Voyager Expanded Books examples.[17] For instance, the *In Memoriam* web, which contains the full text of Tennyson's multilinear poem, not only includes textual variants, critical commentary, and numerous overviews for the poem's imagery and literary relations—all features, in other words, of an electronic book—but also groups of lexias on religion in England, the social and political context, and other elaborations of the contemporary context.

The most important example of a hypertextual electronic library for the humanities is the justly famous Perseus Project, an enormous data base of classical Greek culture. According to Elli Mylonas, managing editor of the project, "Perseus contains eight major classical authors in the original and in translation, the Intermediate Liddell-Scott Lexicon, an extensive overview of classical Greek history and the seeds of a classical encyclopedia with architectural terms and other relevant topics. It also contains entries for about 30 classical sites with detailed site plans and 150 buildings with building plans."[18] The data base also includes descriptions of vases, coins, and sculpture "linked with color photographs of the sites and objects, which can be displayed as video or as digital images" (174). Combined with animation, these digital images permit readers to view all sides of vases and works of sculpture by having them rotate at the reader's command. Perseus, which at present requires a CD-ROM drive and a laser disk player, also features a morphological parser—searching for *ate* will return not only that word itself but also *to eat* and *eaten* as well—and a pathbuilder mechanism.

Most interestingly, despite the fact that Gregory Crane, the project director, is a pioneering advocate of educational hypertext, he and his development team have conceived Perseus primarily as a system-independent data base that will move from system to system as hypertext technology evolves. The version Yale University Press published in 1991, which uses CD-ROM, laser disk, and customized HyperCard 2.0, represents, therefore, only the current (and currently possible) implementation of the data base.

Axial versus Network-structured Hypertext

Hypertext webs, whether read on stand-alone systems or on networks, can have two fundamentally different kinds of structures, the first closely reliant upon that of the linear book and the second realizing the dispersed, multiply centered network organization inherent in electronic linking. In the first decades of the Gutenberg revolution, printing presses, as McLuhan long ago pointed out, poured forth a flood of manuscripts in print form. In a similar manner, one can expect that in the first stages of hypertext publishing, printed books will provide both its raw material and much of its stylistics. The Voyager presentations of both popular and canonical texts, like the currently planned hypertext editions of the works of W. B. Yeats, D. G. Rossetti, and others, necessarily follow the linear structure of the print text as a primary axis of organization. The translation of individual books or subsections of books, such as short stories and poems, into hypertext necessarily produces an axial form of organization in which references, variant readings, and other supplements to the main text radiate from it in the manner of branches from a tree. The conception of the unified main text so characteristic of print technology demands such axial organization, at least for the primary information linked to that text.

Of course, as soon as one either abandons the notion of a single unique text, which some scholars working with manuscript culture have begun to do, or else creates a web composed of smaller individual webs, such as one would do when creating a complete works of a single author, one discovers that amassing a set of local axial structures leads to a network structure. The important capacity of hypertext to permit the reuse of information inevitably creates such networked structures. A hypertext edition of letters or poems, for example, can easily reuse particular bits of information, say, the identity of a correspondent or mention of a repeated motif so that what would have appeared as a single note hanging axially off a linear document now becomes part of a network within which several or many linear documents move.

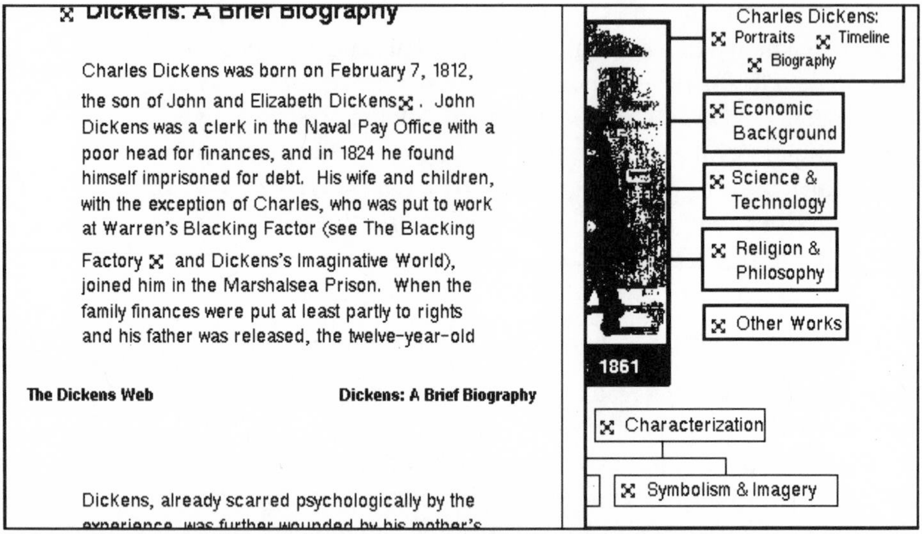

Interleaf WorldView, a system that uses the page metaphor in hypertext. As this snapshot from the WorldView version of *The Dickens Web* shows, this hypertext environment conveys some of the effects of the printed page by retaining a footer containing descriptive information. Although WorldView otherwise has unusually fine screen design and legibility, its use of this virtual footer for a nonexistent page jars the reader in an electronic environment.

Linking, in other words, produces a network organization, and both individual lexia and complete metatexts created originally for use within a hypertext environment will tend, I predict, to take this form, with important implications for the rhetoric and stylistics of hypertextual composing. Such network structure, in which the reader encounters pockets of local organization, produces new habits of reading and writing for which the information regime of print offers at least some precedent. Although books other than those explicitly designed as experimental fiction offer little precedent, newspapers do, for the daily newspaper exemplifies a document composed of discrete subjects often, but not always, grouped according to subject categories, such as local, international, sporting, entertainment, or business news. As one might expect, given that contemporary journalism already relies upon networked digital technology, hypertext researchers have created prototypes for individual customizable electronic newspapers capable of delivering to the individual subscriber either paper or electronic versions suited to their interests, which the system determines, either by the reader's conscious decisions or by assessing the reader's preferences and configuring his or her "paper" according to them.

In addition to this distinction between adaptive hypertext documents and those originally conceived to be read on line, one must also

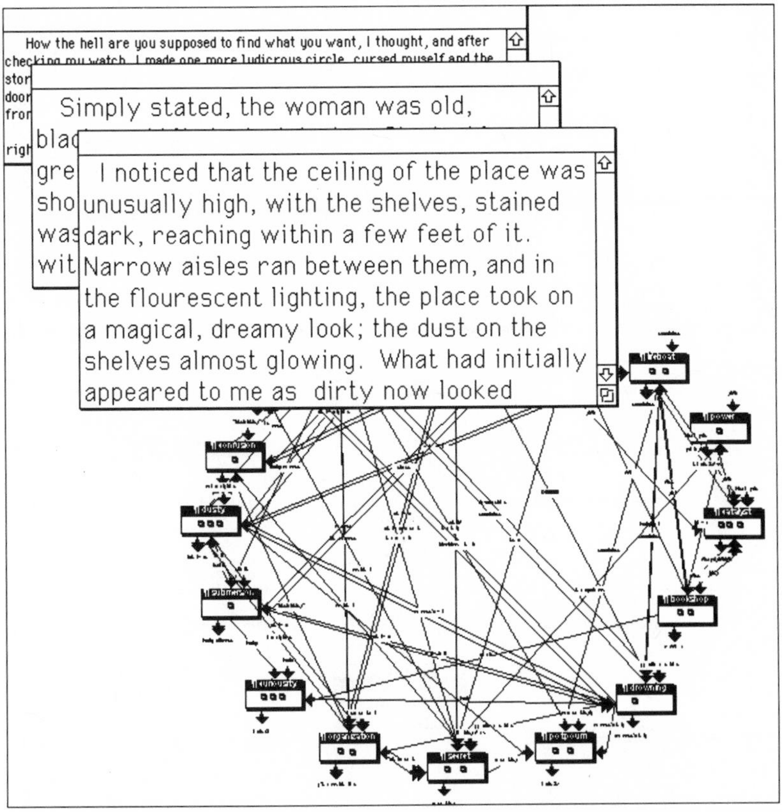

How the hell are you supposed to find what you want, I thought, and after
Simply stated, the woman was old,
I noticed that the ceiling of the place was unusually high, with the shelves, stained dark, reaching within a few feet of it. Narrow aisles ran between them, and in the flourescent lighting, the place took on a magical, dreamy look; the dust on the shelves almost glowing. What had initially appeared to me as dirty now looked

The structure of networked hypertext. In creating a narrative that the reader can enter and leave at any point, Adam Wenger took advantage of the graphic capacities of Storyspace to arrange the individual lexias of *Adam's Bookstore* in the form of a circle or large polygon. (For the sake of legibility, I have increased the font size in two of the lexias in relation to the Storyspace view; in the original, one can easily read the titles of all the lexia icons.)

draw another, more important in a print than in an electronic regime, between a reference book and one meant be read through. Scholars who have consulted on-line library catalogues, the electronic version of the MLA bibliography, or the CD-ROM version of the *Oxford English Dictionary* (*OED*) have already encountered electronic reference works with quasi-hypertextual features. A hypertextual or electronic reference tool still appears as a separate entity when considered as a self-contained, separate document—something easy to do when the electronic reference work either resides in a discrete physically identifiable object, such as a CD-ROM, or exists encoded within a proprietary software difficult to share with commonly available computer environments. However, once such a reference work appears on line within a networked environment, it inevitably loses its separation from other

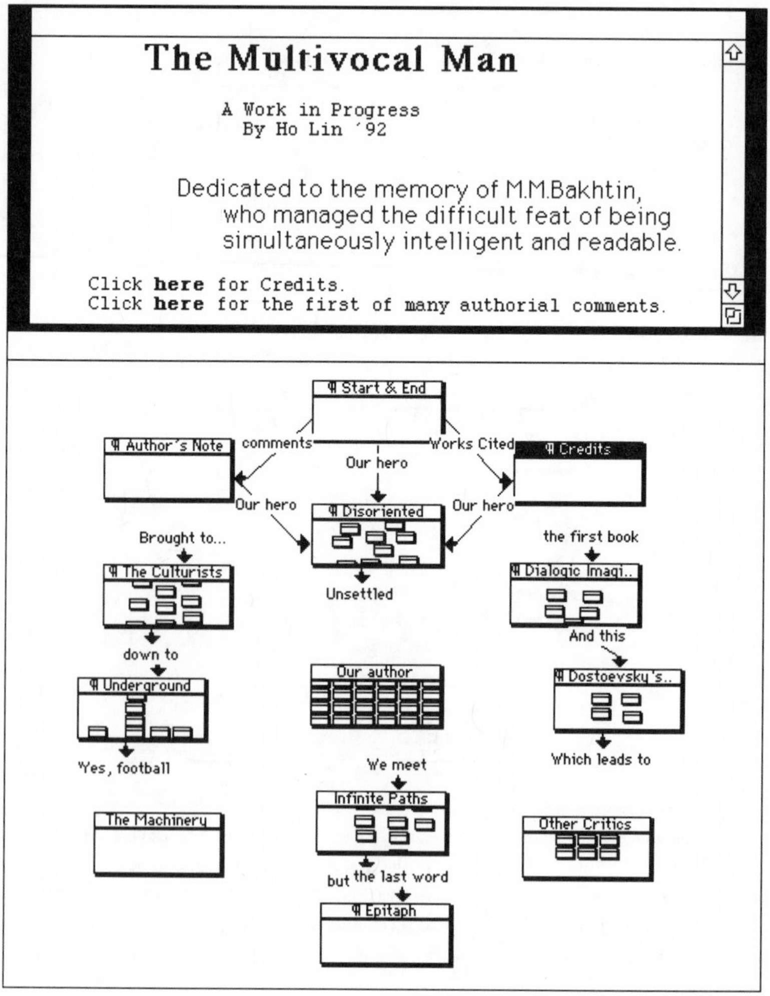

Multilinearity in hypertext. Ho Lin's Storyspace view for his Bakhtinian story, *The Multivocal Man*, uses the graphic features of a system that does not employ the book metaphor. It encourages readers to explore his tale both by following links and by exploring various lines or paths.

texts within it, and the difference between modes and genres begins to blur.

Intermedia, the advanced hypertext system developed at IRIS, includes an electronic version of Houghton-Mifflin's *American Heritage Dictionary.* At any point while working on this system, users can request dictionary definitions of a word. Moreover, since the interface permits morphological analysis, they can also carry out various linguistic exercises, such as using the electronic dictionary to search for words or names used within individual definitions or identifying all words of, say, Norse, Arabic, or Yiddish derivation. The point is that the dictionary, which clearly existed as a discrete body of material within the Intermedia system, appeared to the user so interwoven with the other documents that the distinction and distance between the various modes appeared much smaller. Whether reading materials created by others, or adding one's own to the instructional webs, or writing fiction, the user can always call up the dictionary, consult it, and copy text from it. Simply placing it on line changes the nature of one of the most commonly consulted printed reference works, the dictionary of one's own language. It becomes easier to consult and more convenient as a source from which to take notes—definitions can simply be copied and pasted into one's own document—and it is experienced differently—as close, less distant, from the other works contained in the system. This blurring, as we shall soon observe, has a marked effect on the conception and experience of boundaries and limits in hypertext.

What happens when one creates a hypertext reference work specifically for an electronic environment rather than converting one originally composed for book technology? One great advantage of digitalization lies in the ease with which that form permits manipulation, searching, and (to use the new jargon) re-purposing. In "*Logos* and *Techne*, or Telegraphy," Jean-François Lyotard correctly points out: "Any piece of data becomes useful (exploitable, operational) once it can be translated into information. This is just as much the case for so-called sensory data—colours and sounds—to the exact extent that their constitutive physical properties have been identified. After they have been put into digital form, these items of data can be synthesized anywhere and anytime to produce identical chromatic or acoustic products (simulacra). They are thereby rendered independent of the place and time of their 'initial' reception, realizable at a spatial and temporal distance: let's say telegraphable."[19]

A benign aspect of this telegraphability appears in the brilliantly successful Micro Gallery at the National Gallery, London. This hypermedia guide to the collections, created under the direction of Martin Ellis and Ben Rubinstein, exemplifies a purpose-built hypermedia reference work that moves far beyond the capacity of any printed gallery guide or census of works by providing "a comprehensive and richly interconnected illustrated encyclopedia of the collection."[20] Since the Micro Gallery follows a server-client model in which the computer used by the individual museum goer connects to a central data base, several dozen people can consult the same information simultaneously. More important, because the information is stored digitally, it can be reconfigured according to the needs of different people rather than being preconfigured to meet certain but not other needs. To consult the Micro Gallery, one sits before a large touch-screen color monitor. I last visited London on my way to Amsterdam, and I wanted to see the National Gallery's collection of works by Rembrandt, Vermeer, and other painters I expected to see in the Netherlands. Using the alphabetical guide, I began by touching *V,* thereby bringing up a list of artists whose name began with that letter, including Vermeer. Choosing his name produced a screen containing snapshot-size images of each of his works held by the National Gallery. In the case of some other artists, this first screen also included relevant works in other British museums as well. Choosing one picture gave me information about it and the indication that I could gain additional information about the artist and his times. From that next screen one can access material on the artist's life, contemporary culture of his or her nation and city, and the genre or genres within which individual works appear. Wanting to learn about landscape, history painting, genre, or portraits, one easily obtains basic information about each genre plus its classification into subgenres. Thus, if one wishes to learn more about portraiture, one receives several screens of different categories of portraits, including full-length, three-quarter, allegorical, group, and so on. Each category is represented by a snapshot-sized example, and touching it produces a complete list, again in the form of images accompanied by titles, of works in that category. At any point one can return to the large image of the individual work originally selected.

Such electronic linking permits the museum visitor to place individual works in a wide range of formal, historical, ideological, and other contexts and then, using another feature of the system, to print out an itinerary customized to one's own needs and interests. In addition, the Micro Gallery, whose textual component has been written by curators of individual collections, also contains abundant information best presented by means "beyond the book." The information on one of Vermeer's paintings, for instance, includes diagrams and overlays to explain the light source depicted in the painting, while the lexia containing information about Hans Holbein's *The Ambassadors* employs animation. Between the two men in the painting appears an odd, roughly oval shape that turns out to be an example of anamorphic representation, which only produces a readable image when viewed from a single vantage point at an extreme oblique angle to the picture surface. Requesting information about this part of Holbein's painting produces a screen that depicts the painting hanging on a left-hand wall above a staircase, which is represented in outline or wire-frame mode. Pressing a button on this screen begins an animation sequence in which the viewer appears to move up the stairs until he or she reaches the one point at which the previously unintelligible form becomes understandable as a skull.

Like Titon's project, this work adds capacities, such as reader-controlled animation, that neither print technology nor video and film can include. Like these projects, moreover, the Micro Gallery exists in computer memory and does not employ transitional technology, like CD-ROM or laser disks. Unlike them, however, the National Gallery project does not take the form of a hypermedia extension of a previously existing print text. Conceived as a work meant to be read on a computer terminal, it always exists in potential—and not just because it exists primarily in the form of electronic signals and codes that cannot be comprehended as word or image without a computer and monitor. The Micro Gallery exists as what Espen Aarseth terms "cybertext," text that is generated by the reader's request. It exists as a set of rules and rule-governed possibilities. In other words, the image, say, of X's portrait does not exist somewhere as an image "in there" and, moreover, this image does not exist in one comparatively large size on a particular screen that one receives when one requests that painting and on other screens in smaller size when one requests an artist's works or kinds of portraits. When one requests one of these screens, the computer system instantly assembles it in a tiny fraction of a second, and then it vanishes as soon as one requests another screen.

The Micro Gallery, an interactive cybertext some portions of which are generated on the fly by computation at an individual reader's request, replaces the standard gallery guide—itself a document type of comparatively recent history that took form within a specific social, political, and economic formation. Analogous to this virtual gallery are virtual hypertext resources that take the place of textbooks or even subcollections in libraries. The Intermedia webs created at Brown University and their successors in other environments, including Storyspace, WorldView, and Dynatext, exemplify to some extent such essentially nonlinear documents, and increasingly educators throughout the world have created such webs in a variety of environments.

One brilliantly successful instance of a hypermedia resource originally conceived for the new information medium is Fabio Bevilacqua's *Coulomb and Electrostatics*, intended to "synthesize the research done in Pavia in the fields of history of science, philosophy of science, and science education."[21] After creating a prototype on an Apple Macintosh, Bevilacqua's group at the University of Pavia created their 30-MB web in a DOS environment using Linkway and Storyboard. *Coulomb and Electrostatics* provides "a non sequential and interactive access to information stored as text, graphics, sound, quantitative simulations, qualitative animations, and still and moving colour pictures." The first screen the user encounters, which purposely does not provide a conceptual overview, serves as a reference map divided into three main areas, methodological, educational, and historical. "A special navigation palette is always available on the screen."

Dissatisfied with "traditional textbooks" that failed to "show the most important parts of science, the research patterns, but only the results," Bevilacqua began with a conception of students "as researchers who have to build their own conceptual frameworks" and teachers who are not "keepers of the truth but 'coaches' who help the students in their searching." Students can enter the massive hypermedia web from various points and, once inside, encounter not only what Thomas S. Kuhn calls normal and revolutionary science but also classic scientific experiments presented warts and all—experiments that do not come out the way text books often suggest they did—and evaluations of these classic experiments by famous figures in the history of science. Reading about Coulomb's discovery of electrostatic forces, for instance, the student comes upon both modern presentations of his experiments and beautiful reproductions of diagrams from his original publication. Using the system's animation and computational features, the student can simulate the original experiment, which turns out to produce very little data that supports Coulomb's interpretations. The emphasis throughout falls upon multivocality and problematization, for the reader can move back and forth among two centuries of primary texts and "out" into the worlds of contemporary culture, including issues of science and religion. Considered from the point of view of a print book, *Coulomb and Electrostatics,* like many of the Brown University and Storyspace webs, might seem particularly strange: it does not have a single way to enter its docuverse, and it clearly does not have a single way to exit it either. Furthermore, like other such webs, including the British Micro Gallery, this one obviously embodies abundance, for it clearly contains more than any single reader can be expected to read.

In conclusion, these few examples remind one that the general term *hypertext,* which applies to as many different kinds of works or text objects as does printing technology, includes very different kinds of systems. Therefore, when considering its implications and challenges for theory, one must realize that hypertext can take the form of standalone or networked systems and that they in turn can take the form of read-only, or broadcast, systems, of those that permit readers to create links and brief annotations, or of those that grant the reader full access as a writer. Furthermore, although almost all systems have some elements of hypermedia, since most have the capacity to include images, the capacity among contemporary systems to employ hypermedia varies widely; some use static images, including greyscale monochrome or color, while some can also handle sound and animation. Some of these systems, moreover, have the jerry-built Rube Goldberg appearance of most pioneering technology, because they require separate screens for laser disk information, whether still or cinematic, whereas others integrate all hypermedia functions on a single screen or projected surface.

In addition to such system-generated differences in the individual hypertext document, others derive from their authors, genres, and purposes. Hypertext, therefore, can appear in the form of a single work, which may in turn be a web written for reading on line, one adapted from a print work, or one adapted with such amplification as to become a hybrid; and a web can also take the form of groupings of such subsets. These distinctions may well derive only from the limitations of current data-storage technology, which still encourages configuring sets of lexias as discrete groups. Even so, webs created in systems like Dynatext, Storyspace, and other systems that permit readers to follow links from one web to another always have permeable, blurred boundaries.

Purpose-defined hypertext provides another important category of works in the medium, though, again, such divisions exist only as long as each set of linked documents appears as a discrete unit. If most hypertext webs exist as relatively separate units rather than as nodes or local regions within a giant docuverse, they divide into several genres and modes, including reference, instructional, constructive, and what, for want of a better term, I shall call literary hypertext. Each requires somewhat different stylistics and provides a very different experience to the user. For example, whereas the operation of hypertext and hypermedia reference works such as dictionaries and encyclopedias involves large elements of simple data retrieval and can cause little reader disorientation, certain forms of educational and literary hypertext make exploration, discovery, and even disorientation a crucial part of the reader's encounter with them.[22] Finally, hypertext fiction can have one author (Carolyn Guyer's *Quibbling,* Michael Joyce's *Afternoon,* Stuart Moulthrop's *Victory Garden*) or several (*Hotel*); and since linking blurs all boundaries, it can also embrace nonfiction, instruction, or any other work of hypertext.

What's a Critic to Do?

In *The Post Card* Derrida argues that "an entire epoch of so-called literature . . . cannot survive a certain technological regime of telecommunications," and he adds, "Neither can philosophy, or psychoanalysis. Or love letters."[23] To this list one may add criticism and theory as well, for these certainly will not remain unchanged either. What then will students and theorists of literature do in an electronic realm and, equally important, how will they do it? In particular, what are the implications of this new information regime for what Jacques Virbel, one of the designer's of the proposed Bibliothèque de France Reading Station, calls the "professional reader"?[24] Certainly, as I have argued in *Hypertext,* this new information technology has the power to reconfigure our culture's basic assumptions about textuality, authorship, creative property, education, and a range of other issues. Lyotard is surely correct when he claims that "the spectacular introduction of what are called the new technologies into the production, diffusion, distribution and consumption of cultural commodities . . . [is] in the process of transforming culture" ("*Logos* and *Techne,* or Telegraphy," 34), but he seems far from the mark when he complains of its specific effects.

Electronic textuality brings with it many changes, but not all concern loss, as so many critics of culture seem to believe. Lyotard, for instance, claims that the new information technologies produce effects much like the journalist's rewriting, "which consists in erasing all traces left in a text by unexpected and 'fantasy' associations" (34), but the evidence of hypertext works thus far created, both instructional and literary, suggests that on the contrary electronic linking graphs idiosyncrasy and personal association in particularly liberating ways. He grounds his charge on the doubtful claim, which hypertext linking would seem to contradict, that the "new technologies . . . submit to exact calculation every inscription on whatever support: visual and sound images, speech, musical lines, and finally writing itself," and he argues that "the noteworthy result of this is not, as Baudrillard thinks, the constitution of an immense network of simulacra" but rather the great "importance assumed by the concept of the *bit,* the unit of information." Apparently confusing the bit as unit of digitized information with something equivalent to a sound-bite, Lyotard goes on to propose a kind of tyrannized and therefore tyrannical textuality controlled by "a programmer": "When we're dealing with bits, there's no longer any question of free forms given here and now to sensibility and the imagination. On the contrary, they are units of information conceived by computer engineering and definable at all linguistic levels—lexical, syntactic, rhetorical, and the rest. They are assembled into systems following a set of possibilities (a 'menu') under the control of a programmer" (34–35). Like Baudrillard, Lyotard is, of course, not writing about hypertext, but even so one finds it difficult to follow how he derives his pessimistic conclusion from a standard structuralist and poststructuralist description of language. In fact, like so many other theorists, he falls into the fatal error of failing to see, as have Derrida, Goody, Kittler, McLuhan, and Ong, that language and writing are themselves powerful technologies. Be that as it may, networked hypertext, which offers liberation, idiosyncrasy, and even anarchy, obviates the kind of control feared by Lyotard and other culture prophets who confuse increasingly old-fashioned centralized mainframe computing with the new information technologies as a whole.

Nonetheless, the would-be critic of hypertext does encounter several fundamental problems unfamiliar to the professional reader in the print regime. Modern scholarship and criticism, as Elizabeth Eisenstein and others have shown, depends upon the multiplicity and fixity of the printed book.[25] As Kittler, who draws upon McLuhan, Foucault, and Derrida, correctly points out: "Technologies like that of book printing and the institutions coupled to it, such as literature and the university, thus constituted a historically very powerful formation, which in the Europe of the age of Goethe became the condition of possibility for literary criticism" ("Afterword," 369). Not until readers separated in space and time could refer to the same text did much of what we take to be the normal practice of scholarship come about. At its simplest, the demands of scholarship and criticism come down to being able to refer to a particular text and know that one's readers can consult precisely that text. Hypertext, which permits readers to choose their own paths through a set of possibilities, dissolves the fundamental fixity that provides the foundation of our critical theory and practice.

Before examining the implications of this apparent dilemma more closely, I would like to point out that there are three challenges for scholars, critics, and theorists confronting the new electronic information regimes. First of all, as Lyotard reminds us, the " 'new technologies' should stop being considered as they most often are, as new means, applied to works unchanged in their essence" ("Rewriting Modernity," 148). In seeking to grasp how works change in the context of different information regimes, we must unravel the relations between information technologies, past and present, and cultural assumptions, including our conceptions of literature, theory, self, power, and property. We also have to use various information regimes against each other.

Despite the efforts of Eisenstein, Kernan, McLuhan, Kittler, and others, this task does not come easily to critics and theorists, who tend to naturalize and thus mystify the relations of their practice to all technologies and especially those of the alphabet and the printing press. As Kittler correctly points out, "traditional literary criticism, probably because it originated in a particular practice of writing, has investigated everything about books except their data processing. Meaning as the fundamental concept of hermeneutics and labor as the fundamental concept of the sociology of literature both bypass writing as a channel of information and those institutions, whether schools or universities" ("Afterword," 370). In *The Post Card* Derrida relates a wonderfully apt anecdote about his difficulty in getting literary students to pay attention to the material conditions of the language they read and write. Derrida tells of an American graduate student who was looking for a dissertation topic and to whom he suggested the subject of "the telephone in modern literature." He recounts the conversation: "I spoke to her about microprocessors and computer terminals, she seemed somewhat disgusted. She told me that she still loved literature (me too, I answered her, *mais si, mais si*)" (204). Avital Ronell has taken up the challenge to examine the telephone, and J. David Bolter, William Paulson, Michael Heim, and others have begun to examine the role of electronic textuality as well, so the ground work is being laid for the student of theory who encounters hypertext.[26]

A second major problem that hypertext and other forms of the digital word pose for theory derives from the fact that hypertext readers, who choose their own paths, each read different texts and, in some cases, can never read all of the available text. In large hypertexts and in cybertexts, those unrepeatable documents that are custom or randomly generated, the critic can never master the total text, which thereby becomes what in Aarseth's essay in this volume terms "a readerless text." Few texts, he claims, "drive home the point of the readerless text more abundantly than Raymond Queneau's *Cent Mille Milliards de Poèmes* (1961). In this short book, ten pages are cut into fourteen one-line strips, and the user is invited to flip the strips individually, to form 100,000,000,000,000 different combinations. As it turns out, each of the 140 strips (or textons) is a sonnet line, and the result of any combination is a scripton in the form of a formally perfect sonnet." Critics can never read *all* the text and then represent themselves as masters of the text as do critics in print text. True, one can never fully exhaust or master a particular printed text, to be sure, but one can accurately claim to have read all through it or even to have read it so many times as to claim credibly to know it well. Large hypertexts and cybertexts simply offer too many lexias for critics ever to read. Quantity removes mastery and authority, for one can only sample, not master, a text.

Furthermore, in the nonreproducible text, critics find themselves in a situation analogous to the pre-print world, in which scribal drift insured that one could never be sure that another reader had read precisely the same text. Students of oral and preliterate culture have argued that criticism as we understand the enterprise derives directly from print culture, specifically from printed text's fixity and multiplicity—qualities that permit the critic to write for other readers who can consult the "same" text. What then will the critic do?

The critic has to give up not only the idea of mastery but also that of a single text at all as the mastery and mastered object disappear. In this admission of a relatively weaker, less authoritative position in relation to both text and reader (other readers), the critic, whatever he or she may become, in two ways becomes more like the scientist, who admits that his or her conclusions take the form, inevitably, of mere samples. Like the physicist dipping into a million trillion events, like the drama reviewer discussing only some of many performances, the critic explicitly samples and *only* samples, one must add, by actively participating in text production in a far more active way than ever before.

In looking for a new mantle for the critic to clutch, one might adopt the essentially metacritical procedure followed thus far by most reviewers of hypertext fiction and criticize the system that generates the (eventual) text. Such a project has legitimacy, to be sure, but it restricts the role of critic to metacritic.

The answer to this fundamental question, What will the critic and theorist of literature do about hypertext?, intimately involves the related one, How will the critic do whatever it is he or she will do? Of course, if hypertext truly marks a major paradigm shift, then one can expect that most scholars, critics, and theorists of print-based literature will do nothing at all about it. They will avert their eyes, deny, when pressed, that hypertext fiction or poetry is real fiction or poetry, and in general express great affection for the printed book—even on occasion contrasting the experience of encountering the supposedly denatured and denaturing effects of computer text to that of fondling a Victorian novel bound in rich morocco (even though, to be honest, almost all the books they have ever read turn out to take the form of paperbacks, so misleadingly labeled "perfect-bound," that fell apart, section by section, in their hands and in those of their students). Those increasing numbers of people who like both printed books and their new electronic extensions or partial analogues have several choices. Until the time that computer technology, particularly wide-band networks capable of supporting a widely spread and widely accessible hypertext system, develops to the point that hypertext becomes a major, even if not yet dominant, medium, writers will continue to produce print-based discussions of it; and those discussions, like many in this volume, will relate the two information regimes to each other. One task involves investigating previous major shifts in information technology, such as that from manuscript to print or from craft to high-speed printing. Another closely related task focuses on using the digital word to reveal unnoticed, naturalized, and mystified aspects of print culture. As Baudrillard, Derrida, Haraway, Kittler, Lyotard, Ronell, and others have shown, these aspects involve the theorist as does the specific form of investigation that probes the specific convergences between print-based theory, particularly its poststructuralist forms, and hypertext theory and practice.

Nonetheless, I have to ask again, What is a critic to do? The answer, finally, must be Write in hypertext itself. The answer to the question about what one does comes as yet another of the convergences to which this volume points. After a lecture on the general subject of nonlinearity by Aarseth at the Brown University Computer Humanities Users Group in 1991, discussion moved to the role of criticism and theory in relation to hypertext and cybertext. Several of those attending agreed with Robert Coover's call for a participatory criticism, one that must take place within hypertext and not in print form, which provides inadequate translation from one medium to the other.[27] Aarseth himself offered the model from anthropology of the participant-observer who admits that he or she influences the narrative and thus inevitably colors all results. These suggestions, which turn out to match the kind of work I have seen produced in my courses on hypertext and literary theory, recall Lyotard's insistence in "Can Thought Go on without a Body?" that analogy "requires a thinking or representing machine to be *in* its data just *as* the eye is in the visual field or writing is in language (in the broad sense). It's a matter (to use the attractively appropriate locution) of 'giving body' to the artificial thought of which they are capable" ("Rewriting Modernity," 17). Hypertext theory, finally, might have to be written in the electronic docuverse.

The first attempts to write criticism and theory within a hypertext environment suggest that they inevitably share the medium's characteristic multivocality, open-endedness, multilinear organization, greater inclusion of nontextual information, and fundamental reconfiguration of authorship, including ideas of authorial property, and of status relations in the text. Since I have already discussed these matters (though not with specific reference to writing theory in the new medium) in *Hypertext,* I here propose to examine the closely related matter of the form or genre of such writing, which, again, offers several points of convergence with poststructuralism. What I tentatively term the genre of criticism and theory in hypertext undergoes the kind of sea change one encounters with print-based conceptions of textuality, authorship, and argument; and such fundamental reconception derives from the same factor—linking, particularly in a networked environment. In *Hypertext* I related the occasion on which I realized the inevitable multidisciplinarity of educational experience within a networked hypertext environment: One day, while writing materials about Graham Swift's *Waterland,* a novel that touches upon the antiwar movement in 1973, I observed someone on a nearby machine working on a web about nuclear arms and disarmament. Immediately recognizing that I could provide valuable information for my students by simply linking to lexias in this other web, I did so. The *Context32* materials about Darwinian evolution were also soon linked to those for a biology course. In my earlier discussion I mentioned the way linking encourages author and reader to violate disciplinary boundaries. I did not mention that it also encourages them to violate stylistic and generic ones.

Such boundary crossing in genre and style also occurs repeatedly in work by students in both Robert Coover's hypertext fiction workshops and my courses in theory. For example, Alvin Liu's novel *Bobby Doubleday,* which he wrote on the Intermedia system, in part concerns cloning; reading through his lexias, users suddenly find themselves in materials created originally for a course in cell biology. Ho Lin's *Multivocal Man* takes boundary erasure in another direction. The protagonist of Lin's novel awakes one morning to discover himself transformed, not into Kafka's cockroach but into a literary theory. Unfortunately, the story relates, he has also become invisible to almost every one, with the exception of a university professor of literature who tries, unsuccessfully, to entice him home. Lin presents his story in three fonts, indicating the voices of the protagonist, the narrator, and Bakhtin, each of whose words form entire lexias.

Such use of found objects from outside the textual world appears in early modernist collage and the newspaper headlines John Dos Passos includes in *USA*. The collage method, which Ulmer pronounces the "single most revolutionary formal innovation in artistic representation to occur in our century," provides an entirely appropriate paradigm for both hypertext writing and what Ulmer calls "post-criticism."[28] Collage, or collage-like effects, in fact appear inevitable in hypertext environments, and they also take various forms. Including blocks of nonfictional text or images within a hypertext fiction, as we have seen, provides one way that such collage occurs; it also happens when authors *write with* and, one might say, *along with* texts by others.

One form of this writing with the text of another appears in Stuart Moulthrop's hypertext adaptation of Jorge Luis Borges's "Garden of Forking Paths," in which he not only divides the printed text into discrete lexias but also, as a form of hyper-criticism or post-criticism, adds his own lexias as well.[29] Another instance appears when hypertext authors work in two or more modes and genres that in the world of print would seem entirely different. Observing the hypertext work of students—some instances of which they have integrated into the expanded Storyspace version of *Hypertext* called *The Hypertext and Literary Theory Web* and others of which they create as separate webs—I have noticed that such a collage of modes and genres seems almost inevitable. Given an open-ended assignment involving any sort of writing on, with, or against Barthes's *S/Z,* a significant proportion of student authors chose to use hypertext as a laboratory for theory by attempting to apply Barthesian codes to a variety of works, including the Alice books, Borges's "Borges and I" and "The Book of Sand," and X-Clan's rap "Grand Verbalizer, What Time is It?"[30] One of the most interesting of these projects, Adam Wenger's *Adam's Bookstore,* took the form of a web that interweaves hypertext fiction in the manner of Borges with analytical lexias in the manner of Barthes. Whereas *Adam's Bookstore* places primary, or at least chronologically first, emphasis upon the fiction, Tom Meyer's *Plateaus,* which experiments with the work of Deleuze and Guattari, begins with their texts and then includes large numbers of lexias drawn from Italo Calvino's *Invisible Cities,* Petronius's *Satyricon,* William Burroughs' *Naked Lunch,* his own theoretical writing, and lexias the author imported from discussions in which he participated on Technoculture, an ongoing electronic conference.

In several ways the violation of genre and mode that I have observed in these webs has ample parallels in contemporary theory. For one obvious example let us turn to Hélène Cixous, for as Catherine Clement points out to her in the dialogue that closes *The Newly Born Woman,* Clement herself employs "demonstrative and discursive" discourse but Cixous's "is a writing halfway between theory and fiction."[31] Cixous responds that she in fact uses many forms, including "rhetorical discourse, the discourse of mastery, orally, for example, with my students, and obviously I do it on purpose; it is a refusal on my part to leave organized discourse entirely in men's power" (136). She further claims, "There will not be *one* feminine discourse, there will be thousands of different kinds of feminine words, and then there will be the code for general communication, philosophical discourse, rhetoric like now but with a great number of subversive discourses in addition that are somewhere else entirely. That is what is going to happen. Until now women were not speaking out loud, were not writing, not creating their tongues—plural, but they will create them, which doesn't mean that the others (either men or tongues) are going to die off" (137). Note how Cixous's call for a new discourse that embraces Bakhtinian multivocality and anti-hierarchical rhetoric meets fulfillment in the linked digital word; note, too, how her own practice also anticipates what has become an important mode in the hypertext docuverse.

Like a great many other poststructuralist ideas that appear particularly opaque, bizarre, pretentious, or all three from the vantage point of print-based thought, this blending and blurring of genres makes a good deal of sense in the world of networked electronic text. When Cixous, Barthes, Miller, and other theorists seek to deny a boundary or barrier between theoretical and literary texts, their claims strike many as outrageously pretentious attempts at self-aggrandizement, which the general reader never encounters and at which the writer of poetry and fiction smiles—claims that in a print world have value only, it would seem, in the statusphere of academe. Nonetheless, like Barthes's and Foucault's remarks about the death of the author, Derrida's on textuality, Kristeva's on intertextuality, and so many others, this merging of creative and discursive modes simply *happens* in hypertext.

Furthermore, Ulmer's notion of "mystory" as a novel form of academic discourse provides a model for this effect upon genre and mode, and in so doing it reveals yet another point at which theory and hypertext practice converge. Ulmer originally advanced his ideas of mystory in *Teletheory: Grammatology in the Age of Video,* whose title suggests his emphasis at that period upon a kind of electronically based information technology that has little to do with hypertext.[32] He explains that "one purpose of teletheory is to make personal images accessible, receivable, by integrating the private and public dimensions of knowledge—invention and justification" (39). Ulmer proposes that the border-violating collage-writing of mystory offers a form of academic discourse capable of emphasizing imagination, discovery, and unexpected "crossovers between high and popular culture" (189).[33] "Derrida at the Little Big Horn," the closing chapter of *Teletheory,* and "The Miranda Warnings," which closes this volume, represent Ulmer's print-technology approximations of this new form that combines personal, public, and mythic history.

As these mystories by Ulmer and writing by the increasing number of authors working in hypertext environments show, one task for those concerned with literary and critical theory involves developing new forms of linked electronic discourse. In future, when writing on the net becomes increasingly important, on-line theory and practice may well predominate, though if the coming of print technology in the age of Gutenberg offers a relevant pattern, one can expect that old and new information technologies will exist side by side for a long time to come. If that situation comes to pass, one can also expect that, like video and film, hypertext will have an impact on materials written for print presentation.

Meanwhile, the linked digital word offers a powerful means of understanding by comparison the contemporary and past cultures of book and manuscript. As the essays in this book demonstrate, one means by which to gain insight into our present age of transition takes the form of examining the convergences of contemporary critical theory and hypertext technology.[34]

NOTES

1. For a detailed comparison of three hypertext environments (Intermedia, Storyspace, and WorldView), see George P. Landow and Paul Kahn, "Where's the Hypertext? *The Dickens Web* as a System-independent Hypertext," *ECHT'92* (New York: Association of Computing Machinery, 1992), 149–60.

2. Friedrich A. Kittler, "Afterword to the Second Printing," *Discourse Networks 1800/1900,* trans. Michael Metteer and Chris Cullins (Stanford: Stanford University Press, 1992), 370.

3. The Princeton Interactive Computer Graphics Laboratory team consists of an art historian, Professor Marilyn Lavin, and two software engineers—Brad Gianulis, who began the programming, and Kevin Perry, who has since extended the project. According to Perry, "the software (written in-house) runs on a Silicon Graphics VGX workstation and is based on the Silicon Graphics GL and Inventor graphics programming libraries. The image dataset is currently about 250 megabytes" (electronic mail message, May 10, 1993).

4. Norman Meyrowitz, "Hypertext—Does It Reduce Cholesterol, Too?" in *From Memex to Hypertext: Vannevar Bush and the Mind's Machine,* ed. James M. Nyce and Paul Kahn (San Diego: Academic Press, 1991), 287–318.

5. For Acquanet, see Catherine C. Marshall, Frank G. Halasz, Russell A. Rogers, and William A. Janssen, Jr., "Acquanet: A Hypertext Tool to Hold Your Knowledge in Place," *Hypertext '91* (New York: Association of Computing Machinery, 1991), 261–75, and Catherine C. Marshall and Russell A. Rogers, "Two Years before the Mist: Experiences with Acquanet," *ECHT'92* (New York: Association of Computing Machinery, 1992), 53–62. For the system created by the Darmstadt Integrated Publication and Information Systems Institute and the Gesellshaft für Mathematik and Datenverarbeitung, see Norbert Streitz et al., "SEPIA: A Cooperative Hypermedia Authoring Environment," *ECHT'92,* 11–

21. For MacWeb, see Jocelyne and Marc Nanard, "Using Structured Types to Incorporate Knowledge in Hypertext," *Hypertext '91*, 329–42.

6. See Paul Kahn, "Isocrates: Greek Literature on a CD ROM," in *CD ROM: The New Papyrus: The Current and Future State of the Art,* ed. Steve Lambert (Redmond, Wash.: Microsoft Press, 1986), and Erich Segal, "Lilliputian Leviathans," *Times Literary Supplement,* December 11, 1992, 11.

7. Michael Heim, *Electric Language: A Philosophical Study of Word Processing* (New Haven: Yale University Press, 1987), and J. David Bolter, *Writing Space: The Computer, Hypertext, and the History of Writing* (Hillsdale, N.J.: Lawrence Erlbaum, 1991).

8. See Christinger Tomer, "Emerging Electronic Library Services and the Idea of Location Independence," in *The Digital Word: Text-based Computing in the Humanities,* ed. George P. Landow and Paul Delany (Cambridge: MIT Press, 1993), 139–62.

9. George P. Landow, "Electronic Conferences and Samiszdat Textuality: The Example of Technoculture," in *The Digital Word,* 350.

10. J. Hillis Miller, *Illustration* (Cambridge: Harvard University Press, 1992), 39. On the same page, in a passage that restates what I have elsewhere called hypertext's constructivist theory of education, he suggests that in such an electronic realm "history will much more evidently not be something objectively out there, but something constituted now for some particular purpose, in a transformative act of memory oriented toward the future."

11. Miller mistakenly treats the Intermedia webs, which students in part created, as essentially the same as the broadcast technology of a CD-ROM scholarly edition. He states: "The teaching programmes of the IRIS project, in spite of their attempts to foster the freedom and creativity in interpretation of the student, tend to lay down predetermined tracks leading away from the literary text and the activity of reading it toward the explanatory or causal force of context. Tennyson's 'Lady of Shalott' for example, is explained through 'links' to Tennyson's biography and to historical changes like the building of canal systems in early nineteenth-century Britain" (*Illustration,* 40). Since Miller unfortunately has not had an opportunity either to see the actual webs or to use the Intermedia system, he does not realize that the biographical essay does not in fact explain Tennyson's poem and that no link, explanatory or otherwise, connects the poem and the material on canals. The screen snapshot of Intermedia he includes (38) shows these documents open to suggest how a reader might wish to construct his or her own set of connections. The webs do, of course, have many links, some explanatory or contextual; and the versions in Storyspace, Dynatext, and WorldView also have full-text search mechanisms that permit reader-directed searches. I do not follow his more general objection to providing links to context, which he states in a section on cultural studies that specifically urges placing the "cultural artefact" (15) in the kind of context these hypertext webs offer.

12. John C. Sherris, ed., *Medical Microbiology: An Introduction to Infectious Diseases* (New York: Elsevier Science, 1990).

13. Jeanne Ewert, Terence Harpold, and Alexander Grimwade, *The Keyboard Stacks User's Manual, Keyboard Toolbox 2.1* (Blue Bell, Pa.: Keyboard, 1992), 21.

14. Tim Orren, "Memex: Getting Back on the Trail," in *From Memex to Hypertext,* 319–38, and Randall H. Trigg, "From Trailblazing to Guided Tours: The Legacy of Vannevar Bush's Vision of Hypertext Use," *From Memex to Hypertext,* 353–67, emphasize that, unlike most recent designers of hypertext, the man usually credited with the first conception of it placed chief emphasis on creating and following trails and not on networks of links. See my *Hypertext: The Convergence of Contemporary Critical Theory and Technology* (Baltimore: Johns Hopkins University Press, 1992), 14–18, for a discussion of Bush's relation to contemporary understanding of the medium.

15. Jeff Todd Titon, ed., *Worlds of Music: An Introduction to the Music of the World's Peoples,* 2nd ed. (New York: Schirmer, 1992).

16. Nicole Yankelovich, "From Electronic Books to Electronic Libraries: Revisiting 'Reading and Writing the Electronic Book,'" in *Hypermedia and Literary Studies,* ed. Paul Delany and George P. Landow (Cambridge: MIT Press, 1991), 133–41. The original article, by Yankelovich, Norman Meyrowitz, and Andries van Dam, is reprinted in *Hypermedia and Literary Studies,* 53–80.

17. Eastgate Systems of Cambridge, Massachusetts, published both webs in 1992. *The Dickens Web* matches almost exactly the original Intermedia version created by Julie Launhardt, Paul Kahn, and me—the only changes being some additional illustrations—but Jon Lanestedt redesigned and amplified *The "In Memoriam" Web* by adding more materials, including contextual ones and graphic overview documents.

18. Elli Mylonas, "The Perseus Project: Ancient Greece in Texts, Maps, and Images," *Electronic Books—Multimedia Reference Works* (Bergen: Norwegian Computing Centre, 1991), 174. See also Gregory Crane and Elli Mylonas, "Ancient Materials, Modern Media," in *Hypermedia and Literary Studies,* 205–20.

19. Jean-François Lyotard, "*Logos* and *Techne*, or Telegraphy," *The Inhuman,* trans. Geoffrey Bennington and Rachel Bowlby (Stanford: Stanford University Press, 1991), 50. Lyotard continues: "The whole idea of an 'initial' reception, of what since Kant has been called an 'aesthetic,' an empirical or transcendental mode whereby the mind is affected by a 'matter' which it does not fully control, which happens to it here and now—this whole idea seems completely out of date."

20. Martin Ellis, "The Micro Gallery: A Multimedia Resource for the Gallery Visitor," *Hypermedia and Interactivity in Museums: Proceedings of an International Conference,* ed. David Bearman (Pittsburgh: Archives and Museum Informatics, 1991), 321.

"The Micro Gallery" is now also available in a CD-ROM version for both Macintosh and Windows under the title *Microsoft Art Gallery: The Collection of the National Gallery, London* (n.p.: Microsoft Corporation, 1993). This personal-computer version uses a mouse rather than the original touchscreen interface, and since it can take advantage of the computer's keyboard, which the National Gallery version cannot, it can search for names, places, titles, and so on that readers type in a menu. The fact that this massive hypermedia project is being sold at $75.00 (or the equivalent in other currencies) has important implications for its use in education both inside and outside educational institutions.

21. Fabio Bevilacqua, "Coulomb and Electrostatics: A Hypermedial Approach to History of Physics in Education," manuscript, 1.

22. See Paul Kahn and George P. Landow, "The Pleasures of Possibility: What Is Disorientation in Hypertext?" *Journal of Computing in Higher Education* 4 (1993): 57–78.

23. Jacques Derrida, *The Post Card from Socrates to Freud and Beyond,* trans. Alan Bass (Chicago: University of Chicago Press, 1987), 197.

24. Jacques Virbel, "Reading and Managing Texts on the Bibliothèque de France Station," in *The Digital Word,* 31.

25. See Elizabeth L. Eisenstein, *The Printing Press as an Agent of Change: Communications and Cultural Transformations in Early-Modern Europe* (Cambridge: Cambridge University Press, 1980), and Alvin Kernan, *Printing Technology, Letters and Samuel Johnson* (Princeton: Princeton University Press, 1987).

26. Avital Ronell, *The Telephone Book: Technology, Schizophrenia, Electric Speech* (Lincoln: University of Nebraska Press, 1989); Michael Heim, *Electric Language: A Philosophical Study of Word Processing* (New Haven: Yale University Press, 1987).

William R. Paulson, *The Noise of Culture: Literary Texts in a World of Information* (Ithaca: Cornell University Press, 1988). See also E. S. Turner, "Answering the Call: Alexander Graham Bell's Legacy and Its Far-flung Connections," *Times Literary Supplement,* December 6, 1991, 3–4, which discusses Ronell's book and others on the cultural significance of the telephone.

27. In addition to Aarseth and Coover, Stephen DeRose, David Durand, Elli Mylonas, Richard Ristow, and Alan Renear contributed to the discussion. Taking computer role-playing games as an instance of interactive fiction, Durand offered two diametrically opposed examples of electronic textuality that demand comment upon the social, political, and moral implications of the principles and structures underlying their text production. First, he described John McDaid's *Castle of Greyscale,* in which after the role-player kills a little monster, say, a baby ogre or dragon, the system exclaims, "Look what you did!" and then sarcastically asks if one feels better having killed it. Durand also then pointed out that most interactive fiction and role-playing games force upon one a very different morality than does McDaid's. One cannot, as he once attempted to, act as a pacifist in an electronic world that forces the reader-player to kill or steal booty to survive.

28. Gregory L. Ulmer, "The Object of Post-Criticism," in *The Anti-Aesthetic: Essays on Postmodern Culture,* ed. Hal Forster (Port Townsend, Wash.: Bay Press, 1983), 84.

29. Stuart Moulthrop based *Forking Paths: An Interaction after Jorge Luis Borges,* his 1987 Storyspace web, on Jorge Luis Borges, "The Garden of Forking Paths," in *Labyrinths: Selected Stories and Other Writings,* ed. Donald A. Yates and James E. Irby (New York: New Directions, 1964), 19–29.

30. Karen Kim's *Grains of Sand* focuses upon Borges's "House of Sand," and Jessica Teisch's *Alice's Disorientation* applies Barthes's code to the Alice books. Both are separate, free-standing Storyspace webs, whereas Dexter Flowers' hypertext experiment with "Borges and I," which includes discussions of hermeneutics and contemporary philosophy, and Eliel Mamousette's analysis of the rap song appear linked to materials on Barthes in the *Hypertext and Literary Theory Web*.

31. Hélène Cixous and Catherine Clement, *The Newly Born Woman,* trans. Betsy Wing (Minneapolis: University of Minnesota Press, 1986), 137.

32. Gregory L. Ulmer, *Teletheory: Grammatology in the Age of Video* (New York: Routledge, 1989).

33. Ulmer's description of this video-based educational mode offers another point of convergence with hypertext when he emphasizes its constructivist conception of learning, which he presents with Wittgenstein's metaphor of traversing a landscape that has had such importance with hypertext designers: "To approach knowledge from the side of not knowing what it is, from the side of one who is learning, not from that of the one who already knows, is to do mystory. What is the experience of knowing, of coming to or arriving at an understanding, characterized as following a path or criss-crossing a field, if not narrative experience, the experience of following a narrative?" (*Teletheory,* 106).

34. Since hypertext presents an instance of open-ended, never completed textuality, this introduction appropriately ends by citing convergences that the following pages mention either only in passing or not at all: (1) the notion of hypertext as a prosthesis and Donna Haraway's cyborg paradigm; (2) the intertwined issues of the cyborg, hypertext, and virtual reality as a means of being within the textualized world; (3) *l'écriture feminine, l'écriture hypertextuelle,* and the notes of feminist collaborative authorship proposed by Lisa Ede and Andrea Lunsford in *Singular Texts/Plural Authors: Perspectives on Collaborative Writing* (Carbondale: Southern Illinois University Press, 1990); (4) Foucault's graphing of power relations and status in both hypertext and in the electronic universe of cyberspace; (5) the hypertextual author-function, self-presentation in cyberspace, and conceptions of identity.

BIBLIOGRAPHY

Bass, Randall. "The Syllabus Builder: A Hypertext Resource for Teachers of Literature." *Journal of Computing in Higher Education* 4 (1993).

Baudrillard, Jean. *The Ecstasy of Communication.* Trans. Bernard and Caroline Schutze. Ed. Sylvère Lotringer. New York: Semiotext(e), 1988.

———. *Fatal Strategies.* Trans. Philip Beitchman and W. G. J. Niesluchowski. New York: Semiotext(e)/Pluto, 1990.

———. *Simulations.* Trans. Paul Foss, Paul Patton, and Philip Beitchman. New York: Semiotext(e), 1983.

Benstock, Shari. *Textualizing the Feminine: On the Limits of Genre.* Norman: University of Oklahoma Press, 1991.

Bevilacqua, Fabio. "Coulomb and Electrostatics: A Hypermedial Approach to History of Physics in Education." Unpublished manuscript, 1992.
Bolter, J. David. *Turing's Man: Western Culture in the Computer Age*. Chapel Hill: University of North Carolina Press, 1984.
———. *Writing Space: The Computer, Hypertext, and the History of Writing*. Hillsdale, N.J.: Lawrence Erlbaum, 1991.
Borges, Jorge Luis. *Labyrinths: Selected Stories and Other Writings*. Ed. Donald A. Yates and James E. Irby. New York: New Directions, 1964.
Bush, Vannevar. "As We May Think." *Atlantic Monthly* 176 (July 1945): 101–8.
Cesareni, Donatella. "Ecoland: A Hypermedia Prototype for Environmental Education." Unpublished manuscript, 1992.
Chartier, Roger. *The Cultural Uses of Print in Early Modern France*. Trans. Lydia G. Cochrane. Princeton: Princeton University Press, 1987.
Cixous, Hélène. *Readings: The Poetics of Blanchot, Joyce, Kafka, Kleist, Lispector, and Tsvetayeva*. Minneapolis: University of Minnesota Press, 1981.
Cixous, Hélène, and Catherine Clement. *The Newly Born Woman*. Trans. Betsy Wing. Minneapolis: University of Minnesota Press, 1986.
Conklin, E. Jeffrey. "Hypertext: An Introduction and Survey." *IEEE Computer* 20 (1987): 17–41.
Coover, Robert. "The End of Books." *New York Times Book Review*, June 21, 1992, 1, 11, 24–25.
Crane, Gregory. "Challenging the Individual: The Tradition of Hypermedia Databases." *Academic Computing* 4 (Jan. 1990): 22–26, 31–32, 34–38.
———. "Redefining the Book: Some Preliminary Problems." *Academic Computing* 2 (Feb. 1988): 6–11, 36–41.
Delany, Paul, and George P. Landow, eds. *Hypermedia and Literary Studies*. Cambridge: MIT Press, 1991.
Deleuze, Gilles, and Félix Guattari. *A Thousand Plateaus: Capitalism and Schizophrenia*. Trans. Brian Massumi. Minneapolis: University of Minnesota Press, 1987.
Ede, Lisa, and Andrea Lunsford. *Singular Texts/Plural Authors: Perspectives on Collaborative Writing*. Carbondale: Southern Illinois University Press, 1990.
Eisenstein, Elizabeth L. *The Printing Press as an Agent of Change: Communications and Cultural Transformations in Early-Modern Europe*. Cambridge: Cambridge University Press, 1980.
Ellis, Martin. "The Micro Gallery: A Multimedia Resource for the Gallery Visitor." In *Hypermedia and Interactivity in Museums: Proceedings of an International Conference*. Ed. David Bearman. Pittsburgh: Archives and Museum Informatics, 1991.
Ewert, Jeanne, Terence Harpold, and Alexander Grimwade. *The Keyboard Stacks User's Manual, Keyboard Toolbox 2.1*. Blue Bell, Pa.: Keyboard, 1992.
Foucault, Michel. *The History of Sexuality: An Introduction*. Trans. Robert Hurley. New York: Vintage, 1990.
Geertz, Clifford. *Works and Lives: The Anthropologist as Author*. Stanford: Stanford University Press, 1988.

Greco, Diane M. "Machine Dreams and Cyborg Visions: The Female Self in Cyberpunk Science Fiction." Brown University honors thesis, 1992.

Haan, Bernard J., Paul Kahn, Victor A. Riley, James H. Coombs, and Norman K. Meyrowitz. "IRIS Hypermedia Services." *Communications of the ACM* 35 (Jan. 1992): 36–51.

Heim, Michael. *Electric Language: A Philosophical Study of Word Processing.* New Haven: Yale University Press, 1987.

Henry, Tom. "The Mighty Micro." *Art Quarterly of National College Fund* (1992): 29–31.

Interleaf, Inc. "WorldView Press User's Guide." Waltham, Mass.: Interleaf, 1992.

Joyce, Michael. "Siren Shapes: Exploratory and Constructive Hypertexts." *Academic Computing* 3 (Nov. 1988): 10–14, 37–42.

Kahn, Paul, Julie Launhardt, Krzysztof Lenk, and Ronnie Peters. "Design of Hypermedia Publications: Issues and Solutions." In *EP90, Proceedings for the International Conference on Electronic Publishing, Document Manipulation, and Typography.* Ed. Richard Furuta, 107–24. Cambridge: Cambridge University Press, 1990.

Kernan, Alvin. *Printing Technology, Letters and Samuel Johnson.* Princeton: Princeton University Press, 1987.

Landow, George P. *Hypertext: The Convergence of Contemporary Critical Theory and Technology.* Baltimore: Johns Hopkins University Press, 1992.

Landow, George P., and Paul Delany, eds. *The Digital Word: Text-based Computing in the Humanities.* Cambridge: MIT Press, 1993.

Landow, George P., and Paul Kahn. "Where's the Hypertext? *The Dickens Web* as a System-independent Hypertext." In *ECHT'92,* 149–60. New York: Association of Computing Machinery, 1992.

Launhardt, Julie, and Paul Kahn. "The Educational Uses of Intermedia." *Journal of Computing in Higher Education* 4 (1992): 50–87.

Lyotard, Jean-François. *The Inhuman.* Trans. Geoffrey Bennington and Rachel Bowlby. Stanford: Stanford University Press, 1991.

———. *The Postmodern Condition: A Report on Knowledge.* Trans. Geoffrey Bennington and Brian Massumi. Minneapolis: University of Minnesota Press, 1984.

McArthur, Tom. *Worlds of Reference: Lexicography, Learning, and Language from the Clay Tablet to the Computer.* Cambridge: Cambridge University Press, 1986.

McLuhan, Marshall. *The Gutenberg Galaxy: The Making of Typographic Man.* Toronto: University of Toronto Press, 1962.

Marshall, Catherine C., Frank G. Halasz, Russell A. Rogers, and William A. Janssen, Jr. "Acquanet: A Hypertext Tool to Hold Your Knowledge in Place." In *Hypertext '91,* 261–75. New York: Association of Computing Machinery. 1991.

Marshall, Catherine C., and Russell A. Rogers. "Two Years before the Mist: Experiences with Acquanet." In *ECHT'92,* 53–62. New York: Association of Computing Machinery, 1992.

Meyrowitz, Norman. "Hypertext—Does It Reduce Cholesterol, Too?" In *From Memex to Hypertext: Vannevar Bush and the Mind's Machine*. Ed. James M. Nyce and Paul Kahn. San Diego: Academic Press, 1991.

Miller, J. Hillis. *Illustration*. Cambridge: Harvard University Press, 1992.

———. "Literary Theory, Telecommunications, and the Making of History." In *Scholarship and Technology in the Humanities*. Ed. May Katzen, 11–20. London: British Library Research/Bowker Saur, 1991.

Mossberg, Walter S. "Organizer Program Takes a Leaf from Date Books." *Wall Street Journal*, January 21, 1993, B1.

Moulthrop, Stuart. "Beyond the Electronic Book: A Critique of Hypertext Rhetoric." In *Hypertext '91*, 291–98. New York: Association of Computing Machinery, 1991.

———. *Forking Paths: An Interaction after Jorge Luis Borges*. Unpublished web created in Storyspace Beta 3.3, 1987.

———. "Hypertext and 'the Hyperreal.'" In *Hypertext '89*, 259–68. New York: Association of Computing Machinery, 1989.

Mylonas, Elli. "The Perseus Project: Ancient Greece in Texts, Maps, and Images." In *Electronic Books—Multimedia Reference Works*, 173–88. Bergen: Norwegian Computing Centre, 1991.

Nyce, James M., and Paul Kahn, eds. *From Memex to Hypertext: Vannevar Bush and the Mind's Machine*. San Diego: Academic Press, 1991.

Ong, Walter J. *Orality and Literacy: The Technologizing of the Word*. London: Methuen, 1982.

Paulson, William R. *The Noise of Culture: Literary Texts in a World of Information*. Ithaca: Cornell University Press, 1988.

Queneau, Raymond. *Cent mille milliards de poèmes*. Paris: Gallimard, 1961.

Reid, Elizabeth M. "Electropolis: Communication and Community on Internet Relay Chat." Honors thesis, University of Melbourne, 1991.

Ronell, Avital. *The Telephone Book: Technology, Schizophrenia, Electric Speech*. Lincoln: University of Nebraska Press, 1989.

Segal, Erich. "Lilliputian Leviathans." *Times Literary Supplement*, December 11, 1992, 11.

Selfe, Cynthia L. "Politicizing and Inhabiting Virtual Landscapes as Discursive Spaces." Manuscript.

Sociomedia: Multimedia, Hypermedia, and the Social Construction of Knowledge. Ed. Edward Barrett. Cambridge: MIT Press, 1992.

Steinberg, S. H. *Five Hundred Years of Printing*. 2nd ed. Baltimore: Penguin, 1961.

Storyspace: A Hypertext Writing Environment [earlier subtitle: A Computer System for Reading and Writing]. Developed by J. David Bolter, Michael Joyce, and John B. Smith. Cambridge, Mass.: Eastgate Systems, 1988–93.

Triebwasser, Marc A. "The Electronic Library: The Student/Scholar Workstation, CD-ROM, and Hypertext." Paper delivered at American Political Science Association annual meeting, Washington, D.C., 1988.

Turner, E. S. "Answering the Call: Alexander Graham Bell's Legacy and Its Far-flung Connections." *Times Literary Supplement*, December 6, 1991, 3–4.

Ulmer, Gregory L. *Applied Grammatology: Post(e)-Pedagogy from Jacques Derrida to Joseph Beuys*. Baltimore: Johns Hopkins University Press, 1985.

———. "The Object of Post-Criticism." In *The Anti-Aesthetic: Essays on Postmodern Culture*. Ed. Hal Forster, 83–110. Port Townsend, Wash.: Bay Press, 1983.

———. *Teletheory: Grammatology in the Age of Video*. New York: Routledge, 1989.

User's Guide, Oxford English Dictionary on a Compact Disc. Version 4.10. Fort Washington, N.Y.: Tri Star, 1987.

Yankelovich, Nicole, Norman Meyrowitz, and Stephen Drucker. "Intermedia: The Concept and the Construction of a Seamless Information Environment." *IEEE Computer* 21 (1988): 81–96.

Yankelovich, Nicole, Norman Meyrowitz, and Andries van Dam. "Reading and Writing the Electronic Book," *IEEE Computer* 18 (1985): 15–30.

N O N L I N E A R I T Y

Nonlinearity and Literary Theory

Espen J. Aarseth

2

Electronic writing will require a simpler, more positive literary theory.

—J. David Bolter

The future can only be anticipated in the form of an absolute danger.

—Jacques Derrida

In this essay I outline a theory of nonlinear texts and investigate some of its possible implications for the practice of literary theory and criticism. A nonlinear text is an object of verbal communication that is not simply one fixed sequence of letters, words, and sentences but one in which the words or sequence of words may differ from reading to reading because of the shape, conventions, or mechanisms of the text. Nonlinear texts can be very different from each other, at least as different as they are from the linear texts. In the conceptual framework presented here, the linear text may be seen as a special case of the nonlinear in which the convention is to read word by word from beginning to end. Recently, because of the computer, certain types of nonlinear texts have received attention from educational, technological, and theoretical circles. Now may be the time to broaden the scope of interest and to examine textual nonlinearity from a general point of view.

Over the past two decades, the spread and radical development of the computer as a means of cultural and aesthetic expression has created a challenge to the paradigms of cultural theory that has not yet been systematically answered. Studies of specific computer-mediated phenomena often suffer from a lack of insight into neighboring phenomena, again caused by a missing frame of reference, a general theoretical overview based on a broad comparative study, and a dialectic between neighboring fields. This is not least the case in literary theory, in which technological issues traditionally have been met with very little interest. During the past decade, however, such issues have seen a marked increase of attention, perhaps not totally independent of the successful introduction of electronic word processing as an academic tool. The word processor has served to familiarize the literary scholar with *some* aspects of the new text technologies; but, due to its collaborative and emulative nature (the way electronic word processing assumes the goals of the earlier technologies), the more radical potential of textual computing is easily ignored, and the computer is gratefully perceived as less threatening than it actually is.

This essay, unlike the others in this book, is not primarily concerned with hypertext. Instead, I shall try to take a step back, to investigate the larger repertoire of textual forms of which hypertext can be said to be one. Hypertext, when regarded as a type of text, shares with a variety of other textual types a fundamental trait, which we defined as nonlinearity. It must immediately be pointed out that this concept refers only to the physico-logical form (or arrangement, appearance) of the texts, and not to any fictional meaning or external reference they might have. Thus, it is not the plot, or the narrative, or any other well-known poetic unit that will be our definitive agency but the shape or structure of the text itself. A narrative may be perfectly nonlinear (for example describing a sequence of events in a repetitive or nonsequential way) and yet be represented in a totally linear text.

The advent of computer-mediated textuality seems to have left many of those theorists and critics who noticed it in a terminological vacuum. In their eagerness to describe the brave new reality, they let a few words like *electronic* and *hypertext* cover many different phenomena. Behind the electronic text there is a large and heterogeneous variety of phenomena, and, as we shall see, a computer-mediated text may have more in common with a paper-based one than with one of its electronic brethren.

After considering some fundamental problems with the concept of textuality, I shall propose a typology of nonlinear texts based on principles extracted from various samples, and then I shall outline the main forms of nonlinearity. Since the paradigms and practice of literary theory cannot remain unaffected by its encounter with nonlinear literature, except by pretending it never happened, I both discuss new applications of literary theory and suggest some possible new departures.

Behind the Lines: What Is a Text, Anyway?

The text as a whole and as a singular whole may be compared to an object, which may be viewed from several sides, but never from all sides at once.

—Paul Ricoeur

To present nonlinear textuality as a phenomenon relevant to textual theory, one must rethink the concept of textuality to comprise linear as well as nonlinear texts. "The text," as it is commonly perceived, entails a set of powerful metaphysics that I have no hope of dispersing here. The three most important ones are those of *reading, writing,* and *stability*. Regardless of mutual contradiction, these three work together to control our notion of what a text is. For our purpose, they can be summed up as follows: (1) A text is what you read, the words and phrases that you see before your eyes and the meanings they produce in your head. (2) A text is a message, imbued with the values and intentions of a specific writer/genre/culture. (3) A text is a fixed sequence of constituents (beginning, middle, end) that cannot change, although its interpretations might. In opposition to these notions, I argue that the lessons of nonlinear literature show us a textuality different from our readings (and our readings of "reading"), more fundamental than our messages, and, through the evolving rituals and technologies of use and distribution, subject to many types of change. I do not for a moment believe that my constructed binarism of the nonlinear text and the linear text or any of the other perspectives in this essay are any more free of a metaphysics than any previous textual theory, but I hope they are better suited to identifying some of the relevant issues of textual communication.

My use of the word *text* is seemingly at odds with that of certain schools of textual theory that regard the text as a semantic network of symbolic relations, loosely attached to the notion of the literary work. I do not intend to challenge that idea; I believe that it belongs to a different aspect or level of the same object. We then have two perspectives: the text as a technical, historical, and social object and the text as it is individually received and understood. These aspects, which we might call the *informative* and the *interpretable,* are governed by different rules, but they are interdependent and influence (and sometimes intrude on) each other in many ways.

The informative aspect of the text is usually the harder to see, because it is the most obvious. In addition to its visible words and spaces, which we may call the *script,* a text includes a practice, a structure or ritual of use. Different practices adhere to different texts; we do not read *Peanuts* (the comic strip) the way we read the Bible. Of course, a rich text such as the Bible has many uses and is perused in many ways. I am not talking of interpretation here, just the algorithm and choreography that conducts the script from the text to the mind of the beholder. This may be compared (carefully) to the concept of genre, except that genre is seen prior to the text, and revered or betrayed by it; here it is the other way around.

The relationship between the text and the script requires closer attention. There is, of course, not *one* such relationship but as many as there are technologies and conventions of reading and writing. A simplistic model might depict two of the most common relationships as the following: text subordinate to script (the handwritten letter, the electronic word-processing document) and script subordinate to text (the mass-produced paper copy, the read-only CD-ROM). In the first case, whatever you do to the script affects the text; in the second, it does not. When we look for ways to describe differences between types of text, the word *electronic* usually does not get us very far.

The interpretable aspect of the text is that which makes it different; to be blunt, it is that which makes it worth reading. Formal as well as semantic elements come into play: if a text has an unusual shape, that alone arouses our interest. Most texts, however, are boringly familiar in their shape; we already know how to read them. I intend to deal with the interpretable aspect only insofar as it is affected by my discussion of the informative; to engage it fully here would be (at best) a pointless historic review of the highlights of linguistic and literary theory.

There is a problem here that goes back to a flaw at the heart of my definition of nonlinear text. When I said that a text can be nonlinear by convention, the definition is laid open to interference from the interpretable level. What if a text simply insists on its nonlinearity? Should we take its word for it? There are many such texts; Milorad Pavic's *Landscape Painted with Tea* (1990) comes to mind. From the second half, it can be read as a crossword puzzle, either "across" or "down," following the explicit instructions given on pages 100–101. But what if a text gives us such instructions at the start, then cancels them later on? Or worse, what if the text starts by warning us against possible attacks of illegitimate nonlinearities, then proceeds to order us to go at once to page 50 for further instructions and skip the intervening pages that, we are told, have been contaminated by subversive directions? These hypothetical cases, which are far from impossible, illustrate a peculiar semiotic power of the linear text over the nonlinear: the linear can flirt with nonlinearity, but the nonlinear cannot lie and pretend to be linear.

But let us return to our metaphysical question, which really is a serious one: What is a text? Or, to rephrase it, Which elements and effects belong to the text and which do not? The poststructuralists are fond of discussing this question in (and in relation to) the preface or the foreword, but since I do not have such places at my disposal in this book, but only a chapter, I shall not argue with them. Instead, consider this: does the author's name belong to a text? It is usually only found outside the text—on the cover, in the catalogue, in the book review, and in some cases in the top or bottom margins of the page; but it can be argued that, along with the text's title, which is also found outside the text proper (not "enclosed" in it), the words that make up the author's name are the single most meaningful phrase of the text. Of the text, but not in the text. Imagine the difference between a text by P. G. Wodehouse and a text by Agatha Christie; no problem there. It does not even have to be any specific books; we know the difference anyway. The fact that we may know something about the authors behind these names is not anywhere near as important as what we know about a text, once we know it is by one of them. Once I pick up a book by Ken Follett, I have already started the interpretation of it, long before I have started on the first page. Even if the name itself is unknown to us, its hints of gender and cultural background are meaningful.

Authors have always known these things. In antiquity and the early Middle Ages, some writers would use the name of a famous author to get their ideas read and spread—not as a villainous forgery with the goal of short-term benefit but as a way to enhance the endurance and position of their work. Think of it as a kind of benevolent computer virus. In more recent times, female writers used male pseudonyms: the fiction was even better if a fictitious author could be constructed. Still, "serious" authors use pseudonyms for their less serious work; that way the weight of their "true" name will not mislead their readers' expectations and interpretations. This shift works well even if the connection between the two names is known; it is the name, not the person behind it, that is important. The name belongs to the text, the writer (as in ghostwriter) does not.

Our distinction between the text and the script in the case of mass-produced and -distributed copies leads to the fundamental question of in what sense the script-independent text (the so-called real text behind all the copies) can be said to exist. This distinction may seem so much quaint and unnecessary contentiousness, but as part of the textual ontology—or, to coin a name for our field, *textonomy*—presented in this essay, it helps us to show that the stability of paper-based documents is as much a product of our metaphysical belief in a transcendental text as an inherent quality of the physical object.

Imagine a book in which some of the pages appear to be missing, or the print is unreadable every 16 pages, or some of the pages are repeated while an equal number omitted. Even if this copy is the only one we ever see, we automatically assume that it is not supposed to be this way and that a more correct version exists. It may never have been printed; but to us, who can imagine it perfectly (except for the missing words, of course), it is still more real than the one we are holding. For instance, in Terry Eagleton's *Literary Theory,* there are two chapters bearing the number one; the first titled "Introduction: What is Literature" (p.1), and the other "The Rise of English" (p.17).[1] Since my copy is from the eighth printing (1990) and the book was first published in 1983, it is unlikely that there is a version with only one first chapter, but we nevertheless assume that this is what the text meant, and that the introduction got numbered by mistake. We do this out of lack of respect for the copy; it appears to misrepresent the "real" text, even if such a thing may never have existed. In short, we prefer the imagined integrity of a metaphysical object to the stable version that we observe. Which one is more real than the other? As long as we are able to imagine and reconstruct an ideal version, everything appears to be fine, and our metaphysics remains intact. But what if the flawed version interferes so deeply with our sense of reception that it, in more than a manner of speaking, steals the show? Following our metaphysical logic, we would have to say that a new text had been created, since the alternative would be a script without a text. But, because of its unintentional origin, this new text cannot be metaphysically equal to the text it replaces, and so we are left with a paradox: some texts are metaphysical, some are not, and if we do not know their origins, we have no way to tell the difference.

The alternative, of course, is to abandon the concept of a real text-behind-the-text altogether. On Saturday, February the 7th, 1987, I saw John Boorman's *Zardoz* (1974) at the Bergen Film Club. *Or did I?* As it happened, somehow the reels got mixed up and were projected in the sequence 1, 2, 4, 3, 5. The film is a weird, allegorical adventure, from a barbaric future in which technology has become inexplicable and supernatural to everyone but a secluded group of very bored immortals. The title is an anagramatic allusion to *The Wizard of Oz,* and the story contains many surreal and fantastic elements—not least, it seemed to me, the sudden jump in the narrative, followed after a while by a just as strange flashback. When the fifth reel came on, however, I slowly started to suspect that this rather crude montage technique was neither Boorman nor his film company's doing, but most likely a mistake in "reel time." By then the damage was done, and I had had the confusing privilege of being lost in the materiality of a film—a strangely appropriate experience, somewhat parallel to that of the main character, played by Sean Connery, a barbarian who manages to get into the secret place, the Vortex of the immortals, to see their strange customs and technology (and their eventual destruction) from the inside.

By virtue of the altered sequence, an unintended cinematic experience, a new expression, was created. But was it a new film? I am tempted to answer, *no*. Not because I feel that a film (or any other artistic "work") has to be the intended and consecutive design of a conscious, creative operator, but because both the original and the heretical sequences are based on the same material potential. In this sense, a text or a film is like a limited language in which all the parts are known, but the full potential of their combinations is not. The mutation of *Zardoz* was created by a hidden possibility in its channel, not by the introduction of a new code or principle.

There are many scales of change in a text's metamorphosis: unintentional (the blunders of a typesetter or projectionist in the dark), usurpatory (a re-mix of samples from a musical recording, a hacked version of a computer game), plagiary (one composer's unacknowledged variations on a theme of another), and subversive or estranging (the "cut up" textual experiments of William Burroughs and John Cage), to suggest a few. Some of the results of some of these operations we might accept as authentic new works, others not, according to the cultural legitimacy of their method of construction or their operator; or, in the case of a new aesthetic system, depending on contemporary empathy with the perceived political symbolism of the mode of mutation.

Textual integrity and the border between two works of art—this is hardly a startlingly original conclusion—is a cultural construct. More importantly, as I have tried to show, so is our notion of what constitutes the text itself—not only our conception of its function, meaning, or metaphysical reliability but also what it appears to be made of and what conditions have to be met for us to acknowledge its existence. What remains to be investigated, then, is the possibility that textuality exists beyond metaphysics, through location, anatomy, and temporality.

There is no sense in denying that this crisis of the text (if so pretentious a denotation must be used) is brought about by the digital wonders of the information age—or rather, by the somewhat eschatological claims of the proponents of the so-called new media: "the book is dead," "this is the Late Age of Print," "the electronic text will free us from the tyranny of paper," and "in the future, everyone will be a writer." No doubt, these are interesting times. The problem with terms such as the *electronic text* and the *printed book* is that they are, to borrow a phrase from Clifford Geertz, too "dangerously unfocused" to sustain a precise analysis. Nevertheless, this enthusiastic eschatology forces us to see dusty old things in a new light and perhaps learn a thing or two in the process.

And so the computer—that old, mythological beast—has become instrumental in everyone's quest for a new understanding of the text. The danger of turning this quest into just another metaphysics comes mainly from two sides, both of which it is impossible to avoid altogether: the vigorous rhetoric of the current generation of media prophets urging us to believe in their electronic text; and, more fundamentally, that there *is* such a thing as *the text,* a theoretical entity that defines the sufficient and necessary conditions of textuality, with no regard for practice, history, or technology. (There are also the problems of translation, transcript, pastiche, theft, censorship, editing, variorum editions, incomplete manuscripts, and oral narratives, which will not be discussed here.)

One of the most important ideological aspects of the effects on verbal communication of the present and earlier information technologies is that the transcendental concept of text seems to survive. It does not come to mean something else, like "electronic book," "computer novel," or "virtual document": the electronic text, for all its hype and naiveté, is still a text. If we accept this claim, then it seems clear that textuality cannot be defined in terms of location, anatomy, or temporality. What is the difference, in terms of script, between *Don Quixote* on paper and *Don Quixote* on a screen? I believe they are the same, although I "know" that the ink-cellulose relationship promotes and impedes different rituals of use than does the electron-phosphor relationship.

To clarify the fundamental mechanisms of texts, we should study text as information. This simple and perhaps anticlimactic injunction does not leave the eternal questions of rhetoric and poetics in the hands of the information theorists any more than the fundamental problems of semantics can be solved by phoneticians, but it might give us a more stable object to work with in a time when our old paper-based paradigms seem to disperse on the winds of the rhetoric of the new technologies. Under these circumstances it might seem a suspect move to link our concept of textuality to the very scientific ideology that causes our crisis, the theories of cybernetics and information as conceived by Norbert Wiener, Claude Shannon, and others in the 1940s.[2] However, this is hardly a controversial connection in itself, for the influence of this paradigm on literary theory can be found throughout structuralism and beyond, in the hegemonic works of Roman Jakobson and Umberto Eco, for example. Where this new adaptation might prove to be a radical departure is in the way we shall use it to define textuality independent of its traditional associates, the reader/receiver/audience and writer/sender/author. This move, which might be seen as self-defense, serves two practical purposes: to avoid the rather silly idea that the reader and author are becoming the same person; and to free the text from being identified with its readings and its writings. A text is not what we may read out of it, nor is it identical with what someone once wrote into it. It is something more, a potential that can be realized only partially and only through its script. Furthermore, texts (whether they exist or not), like electrons, can never be experienced directly, only by the signs of their behavior. Texts are cross products between a set of matrices—linguistic (the script), technological (the mechanical conditions), and historical (the socio-political context); and because of the temporal instability of all of these variables, texts are processes impossible to terminate and reduce. This perspective lets us include nonlinear texts, many of which have no author (or even reader) in the traditional sense.

After the tensions and misunderstandings caused by the intrusions of new computer-mediated textualities and the inevitable resistance to them have been absorbed into literary theory, new textual paradigms will eventually emerge. They will no doubt be very different from the perspective presented here, but with a little luck their metaphysics might be informed by the principles behind the lines of the textual technologies, as well as by the metaphors of the latest interfaces.

A Typology of Nonlinear Textuality

The use of the term *nonlinearity* in this essay is grounded in mathematics and not inspired by the modern physical sciences. I emphasize this point not because I want to distance myself from the claims of literary critics, like Katherine Hayles, who employ the term in its latter sense, but because the influence of nonlinear dynamics on recent literary theory should not be confused with the present formal concept of nonlinear textuality.[3] Insights promoted by the metaphors of nonlinear physics aid understanding of nonlinear texts as well as linear ones, but reading a nonlinear text is not the same as a reading informed by research in fractal geometry or chaos theory. The behavior of some kinds of nonlinear texts can certainly be described in terms of unpredictability, self-organization, and turbulence, but for the definition and basic understanding of nonlinear literature we need not look that far.

For a formal definition of our concept, the mathematical branch of topology will suffice. According to my copy of *Webster's New Twentieth-Century Dictionary,* this is the theory of "those properties of geometric figures that remain unchanged even when under distortion, so long as no surfaces are torn." Without too much discordance, I hope, the textonomical version of topology may be described as "the study of the ways in which the various sections of a text are connected, disregarding the physical properties of the channel (paper, stone, electromagnetic, and so on), by means of which the text is transmitted." The original mathematical meaning is transposed from geometry to textonomy rather than metaphorized, because the formalism is left intact. Textual topology describes the formal structures that govern the sequence and accessibility of the script, whether the process is conducted manually (for example, by convention) or mechanically (for example, by computer).

If texts are to be described in topological terms, they must be shown to consist of a set of smaller units and the connections between them. Further, the function of these units must be relevant to our notion of nonlinearity. It is not difficult to partition any text into graphemes (letters), lexemes (words), or syntagms (phrases or sentences), but none of these elements indicates nonlinearity by its presence. As later examples reveal, the position of a single letter or the position of many syntagms strung together can make a text nonlinear. Therefore, the unit for which we are looking is clearly not defined by linguistic form. This unit, which is best conceived as an arbitrarily long string of graphemes, is identified by its relation to the other units as constrained and separated by the conventions or mechanisms of their mother text. It should be noted that these textual units usually do not upset the laws of grammatical language, but that is of no importance to our definition.

As a suitable name for such a unit I suggest *texton,* which denotes a basic element of textuality. In accordance with the concept of textuality developed in the previous section, a more logical name might seem to be *scripton,* but this term posits that the textual unit belongs to the reading process rather than that it inheres in the textual structure as a strategic potential. A scripton, then, is an unbroken sequence of one or more textons as they are projected by the text. Another alternative to *texton* might be *lexie,* after Roland Barthes's *"unités de lecture"* ("units of reading") in *S/Z.*[4] This candidate, adopted by George P. Landow (1992) from an English translation as "lexia," I want to avoid because of Barthes's emphasis on seriality ("*fragments contigu*") and the destructive process of its separation ("*découpé*") from the text.[5] For Barthes, lexies are not the building blocks of textuality but a violent and powerful demonstration of "reading." In sharp contrast to the playful combinatorics of textual nonlinearity, Barthes's motto is clearly *divide et impera.*

In addition to its textons, a text consists of one or more *traversal functions,* the conventions and mechanisms that combine and project textons as scriptons to the *user* (or reader) of the text. We use these functions to distinguish between the variants in our textual typology. A traversal function might be a simple act of accessing a text (for example "pick a random card" or "*Ecc* 12:12b") or it might be a complex set of instructions (for example a computer program such as *Eliza*) that compiles a scripton from textons. Since there is an infinite set of traversal functions, I shall not try to make an inventory of them here but instead describe a set of basic variates that together defines a multidimensional coordinate system into which the functions can be plotted. This proposed matrix, which is clearly incomplete, may be expanded or changed as new traversal functions are discovered, or as existing ones are better understood. The categories I intend to extract are pragmatic and tentative, and will hopefully yield to a more concise model as the research progresses.

Below is a list of the variates, slightly adapted from my *Texts of Change,* in which they are developed and discussed at length and applied to a set of nonlinear texts.[6] Then, by the exploratory data-analysis method known as correspondence analysis, a two-dimensional plot was produced in which the texts formed groups that provided a basis for general classification.[7]

Topology. The fundamental difference is that between the *linear* and the *nonlinear.* A nonlinear text is a work that does not present its scriptons in one fixed sequence, whether temporal or spatial. Instead, through cybernetic agency (the user[s], the text, or both), an arbitrary sequence emerges.

Dynamics. Then there is the difference between the *static* and the *dynamic* text. In a static text the scriptons are constant, whereas in a dynamic text the contents of scriptons may change while the number of textons remains fixed (*intratextonic* dynamics), or the number of textons may vary as well (*textonic* dynamics).

Determinability concerns the stability of the traversal function; a text is *determinate* if the adjacent scriptons of every scripton are always the same, and *indeterminate* if not.

Transiency. If the mere passing of the user's time causes scriptons to appear, it is *transient,* if not, it is *intransient.* If the transiency has the nature of "real time" it is *synchronous;* if the relationship between the user's time and the passing of fictional time is arbitrary, we call it *asynchronous.*

Maneuverability. The question of how easy it is to access the scriptons of a text can be described in terms of traversal functions and their combinations. The most open (or weak) we call *random access to all scriptons;* then there is the standard hypertext traversal function—the *link, explicit access to all scriptons;* the *hidden* link; the *conditional* or *complex* link; and, finally, the arbitrary or *completely controlled access.*

User-functionality. Besides the *interpretative function* of the user, which of course is present in the use of both linear and nonlinear textuality, the use of nonlinear texts may be described in terms of four active feedback functions: the *explorative function,* in which the user decides which "path" to take; the *role-playing function,* in which the user assumes strategic responsibility for a "character" in a "world" described by the text; the *configurative function,* in which textons and/or traversal functions are in part chosen and/or designed by the user; and the *poetic function,* in which the user's actions, dialogue, or design are aesthetically motivated.

Any type of text can be discussed according to these categories; I avoid the primitive and theoretically uninteresting division between electronic and hard copy texts as well as the nebulous concept of interactive fiction. The model is equally applicable to a child's interrogation of a storyteller and a researcher's conversation with an artificial intelligence program, or a radio broadcast of *The Wind in the Willows.*

The best way to test a model is to see how well it stands up to new data. Since I developed mine in 1991, a new text type has appeared, invented by the science fiction author William Gibson. His *Agrippa: A Book of the Dead* (1992) displays its script at a fixed scrolling pace on the screen and then encrypts it by a technique cryptically known as RSA, rendering it effectively unreadable after that one projection.[8] Leaving the more obvious jokes aside (better make reservations down at the library, quick!), this is clearly one more of those one-of-a-kind texts for which "the medium is the message" seems to have been intended. But that should not stop the empirical literary critic. I must admit to a curious feeling of unease here. *Agrippa* perversely obeys the logic of cultural capitalism beyond the wildest dreams of publishers: it is the non-reusable book. At the same time it obviously subverts the metaphysics of textual mass production. How? By being a copy that destroys its text, or a text which destroys its copy? *Agrippa* is a unique lesson in textual ontology, a linear text that seems to flirt with nonlinearity, not through its convention or mechanism but through the difference between its used and unused copies. The individual copy-as-text is linear, because there is only one sequence: first, the decrypted scripton once, then the re-encrypted one for ever after; but the text-as-copy may turn out to be either of the scriptons and is therefore nonlinear. Rather than accept that this paradoxical result undermines my linear-nonlinear distinction, I contend that by destroying its traversal function it exposes the inherent instability of the metaphysical concept of "the text itself." Thus, *Agrippa* becomes nonlinear only if we choose to accept the "text-behind-the-text" as more real than the physical object that can refuse to be read. As for the rest of our categories, *Agrippa* is a rather unusual combination of a static, determinate, and transient text with completely controlled access to scriptons.

As a simplified synthesis of this model I now propose four pragmatic categories, or degrees, of nonlinearity: (1) the simple nonlinear text, whose textons are totally static, open and explorable by the user; (2) the discontinuous nonlinear text, or hypertext, which may be traversed by "jumps" (explicit links) between textons; (3) the determinate "cybertext," in which the behavior of textons is predictable but conditional and with the element of role-playing; and (4) the indeterminate cybertext in which textons are dynamic and unpredictable. The weakness of this simplified model is that some nonlinear texts, such as those that are both static and indeterminate, fall between the generalized categories. However, it is not uncommon in cultural theory that generalization means loss of precision, and it should always be weighed against the usefulness and convenience of the simplification and the fact that a more rigorous and unmitigated model exists.

The rest of this essay discusses each of these four categories, some of the texts that can be said to belong to them, their attributes and peculiarities, and their importance to literary theories and to the practice of literary criticism.

The Readerless Text

Nonlinearity can be achieved in many ways, the simplest of which is a script forking out in two directions on a surface, forcing its witness (the user) to choose one path in preference to another. In such a case (for example, the "dream maps" in Kathy Acker's *Blood and Guts in High School*), the user can immediately afterwards take the other path and thus eventually view all parts of the script simultaneously.[9] The verbal oscillation created by two equally possible combinations, the choice of which is entirely up to the user, produces an ambiguity different from the usual poetic double meaning of a word or phrase, because there seem to be two different versions, neither of which can exist alongside the other, and both obviously different from the text itself. Like optical illusions, we can imagine first one, then the other, but not both at the same time. When we look at the whole of such a nonlinear text, we cannot read it; and when we read it, we cannot see the whole text. Something has come between us and the text, and that is ourselves, trying to read. This self-consciousness forces us to take responsibility for what we read and to accept that it can never be the text itself. The text, far from yielding its riches to our critical gaze, appears to seduce us, but it remains immaculate, recedes, and we are left with our partial and impure thoughts, like unworthy pilgrims beseeching an absent deity.

However, if a text cannot be conquered, it is all the better suited for worship. The wall-inscriptions of the temples in ancient Egypt were often connected two-dimensionally (on one wall) or three-dimensionally (from wall to wall and from room to room), and this layout allowed a nonlinear arrangement of the religious text in accordance with the symbolic architectural layout of the temple.[10]

Without doubt, the most prominent and popular nonlinear text in history must be the famous Chinese work of oracular wisdom, *I Ching* or *Book of Changes,* one of the great classics of antiquity, which was used for thousands of years for meditation and as an oracle. It is not, as is sometimes stated, the oldest text in Chinese and world literary history, but it is well over three thousand years old and originates from the symbol system said to have been invented over five thousand years ago by the legendary Fu Hsi.[11] Other notables, among them King Wen, the Duke of Chou, and Confucius, have developed and annotated the text down through the ages; and the text is still being rewritten and mutating, adapting to modern society and its paradigms.[12]

I Ching is made up of sixty-four symbols or hexagrams, which are the binary combinations of six whole or broken ("changing") lines ($64 = 2^6$). A hexagram (such as nr. 49: ䷰ *Ko/Revolution*) contains a main texton and six small ones, one for each line. By manipulating three coins or forty-nine yarrow stalks according to a randomizing principle, textons from two hexagrams are combined, producing one out of 4096 possible scriptons. This scripton contains the answer to a question the user wrote down in advance. The extremely clever openness of the formulations, the sense of ritual involved in throwing the coins or stalks, and the strangely personal communication between the user and the book almost always make an answer extracted from *I Ching* seem relevant and sometimes even divinely inspired.

Unlike historic texts with a fixed expression, such as *Beowulf*, *I Ching* seems to speak uniquely to us across the millennia, not as a distant mirror that can be understood in a philological or romantic sense but as an entity that somehow understands us and exists for us. This almost religious effect can be partly explained by the repeated updates and the fact that the text was intended to be useful and directly relevant to events in people's lives, but it seems to me that it is the explicit and elaborate ritual, largely unchanged through the ages, that creates the textual *presence* that allows us to be naive users—not readers but agents of the text, closely related to the users of three thousand years ago, despite the epistemological interventions of time and culture. The *Book of Changes* may not be the world's first text, but it is certainly the first expert system based on the principles of binary computing that very much later became automated by electricity and the vacuum tube.

Both types of text discussed so far seem to reject the presence of the traditional reader figure, as it is implied and applied in the theories of literature. As an individual, this pale and uncontroversial character never mattered much to us critics anyway, and then only as a construct on which to hang the baser pleasures of the text; he is our poor and predictable cousin, slave to the rhythm, lost in the textual pleasure dome like the ball in a pinball machine. Later, for the reader-response theorists, he became a thumbtack with which to pin down the variable of literary meaning when it could no longer be located in the text. Active or passive, the reader is always portrayed as a receiver of the text, going quietly about the business of consuming, constructing *meaning only*, a fixed but evolving character at the end of the text's production line, defined by the conventions and strategies of reading. Of course, it can be argued that this relationship is no different for nonlinear texts, once the shock of an alien form is gone and the particular convention is understood and mastered. This counterpoint, which may be called the *Verfremdung*-argument, has much merit, but it ignores the fact that the understanding (beyond trivial) of a nonlinear text can never be a consummate understanding, because the realization of its script (and not just its meaning) belongs to the individual user, who is acutely aware of his or her own constructive participation. Since the object is unstable both in a syntactic and semantic sense, it cannot be read, only glimpsed and guessed at. Much of the initial discomfort felt by the user of a nonlinear text is caused by its not behaving as a real text should; once the strangeness is gone, the user knows what to expect, which is not to expect everything. The users learn to accept their position as agents of the text, sometimes happily, as in the case of the *Book of Changes,* and sometimes unhappily, as with the forking directions texts. The difference between these two types of experience can be explained by the presence or absence of an established (meaningful) ritual, which must absolve the user from the burden of reading, which in the case of nonlinearity may be defined as the frustrating attempt to harmonize contradictory scriptons from the same text. The user of *I Ching* relates the scripton directly to his or her individual situation, and the interpretation, following the ritual of producing the hexagram, can only be done by the individual.

This fall from readership should not be confused with the clever destabilization effects of so-called metafictions, in which the opposite point—readership confirmed—is made. Even (and especially) the famously "unreadable" texts subversively observe the metaphysics of the general reader: the door would not be locked if the owner did not believe in thieves.

Few texts drive home the point of the readerless text more abundantly than Raymond Queneau's *Cent Mille Milliards de Poèmes* (1961).[13] In this short book, ten pages are cut into fourteen one-line strips, and the user is invited to flip the strips individually, to form 100,000,000,000,000 different combinations. As it turns out, each of the 140 strips (or textons) is a sonnet line, and the result of any combination is a scripton in the form of a formally perfect sonnet. Here is sonnet number 65 957 658 052 316:

> Quand l'un aveque l'autre aussitôt sympathise
> que convoitait c'est sûr une horde d'escrocs
> des êtres indécis vous parlent sans franchise
> il ne trouve aussi sec qu'un sac de vieux fayots
>
> L'un et l'autre a raison non la foule insoumise
> qui clochard devenant jetait ses oripeaux
> aller à la grand ville est bien une entreprise
> l'enfant pur aux yeux bleus aime les berlingots
>
> Du pôle à Rosario fait une belle trotte
> on giffle le marmot qui plonge sa menotte
> lorsqu'on revient au port en essuyant un grain
>
> Ne fallait pas si loin agiter ses breloques
> on transports et le marbre et débris et défroques
> la gémellité vraie accuse son destin.

This may not be the most exciting of lyrical poetry, but it is unique in a very special sense: I have never read it before, and chances are that neither has anybody else. Who wrote it? Was it me, or Queneau (and if so, in 1961 or 1992?), or perhaps the text itself? Will anybody ever read number 65 957 658 052 317? For one person to read all the sonnets is clearly impossible, and even a very small fraction—say ten million—would take at least one hundred years. *Cent Mille Milliards de Poèmes* effectively mocks the theoretical notions of writer and reader, while the power of the text is cleverly demonstrated. (What it does to our notion of the sonnet is perhaps better left unsaid.) "Obviously the possibilities of the book as format are being strained to the limit," comments William Paulson, who goes on to propose *Poèmes* as "an ideal candidate for a computerized version."[14] Contrary to Paulson, I suggest that the fact that it *is* a book is just as significant; and if it seems easy to implement as a computer program, that is because of the simple and unstrained elegance of its idea.

The difference between these experiences and my experience with Boorman's *Zardoz* is that in the latter case I could, based on my cultural competence, deduce the actual existence of a version that was independent of me and the possibility of a proper reading that could be conducted by an easily imagined proper reader, but not by me. In other words, I rejected my reading because it told me that I was not a real reader, since what I was reading was not the real text. The shock of discovering that one is not a reader can only happen (and only accidentally) with a linear text, because that is the only text in which the metaphysics of a real reader has any credibility and the only text in which the reader can exist as a reducible, accountable figure. In addition, *reader* has—until now—always been defined by literary theorists with only the linear text in mind. If we want to know what is going on between nonlinear texts and their users, we must come up with a concept that implies both more and less than reading and redefines literary satisfaction as well as hermeneutic behavior.

Hypertext Is Not What You (May) Think

Hypertext, for all its packaging and theories, is an amazingly simple concept. It is merely a direct connection from one position in a text to another. However, when we speak of hypertext, it can signify at least three different things: (1) the general concept, as outlined above; (2) an implementation of the concept, usually a computer application called a hypertext system, with idiosyncrasies and enhancements that make it different from other systems; and (3) a text embedded in (and defined by) such a system. As an unfortunate result, many assumptions made about the general concept of hypertext are really about a specific implementation. Added to that are the political conjectures about the benevolent effects on the structures of power between writers and readers, teachers and students, government and the public, in which the good guys seem to be winning, at least in theory. Only the first of these relationships will be discussed here, and only because of the assumptions about the effects of hypertext upon the figures of author and reader.[15] (Of course, implicit in the term *hypertext* is a sphere of meanings beyond the operational. Those who would play on this potential cannot completely escape its dark side: the excessive, the abnormal, the sickly.)

Although the term *hypertext* was first used by Theodor H. Nelson in 1965 (compare Nelson 1987), the modern origin of the idea is generally accepted to stem from Vannevar Bush, whose article "As We May Think" (1945) described a possible solution to the scientist's problem of keeping up with the "growing mountain of research," in the form of a "sort of mechanized private file and library," a machine for storing, annotating, retrieving, and linking information: the *memex*.[16] Although Bush emphasizes the "trail"—the linear ordering of interesting items from the "maze of materials available"—he allows his user to go off on little side excursions. Bush was no techno-pessimist (at the end of the article he even envisions the neural jack of the 1980s cyberpunk science fiction!), and we can hardly blame him for not coming up with a complete "web view" on hypertextuality in 1945. But it should be pointed out that in his fascinating vision—his *poetics*—nonlinearity is as much a problem (the "maze") as a solution (the "trail"). Where he clearly concurs with his apostles is in his focus on user-created links and annotations. This may seem more radical than it actually is, with subversive political consequences for the world of literature and art; but Bush's user is clearly modeled on the traditional academic author, who can carry out his critical comparisons and annotations of sources with the same serene distance as before, only much more efficiently.

The principle of hypertext should not be linked to a particular ideology or poetics because it can be used (and of course misused) by many. Moreover, when as literary critics we examine a hypertextual text, we should take care not to confuse its interpretation with the author-reader relationship made possible by the ideology of its hypertext system and then assign the conclusions to a general theory of literary hypertext.

Hypertext theorists frequently employ spatial imagery to describe the relations made possible by links and textons: maps, three-dimensionality, textual landscapes, navigation, topography, and the like. This rhetoric fails to hide the fact that the main feature of hypertext is discontinuity—the jump—the sudden displacement of the user's position in the text. Pure hypertext is actually among the least topographical modes of nonlinearity. To ease this situation, hypertext systems often introduce additional features: overviews, index views, web views, texton lists, and so on. Some would undoubtedly argue that these instruments are also hypertext, but since we would recognize a text as hypertext without any of them, we should also endeavor to discuss the literary ramifications of hypertext without them. When they are included in a literary hypertext, they substantially affect the textual ritual, usually to a point at which it is difficult to speak about the same text.

A text that already has become canonical in the discussions of literary hypertext is Michael Joyce's *Afternoon, a story*.[17] Comprising (according to the information supplied at startup) 539 textons and 950 links, *Afternoon* both celebrates and subverts hypertext structure. The first of its kind, it intriguingly demonstrates the potential of hypertextuality for literary experiment and explores the effects of nonlinearity on narration.

There are no visible links in *Afternoon,* and the user may click on any word in the scriptons to see if they yield (link to) something special. If they do not, or the user presses the return key, the next default scripton in the present chain occupies the screen. In addition, the user may call up a menu with explicit links, but this can be a disruptive element in the otherwise suggestive and enigmatic ride on the link stream. To complicate matters, some links are conditional; they are available only if the user has earlier traversed certain unspecified scriptons. As anyone familiar with hypertext programs knows, this interface is very unusual: an invisible link is as unheard of as a newspaper article without a headline. The conditional link is just as uncanny and makes the text "seem to have a mind of its own."[18] Thus *Afternoon,* arguably the first literary hypertext, turns out to be something more: a cybertext disguised in hypertext's clothing.

It is hard to classify *Afternoon* as a narrative (or "a story," as the text paradoxically titles itself). Although within most of the individual scriptons the voice of a first person narrator relates events to a narratee in a traditional manner, the unpredictable changing of scenes (as one trail of related scriptons abruptly stops and another begins) constantly undermines the would-be reader's attempt to identify with the narratee, as well as the identification of the narrator and the (implied) author or exo-narrator, as it were. In *Afternoon* there seems to be an anti-narrator at work, giving the narrator (and me) a hard time. In linear experimental texts the subversive effect is sometimes achieved by a "distance between narrator and narratee" and sometimes by the "loss of narratee"—the narrator as solipsist.[19] In *Afternoon*, however, the relation between narrator and narratee appears relatively normal; while the distance between the user and narratee on one side and narrator and author on the other is stretched to the limit by the unreliable links. Far from feeling like Landow's "reader-author" (117), who has no problem constructing "meaning and narrative from fragments provided by someone else," I felt constantly sidetracked, turning and turning in the dilating text, dead sure that important things were being whispered just beyond my hearing. I cannot deny that it was a very fascinating literary experience.

It can be argued that the text I encountered was (in more than one sense) not the same as the one discussed by Stuart Moulthrop, J. David Bolter, and Landow. From their accounts it appears that they used a different and more advanced version of *Afternoon*'s hypertext system, the "author version" of Storyspace, which allows writing and adding links, and most significantly contains a global view, a graphical representation of the topological relations between all textons and links. My version was in Readingspace, the stand-alone reader program that *Afternoon*'s publisher distributes. Consequently, my encounter, "one scripton at a time," with *Afternoon* was very different from theirs; for the global view, even if they did not use it, gave them a safety net that I lacked. While I was lost in the labyrinth, they could be "up there" with its creator—but only up to a point. Whatever changes they might impose, it would only be on their own copies; Joyce's text would stand unchanged. In this, hypertext is not different from paper-based linear texts. The balance of power between readers and writers is not changed by hypertext alone, nor by its enhancements, but by the political and economic logic of society (to use some slightly inaccurate clichés). This may change, under the influence of technological change and other things; but until it does, hypertext is just one more "instrument in some representational enterprise," to borrow a phrase from Samuel Delany.

To expand the notion of hypertext by subsuming other computer-mediated textual communication phenomena such as Usenet (see Bolter, 29) or intertextual allusion (see Landow, 10) will only render the concept useless for critical discourse. Landow's term "implicit hypertext" implies that an allusion and a link are essentially the same, but we only need a hypertext with both links and allusions to see that they work differently and must be considered two separate literary instruments. Bolter, eager to proclaim the end of "the printed book," plays along with the metaphysics of logocentrism and reduces print on paper to barely a corner of its multiform nature: "A printed book generally speaks with a single voice and assumes a consistent character, a persona, before its audience."[20] For "the electronic text," however, this no longer applies, because "it is not a physical artifact." To go against Bolter's rhetoric, I would say that instead of having two sets of opposed attributes, one connected to the "printed" and one to the "electronic" text, we have a number of different text types, some paper based and some digital, with the greater variety among the digital ones, and the paper based most centrally placed. Thus, there may be more difference between two digital texts than between either of those and a paper text. Allusion, reference, quotation, and linking are all *different* functions of intertextuality, just as Usenet newsgroups, electronic mailing lists, hypertext systems, paperback bestsellers, and flysheets represent different modes of textuality.

As the analysis of *Afternoon* indicates, literary hypertexts seem to pose interesting perspectives for students of literature. The question of nonlinear narrative versus anti-narrative should not be decided by the evidence from only one text (even if it exists in two versions), and perhaps we need a new terminology that lets us name the representation and composition principle that relates to nonlinearity as narrative relates to linearity.

However, one traditional term seems almost perfect to describe literary hypertexts. *Afternoon* does not represent a break with the *novel.* On the contrary, it finds its place in a long tradition of experimental literature in which one of the main strategies is to subvert and resist narrative. The novel ("the new"), from Cervantes to the *Roman Nouveau,* has always been an anti-genre, and *Afternoon* is but its latest confirmation.

Death and Cybernetics in the Ever-ending Text

I'm not sure that I have a story. And if I do, I'm not sure that everything isn't my story.

—Michael Joyce, *Afternoon, a story*

If literary hypertext is a new form of computer-mediated textuality, cybertext is a fairly old one, going back to the 1960s if not longer. *Cyber* is derived from *cybernetics,* the name of Norbert Wiener's science of "control and communication in the animal and the machine," again derived from the Greek *kybernêtês, steersman* (compare *governor*). A cybertext is a self-changing text, in which scriptons and traversal functions are controlled by an immanent cybernetic agent, either mechanical or human. There are many species of cybertext, and my distinction between determinate and indeterminate tries to set up an important division between two main groups: those that can be predicted (for example, one set of user actions will always yield the same set of scriptons) and those that cannot. The second group will be discussed in the next section.

The history of computer-mediated cybertexts can be traced to two different sources, both originating from fields of computer science, and both with their memorable ur-texts. The first, *Eliza,* created by Joseph Weizenbaum in 1966, was an early success in the field called artificial intelligence. The mother of all dialogue programs (*Parry, SHRDLU, Racter,* and countless others), *Eliza* played the part of a psychotherapist, asking the user questions and constructing further questions using information from the answers. Usually, dialogues turned rather Pinteresque as soon as the users discovered *Eliza's very* mechanical nature; but Weizenbaum's invention effectively demonstrated man's needs for communication, no matter with whom (or indeed *what*), and an important literary genre—the artificial conversationalist—was born.

The other source is known as the classic game *Adventure,* the first of the highly popular computer game genre of adventure games. According to Jon Lanestedt, *Adventure* was first a landscape simulation of Colossal Cave in Kentucky, topographed as a Fortran program by William Crowther at the end of the 1960s, then enhanced by Don Woods to attain its adventure form, and later modified and ported by others to countless computer platforms as the home-computer explosion started at the end of the 1970s.[21] Its technical structure became the paradigm for a very large number of similar games, even after more advanced types, such as Infocom's *Zork,* became commercially available.

The basic structure of *Adventure* can be described not as a topography but as an *ergo*graphy, the textually represented laborious progress of the main character/narratee/user; the text's "you." *You*'s task is to find all the treasure and kill the appropriate monsters while avoiding getting killed or stuck or lost in the topographical maze. The user controls *you* by typing commands, such as "kill troll," or "grab gold," that are interpreted by a simple verb-object parser. Directions can be specified by simple letters: "n" for "north," "d" for "down" etc. Depending on the user's input, the text will issue short scriptons describing the landscape, possible exits to the next room, any objects lying about, or the result of the user's last command. Here is a short sample of the start of a session with *Adventure* (my commands are in capital letters):

Welcome to Adventure!! Would you like instructions?

N

Please answer the question!

NO

You are standing at the end of a road before a small brick building. Around you is a forest. A small stream flows out of the building and down a gully.

BUILDING

You are inside a building, a well house for a large spring.

There are some keys on the ground here.

There is a shiny brass lamp nearby.

There is food here.

There is a bottle of water here.

TAKE KEYS

Ok.

. . . .

LEAVE

You are at end of road again.

DOWN

You are in a valley in the forest beside a stream tumbling along a rocky bed.

DOWN

At your feet all the water of the stream splashes into a 2-inch slit in the rock. Downstream the streambed is bare rock.

DOWNSTREAM

You don't fit through a two-inch slit!

You're at slit in streambed.

Adventure and most texts like it are determinate, intransient, and intratextonically dynamic, with completely controlled access to scriptons. The user's function takes the form of role-playing, since the user assumes strategic responsibility for the narratee. As with *Afternoon,* these texts often give me a feeling of being lost, the feeling that the real action is taking place elsewhere in the text; but in adventure games the ennui is usually replaced by death, when the *you* has reached a dead end in the topography or invoked some deadly response by a wrong action. Death in the cybertext is a strange kind of death, however, in relation to death both in fiction and in real life. Rather than signifying closure—the end—"cyberdeath" signifies a sort of reincarnation of the main character: death implies beginning. This phenomenon most clearly establishes the difference between main character, narratee, and user. The main character is simply dead, erased, and must begin again. The narratee, on the other hand, is explicitly told what happened, usually in a sarcastic manner, and offered the chance to start anew. The user, aware of all this in a way denied to the narratee, learns from the mistakes and previous experience and is able to play a different game.

Just as death in the determinate cybertext is a kind of unend, the end of the cybertext is a kind of undeath also contrary to fiction. The end of a cybertext (when the user quits) can be either successful (the user wins) or unsuccessful (the game is not solved). The first case denies the satisfaction that can be experienced at the end of a good, traditional epic, since the *you* remains in the text after completing the adventures, but there is nothing more to do. Even when the text includes some sort of ceremony of victory, it cannot provide the traditional build-up and release of tension that the readers of fiction normally expect. In Aristotelian terms, the end is marked by peripety not catharsis. If the end is unsuccessful, this too means abandonment of the *you,* which then remains in the text as a ghost in the machine: not living, not properly buried, and with a cause left unfinished.

If the absent structure of narrative is the key problem in literary hypertext, in determinate cybertext the absent structure is the plot. Since without a user there can be no action (*praxis*) in a determinate cybertext, the concept of story (*fabula*) is meaningless. In fiction the story determines and hides behind the plot, which produces the action, whereas in cybertext the plot itself is hidden, and so the discursive causality is reversed: action determines (or seeks in vain for) the plot, which if found does not produce anything interesting, only (barely) closure. Although there is a narrator, because of the narratee's significant interruptions there can be no narrative, only narration. The goal of this dialogue is to try out possible plots until the shoe fits: the user is playing for the plot.

Anthony Niesz and Norman Holland, in their early article on what they called "interactive fiction" (a concept that corresponds to determinate cybertext, if one disregards their definition of it), contend that "Interactive fiction has become possible only with the advent of high-speed digital computers that are capable of handling words."[22] However, when they compare computer-based adventure games to paper-based ones, the only difference they can find is that the latter do "not yield the sense of true dialogue that one gets from computerized interactive fiction." What they mean is that the user does not type words on the screen and watch the response. (The "sense of true dialogue" is hard to take seriously.) In fact, a game book such as *The Money Spider* (of the type that instructs, "If you want to hear about Schmidt, turn to 270, and if you want to hear about Popper, turn to 90") tells the user to write on its pages to map progress.[23] When classified by the categories of the variate model, *The Money Spider,* just like *Adventure,* is determinate, intransient, and intratextonically dynamic (since the user by writing changes at least one texton), with completely controlled access to scriptons (it is possible to cheat, of course, but that can be done in *Afternoon* too). This is no coincidence, because the game book genre was in part inspired by and adapted from the computer-mediated adventure game: an interesting example of how "the printed book" can subsume "the electronic text," if the market demands it.

"The Lingo of the Cable": Travels in Cybertextuality

As the field of artificial intelligence expanded, it soon overlapped with that of topography and world simulation and produced story generators and models for representing actions and characters.[24] Later, research took an explicit interest in the adventure game, developing complex models of the interaction between a user-controlled character and artificial persons within a simulated world, for example, the Oz project of the Simulated Realities Group at Carnegie Mellon University.[25] Such systems can be classified as indeterminate cybertexts, since the level of complexity and the flexibility of user input, like explicitly programmed random behavior, make scriptons unpredictable. Interestingly, a main goal of adventure game theorists such as Brenda Laurel and others is to be able to control what they call the plot. The user-character will be allowed some leeway, but by use of Playwright, an expert system with knowledge of dramatic structure (perhaps not totally unlike an intelligent version of *Afternoon*'s anti-narrator), the situations and actions would be carefully orchestrated to fit its model of appropriate drama. Although this aesthetically motivated poetics has the goal of creating well-formed dramatic unity, it is hard not to see the potential for conflict between the user and this *deus in machina.* As the history of the novel has shown, the forces of carnivalism will work centrifugally against the law of genre in any simulated social situation. At last, in the cybertext, the user can become a little akin to an author—*not,* I hasten to add, to the author of the cybertext (and perhaps the conception of author should not be stretched this far), but perhaps, say, to a novelist of the nineteenth century.

The early determinate texts, such as *Adventure* and *Eliza,* seemingly invited the user to participate, but soon revealed that this was impossible, and that subordination was the name of the game. The user could only fill, or more typically fail to fill the narrow track of the text's hidden "plot"; and the texts evolved to play on this failure, as testified by the often (and sometimes unintended) ironic and humorous response to the user's contra-generic activities (for example, "drop dead"—"You're not carrying that!").

Indeterminate cybertext should be seen as a movement not against, but *beyond* genre. As the simulation of social structure becomes richer, plot control becomes increasingly difficult; and it is easy to predict the decentered cybertext in which stories, plots, and counterplots arise "naturally" from the autonomous movements of the cybernetic constructs. Already free of narrative, this Baudrillardian nightmare—if that is what it is (compare Moulthrop, "Hypertext and 'the Hyperreal'")—promises many more escapes: from plot and plotters (authors and author-machines), from genre and contra-generity, and from the social self. If it succeeds, the textual pleasure machine could be said to have escaped even from simulation and become an emulation, a "supplement" as dangerous as they come.

As always, we do not have to wait for the textual machines to catch up. They already have. The telegraph, "the singing wire," is a conspicuously unsung hero in most histories of communication.[26] Invented in 1793 by Claude Chappe, the first modern telegraph was optical, not electric, implemented as a chain of semaphore towers in France. Later the American Samuel Morse constructed his electromagnetic telegraph, and in 1844 set up a line between Baltimore and Washington, thus redefining the meaning of the word communication. A reason for media theorists' omission of the telegraph could be that it is categorically unclean, depending equally on material and immaterial technologies, and therefore an embarrassment to the great divide between print and electronic media.

From the start, the electric telegraph was used for textual fun and games. Marshall McLuhan tells this story: "When a group of Oxford undergraduates heard that Rudyard Kipling received ten shillings for every word he wrote, they sent him ten shillings by telegram during their meeting: 'Please send us one of your very best words.' Back came the word a few minutes later: 'Thanks.'"[27]

This is not the place to retrace the fundamental changes to society, time, and space brought about by the telegraph, but it should be noted that telegraph and later the telex was *the* method of instant global textual communication during a period of more than a hundred years, before digital computer networks came into being in the 1960s and '70s. However, with the computer's ability to handle more than two communicators simultaneously, new types of nonlocal textual fora were made possible. First there were the mainframe computers with their user communities sending messages to each other and so forth, then communication between computers (and their users) over a distance, by telephone wire or dedicated cable networks. With the emergence of the networks and the use of modems, many different kinds of textual communication evolved, from e-mail via mailing lists and newsgroups to so-called on-line chat, such as the interesting phenomenon Internet Relay Chat.[28]

At the end of the 1970s, with the spread of the highly popular *Adventure* over the networks, it was to be expected that someone should combine instant textual communication and adventure gaming. In the fall of 1979 at Essex University, Roy Trubshaw started the development of the Multi-User Dungeon (MUD) on a DEC system-10 mainframe, a task taken over by Richard Bartle in the summer of 1980.[29] The first MUD was a successful game, with users scoring points by killing each others' characters or finding hidden treasures and eventually reaching the powerful status of wizard, but it was also much more than a game; it was a cyberplace where people could enjoy complete anonymity and freedom from their social and physical selves and take on any persona they could think of, doing things with words that they would normally never do. Thus a new mode of textual expression was initiated, different even from the telegraph: the user had to be very quick, and formulate short, unretractable sentences in seconds, or die. Dorothy Parker and Ernest Hemingway would have loved it.

Like *Adventure* before it, MUD spread out globally on the academic computer networks, was soon copied, and changed into other types of multi-user texts. In the summer of 1989 at Carnegie Mellon University, James Aspnes programmed a MUD with a significant new feature: in addition to creating their own characters, the users were allowed to expand the MUD's textual descriptions, adding their own landscapes to the topography of the MUD. This MUD, known as *TinyMUD* and reachable from any computer linked to the global Internet, emphasized social interaction and building. There was no merit system; if your character was killed, it simply got an insurance fee of 50 pennies. The co-creativity of the users was a very anarchic step from the first MUDs. *TinyMUD* lasted from August 19, 1989, to April 28, 1990, when its data base of descriptions became too big to handle, filled up by more than 132,000 user-defined objects, each of which could contain several textons.

When regarded as literary objects, MUDs seem to defy every concept of literary theory. Every user has a different (or several different) and partial perspective(s), and the users bombard each other with textons meant only to last as long as they are not scrolled off the screen. MUDs are like constantly meandering rivers, developing new courses that cross and re-cross each other and are filled with all sorts of peculiar flotsam and jetsam. And suddenly, in the middle of chaos, a group of characters may start singing in unison the Yoyodyne song from Thomas Pynchon's *The Crying of Lot 49*: "High above the LA freeways, / And the traffic's whine, / Stands the well-known Galactonics / Branch of Yoyodyne."[30] Strange things happen at sea.

Compared to a nineteenth-century novel, *TinyMUD* appears totally different: transient, dynamic, indeterminate, with explorative, role-playing, configurative, and poetic user-functionality. And yet, this is literature: letters, words, and sentences are selected, arranged and disseminated to delight, impress, or enrage an unknown audience. The scriptons, which can be funny, poignant, sleazy, silly, obnoxious, or noisy, usually come in a heterogeneous mix. With more than twenty characters in the same room, it takes a hardened "MUDder" to keep track of what is going on. Special-purpose MUD-client programs that have been developed to run on the user's local machine and ease communication provide functionality that is not part of the MUD itself, such as filtering out noisy characters and automating often-used commands. Not all characters one meets on a MUD have real persons behind them, and several characters might be played by the same person. An early automatic character (so-called bot) on *TinyMUD* was called Terminator, had its own office, and was, like its cinematic namesake, programmed to kill. If you paid it 200 pennies it would go and pester any character you specified. Bots were simply external programs built using various artificial intelligence techniques and logged on by their creators to *TinyMUD* just like human players, but usually recognized by their somewhat poor communication skills.

A discussion of MUDs in terms of authors and readers is irrelevant: a MUD cannot be read, only experienced from the very narrow perspective of one or more of the user's characters, with a lot of simultaneous scriptons being beyond reach; and the user cannot be sure that a particular contribution will ever be experienced by more than a few people, or, since the other characters might all be artificial persons or controlled by the same real person, by anyone at all.

The Limits of Fiction

An important issue raised by both determinate and indeterminate cybertexts is their relation to the ontological categories of textuality: fiction, nonfiction, poetry, drama, etc. In the case of cybertexts such as *Adventure* and *TinyMUD,* the most obvious choice, fiction, is not obvious enough. *Adventure* invites a belief from the user, but this is not the same belief or suspension of disbelief that must be sustained by the user of realistic or fantastic novels. Cybertextuality has an empirical element that is not found in fiction and that necessitates an ontological category of its own, which might as well be called simulation.

In fiction the user must construct mental images that somehow correspond to the world described in the text. The user is responsible for the images, but the text is in control and can dictate changes without any deference to external logic. From the user's perspective, fictions are neither logical nor illogical. If the fiction claims that elephants are pink, then in the fiction they are, because nobody is "there" to contradict it. A fiction, then, is not about something that does not exist but about something that it is meaningless to contradict.

In *Adventure,* the responsibility for coherence is shared between the user and the text. If the you-character drops a sword in one place, leaves, and comes back, the sword is still there. In other words, there is a systematic contract between text and user, like the causal one that exists in the real world and which, unlike fictions, can be empirically tested. In *TinyMUD* the simulation of reality is even closer to the real thing, since the conversations the user's character conducts with other characters often have the signs of real conversations.

Simulations are somewhere in between reality and fiction: they are not obliged to represent reality, but they do have an empirical logic of their own, and therefore they should not be called fictions. Unlike fictions, which simply present something else, cybertexts *represent* something beyond themselves.

The Rhetoric of Nonlinearity

As we have seen, the profound challenge of nonlinear texts to the basic concepts of literary theory makes it difficult to discuss them in common literary terms. Even to the extent it is still possible, it should be done with caution; and if we can be sure of nothing else, we may be certain that contradiction will be the uninvited master trope of our discourse. But still—what kind of (literary? semiotic?) phenomenon is nonlinear textuality? Is there a name or recognized class for the device (or better, set of devices) of nonlinearity? Do some domains of literary theory lend their vocabularies more easily to its description than others? (If so, those are the ones most worthy of suspicion.) As the advocates of hypertext enthusiastically remind us, it can be found as fiction, poetry, textbooks, encyclopedias, and so on; so nonlinearity as the superset of hypertext is clearly not a literary genre, or a type of poetic expression or discourse. This problem of classification can also be described in semiotic terms, but mainly to the effect that a text type (in our nongeneric sense) is a signification system, "an autonomous semiotic construct that has an abstract mode of existence independent of any communicative act it makes possible," which does not really answer the question.[31] To semiotics, texts are *chains* of signs, and therefore linear by definition.[32]

If we turn to rhetoric, we see that nonlinearity is clearly not a trope, since it works on the level of words, not meaning; but it could be classified as a type of figure, following Pierre Fontanier's taxonomy of tropes and figures. In the second part of his classic inventory of rhetorical figures, *Figures du Discours,* Fontanier defines "*les Figures non-Tropes*" —the figures other than tropes.[33] These he divides into several classes: construction-figures, elocution-figures, style-figures, and thought-figures, with various subclasses including inversion, apposition, ellipsis, and repetition. Among these classes we could place the figures of nonlinearity, with the following set of subclasses: forking, linking/jumping, permutation, computation, and polygenesis. These subclasses can be further divided, of course; and more importantly, instances from different subclasses (and from traditional ones such as repetition and topography) can combine to constitute a text type.

Compared to the textual typology presented earlier, this perspective has the advantage of connecting to a traditional concept of literary theory, the figure. In this, however, the idea of rhetoric is even farther removed from its origin as a theory of speech. But since the non-tropic figure is the concept for unusual positionings of words, it might not be totally unjustified.

In terms of the simplified hierarchy of nonlinear texts, these classes of figures belong to the following levels: *forking,* found in the spatially nonlinear text; *linking/jumping,* belonging to the stratum of hypertext; *permutation, computation,* and *polygenesis,* all found in both determinate and indeterminate cybertext. Whereas a user-created permutation is determinate (for example, Queneau's *Poèmes*), a computed permutation may be determinate or indeterminate (for example, *I Ching*). A computation may be determinate or contain a random function that makes it indeterminate. Polygenesis can be determinate (for example, when the user types a sentence to *Eliza,* its response can be predicted) or indeterminate (as in the MUDs). A further classification of the figures of nonlinearity, such as distinguishing between different types of forks, links, random functions, polygenetic modes, and so on, will not be undertaken here.

The Corruption of the Critic

How can literary theory attack the textualities of nonlinearity? How can we cut them up, read into them, de-scribe them so they fit in our narratives? How can we link them to our totems and control their hidden mechanisms? Hypertext seems already well on its way into the canon. Is this a good sign? Conquests, unlike discoveries, are seldom accidental. On the other hand, there is no such thing as literary theory; there are only theories and theorists. And texts. Literary theory, more than most academic disciplines, has always been uncentered and fragmented, a widening gyre of readings and interests linked to countless philosophies, like a true Barthesian *texte scriptible*. So if hypertext should find a home, why not here?

This essay will not answer any of the big questions: What will hypertext do to the ways we think about texts? How will it resist the ways we are going to think about it, and be remembered as something other than an in-house pet, a dead tradition of literary experiment, explained and packaged from the start? How will the powerful but extremely primitive logic of the link affect our discursive methods?

If hypertext has connected well with literary studies, cybertext, a much older textual phenomenon, has gone by largely unnoticed. An article or two, a few doctoral dissertations; the lack of interest is significant, and may have several causes. One is obvious: adventure games are *games,* and that is not our department. Neither is the similarity between *I Ching,* Queneau's *Poèmes,* and *Adventure* too striking at first sight. Perhaps, also, the adventure game, for all its trivia and popular appeal, is too radical to be recognized, because it disfigures not only the reading process but also the reader. Literary critics have generally scorned prosaic texts that too openly captured their users—in which the relationship between reader and narratee became too intimate, lacking ironic distance or *Verfremdung*. Like the telegraph, such texts fall between accepted categories, in this case between lyrical poetry and prose. *Afternoon* on the other hand, with its subversive anti-narrator, has seemingly no problem with this, and can be welcomed and configured into literature and the literary.

The key difference between *Afternoon* and cybertexts such as *Adventure* and *TinyMUD* is what the virtual reality researchers call immersion: the user's convinced sense that the artificial environment is not just a main agent with whom they can identify but surrounds the user.[34] In cybertextual terms we could say that the user assumes the strategic and emotional responsibility of the character, or that the distances between the positions of main character, narratee, and user have collapsed.

To the critical institution, this ontological embarrassment becomes an ethical one. How can we be critics if we can no longer read? How can reviewers of cybertexts face the fact they probably missed large numbers of scriptons? And worse, not only will we have to admit that we barely made it to first base, but in the exploration of indeterminate cybertexts we will be reviewing the results of our own strategic and creative investments.[35]

Problems of "Textual Anthropology"

This crisis in criticism might not amount to anything terrible, but it could be used as a new departure for literary hermeneutics. After the celebrated deaths of the author, the work, and reading, the text is now giving up the spirit, betrayed by its most trusted companion, the signifier. What is left is linear and nonlinear textuality, or better, linear and nonlinear textualities. This empirical evolution makes possible a shift in method from a philological to an anthropological approach in which the object of study is a process (the changing text) rather than a project (the static text). On-line phenomena and particularly the MUDs, with their fluid exchanges of textual *praxis,* offer unique opportunities for the study of rhetoric, semiotics, and cultural communication in general.

MUDs and similar nonlocal forms of instant textual communication can be studied from many perspectives in the human sciences; psychological, sociological, anthropological, linguistic, philosophical, historical, etc. Shades of these will inevitably find their way into the literary and textual perspectives that we might expect from our own discipline. If literary theorists and critics do engage in the study of indeterminate cybertexts, it should be with an awareness that the old role of *a posteriori* investigator no longer suffices. Like the user, the critic must be there when it happens. Not only that but, like the participant observer of social anthropology, he or she must make it happen—improvise, mingle with the natives, play roles, provoke response.

What, may we ask, will then be the difference between this literary anthropology and a real anthropologist's investigation of on-line phenomena? In other words, what keeps criticism from changing into a sub-discipline of traditional social anthropology? First, it must be noted that social anthropology and literary theory already have several perspectives and goals in common, and a recent history of mutual influence. In cultural anthropology, cultures are treated as texts to be interpreted and subjected to critique,[36] and even the problem of anthropological method as a literary process has become a concern.[37]

In the transient social textualities, the ontologies of the two traditions might seem to converge, and the boundaries between cultural anthropology and literary theory may appear fuzzier than ever. It could therefore be useful to explore some problems and conflicts of perspective that might await eventual partnerships of the two fields. Since MUDs and other indeterminate cybertexts are closed signification systems, that is, textual types, they should not be analyzed as traditional cultures or subcultures. The postorganic anthropology solicited in a recent essay on the phenomenon known as cyberspace is perhaps just another term for what literary critics have been doing since Plato.[38] To be analyzed and defined, a culture must be shown to exist independently of any one signification system. When a science starts to confuse its metaphors with its empirical substratum (for example when "texts" become texts), it is dangerously close to becoming a mythology. An anthropology of MUDs, for instance, should not see as its primary object the rituals and interactions between the characters inside, but rather the relation between the outside participants (the users) and their inside symbolic actions. Literary theory, on the other hand, should not focus on the social behavior made possible by textual symbols, but on how the sign system is used to construct and explore the possibility of a text-based representation of identity. If a cooperation between anthropology and textual criticism is to be achieved, the two disciplines should not try to do each other's work, or mistake the other's ontology for its own.

囍

After these speculations the question remains: What will the study of nonlinearity and cybertextuality do to literary theory? At this point there can be no clear answer. Between the blurry promises of technology and the sharp edges of political reality there is, in the words of Jacques Derrida, "as yet no exergue." This essay has attempted to create a usable terminology for the study of a wider range of textualities than has hitherto been acknowledged by the field of literary study and to point to some current problems and challenges in the study of computer-mediated textualities. As we have seen, fundamental structural terms like *story, plot, fiction,* and *narrative* are not always suitable to describe the nonlinear textualities. To use them without qualification is clearly irresponsible. The figures of nonlinearity suggest that one must revise literary terminology and poetics in order to avoid further confusion and unnecessary ambiguity. Some of my reconfigurations of these literary and theoretical concepts might turn out to be unnecessary, and others are probably not radical enough. As I have shown, in addition to hypertext there is a wealth of nonlinear text types, from ancient inscriptions to sophisticated computer programs based on the latest semantic research. I have not tried to present an exhaustive empirical survey of such types or to give a detailed historical exposition of the development and spread of textual nonlinearity. Others are very welcome to either of these tasks; I have no intention of taking them on. Nor do I believe that there is any need to construct a historical tradition of nonlinear literature, as the specimens I have seen so far seem to be different from and isolated from each other rather than belong to anything that can reasonably be characterized as a common genre. There are undoubtedly local traditions, but nonlinear strategies appear to rise out of a prevalent and trans-historic need to compose a practical effect, perpendicular to linear textuality, but usually with a specific and constructive or subversive rather than sensationalistic or frivolous objective.

When confronted with new data that is recognized as relevant but unusual, an academic discipline such as literary studies can employ at least two different tactics to harmonize the situation. The existing theories may be used to grasp and focus the new material (the intruder is tamed), or the new material can be used to reevaluate and modify the old perspectives (the field is changed). Here I have focused not on the effects and insights produced by the various branches of literary theory when applied to nonlinear texts but on the potential for new perspectives on literature in general that the study of nonlinear textuality might bring us. Nonlinear texts and literary theories may have a lot to say to each other, but we should not let only one side do all the talking.

NOTES

1. Terry Eagleton, *Literary Theory: An Introduction* (Minneapolis: University of Minnesota Press, 1983).

2. Norbert Wiener, *Cybernetics; Or, Control and Communication in the Animal and the Machine* (New York: Technology, 1948).

3. N. Katherine Hayles, *Chaos Bound: Orderly Disorder in Contemporary Literature and Science* (Ithaca: Cornell University Press, 1990).

4. Roland Barthes, *S/Z* (Paris: Seuil, 1970), 20.

5. George P. Landow, *Hypertext: The Convergence of Contemporary Critical Theory and Technology* (Baltimore: Johns Hopkins University Press, 1992).

6. Espen Aarseth, *Texts of Change: Towards a Poetics of Nonlinearity* (c.phil. diss., unpublished, University of Bergen, Department of Comparative Literature, 1991).

7. See Michael J. Greenacre, *Theory and Applications of Correspondence Analysis* (London: Academic Press, 1984).

8. William Gibson, *Agrippa: A Book of the Dead* (New York: Kevin Begos, 1992).

9. Kathy Acker, *Blood and Guts in High School* (New York: Grove Press, 1978), 46–51.

10. Rolf Gundlach, "Tempelrelief," in *Lexicon der Ägyptologie* (Wiesbaden: Otto Harrassowitz, 1985), 6:407–11.

11. James Legge, *I Ching: Book of Changes* (1888; Secaucus, N.J.: Citadel Press, 1964), 7.

12. C. G. Jung, foreword to *I Ching or Book of Changes*, trans. Cary F. Baynes from a German translation by Richard Wilhelm (1950; London: Arkana/Penguin, 1989), lvii–lxi.

13. Raymond Queneau, *Cent Mille Milliards de Poèmes* (Paris: Gallimard, 1961).

14. William Paulson, "Computers, Minds, and Texts: Preliminary Reflections," *New Literary History* 20 (1989): 297.

15. For critical views of political claims about electronic media in general, see James W. Carey, *Communication As Culture: Essays on Media and Society* (Boston: Unwin Hyman, 1988), especially "The Mythos of the Electronic Revolution," and about hypertext, Stuart Moulthrop, "You Say You Want a Revolution?: Hypertext and the Laws of Media," *Postmodern Culture* 1 (May 1991).

16. Theodor Holm Nelson, *Literary Machines*, ed. 87.1 (Swarthmore, Pa.: Theodor H. Nelson, 1987), and Vannevar Bush, "As We May Think," *Atlantic Monthly* 176 (July 1945): 101–8.

17. Michael Joyce, *Afternoon, a story* (Cambridge, Mass.: Eastgate Systems, 1990). For discussions of *Afternoon,* see Stuart Moulthrop, "Hypertext and 'the Hyperreal,'" *Hypertext '89* (New York: Association of Computing Machinery, 1989), 259–67; J. David Bolter, *Writing Space: The Computer, Hypertext, and the History of Writing* (Hillsdale, N.J.: Lawrence Erlbaum, 1991); and Landow, *Hypertext.*

18. Moulthrop, "Hypertext and 'the Hyperreal,'" 239.

19. Inger Christensen, *The Meaning of Metafiction: A Critical Study of Selected Novels by Sterne, Nabokov, Barth, and Becket* (Bergen: Universitetsforlaget, 1981), 141–43.

20. Bolter, *Writing Space*, 7.

21. Jon Lanestedt, *Episk Programvare—En Litterær Teksttype? [Epic Software—A Literary Text Type?]* (c.phil. diss., University of Oslo, 1989). William Crowther and Don Woods, *Adventure*, this version implemented by Gordon Letwin (IBM/Microsoft, 1981).

22. Anthony J. Niesz and Norman N. Holland, "Interactive Fiction," *Critical Inquiry* 11 (1984): 113.

23. Robin Waterfield and Wilfred Davies, *The Money Spider* (London: Penguin 1988).

24. See James Richard Meehan, *The Metanovel: Writing Stories by Computer* (Ph.D. diss., Yale University, University Microfilms International, 1976); Roger

C. Schank and Peter Childers, *The Cognitive Computer: On Language, Learning, and Artificial Intelligence* (Reading, Mass.: Addison-Wesley, 1984); and Michael Lebowitz, "Creating Characters in a Story-telling Universe," *Poetics* 13 (1984): 171–94.

25. Brenda Laurel, *Computers as Theatre* (Reading, Mass.: Addison-Wesley, 1991).

26. Cf. Carey, *Communication As Culture*, ch. 8.

27. Marshall McLuhan, *Understanding Media: The Extensions of Man* (New York: Penguin Books/Mentor, 1964), 225.

28. Elizabeth M. Reid, *Electropolis: Communication and Community on Internet Relay Chat* (honors thesis, University of Melbourne, 1991).

29. Richard Bartle, *Interactive Multi-User Computer Games* (parts from a research report commissioned by British Telecom, disseminated by the author, 1990).

30. Thomas Pynchon, *The Crying of Lot 49* (London: Picador, 1967).

31. Umberto Eco, *A Theory of Semiotics* (Bloomington: Indiana University Press, 1979), 9.

32. Louis Hjelmslev, *Prolegomena to a Theory of Language* (1943), trans. Francis J. Whitfield (Madison: University of Wisconsin Press, 1961), 30.

33. Pierre Fontanier, *Les Figures du Discours* (1821–30; Paris: Flammarion, 1968), 271.

34. Howard Rheingold, *Virtual Reality* (New York: Summit Books, 1991).

35. See also Richard Ziegfeld, "Interactive Fiction: A New Literary Genre?" *New Literary History* 20 (1989): 341–72.

36. George E. Marcus and Michael M. J. Fischer, *Anthropology as Cultural Critique: An Experimental Moment in the Human Sciences* (Chicago: University of Chicago Press, 1986).

37. Clifford Geertz, *Works and Lives: The Anthropologist as Author* (Stanford: Stanford University Press, 1988).

38. David Tomas, "Old Rituals for New Space," in *Cyberspace: First Steps*, ed. Michael Benedikt (Cambridge: MIT Press, 1991), 31–47.

Wittgenstein, Genette, and the Reader's Narrative in Hypertext

Gunnar Liestøl

3

Philosophy in an Album

Hypertext reconfigures the way we conceive of texts. The facilities of manipulation, individual navigation, and freedom from given, authoritative structures provide us with new practices of writing and reading. However, the conduct of traditional print-age reading and writing has always been subject to complications and opposition. A brief examination of the way Ludwig Wittgenstein encountered severe problems with his own print-conditioned reading and writing practices has much to offer anyone interested in the relations between hypertext and theory.

In the preface to *Philosophical Investigations* Wittgenstein reflects upon his difficulties giving his thoughts an adequate linguistic representation in traditional forms:

> I have written down all these thoughts as *remarks,* short paragraphs, of which there is sometimes a fairly long chain about the same subject, while I sometimes make a sudden change, jumping from one topic to another.—It was my intention at first to bring all this together in a book whose form I pictured differently at different times. But the essential thing was that the thoughts should proceed from one subject to another in a natural order and without breaks.
>
> After several unsuccessful attempts to weld my results together into such a whole, I realized that I should never succeed. The best that I could write would never be more than philosophical remarks; my thoughts were soon crippled if I tried to force them on in any single direction against their natural inclination.—And this was, of course, connected with the very nature of the investigation. For this compels us to travel over a wide field of thought criss-cross in every direction.[1]

Wittgenstein makes two prominent and interrelated points here: First, he worked laboriously to convey his thinking by means of a form of representation adequate to certain conventions of writing. Second, he perceived that the one-dimensionality these conventions demanded was incompatible with the way he actually thought.

Such a conflict between thought and text, such a struggle with technologies of expression, parallels the motivation behind the conceptual evolution of hypertext in the writings of pioneers like Vannevar Bush, Douglas C. Engelbart, and Theodor H. Nelson.[2] Wittgenstein's experience and solutions to the problem of representing his thoughts both exemplify the needs that prompted the development of hypertext and provided workers in the field with models of knowledge.[3]

From the outset Wittgenstein had a definite idea of how he should (or was expected to) present his work. In accord with contemporary principles of genre, he wanted his "thoughts to proceed from one subject to another in a natural order and without any breaks." This description echoes the classical treatise form that dominates philosophy from Plato to Hegel (and beyond). Wittgenstein, dissatisfied with writing according to contemporary academic conventions, found it difficult to reduce complex thought structures into the continuous linear form of a written text. His remarks remind us of the many constraints embedded in the institutions of presentation and print, constraints which presently seem relevant to the problems of composing as well as studying hypermedia as a mode of communication.

Central to Wittgenstein's conception of a book without breaks lies an implicit theory that language mirrors reality in a one-to-one ratio. In Wittgenstein's case this idea connects to the picture theory advanced in his earlier philosophy that presupposes that the structure of facts in the world is identical to the structural relationships of words in language.[4] These assumptions further imply that the "single directedness" at the topical level necessarily relates to an identical structure at the level of verbal representation. Consequently, the natural, successive order of the subject matter should easily find its expression in a continuity of equally progressive movement in their final written form. However obvious the internal logic of this idea of language seems, Wittgenstein could not adapt his endeavour to the conditions of the model. In fact, he came to realize that his philosophical thinking opposed this particular kind of textual organization. The philosophical argument of *Investigations* also implies a fundamental attack on this narrow notion of language and reality. After several unsuccessful attempts at constructing a book compatible with his preconceptions, Wittgenstein reconciled himself to never being able to write anything more than philosophical remarks. The quest for continuity and linear, successive order gave way to a form in which something analogous to a hypertext lexia, the paragraph, became the largest textual unit, since it provided a form flexible enough to accommodate the complexity and multidirectedness of the subject matter.

Many of the philosophical problems Wittgenstein addressed in the early parts of *Investigations* had been discussed by philosophers before him, particularly Plato and Hegel. In *Theaitetos* Plato treats similar topics by means of the dialogue form.[5] The young student Theaitetos is continually forced to articulate definitions of knowledge in reply to Socrates, who constantly confronts him with counter-examples. This oscillation between theoretical attempts and critical examination forms a successive, well-ordered movement of thought and investigation. In Hegel's *Phänomenologie des Geistes* the discussion is more formalized.[6] The first chapter, in which Hegel discusses what he terms sense-certainty, proposes a theory of knowledge tested against examples supposed to confirm it. However, the theory needs continued adjustments, and in the end the position is abandoned. On the ruins of this theory another, wiser attempt is made. Thus the book depicts a dialectic evolution of the mind which progresses steadily towards more and more advanced states and conceptions of self-knowledge. In contrast to Wittgenstein, Plato and Hegel succeed in presenting their thoughts in a sequential order without breaks.

Wittgenstein's fragmented form on the other hand gives room for multidirected movements. Thus, the constellation of short remarks with his sudden changes, criss-crossing, and jumping around became the final form of *Investigations* and contrasts to the book he originally intended to write. Breaking with the unified model of language and reality, it instead presents a practice and a picture of writing that resist preconceived order but that acknowledge diversity and difference. To present his philosophy, Wittgenstein claimed a looser textual organization and arrangement that obviously parallel the acclaimed liberation and decenteredness of hypertextual structures.

Wittgenstein's effort with textual organization shows unconventional methods and illuminates the form of the final version. Scholars involved in providing a machine-readable, hypertext version of Wittgenstein's *Nachlass* have described the process of his work with various versions of the manuscripts. His notes and remarks went through a long process of rearrangement and editing before reaching final form. He would, for example, insert a fragment that had first appeared in a hand-written notebook into a volume along with other material, later moving it to a typescript. During this transference he might alter words or insert the original remark into a larger paragraph. Finally Wittgenstein would cut up the typescript into paragraphs and start over again rearranging the various paragraphs.[7] This laborious procedure of preparation is in principle very similar to the sort of brainstorming and cut and paste techniques that can easily be carried out with a hypertext editor like Storyspace.[8] For Wittgenstein this textual fragmentation and the flexibility of constant rearrangement was intimately and necessarily related to his way of thinking and "connected to the very nature of the investigation."

One of the books published by Wittgenstein's literary executors contains a collection of fragments found in a box file. The fragments were cut from his extensive manuscripts, and some of them were found clipped together whereas others lay loose in the box. According to his executors, these fragments formed a collection quite distinct from the remarks found elsewhere in the *Nachlass*.[9] We will never know exactly how Wittgenstein worked this manuscript material: it could have been a means which allowed him a flexible format suited to the nature of the problems he was dealing with; he may have created a collection of text unconstrained by the bound book; or perhaps the collection provided a way of conserving the dynamics of his thoughts. Wittgenstein at one time also planned a numbered coding system that could present the interrelated network in which he wanted his remarks organized and conceived (Bolter, *Writing Space,* 115).

In his preface Wittgenstein gives a figurative description for this laborious process of textual production and organization. The reader is invited to think of the text in a topographic way, as travels "over a wide field of thought criss-cross in every direction":

> The philosophical remarks in this book are, as it were, a number of sketches of landscapes which were made in the course of these long and involved journeyings.
>
> The same and almost the same points were always approached afresh from different directions, and new sketches made. Very many of these were badly drawn or uncharacteristic, marked by all the defects of a weak draughtsman. And when they were rejected a number of tolerable ones were left, which now had to be arranged and sometimes cut down, so that if you looked at them you could get a picture of the landscape. Thus this book is really only an album. (vii)

Wittgenstein moves from the *literal* reality of his presentation and seeks to illustrate the process of his work by using a complex of metaphors taken from the *visual* mode of representation. The writer presents himself as a painter. This movement from literal to visual is concluded in the last sentences. The sketches have been rearranged and altered but, seen together as a collection, their constellation conveys a picture of the landscape. "Thus this book is really only an album."

Again he reduces his work to something that could not match the expectations of a "real book." Failing at adaption, he can "only" present us with another form: the unpretentious format of an album.

Wittgenstein's figurative presentation of his method reveals a relationship between the structure of *Investigations* and his involved journeyings among the different topics of the thought landscape. He describes three orders of organization in the process that leads to the published text (album): landscape, sketches, and published remarks. First, the philosopher carries out field work in the thought landscape. While moving around in this imaginary space the philosopher makes written descriptions of the scenery from different positions and in various directions. These notes or sketches form a topography of the landscape. Before the philosopher arrives at the final order of the published book, he selects, alters, and rearranges this material.

Given Wittgenstein's struggle to escape the limitations of the linear book and to establish a procedure of work and a form of expression capable of mediating the complexity of his endeavour, it is no surprise that parts of his work have been transferred into electronic text environments with hypertext facilities. *Philosophical Investigations* itself consists of seven hundred segments or paragraphs, none longer than a page and some only a sentence in length. Nonetheless, this book is *not* a hypertext any more than are other texts with allusions, references, digressions, paragraphs, or footnotes. Despite his mention of sudden changes, jumping around, and criss-crossing, Wittgenstein's written text is as linear as any. Each fragment is numbered and ordered in a long fixed chain from one to seven hundred and displayed over several hundred numbered pages. Wittgenstein broke the conventions of linear reference by his use of language, but he stayed within the constraints of printed text as a physical marker for information and meaning. His jumping and criss-crossing exist on a thematic level distinct from the written and alphabetically ordered paragraphs. We must distinguish the nonlinearity in the structuring of his thoughts from the linearity of its literal representations by means of ink and paper as information markers (nonlinear at the level of signifieds but linear at the level of signifiers). In Wittgenstein's text the alphabetic linearity of written language mediates the nonsequential and nonsystemic order of his thought landscape, characterized by the metaphors of more or less adequate "sketches." Linearity here represents nonlinearity, just as nonlinearity in other contexts may represent linearity. This paradox dissolves when one considers the different types or *levels of linearity* involved. Although he maintained a flexible, dynamic, and manipulative attitude in the editorial process, Wittgenstein does not question the physical status and stability of textual representation in his final work. But considering the focus on visuality and the perspicuity evoked by the album metaphor, Wittgenstein gives directions for the users of his work which suggest a different attitude to philosophic texts.

In ancient Rome the word *album* (from the Latin *albus*, meaning "white") designated public boards, coated with white chalk, upon which documents were inscribed or posted much as they are on modern bulletin boards (both hard-copy and electronic). This form of message exchange displays a contingent relationship between posted or inscribed documents. Each message is individual and self-contained, their common grounds are their creators and the community they address. The album format characteristically lacks a strict successive organization of messages and meanings. Instead, the family album tells stories by means of snapshot, and its effects have little in common with the constrained structure of linguistic articulation. On the other hand, the album generates the richness and variety of a pictured whole constituted of the individual clips as punctuations of time and place. Wittgenstein wants his philosophic album of sketches to give the readers a *picture* of the whole. Direct theoretical communication would command a unity in expression not compatible with the variety and diversity of the subject matter. Thus, instead of creating one essential text relating all aspects to a monolithic whole, he had to develop a fragmented collection that conveyed difference and complexity by means of indirect communication. This album mode of message exchange, which seems relevant to the qualities of hypertext, is discussed in a later section of this essay.

Story and Discourse

In presenting one of the key distinctions in narratology Gerard Genette turns to the film semiotician Christian Metz:

> Narrative is a . . . doubly temporal sequence . . . : There is the time of the thing told and the time of the narrative (the time of the signified and the time of the signifier). This duality not only renders possible all the temporal distortions that are commonplace in narratives (three years of the hero's life summed up in two sentences of a novel or in a few shots of a "frequentative" montage in film, etc.). More basically, it invites us to consider that one of the functions of narrative is to invent one time scheme in terms of another time scheme.[10]

This temporal duality, which is central to all storytelling, may also serve as the basis for identifying the specific characteristics of hypertextual narratives. In theories of narrative the distinction between the story told and the telling of the story has appeared in numerous constellations and contexts. In this section Genette's categories are used as a starting point.[11]

In a movie or a novel, the discourse line is *always* linear. The cinematic apparatus of displaying a film and the social conventions of attending one rely on linearity for their existence. To construct a motion picture one must experience the pictures frame by frame, one after the other, usually 24 or 30 times a second; to read a novel in English one must add letter to letter, word to word, sentence to sentence, from left to right, top to bottom, in order to achieve any meaning at all. This one-directional chronology, or temporal linearity, is necessary and transcendent when related to the units actually organized in this way, whether they be pictures, words, or sounds. The linear organization of Wittgenstein's text, for example, is a discourse: a narrative that tells a story, the story of the protagonist's "involved journeyings." Genette's discussion of order, duration, and frequency clarifies the temporal distinction between story and discourse with regard to hypertexts.

Order concerns the chronological location of story elements in relation to discourse elements. Most narratives do not have synchrony between discourse time and story time. The movie *Citizen Kane,* for instance, is mainly told in flashbacks; it shows anachrony between the chronological order of the story elements and the elements of discourse. The first element in discourse time, Kane's death in his bedroom at Xanadu, is almost the last on the story line. The criss-crossing or zeugmatic relationship between the two time schemes may be represented as follows:

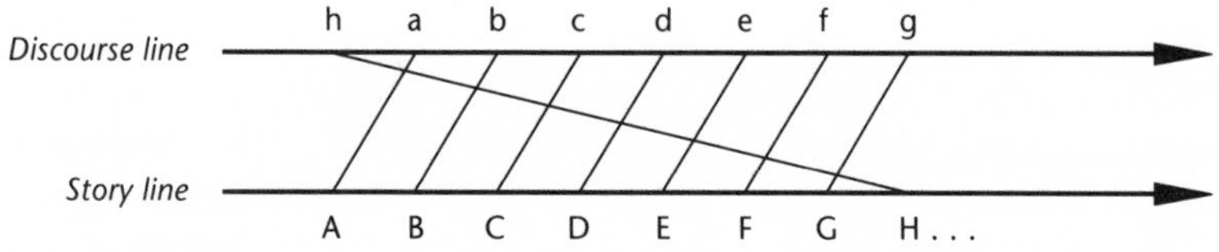

This relatively perspicuous relation between story and discourse is present in most fictional film and literature. However, the relation vanishes or becomes nearly irrelevant in works by many avant-garde authors and directors. In television and newspaper journalism, documentary films, and academic and scientific texts, the distinction may to some extent be functional. Wittgenstein's text has no equivalent to the fictional story line of Charles Foster Kane's life, although it both describes actions and happenings and contains dialogue. Wittgenstein's frustration, one might say, consisted in the fact that his subject matter would not permit him to construct a continuous story line that its discourse could mirror. Instead, the discourse line signifies and displays more of a spatial order at the signified story level.

In contrast to *Philosophical Investigations*, the story line of Hegel's *Phänomenologie des Geistes* is articulate, linear, and well established within the constraints of contemporary novels. In Hegel's text (story) the spirit is hero, and its quest is absolute knowledge of itself and the world, which it gains through a long inclination of philosophical experience. Order concerns relations of story elements and discourse elements in time, but it also describes the relation between the reading of hypertext and the order in which the information exists as stored and independent of that reading.

Genette also discusses the relation between story and discourse in terms of duration (the time it takes to tell about events in the story compared to the actual time of the events in the fictional universe) and frequency (the relation between repetitive capacities of story and discourse). Before returning to this idea of order in hypertexts I will examine the relevance to hypermedia of these other two categories.

Duration, which concerns the time and speed of story and discourse, divides into five categories: summary, ellipsis, scene, stretch, and pause:

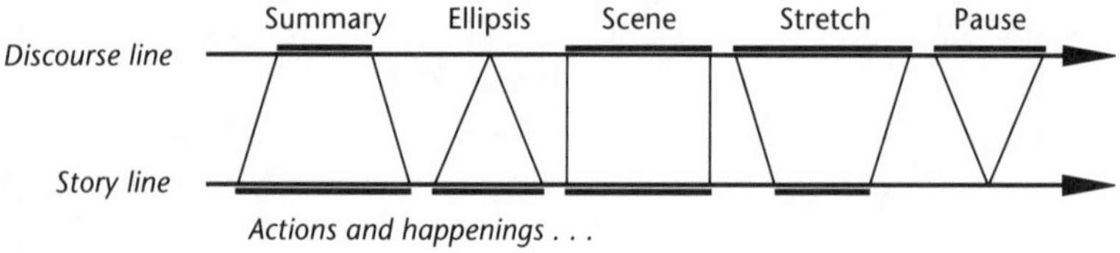

Summary and ellipsis have shorter duration than story time. Cutting or montage are the necessary techniques for this in film, like the breakfast scenes in *Citizen Kane,* which in a few seconds tell the story of Kane's first marriage. Ellipsis refers to parts of story time that do not have any representation in discourse time. It follows that ellipsis is a necessary element in summary. Interactivity in hypermedia allows the user to choose the speed, quantity, and quality of information. By jumping from one node to another, the user creates summary and ellipsis. In hypertext and hypermedia, browsing parallels summary and ellipsis, for choosing not to follow a link creates ellipsis, by means of which the articulated discourse is made "shorter" than other possible durations of the potential text.

Story time and discourse time are identical in a scene. Whereas in a film unedited shots in normal motion are all scenes, in hypermedia the equivalent may be just the same as watching a video clip of some action or happening that is not rearranged by editing or manipulated in some other form.

Stretch occurs when discourse time is longer than story time, as in, for example, slow motion in film or extremely detailed descriptions and stream-of-consciousness in literature. In hypertext, the reader creates stretch by following links that lead to more material on the same topic, since this procedure extends the discourse. It also expands the amount of information in the read text, whether fiction or faction. (Applied to hypermedia, Genette's "pause" could refer to a still photograph or other illustration.)

The concept of duration, which has particular relevance to hypertext, may prove useful to more critical analysis of specific texts. The stretch metaphor clearly focuses attention on hypertext's fundamental qualities of flexibility and openness. Nelson coined the term *strechtext* as a special variant of hypertext; the related term *elastic* has been used in the same sense when describing the hypermedia journal *The Elastic Charles*.[12]

In hypertext the reader relates to a discourse line (time) that exists only as storage absent from the surface of the screen. The variations of duration in hypertextual readings (discourse) become variations of the discourse as stored, possible readings. In traditional fiction the variations of duration are fixed and stable once the text is written. In hypertext fiction on the other hand, the reader is in principle free to manipulate a scene—to compress it or decompress it. The reader can shrink a scene into a summary or an ellipsis or, if the stored discourse has the necessary qualities, expand it. In the act of reading a hypertext fiction the durative relation between story and discourse is both open and closed; the act of reading is at the same time the act of choosing and deciding between the various kinds of duration.

Frequency, Genette's third category, concerns the number of references between story line and discourse line and subdivides into singular, repetitive, multiply singular, and iterative.

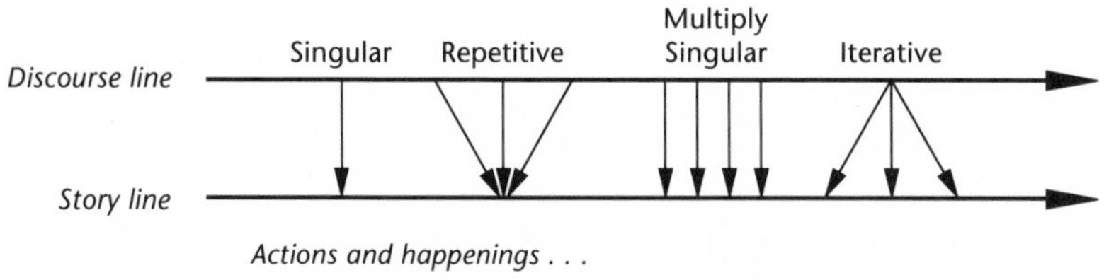

Under "singular" one discourse element refers to one story element only once. This is the usual frequency of representation and reference in a synchronous narrative. In hypertext, singularity could refer to one node signifying one event being visited only once.

When the same event in story time is referred to more than once in discourse time it is described as being repetitive. Thus, Wittgenstein's text is repetitive when he talks about entering the same place in the thought landscape from different directions. Cubism in painting represents a form of repetition that looks at an object twice but from different angles. Similarly, repetition appears in hypermedia both when one activates the same node more than once and when different nodes relate to the same topic.

Multiple singularity incorporates individual but similar elements in discourse time which refer to individual but similar events in story time. In many Hollywood film productions, the form of presenting front pages in spinning newspapers is an example of multiple singularity (as is the case with the reporting of Susan Alexander's opera performances if we stick to *Citizen Kane* as example). The equivalent in hypermedia could take the form of selecting similar nodes that refer to similar events.

In Genette's *iterative*, several incidents on the story level are referred to from one element of discourse. A node that summarizes the whole of a hypertext, like an extended table of contents, is iterative. Summary nodes and overviews are also iterative. Hypertextual navigation tools, like Intermedia's Web View and Storyspace's Roadmap, also contain iterative elements.[13] Iterativeness is also summary and ellipsis seen from another angle.

In the case of frequency (as with duration) the hypertext reader moves at a level in a "hyper" discourse created by the act of reading above and in addition to the traditional discourse line. Although free to move between the different variations, the user is constrained by the potential of the stored discourse (lines). An element of read discourse may in one constellation be repetitive but turn up at another place in the syntagmatic chain as a part of an iterative reference.

Although Genette developed these categories as a means of analyzing narrative structure in the writings of Marcel Proust, they are helpful in making sense of hypertexts. With hypertext and hypermedia something new is added to the story-discourse dichotomy. A third level, or a third line is introduced that may be called the discoursed text or *discourse-as-discoursed*—the actual use and reading of the digitally stored text. It is, in other words, the creation of a path based on the selection and combination of elements existing in a spatial and non-linear arrangement of nodes and links. The chronology of the story line may remain intact depending to a certain extent on fictiveness in the text. The discourse line, however, divides into two different levels: the discourse as a nonlinear text stored in space and the discourse as discoursed, as actually read. The actual way discourse-as-discoursed generates clearly has an effect on story and produces two story levels. There is one possible or potential story-as-stored and one actual story articulated by discourse-as-discoursed. This distinction is primarily of interest in fictional text, but is also of relevance to scientific or academic writing, in which quest for knowledge substitutes for traditional story.

The different levels may be presented as follows:

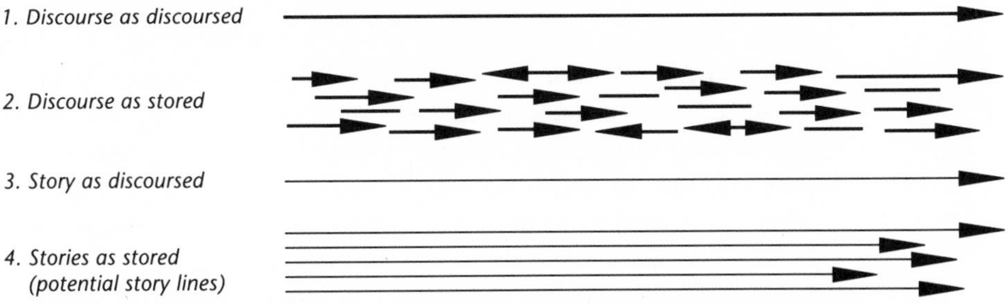

The icons at the discourse-as-stored level suggest different rules of linearity found in various types of media: "→," one-directional (spoken and written language, video); "↔," bidirectional (palindromes and reversible video and audio); and "—," nondirectional (pictures, still images).

Take the example of Michael Joyce's *Afternoon,* the work scholars and critics most frequently refer to when discussing hypertext narratives.[14] Within the frame and constraints conditioned by the hypertext author's choices of information, composition, software, and linking structures, the discourse-as-discoursed can take an unlimited variety of configurations and orders, which produce different and even contradictory story lines. The potential for syntagmatic variations increases radically when not only can the order of stable discourse-as-stored elements continually recombine but, in addition, signifieds (story content) can exclude each other by referring to contradictory events, events which both take place and do not take place. As a message independent of the reader, *Afternoon* exists as levels 2 and 4, discourse-as-stored and stories-as-stored. When the message is consumed or created by the reader during the interactive process of selection and combination, levels 1 and 3 emerge, discourse-as-discoursed and story-as-discoursed. The special effects of hypertext fiction, which distinguish it from traditional fiction, emerge in the dialectic relationship between levels 1 and 3 on one hand and 2 and 4 on the other–dialectic because the selected information continually is read in the context of the whole, both as stored and as previously articulated. This contextual totality in dynamic change continually alters the significance of selected elements.

In reading hypertext fiction the reader not only recreates narratives but creates and invents new ones not even conceived of by the primary author. In hypertext fiction the key principles of narrative structuring, and thus the basic operations of authorship, are transferred from author to reader, from primary to secondary author. The above application of Genette's concepts shows that one of the defining characteristics of hypertext, from the reader's point of view, is to engage in the selection and combination of different modes and techniques of narrative construction and composition. With hypertext fiction the reader is invited to take interactive part in the operations of what we may call the narrative machinery.

Since Genette's terminology originally applied to discourse time and story time, the equivalent of levels 1 and 3, there are no predefined rules for how to employ it when analyzing hypertexts; both levels of discourse may be selected as points of departure, but critics may also focus on the relationship between the two. In the exposition above I have made no fundamental distinction between these two applications.

Implications of Ancient Rhetoric for Hypertext

To complete the process of telling a story—of exchanging a narrative—the receiver must be constructive and produce or reproduce a coherent understanding of the message. Meaning is never contained or guaranteed by the text alone but requires the reader's engagement and creative relationship to the text. The user relates to the given parts and generates a whole that makes sense in the receiving context. The role of the reader in constituting textual meaning has always been central in narrative theory and general poetics. When focusing on the special kind of relationship between receiver and message in communication by hypertext, Landow discusses a relevant passage from J. Hillis Miller's study of a text by Heinrich von Kleist about a political speech by the French politician Mirabeau:

> The speaker posits a "syntactically incomplete fragment, says Kleist, without any idea . . . of where the sentence is going to end, [and] the thought is gradually 'fabricated' "; and Kleist claims that the speaker's feelings and the general situa-

> tion in some way produce his proposals. Disagreeing with him, Miller argues in the manner of Barthes that Mirabeau's revolutionary "thought is gradually fabricated not so much by the situation or by the speaker's feelings," as Kleist suggests, "but by his need to complete the grammar and syntax of the sentence he has blindly begun." (*Hypertext,* 116–17)

Landow suggests that this "in-process generation of meaning," central as it is to contemporary criticism and its attack on the traditional conceptions of self and author, also characterizes the reading process in hypertext. Production and consumption of hypertext, says Landow, "forces us to recognize that the active author-reader fabricates text and meaning from 'another's' text in the same way that each speaker constructs individual sentences and entire discourses from 'another's' grammar, vocabulary, and syntax" (117). In hypertext the in-process construction of meaning is rediscovered not only in the author's but also in the reader's position—the reader becomes secondary author within the constraints laid down by the primary author. This displacement of authoring from sender to receiver redefines the reader's position and makes it more like that of the traditional speaker. The reflections surrounding Kleist's example and the special focus on the speaker give us an opportunity to examine some relevant aspects of ancient rhetoric.

A growing body of scholarly texts has dealt with the relationship between hypertext and rhetorics.[15] In these studies the five components of what Roland Barthes calls the "rhetorical machine" (the "*techné rhétoriké*") have been given little attention. In his essay "The Old Rhetoric: An Aide-Mémoire" Barthes presents the different "mother-operations" which in classical conceptions of rhetoric surround the speaker before and during the delivery of a speech.[16] To test the relevance of this classification system I shall transfer it to the hypertext reader. Ancient rhetoric describes the operations recommended before performing a speech; these operations also relate to the actions performed by the receivers of hypertext and hypermedia messages.

In the first operation, *inventio* (*euresis*), the speechmaker gathers elements of what is to be said. Inventio is a discovery, not an invention, in which the speaker relates to existing topics, places or loci, commonplaces, for proof and persuasion. The proofs of inventio are either within-techné or outside-techné, *techné* meaning "a speculative institution of the means of producing what may or may not exist" (Barthes, 53). Proofs (elements) that are techné-independent are found outside the orator, the operator of techné. Proofs within-techné, on the other hand, depend on the orator's powers of reasoning and imagination. In the operation of inventio the orator collects proofs from different *topoi*, selects ready-made elements from a repertoire, and forms the unorganized raw material of the speech.

Readers of a hypermedia message act within a similar structure: they select existing elements or nodes from the message material and read in their given shapes (outside-technè). But elements existing as complete documents or nodes in the hypermedia message may be only partially selected, dependent upon the reader's punctuation in the chain of signifiers. The reader may read a whole node or only parts of it before following a link. This manipulation and imposing of a different order (*ordo artificialis*) upon the given structure of stored segments in the message (*ordo naturalis*) may be characterized as an operation of the orator (hypertext reader) within-technè.

Next, following the foundation of traditional dramatic principles of composition with beginning, middle, and end (*exordium, narratio, confirmatio,* and epilogue), the act of *dispositio* (*taxis*) orders what inventio has found. Of special interest for our purpose is the existence of a movable element, abstracted from the fixed parts, *egressio* or *digressio*—a piece of speech detached from the main subject and related to it only by a very loose link. This movable unit, mostly used in a signature function displaying the orator at his most brilliant, shows that although the rules of rhetoric are rather rigid, they enable flexibility and interchangeability between the elements of inventio and the successive arrangement of dispositio. The orator has an option to choose the syntagmatic order of dispositio when facing the already elected element of inventio. And this is of course exactly the case with dispositio in the act of reading a hypermedia message. In the act of selecting nodes and following links, of consuming the nonlinearly stored documents, the hypermedia reader performs dispositio.

When the orator puts into words elements of speech found in inventio and arranged in dispositio, he reaches the stage of *elocutio* (*lexis*), the figurative or other embellishment that makes argument persuasive. During the recent revival of scholarly interest in rhetoric this operation has received the most attention, despite being responsible for the negative connotations of the word *rhetoric.*

Elocutio in computer discourse concerns not only linguistic ornaments but also the graphic layout on the screen and the way signs and icons trigger action and interaction. In hypertext, interface design, layout, the information value of link icons, and so on all belong to elocutio. (The desktop metaphor, for example, was originally created to persuade people—to ease the use of technology and thereby to increase the sale of computers.) A question under elocutio might be which metaphor is "best" for the delete function: the trashcan icon on the Macintosh or the recirculation icon on the NeXT computer.

The renaissance of rhetoric has focused mainly on written texts. Barthes's survey is an example of that: "The last two (Actio and Memoria) were rapidly sacrificed, as soon as rhetoric no longer concerned the spoken (declaimed) discourse of lawyers or statesmen, or of 'lecturers' (epideictic genre), but also, and then almost exclusively, (written) 'works' . . . and since they have given rise to no classification (but only to brief commentaries), we shall eliminate them here from the rhetorical machine" (51). Electronic culture forces us to reevaluate these neglected operations.

Actio (*hypocrisis*) concerns performing the discourse like an actor with gestures and diction. The ancient concept of actio has two relevant links to hypertext and computer communication: actio as "inter-actio-n" (man-machine interaction) and actio as acting when the user is given a role according to which characteristics she or he acts and interacts.

Actio as inter-actio-n is exactly what Kleist describes as Mirabeau's relation to the general situation and to his audience. Mirabeau's speech act is a product of his interaction with his immediate surroundings. In reading hypertexts the user performs or acts, not facing an audience but interfacing with a computer. User and computer exchange information, but they do not engage in social interaction; and the computer is not a social being but only mediates operations and information invented and made possible by social beings. Identification with a role is to some extent present in all communication, but it increases dramatically in collaborative computer environments, such as role-playing games in the form of multi-user dungeons (MUDs), in which each participant acquires various characteristics and interacts according to those qualities.[17] In such environments actio as acting becomes relevant.

Memoria (*mnémè*) concerns the strategies and techniques of committing the speech to memory.[18] The techniques for remembering where you are in a train of thought when presenting a speech involve navigation. And navigation has been a major concern to hypertext research and development. Any speaker or subject is positioned in the temporal context of past, present, and future and must navigate according to what has been said, what is being said, and what is going to be said. Numerous aides-mémoire have been created for orientation within this situation. The main problems of disorientation in reading hypertexts follow the same pattern: where have I been, where am I, where am I going, and how am I going to get there? The problems of navigating in hypertext have been elegantly solved in Intermedia's system-generated navigator, the Web View.[19]

In memoria it is recommended that one imagine a building with as many levels and rooms as required. In the rooms of this imaginary construct pictures are placed on the walls. These images represent visually the topics of the speech. In making an imaginary walk through the building the speaker can then remember the order and succession of elements of the speech by associations related to the images. The rules for "places" and "images" in memoria serve as navigational devices that inform the speaker of what has been said, what is presently being talked about, what there is left to say, and in what order it will be said. In recent years numerous applications have exploited the knowledge implied in mnemonics: "Information Visualizer," an interface project at Xerox PARC,[20] and "Abulafia," a HyperCard-based information organizer that Geoffrey Bilder developed at Brown University, are directly inspired by the art of memory. "The Virtual Museum," a CD-ROM produced by Apple Computer, is an example of an electronic publication using the principles of virtual memory and the analogy to museum exhibits for information organizing.[21]

The basic elements of the graphical user interface exploit the same principles for orienting users. For example, to dispose of a document, the user of a Macintosh desktop computer employs the mouse to activate the function and then to drag the document icon to the lower right corner of the screen (place) and put it "into" the icon named "trash" (image). Vannevar Bush's original idea of an information machine, the *memex* (*mem*ory *ex*tender), and the conviction that procedures of unconscious information processing could be externalized and provide the structure for mechanical storage and retrieval, was based on similar principles. Wittgenstein's use of the landscape metaphor applies the principles of memoria to achieving structure and navigation in opaque information spaces.

Barthes excludes memoria and actio, believing them to be residual elements of oral culture that are superfluous within writing and print technologies. The fact that these operations gain new relevance from hypermedia supports Walter J. Ong's key argument that electronic culture, including computer technology, forms a secondary orality, an orality one step beyond literacy but dependent upon it.[22]

Elements in the relationship between oral speech and the two authoring levels of hypermedia communication can be displayed as follows:

		Hypermedia Communication	
	Oral Speech	Author/Sender	Reader/Receiver
INVENTIO	Discovering and selecting speech elements, "proofs"	Selecting/producing multiple media information	Selecting/manipulating nodes/ documents to read/consume
DISPOSITIO	Combining the selected elements	Combining selected and created elements. Link structure	Combining selected elements by reading. Following links
ELOCUTIO	Adding ornament to the speech for reasons of persuasion	Deciding layout, destination, and anchors. Normative rhetorics	The eloquent mastery of navigating and reading hypermedia texts
ACTIO	Performing the discourse like an actor: gestures and diction	Performing the writing in interaction with computer	Performing the reading in interaction with computer
MEMORIA	Organizing and structuring information in memory	Graphical representation for purpose of navigation (computer memory)	Individual use of navigational device

If we link the rhetorical perspective to that of narratology, we see that the primary author (author-sender) of hypertexts produces discourse-as-stored whereas the secondary author (reader-receiver) produces discourse-as-discoursed. While the narratological perspective primarily concerns the secondary reader's operation of dispositio (and to some extent inventio), the rhetorical perspective places the hypertext reader in a context which includes more of the operations involved in the act of hypertextual reading. Both the narrative and the rhetorical perspectives offer extensive arsenals of concepts to help our critical understanding of this reader-dominated medium.

From Nonlinearity to the Multiplication of Linearities

Order and pattern of some kind are necessary ingredients in all forms of communication. Nonlinearity has generally been seen as one of the distinguishing hallmarks of hypertext, which is most often defined as nonlinear or nonsequential reading or writing. It is nonlinear because readers can choose their own order of acquisition, according to their own needs and interests. The reader is no longer totally controlled and limited by the author's decisions concerning structure and succession. A traditional text of print and book technology is prelinked by the producer, and the reader is supposed to always behave within and be conditioned by the constraints of that arrangement (and agreement) but is free to conceive of the text's signifieds in a variety of combinations. However, in hypertext it is the physical status and position of each node (text element) itself which is supposed to be manipulated. Not only the author but also the reader takes an active part in the manipulation of message material. The linear chain provided by the author in traditional texts is thus replaced by a nonlinear constellation of text chunks from which the reader can choose individualized (customized) routes. Hypertext then has the potential to liberate readers from the linear dominion of physically stable media. As a consequence, the bonds to the author are weakened, noise is introduced to the channel, and predictability in communication is reduced. A central question, however, is to what extent hypertext and hypermedia really are nonlinear media and how comprehensive the nonlinear structures are. The questions arise as to what is actually nonlinearity in different systems of communication and at what levels of organization it exists. When reflecting upon problems in relation to the linear-nonlinear dichotomy, one inevitably touches the intriguing relationship between spatial and temporal dimensions. As we shall see, both linear and nonlinear patterns of organization exist and are generated in the changing contexts framed by time and space.

In all circumstances in which subjects engage the world and interact with it—whether by eating, moving, sensing, talking, reading, or writing—their actions can be conceived of in terms of selection and combination. In hypertext the actions of choosing and combining the elements of discourse (as stored)—and thereby creating the actual discourse (as discoursed)—are similar to basic operations in other forms of human communication and interaction. Film editors experience the same moments of decision when they piece together individual frames into a roll of film. This kind of selection also characterizes human language. When talking, we add words from the paradigmatic dimension of language and order them into the syntagmatic chain of speech. Even in nonverbal communication we go through the same operations of selection and combination. For instance, when we dress, we select items from our wardrobe and combine them into a particular day's mode of dressing. Then, consciously or not, we communicate messages to the people with whom we interact in the social reality of everyday life.

Reading hypertext differs in one important way from editing film or choosing one's clothing for the day, since the combined elements are processed in a way that differs from reading video clips and written text. We cannot stress any strict linear order in dressing, because the same rules of linearity do not apply. When regarding another individual's clothing, we follow no rule that determines in which order we read the outfit, say from top to bottom. This example connects to the types of nonlinearity, or rather other rules of linear organization, that exist on the computer screen. The screen occupies a third position, between the three dimensions of space and the one dimension of time. The screen and what it presents is a manifestation of the present, between past and future. Therefore the movement from space to time and the reduction from three dimensions to one both halt at the position of the screen and its flatland of two dimensions. Obviously, the design and composition of elements on the screen are of central importance to any critical study of hypermedia texts. The complication of relating time to the acquisition of still images can very easily be reduced to bioneurological aspects of perception, which are not of interest here. However, still images often present sequences of actions over time and thereby present narrative rules for successive relations of pictorial elements.[23]

Interaction unfolds at the intersections of linearity and nonlinearity and of time and space. At the core of interaction one finds the operations central to all communication and exchange, including language: selection (inventio), combination (dispositio), and the intimate relation between the axis of the message and the axis of the code. A variety of conceptual pairs originating in the structuralist study of language relate to this distinction, one that also parallels the distinctions between linear and nonlinear and between time and space: contiguity and similarity; *parole* (speech) and *langue* (language); diachrony and synchrony; syntagmatic and paradigmatic; metonomy and metaphor; displacement and condensation; and succession and simultaneity. Starting with Saussure and the general study of language, this paradigm of distinctions developed under the names structuralism, semiology, and semiotics into an interdisciplinary movement with tremendous impact on disciplines within the human and social sciences. For anthropology, psychoanalysis, literature, film studies, and archaeology, language has provided a paradigm. Several questions of comparison have come forward: "Is myth a language?" (Lévi-Strauss); "Is the unconscious structured like a language?" (Lacan); "Is film a language?" (Metz); "Is there a rhetoric of the image?" (Barthes). Similar questions arise in relation to hypertext: Are the systems of information we call hypertextual structured like a language? And should such systems be described accordingly? One might say that discourse-as-discoursed is an articulation of the system and its structure, but this claim does not mean that the stored information is necessarily like language or even comparable to it. Language is obviously the most advanced form of human communication, but not all communication is language. Using language as the primary paradigm of understanding, other and different modes of communication may very easily become reductionist.

Language is basically a digital coding system, whereas hypertext has both analogue and digital elements. Furthermore, articulation in hypertext takes place not at the level of letters and words but at the level of discourse. The form of articulation we find in hypertextual reading, the discourse-as-discoursed, is not a linguistic utterance. It remains for discourse analysts to decide what kind of utterances or articulation the reader encounters in hypertext and hypermedia messages—both as stored and as discoursed.

Returning to the relationships of linear and nonlinear and temporal and spatial, one must distinguish between nonlinearity in time and nonlinearity in space. Nonlinearity in time is imaginary; it is a fundamental contradiction of terms and necessarily impossible. *Time is linear,* at least the time that is required to read and write hypertexts. Reading and writing are linear phenomena; they are sequential and chronological, conditioned by the durative ordering of time, although their *positions* as stored and *in space* may have a nonlinear organization. But once a word or a sentence is read, it is chosen and taken out of its nonlinear context and positioned as a sequence in the linear chain and in conditioned time. However discontinuous or jumpy the writing or reading of a hypertext might be, at one level it always turns out to be linear.

The temporal linearity of reading a hypertext can easily be studied in Intermedia's dynamic navigation tool, the Web View. The main function of the Web View window is to represent graphically the user's current position and options. In the case illustrated, Web View shows that the documents or nodes visited by the reader thus far are organized nicely along a single line. It also shows the exact times each node was visited. From the reader's present position, at the document named "Levels of linearity," the user can choose among several alternatives, including revisiting the documents already visited, and each option represents access to the complex structure of the whole system. Thus, nonlinearity exists only as positions *in space,* different alternatives of which one may choose only *one at a time.* But in the act of choosing, when one selects the next node to consume, one moves from the dimension of space to the dimension of time. So the moment one reaches into nonlinearity by clicking on one of the icons in the graph, one reduces nonlinearity to linearity. We cannot escape. We always find ourselves at the intersection of time and space, and this situation frames all our actions. It is the *origo* where history and stories are created and where we all live our lives. Nonlinearity, one might say, is

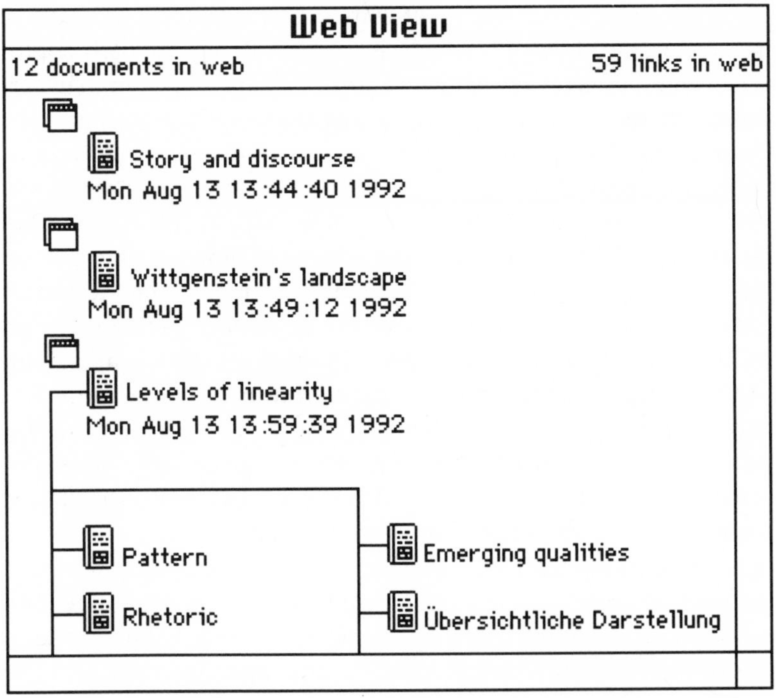

never actually experienced directly. It exists only as a logical negation and at a distance in both time and space.

The narratological perspective suggested earlier makes the movement from the nonlinearity of space to the linearity of time equivalent to the generation of a discourse-as-discoursed based on discourse-as-stored. From the rhetorical perspective of the secondary author, all the documents that can be reached from the Web View belong to the operation of inventio. The documents displayed (the visited nodes) form a dispositio, and thus a node may simultaneously form part of both inventio and dispositio. The structure of the Web View window seen as a whole offers a graphical metaphor for memoria.

Returning now to temporality, one may refer to Kant and state that time is the form of representation a priori; that is, time is a transcendental form of perception and is not empirically given.[24] It thus presupposes all representations and objects in time (and space), including hypertext nodes and links. At the most fundamental level, Kant's transcendental deduction of time and space formulates the frame for storing and processing, selecting and combining, and consuming and creating meaning in all human environments.

Let me elaborate on this point with an example. Imagine that one has a stack of cards lying on a table (cards provide a particularly appropriate example, given the extensive use of the card metaphor in hypertext circles, as in, for example, NoteCard, HyperCard, and SuperCard). One is primarily concerned with the relationships between the individual cards and the rules determining these relationships. The ways in which one perceives and interacts with such a collection of entities depend upon context and upon the rules one follows. If one picks up one card at a time, thereby acquiring the information and meaning it conveys, one has "followed" one rule of linearity—temporal linearity—by reading the cards in a successive order. This temporal linearity is always present no matter how nonlinear or chaotic a situation may be. The physical arrangement of the cards in a stack can be seen as a form of spatial, specifically vertical, linearity given by whoever provided the stack. This order of vertical linearity is activated and followed when one picks one card at a time from top to bottom.

However, if one follows an instruction "Pick three cards at random," the vertical linearity loses its dominance and the stack becomes perceived as a collection of equal opportunities. The stack is not linear in this context, since its vertical, top-to-bottom linearity is negated. The various cards may also be spread out on the table and not selected by hand but just scanned by the eye. The linearity produced then, the succession of perception, is subjective and independent of any external or physical rules other than the given arrangement. The agreement to make a random selection, whether by hand or eye, turns linearity into nonlinearity, but again the selection of the cards is subsumed under the order of temporal linearity. Temporal linearity is a product of the present and can, if wanted, be maintained and stored. One may hold the cards in one's hands, thereby imposing a successive order from left to right. Now one has created yet another form of linearity: a rule for spatial organization of the cards representing the order in which the cards were selected, so that spatial linearity represents temporal linearity, which is the basic metaphorical function of the line. This hand-held order may similarly be rearranged by additional actions of selection and combination, and so on.

This simple example demonstrates that linearity in the form of orders of linear and successive organization exists at several levels in both spatial and temporal constellations and that it depends upon which rules are applied in specific contexts. The way one produces and experiences linearity and nonlinearity in hypertext is context dependent. The number of constellations of succession and rules of linearities increases as the variety of information types increases—numbers, words, still pictures, moving images. Cards may also generate narratives. The Tarot, for example, is a complete system of divination, which means that its cards claim to represent all fundamental forces at work at all levels of nature, including humanity. The infinite variety of life results from the different combinations, patterns, and sequences of these forces reflected in the random patterns and combinations of the cards. Used in fortune telling, the Tarot cards articulate a discourse based on random selection, which the fortune teller interprets to produce stories about a person's future.

When one moves from verbal hypertext to hypermedia's activation of multiple senses, the variety of linearities increases. As Ong points out: "Sight isolates, sound incorporates."[25] Different senses favor different media and different types of communication. Orality favors hearing, whereas literacy favors the visual faculties. Hypermedia integrates the two.

The kinds of linearity discussed so far are all unidirectional. Reading, writing, and speaking cannot be reversed, although the direction of apprehending written texts varies depending on the language: left to right or right to left, for instance. (Spoken language, in contrast, generally has only one orientation, that of time.) However, the occurrence of symmetrical combinations of letters and words (palindromes) provides a very limited bidirectional linearity in writing. In Latin, the bidirectional qualities of words were used in magic; the so-called devil's square is a well-known example that exists in different combinations:

S A T O R	S A T A N
A R E P O	A D A M A
T E N E T	T A B A T
O P E R A	A M A D A
R O T A S	N A T A S

In hypermedia, bidirectional linearity becomes significant when one considers temporal and dynamic media, audio, and especially video. In a digital video medium, symmetrical shots neutral to motion may play an important role. Panning across a landscape may in principle be reversed with the effect of forming a reverse but different shot. The direction chosen is basically context dependent and is conditioned by the preceding and following shots or nodes. One may enter a hypertext document at any point. In hypermedia systems, bidirectional video has already proven useful as a device for navigation and dynamic representation of objects (artifacts). Productions like "The Virtual Museum" exploit the neutral, symmetrical qualities of digital video motion.

Hypermedia and the manipulative power of digital video can exploit these qualities, and video palindromes may eventually emerge as a central figure in digital media and communication, especially for three-dimensional navigational interface designs (virtual reality) and documentation of objects and landscapes.

In music the concept of linearity extends in yet another direction. Along the syntagmatic message or discourse line, melody is linear because displayed over time. Harmony appears when several voices (polyphony) at the same time make up parallel lines. In hypermedia the simultaneity found in harmony appears when sound is displayed parallel to text, video, or both. These elements form constellations of parallel linearity. This observation about hypermedia echoes Genette's concept of multiple singularity between story and discourse but presupposes that information is simultaneously displayed from *distinct* information channels.

The complexity of linearities in hypertext and hypermedia, which exists at many levels, depends upon different perspectives and contexts. Thus, the flexible collection of intersecting context-dependent linearities should, as suggested by Landow, be conceived as *multi*linear and *multi*sequential instead of as the negatives *non*linear and *non*sequential (*Hypertext,* 4). Multilinearity or -sequentiality are not pure negations of line and sequence but designate complex structures of various kinds and occurrences of linearities or, rather, multiplication of linearities. *Nonlinear,* on the other hand, is an empty term in the discourse on hypermedia that only shows how preoccupied writers on the subject have been with defining hypermedia in opposition to traditional media. It is my purpose here to stress continuity, relation, and connection rather than negation, difference, and distinction.

Emerging Qualities of the Hypermedia Message

With technological innovation, new qualities and capabilities of expression necessarily emerge. The transitions from writing to print and from silent film to talkies were additions to the register of expression, changing the form and content of the communicable information. What then are the characteristics of the hypermedia mode of communication and what are the emerging qualities of the hypermedia message? From the literary theorist's point of view the importance of hypermedia lies in the reconfiguring of author-reader relationships.[26] Hypertext redefines the authority of the author, implied or explicit, and the reader gains more control.

Hypertext and hypermedia applications have so far been dominated by stand-alone packages of information. However, if hypermedia facilities are to have extensive impact on the society of information exchange, they must be implemented and proven useful in communicational relationships. Evolving within the general framework of Vannevar Bush's classic vision of the memex as a personal library and file cabinet, hypermedia has proven itself in two different but closely related formats: as resource and as environment.[27] In hypermedia resources, the user can read, copy, and navigate through a large multimedia data base with hypertextual linking, but the information remains fixed; new documents cannot be added, and the structural relationship of the material is given. In a hypermedia environment, on the other hand, the reading subject does not interact from an external position but from one within, by adding documents and links, thereby changing the structure and content of the system.

Hypermedia resources and environments do not yet form part of ordinary systems of interpersonal communication. Their readers are not concerned with senders' intentions and motivations or with the whole system as a message. Within hypermedia environments, communication may take place between users, but the texts exchanged are rarely multinode messages. Single-node messages are frequently exchanged in the form of electronic mail, which may be integrated into hypermedia environments of senders and receivers. A focus on the hypermedia message as a multinode message seems to be missing in the development of hypermedia communication. Such a hypermedia message not only forms a part of an environment but is itself a hypermedia system, an aggregate of documents and nodes linked in a structure which provides multisequential readings and a variety of articulations.

The application of hypermedia to systems of communication has both advantages and disadvantages. Our narrative and rhetorical approaches both show that the acquisition of information is increasingly left to the reader, for hypermedia messages give rise to individual preferences and inclinations. Hypermedia is a pronounced receiver medium. However, multilinearity and the reader's increased influence on meaning production also have a negative side: the efficiency of communication decreases. The phenomenon of hypermedia communication therefore seems problematic: the moment one stresses the defining qualities of hypermedia, its potential as a means of conventional information exchange disappears. Hypermedia messages may transport large quantities of varied information but not necessarily at a satisfactory level of precision. How may this paradox be solved? In such a situation it is important to remember and reflect upon the connections between the new medium and established routines and types of communication.

As we have seen, the transference of power between communicators and their relationship to the means of information is modestly suggested in Wittgenstein's comments upon his own philosophic writing. His application of the album metaphor and his move from a literate to a figurative mode of representation implies a change in attitude in which *looking* becomes important at a level other than the literal *reading*. Wittgenstein's request for an attitude of looking instead of reading parallels the distinction between showing and telling in modern literary theory, especially in the Anglo-American tradition. The telling-showing dichotomy is—mistakenly, some would say—traced back to Plato's opposition between *diegesis* and *mimesis*. For Plato, diegesis appears when "the poet himself is the speaker and does not even attempt to suggest to us that anyone but himself is speaking."[28] With mimesis, on the other hand, the poet purposes to create an illusion that it is not he or she who speaks. Thus indirect speech is diegetic whereas dialogue, monologue, and direct speech in general are mimetic. The work of Anglo-American critics takes up this opposition as telling and showing, with a normative emphasis upon showing as the more artistic form of expression. Perry Lubbock insists that "the art of fiction does not begin until the novelist thinks of his story as a matter to be shown, to be so exhibited that it will tell itself."[29] Contrary to Lubbock, Wayne Booth emphasizes the qualities of telling over showing.[30]

In *Narrative Discourse,* Genette, however, argues convincingly that "no narrative can 'show' or 'imitate' the story it tells. All it can do is tell it in a manner that is detailed, precise, 'alive,' and in that way give more or less the *illusion of mimesis*" (164). The crucial distinction, therefore, exists not between telling and showing but between different kinds and levels of telling. Language can only imitate language directly, or as Genette puts it: "The truth is that mimesis in words can only be mimesis of words." Since language is a digital system for coding information, it can only produce analogue representations indirectly and mediated by the coding system itself. In literature, showing is a function of telling and is made possible by it, just as multilinearity is a function of linearity. Basically, all literature takes the form of telling, for only in that condition can it present itself as different levels of showing. In general, telling is the means of precision whereas showing is indirect and ambiguous, since the receiver must fill in and thereby complete the message. Showing works as a whole, an overall picture generated by the reader by connecting the given information. The reader's activity and participation in the construction of meaning increase when the system of communication involved moves from a mode of telling to that of showing.

The telling-showing dichotomy in literature parallels a distinction between fiction and poetry on one side and general nonfiction literature on the other. At yet another level it parallels the difference between the aesthetic and the practic-theoretic domains of experience. Artistic expression has always been opposed to conceptual and theoretical knowledge. It has been considered a different kind of experience and communication, based primarily on feeling and emotion as opposed to intellect and reason. Kant, for example, in his *Kritik der Urteilskraft*, presents the beautiful (*das Schöne*) as a form of representation so rich with information and meaning that it cannot be adequately represented by any concept of the understanding.[31] Indirect communication has a long tradition in philosophy, not only as a subject matter in aesthetics but as a form of representation, from the dialogue format (mimesis) in Plato's work to the evolution of philosophical self-consciousness in Hegel. Even Kant's rigid system has an opening for the figurative and indirect when he utters the need to look upon his theoretical philosophy as an *architecture* of pure reason.

In §122 of *Philosophical Investigations* Wittgenstein elaborates on what the album metaphor in his preface only suggests. A general theme in Wittgenstein's later philosophy involves his rejection of the idea that philosophy takes the form of theory that can explain the nature of knowledge, since this task necessarily gets tangled up in the problem of self-reference: in order to explain the conceptual construction one applies concepts that remain unexplained. Wittgenstein avoids such regression by practicing a method that attempts to get a "clear view" of language and philosophical problems. "The concept of a perspicuous representation [*Übersichtliche Darstellung*] is of fundamental significance for us. It earmarks the form of account we give, the way we look at things." And this method has a certain content and purpose: "A perspicuous representation produces just that understanding which consists in 'seeing connections.' Hence the importance of finding and inventing *intermediate cases* [*Zwischengliedern*]" (§122). The sketches and paragraphs in *Philosophical Investigations* describe and display language games rather than representing a privileged, theoretical position. Therefore, "the language-games are rather set up as *objects of comparison* which are meant to throw light on the facts of our language by way not only of similarities, but also of dissimilarities" (§130).

Wittgenstein's project is not to advance new theories or explanations in philosophy: "Philosophy simply puts everything before us, and neither explains nor deduces anything" (§126). His counter-strategy involves presenting descriptive examples that in a paradoxical way relate to philosophical problems and theoretical presuppositions both displayed in the text and present in the reader's understanding. This goal is achieved by presenting the reader with examples that on one side are diverted from a presupposition and apparently compatible with it but which from another perspective turn out to overthrow the theory.

This dimension of Wittgenstein's text has been related to aesthetics by the philosopher Viggo Rossvaer: "Indirect communication is an art form. The formation of messages that are completed by the addressee's recreation of it is a philosophical art. The mastery of this art consists in the formulation of symbols that are intrinsically ambiguous, manifesting the unity of saying and showing as a contradictory unity of opposing tendencies."[32] Such an interpretation makes sense of Wittgenstein's palpable humility in describing his own work in the preface. *Philosophical Investigations* as a whole becomes an example that shows that the format he was unable to realize, the book-without-breaks, in fact was a mistake, and the book itself ridicules and dismisses it. In the preface then, the art of indirect communication takes the form of irony.

Rossvaer's identification of indirect communication in the case of Wittgenstein and its implied reconfiguration of author and reader can also be seen as a description of the hypermedia message: "In indirect communication, the addressee also becomes the sender of the message he receives since he must himself give it direction and application. To receive the message as an indirect form of communication one must recreate the message. The message can only be validly applied by means of the addressee's own self-knowledge, even if the message is *formulated* by someone else. It takes two persons to make up *one* message" (29). This "aesthetic" aspect of conceiving relationships in description, understanding, and knowledge is also central in the work of Gregory Bateson: "By *aesthetic,* I mean responsive to the *pattern which connects.*"[33] The phrase "the pattern which connects" describes a strategy for thinking about organization in communication and exchange, since "the right way to begin to think about the pattern which connects is to think of it as primarily a dance of interacting parts" (33).

This interrelated and dynamic approach has been applied to media analysis by Anthony Wilden in describing the effects created by decontextualization of film texts by means of videotape montage.[34] Wilden and his students edited a collection of selections from classic Hollywood dance films. Consisting of nineteen individual numbers, *Women in Production: The Chorus Line* is a fifty-five-minute-long montage displaying how the codes of the Hollywood musical depict social relations of class, race, and gender. Both the participants in the editing process and the viewers of the completed montage developed media literacy. Wilden points out that the group became aware that although television and video media are highly developed in the industrialized countries, media literacy remains largely inarticulate, unconscious, and unrecognized. In recontextualizing the film texts by taking the various dance numbers out of their original environment and putting them into the context of each other, a new level of communication emerged which increased the available information in the film clips:

> Without at first realizing it, we were transforming what would ordinarily be merely message information—the actual details of a given production number in a particular film—into coding information—the repetition in many modes and styles of the basic semiotic patterns of the Hollywood musical. What had previously been invisible, unnoted, or disregarded as noise emerged, as if from nowhere, as novel information. Pattern after pattern joined the patterns that connect. (286–87)

The editing of this videotape montage may to a certain extent be compared to a reading or articulation (discourse-as-discoursed) of a hypermedia message, as a selection and combination of film segments taken from a larger repertoire of films. The abolition of hypermedia communication as a paradox appears in the focus on hypermedia as a means of indirect communication, a medium dominated by showing. A mode of mediation in which the purpose is not to present a linear structure but to take advantage of dynamic network structure to exchange "perspicuous presentations" generating "that understanding which consists in 'seeing connections'"—"the pattern which connects." What then are the implications of this perspective upon hypermedia? Which patterns do the users' interaction with the hypermedia message generate? Within the frame of this essay the answer can only be general, and I shall limit myself to the media literacy.

Wilden defines media literacy as "literacy in communication, whatever its shape and form" (299). If recontextualization plays an important role in generating new information and new levels of communication in the videotape montage, this fact has consequences for hypermedia. Since readers of hypermedia to some extent take up the position of authors, the contextual change of the informational elements and the types of media becomes of central importance. The computer's digital coding of information makes it possible for the traditional media to combine in discourse that integrates numbers, words, drawings, graphics, photo, audio, and video. The computer has become an inclusive supermedium capable of connecting various media independent of the institutions in which they usually appear: written language, graphics, and photography from book and print culture; audio from radio and telephone; and video from cinema and television. Various media institutions have shaped different forms of expressions but have also protected these forms from each other. Hypermedia separates individual information technologies from their comprehensive social, technological, and economic apparatuses and mixes them in a manner previously impossible. This recontextualization combines older information media independent of their previously protecting environments. The direct juxtaposition of verbal text and video, for example, makes one immediately experience similarities and differences between the two types of information.

Hypermedia communicates not only different topics in diverse and complex ways but also the distinctive character of different forms of information, qualities inaccessible when they appear in protection of their mother institutions. By changing the relationship between language and figurative representation, between text and pictures, hypermedia creates new conditions for experiencing information and meaning. Wilden amplifies his definition of media literacy in a way that clearly is valid for descriptions of the experiences of hypermedia: "Media literacy is the capacity to combine the digital precision and low diversity of language (which is predominantly digital and iconic) with the analog and iconic ambiguity and high diversity of visual and other non-verbal modes of communication" (299). Creating a discourse (as discoursed) from the discourse-as-stored is a constant recontextualization best conceived as a montage, since no node conveys a meaning neutral and independent of context (something apparent in the works of the Russian film theorist and director Sergei Eisenstein). However, one important feature distinguishes the editing of the montage from the "editing" process in hypermedia consumption. In hypermedia the user faces a multimedia and multilinear information space from which pieces of information can be picked up and displayed on the screen, and each selection reconfigures the message as a whole.

In all reading of printed texts the knowledge of the text's physical organization as a fixed entity acts as a major element in the reading process, and the unchangeable structure guarantees a frame for the reading. The combination of that-which-is-read, the text, may differ from the order of the signifier; but the physical organization stands as a dominant succession that at the most fundamental level, as a contract, may not be broken. In addition, the subject has the constant digressions and rearrangements and reconfiguring of information by means of connotation and association.

This constant recontextualization reaches a new level with hypermedia, because the whole with which the reader compares that-which-is-read exists only as a flexible, unstable whole, an information space constructed by the reader's interactions with the text. These flexible and changing relationships between part and whole, text and context, that which is read and that which is to be read, create a dialectic process, a rereading of old and new information in changing contexts that again transforms the circumstances in which we experience various modes of coding information. In hypermedia communication the subject reads against an unstable textual order (the material of the hypermedia message). It has an order of a very different kind than do printed texts. The meaning and understanding of the message lies in the relationship between what is consumed and knowledge of the general structure. This oscillation between articulated part and a flexible multilinear whole is the place at which the emerging qualities reside. In hypermedia this dialectic oscillation conveys a different potential than traditional texts, because discourse-as-discoursed relates to a textual structure that the user continually recontextualizes, thereby confronting the informational content with situations unprotected by context.

Hypertext and hypermedia are means of information exchange that combine modes of telling and showing in innovative and provocative ways, and, given the reconfiguration of author and reader relations, they emerge as media dominated by the mode of showing. Although hypertext fictions exploit this potential of electronic media, few nonfictional or educational applications have done so. Gregory Ulmer provides a rare exception. He describes a hypermedia essay that focuses on many of the same theoretical implications of using non-print media that I have discussed. Inspired by Walter Benjamin's Arcade project and the *mise an abyme* structure, Ulmer relates the telling-showing dichotomy to the characteristics of hypermedia:

> The *mise an abyme* is a reflexive structuration, by means of which a text shows what it is telling, does what it says, displays its own making, reflects its own action. My hypothesis is that a discourse of immanent critique may be constructed for an electronic rhetoric (for use in video, computer, and interactive practice) by combining the mise an abyme with the two compositional modes that have dominated audio-visual texts—montage and mise en scene. The results would be a deconstructive writing, deconstruction as an *inventio* (rather than as a style of book criticism).[35]

My essay has touched upon at least three interrelated main aspects of hypertext and hypermedia: (1) the *interactivity* between user and information (subject and text) that makes nonlinear navigation in, and random access to, the information space possible; (2) the *integration* of different types of media: verbal text, photographs, sound, and video—a complexity of combinations that exceeds all previous communications media and makes hypermedia incompatible with both book and video technology; and (3) the *inclusion* of context as both quantity and quality. Interaction concerns the subject's relationship to the message, integration primarily concerns the status of the message, and inclusion deals with the relation of the message to its reconfigured contexts and environments. Joined together as a whole in the mode(s) of hypermedia communication, these deeply intermingled aspects are not the sum of their parts, not even *more* than the sum, but simply *different* or *other* than the summation of their preceding elements. Consequently, this multifaceted mode of expression encourages interdisciplinarity.

My purpose here has been to emphasize the importance of continuity in order to prevent us from breaking the patterns that connect old competence and new technology. It is important to make integration central, integration of both different media and relevant theories. The emerging potential of media integration creates the theoretical challenge of hypermedia which lies in the forthcoming theoretical integration. This is especially the case for literary theory which for so long has enjoyed a hegemonic position.

NOTES

The ideas presented in this essay were first expressed during a talk at Brown University's Computer Humanities Users Group (CHUG) in April 1991. I am grateful to George P. Landow and Andrew Morrison for helping me to give these ideas a readable form.

1. Ludwig Wittgenstein, *Philosophical Investigations* (Oxford: Basil Blackwell, 1953), vii.

2. Wittgenstein's preface was written in 1945 and coincides with the publication of Vannevar Bush's now-classic essay, "As We May Think," *Atlantic Monthly* 176 (July 1945): 101–8, which has come to mark the conceptual beginning of hypertext, while the actual implementation and terminology of hypertext first appeared with the works of Engelbart and Nelson twenty years later. See Douglas C. Engelbart, "The Augmented Knowledge Workshop," in *A History of Personal Workstations,* ed. A. Goldberg (Reading, Mass.: Addison-Wesley, 1988), 187–336. Theodor Holm Nelson first employed the terms *hypertext* and *hypermedia* in "A File Structure for the Complex, the Changing, and the Indeterminate," *ACM Proceedings of the 20th National Conference* (New York: Association of

Computing Machinery, 1965), 84–100. I do not know of any immediate link between Wittgenstein and Bush other than that both trained as engineers, but the philosopher's dissatisfaction with conventions of writing and the scientist's idea of a new machine for the extension of man's thinking show similar interest in adapting new ways of handling information.

3. See J. David Bolter, *Writing Space: The Computer, Hypertext, and the History of Writing* (Hillsdale, N.J.: Lawrence Erlbaum, 1991), 115. It has further been asserted that Wittgenstein's procedures have been an inspiration for developments in educational hypertext, see George P. Landow, *Hypertext: The Convergence of Contemporary Critical Theory and Technology* (Baltimore: Johns Hopkins University Press, 1992), 122.

4. See Ludwig Wittgenstein, *Tractatus Logico-Philosophicus* (London: Routledge & Kegan Paul, 1971), 31–42.

5. Plato, *Theaitetos*, in *Gesammelte Werke*, ed. Ernesto Grassi and Walter Hess (Hamburg: Rowolt, 1977), 4:103–81.

6. See Georg Wilhelm Friedrich Hegel, *Phänomenologie des Geistes* (Frankfurt: Suhrkamp Verlag, 1977), 82–93.

7. Claus Huitfeldt and Viggo Rossvaer, *The Norwegian Wittgenstein Project Report 1988* (Bergen: Norwegian Computing Centre for the Humanities, 1988), 2.

8. Storyspace, developed by J. David Bolter, Michael Joyce, and John B. Smith (Cambridge, Mass.: Eastgate Systems, 1988–93).

9. See Ludwig Wittgenstein, *Zettel*, ed. G. E. M. Anscombe and G. H. von Wright, trans. G. E. M. Anscombe (Oxford: Basil Blackwell, 1977), iv.

10. Christian Metz, *Film Language: A Semiotics of the Cinema*, trans. Michael Taylor, quoted in Gerard Genette, *Narrative Discourse: An Essay in Method*, trans. Jane E. Lewin (Ithaca: Cornell University Press, 1983), 33.

11. Genette presents his position in both *Narrative Discourse* and *Narrative Discourse Revisited*, trans. Jane E. Lewin (Ithaca: Cornell University Press, 1988). For Genette's relevance to film, see Seymour Chatman, *Story and Discourse: Narrative Structure in Fiction and Film* (Ithaca: Cornell University Press, 1983).

12. See Hans Peter Brøndmo and Glorianna Davenport, "Creating and Viewing 'The Elastic Charles: A Hypermedia Journal,'" in *Hypertext: State of the Art*, ed. Ray McAleese and Catherine Green (Oxford: Blackwell, 1990), 43–52.

13. On the IRIS Intermedia Web View, see Kenneth Utting and Nicole Yankelovich, "Context and Orientation in Hypermedia Networks," *ACM Transactions on Information Systems* 7 (1989): 58–84.

14. For description and analysis of *Afternoon*, see Bolter, *Writing Space*, 123–28, Landow, *Hypertext*, 113–15, and the chapters in this volume by J. Yellowlees Douglas and Terence Harpold.

15. For a brief overview see Stuart Moulthrop, "Beyond the Electronic Book: A Critique of Hypertext Rhetoric," *Hypertext '91* (New York: Association of Computing Machinery, 1991), 291–98.

16. Roland Barthes, "The Old Rhetoric: An Aide-Mémoire," *The Semiotic Challenge* (Oxford: Blackwell, 1988), 11–95.

17. See Espen Aarseth's discussion of cybertext and MUDs in this volume.

18. See Frances Yates, *The Art of Memory* (Chicago: University of Chicago Press, 1966).

19. See George P. Landow, "The Rhetoric of Hypermedia: Some Rules for Authors," *Hypermedia and Literary Studies*, ed. Paul Delany and George P. Landow (Cambridge: MIT Press, 1991), 81–103.

20. The Information Visualizer: An Information Workspace, developed by Stuart K. Card, George G. Robertson, and Jock D. Mackinlay (Palo Alto, Calif.: Xerox Palo Alto Research Center).

21. "The Virtual Museum: Interactive 3D Navigation of a Multimedia Database," developed by Gavin Miller et al., on *The Virtual Museum Release 1.0* (CD-ROM) (Cupertino, Calif.: Apple Computer, 1992).

22. Walter J. Ong, *Orality and Literacy: The Technologizing of the Word* (London: Methuen, 1982), and *Interfaces of the Word* (Ithaca: Cornell University Press, 1977).

23. See for example Nelson Goodman, "Twisted Tales; Or Story, Study, and Symphony," in *On Narrative,* ed. W. J. T. Mitchell (Chicago: University of Chicago Press, 1981), 99–117.

24. Immanuel Kant, *Kritik der reinen Vernunft*, ed. Raymund Schmict (Hamburg: Felix Meiner Verlag, 1976), 63–93.

25. Ong, *Orality and Literacy,* 72.

26. See Landow, *Hypertext,* 71–119.

27. George P. Landow and Paul Delany, "Hypertext, Hypermedia, and Literary Studies: The State of the Art," in *Hypermedia and Literary Studies,* 32–35. This distinction parallels Michael Joyce's opposition of "exploratory" and "constructive" hypertexts; see Joyce, "Siren Shapes: Exploratory and Constructive Hypertexts," *Academic Computing* 3 (Nov. 1988): 10–14, 37–42. To this opposition Moulthrop has further added "deconstructive hypertext."

28. Plato, *Republic,* in *Plato: The Collected Dialogues,* ed. Edith Hamilton and H. Carius (Princeton: Princeton University Press, 1963), 638.

29. Shlomith Rimmon-Kenan, *Narrative Fiction: Contemporary Poetic* (London: Methuen, 1983), 107.

30. Wayne C. Booth, *The Rhetoric of Fiction* (Chicago: University of Chicago Press, 1961).

31. Immanuel Kant, *Kritik der Urteilskraft* (Hamburg: Felix Meiner Verlag, 1974), 167–68.

32. Viggo Rossvaer, "Philosophy as an Art Form," in *Wittgenstein—Akten eines Symposiums in Bergen 1980,* ed. Kjell S. Johannessen and Tore Nordenstam (Wien: Hölder-Pichler-Tempsky, 1981), 29–30.

33. Gregory Bateson, *Mind and Nature: A Necessary Unity* (New York: Bantam Books, 1988), 8.

34. Anthony Wilden, *The Rules Are No Game: The Strategy of Communication* (London: Routledge & Kegan Paul, 1987), 286–87.

35. Gregory Ulmer, "Grammatology Hypermedia," *Postmodern Culture* 1 (1991), 1–19.

The Screener's Maps: Michel de Certeau's "Wandersmänner" and Paul Auster's Hypertextual Detective

Mireille Rosello

4

Imagine that this is 2084 (or any other symbolically loaded science fiction historical landmark) and that you are trying to explain to a group of young school children what it meant to "read" before the times of hypertexts. The word *reading* having since then fallen into disuse, you could preface your hypermedia presentation by explaining that *reading* was the activity performed by *readers* and that the closest modern equivalents might be *screening* and the *screener*. You might want to point out, however, that the screener corresponds both to the reader and to what used to be called the writer, it having previously been assumed that readers and writers were to be carefully distinguished. You could explain that reading a single object called a *book*, for instance a novel by Colette entitled *La Chatte*, could require an enormous amount of preliminary work and physical exertion: a reader would have to take a trip to a place called a library or to a bookstore, borrow or buy the book, or order it and wait, and might have to settle for a translation (for linguistic frontiers still very much coincided with national borders at that time). Then one would have to carry the object back home. Books were made of sheets of paper, called pages, that were turned over one by one to read them. Each page had a number, and it was more or less assumed that one would read the book from beginning to end. There were exceptions of course: some writers liked to experiment with fragments and nonlinear writing, but it was considered revolutionary and bold. Generally speaking, nonlinearity was a second best, a second best to literature in the case of directories, catalogues, files, or even encyclopedias, and a second best to creative writing in the case of critical articles whose authors already knew how to use footnotes and indexes and tables of contents but considered them marginal and secondary to their thinking. The process of reading a book was supposed to have a beginning and an end determined by the object itself, although linearity was still arbitrarily interrupted by readers, since most people did not finish a book in one sitting: some used to read a few pages every night before going to sleep, or they would read the book while being transported to work. Once read, the book usually ended up on a shelf; at the end of a career, a professional reader (a professor of literature for example) would usually live in cramped corners, pushed out of his or her home by hundreds and hundreds of once-read and rarely glanced at original editions or books of criticism.

Now imagine that we are in 1993 but that hypertext has not been invented yet. Then, I could describe the invention of hypertext as the very cultural and discursive phenomenon which allowed me to imagine the above scenario, to defamiliarize the reading process and the book as object, and to question the apparently transparent features of the printed medium. My first paragraph is a fiction of scientific history—or the fiction of science rather than science fiction—but if it appears fantastic to our sense of reality, it is not because hypertext does not yet exist but because most of what is described and explained above usually goes without saying, usually falls within the apparently unrelated yet symmetrical, categories of common sense, the obvious, silence, the norm, or the mandatory.[1] In the same way as a glossary of Jamaican Creole words at the end Michelle Cliff's books will be useless and perhaps insulting to Jamaican readers, a story of how books are read seems redundant and hardly worth telling in 1993.

In a hypertextual and hypothetical future, I might not read *La Chatte* as such or any text defined by a single and unchanging title. I might never have to buy a book again. I might be sitting in front of a terminal that would let me screen some equivalent of a "text" (a theoretically infinite textual or visual or aural space) via some kind of networking facility. Buying a book would probably be replaced by some form of electronic subscription or on-line charging system. Moreover, the concept of a single work identified by an author, a title, or a genre may not be very useful in this future. A hypertextual version of *La Chatte* would be linked to many other documents, and if linking has become commonplace, there is no telling how borders between texts will have been reappropriated and reimagined. If current, rapidly evolving (or already obsolete) programs such as HyperCard, Intermedia, and Storyspace are any indication, the travel metaphor may well have replaced, or transformed, the idea of reading as we now understand it, altering related concepts such as footnotes, quotations, tables of contents, indexes, and even the definition of genres of discourse, such as the opposition between fragments and linearity, literary genres, and concepts of authorship, readership (Landow, *Hypertext*).

Consequently, I will not be talking so much about hypertext per se as about the multifaceted layers of commentaries on hypertext which are gradually becoming familiar even to people who have never experimented with hypertextual designs. More specifically, I look at how hypertext reveals that the metaphorical system governing our conceptualization of reading is transparently dependent on the print medium. Whether it becomes dominant or goes down in history as a failed experiment, hypertextuality will have had the merit of questioning the status of the book as a privileged vehicle for narratives, by raising ideological and practical issues, two of which I analyze in this article: the relationship between reading and technology and the redefinition of how bodies move or write themselves in space.

Did You Say *Technology?*[2]

When I started writing this article, I realized that I was addressing those of my colleagues and friends in the humanities who will not follow me onto the mine field of what they call technology, even if we share interests in every other theoretical pursuit. I would like to convince them that thinking about hypertext is not different from thinking about nationalism, cultures, gender, or storytelling, because it also entails a redefinition of the relationship between bodies and spaces. Yet, most of the colleagues who have helped me grow by sharing their insights about theories of literature and culture seem hostile to, or frightened by, technology and, sometimes, determined to protect the sacred land of culture from the evils of inhumane and would-be scientific gadgets.

Perhaps I should point out that I am not sure why hypertext should be put under the category of technology (as opposed to literature for example): once, I had to persuade myself that I was using the word *technology* as a synonym for "machines that I cannot afford (financially or ideologically) or do not know how to use." Today, I wonder if the same logic is not at work when one systematically presupposes that hypertextual experiments belong to the (admittedly unromantic and threatening) category of technology. When I first came to the University of Michigan as a foreign student, I had never used a typewriter. No professor in France had ever suggested that we use one of these noisy and ugly contraptions, and, for all I remember, we apprentice intellectuals would have thought it indecent to resort to such "technology" to produce literary criticism. Typewriters, in our leftist and unknowingly elitist group, were probably associated with the world of bourgeois and materialistic business people. Typing was viewed as a professional skill which only secretaries mastered as a result of specific training, not to mention that typewriters were considered horribly expensive and therefore undemocratic. After one term of graduate studies in a North American institution, it soon became obvious that the matter was not open to discussion. My theoretical, political, and economic objections were greeted with raised eyebrows or sympathetic incomprehension; and I began to realize that if I did not abide by what I then perceived as a rather intolerantly enforced unwritten rule, I would simply not get a degree. The stakes were rather disproportionate. One does not wage a lonely war against deceptively invisible culturally dominant items. I therefore gave up on the idea of converting America (at the time, I thought of America with one big capital A) to the sensual, creative, democratic beauties of handwriting. I resolved to learn how to type. I would purchase or borrow a typewriter.

As destiny would have it, I was saved by a historical bell: in 1985, the University of Michigan campus was flooded with the first wave of microcomputers. I started my dissertation on the first generation of Macintoshes, spending my nights at the well-heated, well-lit computer center, discovering at the same time how to write a thesis and how to use an electronic environment, which in turn taught me that index cards, bibliographies, texts, and quotations could be thought of as different hierarchical levels of writing rather than as different literary genres. The question of which typewriter to buy or rent instantly became obsolete, and, seven years later, the fact that I still cannot type properly and do not own a typewriter is moot. My point is that technology saved me from technology, or that there is probably no such thing as a nontechnological writing environment.

If one agrees that "technology," like "power," tends to function like a transparent convention influencing the way in which we each make sense of our reality (that is, narrativize our problems), then trying to ignore hypertexts will not make technology go away. The dominant print medium is the (by now proverbial) always already of technology, and hypertextuality may well be the fragile and nonviable emerging end of some hegemonic iceberg. And if technology is Monsieur Jourdain's prose, it might be more useful to reflect on what specific ideological changes obtain when one shifts from one form of technology to another than to strive for the elimination of technological pollution from the not-so-pure rivers of literature. I wonder if the skills one needs to navigate comfortably within hypertext will soon become as necessary to one's social and professional survival as the enormous apparatus of transparent knowledge one requires to use books and typewriters or word processors.

Granted, hypertext is not word processing, and I do not intend to confuse the two. In the same way as I knew what a typewriter was, even though I was convinced that using one would be bad for my soul, most academics, I suspect, are aware that word processors exist and perhaps, even if they have never used one, know enough to make an educated (ideological) decision about whether to adopt or reject them. No unwritten rule absolutely demands that critics, writers, or students "compose at the keyboard" (at least for another few years or decades). Enthusiastically embracing the new possibilities is still potentially as fashionable or socially acceptable as stoically resisting the call of incessant advertisement.[3] Hypertexts, on the other hand, are not exactly the most common cultural products, even for people who routinely work with computers.

Critics or students of theory and literature who have never heard of hypertextuality may wonder if it has anything to do with intertextuality. And readers who have lived a happy and productive life without studying Barthes, Kristeva, or structuralism will naturally (and, at present, correctly) assume that a hypertext is a text with some "hyper" features. The prefix and the whole word evoke science fiction, futuristic fantasies, mysterious attributes. There is something both infinite and high-tech about hyper things. "Super"-items, on the other hand, are already a little passé, almost obsolete. Superman still dreamed of individualistic heroic deeds; he still belonged to the tail-end of epic modernity; he was still a white, straight, male more-than-human rather than a cyborg. Hyper-*beings* on the other hand (who would dream of a generation of hyper-gender-specific-bodies?) are on the side of post-postmodernism; they evolve in the imaginary space of disembodied and optimistically cynical cyborgs (Haraway, *Primate Visions*). A *supertext* would be grotesque among scholars of literature, theory, and culture, who tend to believe that God died at the beginning of the century and who are not too patient with substitute Ur narratives.[4] A supertext would probably sound like a commercial: it would be efficient, down-to-earth, manageable. A superpoem is an oxymoron. Hypertexts, on the other hand, may be slightly amusing because they are on the verge of grandiloquence, but they are intriguing because whoever trades on hyper-ground in the 1990s is bound to have a vision, some wild (and perhaps self-centered) faith in the evolving future of literary and cultural forms, and also a slight tendency to celebrate unfinished projects.

Compared with word processors, which, in the space of a few years, have become commonplace and banal (most of the time they work very well), hypertextual environments have remained almost as "outlandish"[5] as when Ted Nelson popularized the concept.[6] Not everyone has heard of, let alone used, Storyspace, Guide, or Intermedia; and HyperCard users are not necessarily interested in hypertextuality. Hypertextual experiments are often carried out within the limits of academic units and Hypertext fiction, such as Michael Joyce's *Afternoon* or Stuart Moulthrop's *Victory Garden*, is still an emerging practice.[7] But even as I cannot say at this time that hypertext really exists as an element in Western culture, some(hyper)thing is being celebrated or criticized in a rapidly growing number of printed texts. Interestingly enough, articles published in newspapers and those published in scholarly journals during the late 1980s and early 1990s do not agree on the level of reality one should grant hypertexts. Authors seem either to suggest that the print medium is already anachronistic or, on the contrary, to insist on the radical and futuristic nature of hypertextual experiments and on the tremendous amount of hostility they are bound to generate among conservative thinkers. In "Computers, Minds, and Texts: Preliminary Reflections," William Paulson, one of the authors who suggest that electronic systems have already displaced traditional reading, writes: "*Everyone by now* realizes that electronic storage and retrieval systems can supplant the printed page as the medium or element of written language. Computers are fast replacing pen and ink, and could literally replace the book, though that will not happen soon and may not happen at all" (293, my emphasis).[8]

Paulson's vision is reassuring, because he does not turn his conclusions into prophecies but he does not hesitate to describe the present as the historical site of a major conceptual change, involving every one of us. In "Into the Electronic Millennium," published three years later, in 1991, Sven Birkerts goes even further: instead of proposing his own version of what he feels everyone around us knows, he chooses to interpret one anecdote as the final proof that books are definitely obsolete. The interpreter's tone is slightly apocalyptic in spite of the apparently banal character of the story he tells. Birkerts explains that, as the co-manager of a used bookstore in Ann Arbor, he was "often asked to appraise and purchase libraries—by retiring academics, widows and disgruntled students" (Birkerts 14). Apparently, such categories of people are unremarkable sellers of libraries. It is probably considered normal that they should be unhappy or in financial trouble; they are unworthy of further analysis. But Birkerts' story is about the exception to the rule, about a professor who was selling his impressive library for another reason. When asked if he was moving, the "ex-professor" is quoted as having said that he was "getting out," "out of books," that he was "changing [his] life" and that his books "represent[ed] a lot of pain to [him]" (14). This out-of-bookish-hell-and-into-outlandish-paradise narrative structure is interesting not only because of the dream/nightmare paradigm involved but also because of the teleological myth unfolding in the story. Books appear to be a thing of the past which will not coexist peacefully with other forms of textuality. Books are also a *space* within which one is enclosed and which one must leave in order to avoid painful consequences. The story is completed with a trip to the dungeon of doom, the professor's basement, which predictably reveals the cause of this remarkable sell out: the basement is a shrine, in the middle of which sits the source of all this narrative energy—a computer. Birkerts admits that he has no idea what the computer is used for but that the machine does remind him of an "exhibit in the Space Museum" (14). In the absence of all other hypertextual evidence, I will note that, once again, *space* seems to be the recurrent key word in such discourses, and that like technology, hypertextual logic is beginning to remind me of the Would-Be Gentleman.

In Birkerts' article, the episode becomes a sort of primal scene, a "kind of marker in my mental life" (14). The professor is one of those "new men and new women who had glimpsed the future and had decided to get while the getting was good." He needs to "burn bridges," because "a change is upon us—nothing could be clearer. The printed word is part of a vestigial order that we are moving away from" (14). In the same way as I remember the first generation of Macintoshes as a historical landmark which changed my conception of writing, the ex-professor's decision finds its way into Birkerts' narrative as the undeniable evidence that a major change is taking place. And what strikes me in our similar way of telling the story is that we seem to be searching for some proof that something has already happened, while at the same time relying almost exclusively in our daily practices on a medium which we suspect is obsolete.

The same remark holds for critics who choose to celebrate or criticize what they think hypertext is or will be. A sense of great danger often pervades our discourse, as if hypertext had a life of its own, as if our commentaries were somewhat outside reality, as if the discourse which we produce about hypertext had no power to shape its future. Yet there is no reason to assume that everyone will experience hypertext in the same way. A subject's race, culture, and sexuality will certainly be relevant factors, even if hypertexts, in turn, lead to a redefinition of such terms. It is not too early to tell—rather, the time has come to make sure—that hypertext is or will be used in such a way that even the marginal collective, which is traditionally so estranged by machines, will have a say in the creation of hypertextual narratives.[9] In a sardonic article entitled "Extra-Sensory," George Scialabba pictures hypertexts as monsters, as an exaggerated by-product of late capitalism and social inequalities: "To suggest that humankind is now ready to *leave behind* verbal literacy when only a tiny, fortunate fraction have savored its pleasurable possibilities to the full, is not hubris. It is fatuity; worse, cruelty. . . . The electronic millennium is now a threat rather than—what it may yet prove to be, in the *farther* reaches of cultural evolution—a promise" (17, my obsessive emphasis).

It seems to me that whether hypertexts are a threat or a promise depends on precisely how we shape them now. And the forms they will take may very well depend on how we talk about them now, and on who decides to use them for whose benefits. At this point, hypertexts are neither a threat nor a promise, because for a good 90 percent of the population they remain a dream, or a nightmare. For better or for worse, I have inherited the post-Freudian belief, or suspicion, that dreams are not useless. And even if I have outgrown the belief that my dreams reveal something hidden and function as signs, I would not want to dismiss them as irrelevant to my cultural environment. Of course, one does not use the same (discursive) tactics when talking about a dream or a nightmare (be they collective) and when using words as an attempt to solve immediate problems which are clearly identified and obviously require attention. In other words, I don't claim that hypertexts could help the homeless or constitute effective solutions to racist behavior or inner-city disasters. On the other hand, I blame my lack of imagination, and not hypertext, for the missing link. And I also do not need cataclysmic prophecies to be aware that hypertextual environments could also exist side by side with, or even perpetuate, a system which tolerates such problems.

People who are actively involved in hypertextual experiments are frowned upon as mad scientists, but the ways in which hypertexts will be used depends on their efforts. Teams of researchers are willing to bet that eventually their work will not be dismissed, that they are not going off at a tangent (is hypermedia research tenurable?). Of course, they may become the heroes of future comic films to be shown in museums together with the first inventors of flying machines, whose trials and errors have been recorded on precious and hilarious black and white movies. It could be that our present hypertexts will eventually appear to have been flapping their electronic wings in a most hopelessly ineffective and naive manner, in spite of our impression that pioneers are standing on the cutting-edge of technology. But whether the first hypertexts are to be forgotten as origin because the medium has become totally hegemonic or whether they will go down in history as bloopers, they can serve a purpose today: from a cultural or literary point of view, one of the most interesting areas of study may well be the analysis of the invisible interconnection between reading (the relationship between the body and the text) and mapping (the relationship between bodies and space).

The "Exploitation" of Space

Writing is always spatial and each technology in the history of writing (e.g. the clay tablet, the papyrus roll, the codex, the printed book) has presented writers and readers with a different space to exploit.

—J. David Bolter, "Topographic Writing"

To exploit indeed. What else do I know about space at this point except that I am supposed to "exploit it," use it, appropriate it? As Gregory Ulmer has perceptively pointed out, in his "Grammatology Hypermedia," the metaphors used in hypermedia are rapidly solidifying into conventions and thus escaping theoretical scrutiny. The travel metaphor, "used to characterize the retrieval of . . . information," is problematic, especially when associated with "an analogy between the mastery of a database and the colonization of a foreign land." For Ulmer,

> The idea was to expose the ideological quality of the research drive, the will to power in knowledge, by calling attention to the implications of designing hypermedia programs in terms of the "frontiers" of knowledge, knowledge as a "territory" to be established. The goal is not to suppress this metaphorical element in design and research, but to include it more explicitly, to unpack it within the research and teaching activities. In this way stereotypes may become self-conscious, used and mentioned at once in the learning process.

Reading, interpreting spaces, and drawing maps are activities so intricately intertwined that it is difficult to separate them, and one can hardly change without the others' doing so. The way we use maps usually defines us as one of two vastly different kinds of travelers. There are basically two ways of appropriating space: one may either trace a path where none existed before or use an already constituted map. Two paradigmatic travelers are thus distinguished, the former image evoking discoveries, new frontiers, explorers, the glamor of adventure but also the traumatic encounter of colonization, of imposing grids upon others; the latter a process of choices and selections, in which the traveler picks his or her way through an already existing network of connections and nodes. Such map reading entails distinguishing between straight lines and detour, fast lane and scenic route; it requires interpreting a no-left-turn sign or understanding the implications of a one-way street or of cutting through. Using a map in this way entails a (possibly intuitive) theory of linearity and digression; it invites oppositionality.[10] In hypertext, I strongly suspect, the difference between the two kinds of travelers will collapse at the same time as the reader and the writer are redefined as screeners.

It may be all the more important to tease out the ideological implications of the pre-map, post-map paradigm as the metaphor of navigation is so powerfully associated with hypertext. Webs, in Intermedia, are represented as a series of vectors linking little square documents. One of the most frequent visualizations of hypertextual spaces is series of lines at the intersections of which lie the nodes, or documents.[11] The organization of a document as a main text followed by a series of end notes, an index and a bibliography (conceived of as distinct and self-contained spaces each with its own textual identity) is replaced by an infinite web of interconnected crossroads.

One of the problems raised by the map metaphor, however, is that it implies a body circulating among fixed, immobile roads. In a map, changing spaces (the construction of a new road, the destruction of a bridge by a natural disaster, a road closed by a snowfall) are the exceptions worth noting. Until proven otherwise, if Aix-en-Provence is north of Marseilles, then Marseilles is south of Aix, and I rely on such theoretically relative measurements to make absolute travel plans for my embodied self. The print medium, with its share of going to the library, carrying the book home, sitting down with a good book, does not radically revise the map. But in hypertext, where what travels is weightless information, I may well need, eventually, to re-imagine the relationship between my body and space; and if I have to rethink the way in which I orient myself in space, I may well have to redefine the way in which I read maps. Unfortunately, I may be caught in yet another recursive loop: maps are themselves a reflection of how we construct space, of what we consider linkable, bridgeable, or off limits, out of bounds, or the same and different. And if our ways of traveling change, for a while the old maps, adapted to different ways of moving, may be the only way we have of imagining our relationship with space.

For example, how do I describe the experiences undergone by the heroes of *The Fly* or of *Star Trek*? Here are people who transgress the limits of their own bodies and move through space thanks to science fiction technology. Perhaps instant transportation is just as powerful to contemporary dreamers as flying was at the beginning of the century. But if I insist on talking about moving through space or instant transportation, am I not refusing to create new discourses appropriate to a new knowledge? Should I not adopt different criteria and different maps? For example, let us assume that I can find myself in Amsterdam at one given moment and in New York a fraction of a second later, with no means of technological transportation to mediate between space and my body. It could be that, in 1993, the only satisfactory narrative to describe the nature of such an experience would be to say that I have "traveled" "through" space: I am still traveling, but travel is seen as better, faster. Science has found a more convenient way of covering the distance that separates two points on a map. Yet, we could also decide that it is time to alter radically our perception of how a body and space relate to each other: for example, instead of a map representing cities (points) connected by roads (lines), we could think of lists of names (or rather clusters, to avoid the orderly nature of lists). Imagine a map with no picture, no links, simply names forming sets, the names of which share the attribute of allowing bodies to find themselves at one point or another without traveling. The names of points, cities, entities belonging to the same set or network or web would not be "close" or "far" away from each other. In fact, it would be impossible to tell just by looking at such a map what lies "in between" such points or if one of the nodes is in the same country or region as another.

If such maps became commonplace, I wonder how literary critics would redefine notions of literary influence or communities, for such concepts depend on how we imagine contact, in time and in space. What would become of Edouard Glissant's celebration of "creolization" if cultures could not be imagined as inherited knowledge, as the link between individuals sharing social and also contingent or essentialist characteristics (Glissant, *Poétique de la Relation*)? The concepts of colonization and even nationalism or regionalism require that we imagine space as a horizontal surface divided into distinct and self-contained territories whose supposed sovereignty and identity are only put to question by the presence of unstable frontier lands. But whether one re-conceptualizes the border as another specific territory with its own practices and politics of identity or insists on the forever unstable quality of cultural hybridity or *métissage,* whether Chicano and Chicana scholars analyze the borders as a new space or deconstructionists study the infinite regress of the margins of texts, we are not leaving the bidimensional space of road maps (Anzaldúa, *Borderlands*; Anderson, *Imagined Communities*; and Glissant, *Poétique de la Relation*). I wonder if hypertexts will be both the cause and the consequence of our need to invent multidimensional thinking about cultures, "contact zones"

(Pratt, "Arts of the Contact Zone"), gender, and oppositionality. Perhaps a new geometry of space is needed in order to invent communities that will have little to do with proximity and context.

Denatured Contexts

The formulation of a new geometry may be a delicate transition, because it seems to run against the grain of the recent focus on (political and historical) contexts: this is not to say that scholars who insist on the importance of the cultural and harshly criticize formalist literary theories are willing to ignore the seemingly irrevocable "denaturing" (Hayles, *Chaos Bound*, 265 ff.) process undergone by language, reality, and the subject. Even if the feud between essentialism and constructionism seems unnecessarily manichean in the light of recent subtle and sophisticated reconstructions of identity (Haraway, *Primate Visions*; Butler, *Gender Trouble*; Miller, *Getting Personal*), context remains the link between literary universes and the possibility of social intervention. But refusing to dissociate literature from racial or gender or cultural politics is not enough if the definition of the context remains saturated with invisible conventions. And these conventions will be exposed, and questioned, if print loses its monopoly. How can I historicize my hypertextual thinking if my definition of context is historically anachronistic and my new screening experiments are stuck in a no-man's-land of a desire for both new contexts and the familiar old configurations?

In *Chaos Bound,* Katherine Hayles examines what happens to our definition of context when it is, like other concepts, denatured by television hypertextuality.

> Far from being confined to the kind of events that make newspaper headlines, [denatured contexts] are extremely common. Take MTV as an example. Turn it on. What do you see? Perhaps demon-like creatures dancing; then a cut to cows grazing in a meadow, in the midst of which a singer in blue hair suddenly appears; then another cut to cars engulfed in flames. In such videos, the images and medium collaborate to create a technological demonstration that any text can be embedded in any context. What are these videos telling us, if not that the disappearance of a stable, universal context *is the context* for post modern culture? (272)

She concludes, "So thoroughly has the context been denatured that it may be only a matter of time before the distinction between text and context collapses altogether" (275).

Given that I am not ready to renounce the rich array of knowledge and discursive techniques one can tap by studying what one now thinks of as the context, it might be crucial at this point to make sure that, if the "new kinds of units, context-plus-text" (Hayles, 274) do emerge, the transition is not operated at the expense of what used to be the context. How, and by whom, is value (literary, social, political) reintroduced when one watches the video described by Hayles in the midst of other such discontinuities? How could I use the disjunctive and nonlinear qualities of hypertexts to make points which usually require the familiar rhetoric of critical arguments?

The story according to which hypertext will be a valuable asset to professors of literature, because it will teach undergraduates how to "read," rests on the assumption that an educated reader will have much more contextual knowledge at his or her disposal (Conklin, "Hypertext"). Hypertexts would certainly constitute an ideal instrument to provide students with historical references, with translations, with bibliographical annotations, in short, with encyclopedic knowledge which one does not expect inexperienced researchers to dig up on their own. Obviously, if one plans to lecture on the historical background or the author's biography as part of a survey course, then hypertext is indeed a useful tool for students' independent exploration of these subjects. But then we are using technology as a way of reinforcing the old paradigms; we assume that the distinction between educated readers and bad readers is essentially a question of what (legitimate) references and ultimately what (fashionable) canon one is able to draw upon. It seems very dangerous to assume that each student will learn a great deal simply by following the same erudite associations as the scholar who developed the material. Rather than opening up an infinite field of connections, such an assumption might end up reinforcing, in the reader's mind, the impression that only those connections made by the authorities are legitimate.

On the other hand, I am aware of opening a can of wriggling paradoxes: it is true that hypertextuality makes the study of context easier and more meaningful,[12] but at the same time, it is an environment most likely to make the very notion irrelevant and obsolete: hypertext enriches the context even as it contributes to making it redundant.

So far the video described by Hayles bears little resemblance to the literary stacks or webs created by literary scholars. After all, people born before 1970 have been raised as book consumers, and even those who try to oppose the system will do so without being able to shed conditioned reflexes they acquired as readers and writers. When creating a web or a stack, developers, by their own admission, usually rely heavily on concepts that are being dismantled by hypertextuality. As a result, hypertexts are dependent upon traditional definitions of the concepts of author, work, period, century, literary influence, literary movement, etc. The way in which Zola's work was influenced by, or influences, his own period is easily explored in hypertext, but hypertext also draws attention to the arbitrariness of such a way of linking bits of information.

One could thus decide to use hypertext to reinvent the very notion of context, rather than as a privileged tool to teach context as we now understand it. Instead of importing historical, social, or literary background into hypertextual webs in order to supplement our primary texts, we might, for example, wonder what kind of context is being created as the result of experimenting with apparently arbitrary connections. By arbitrary, I do not mean the kind of accepted arbitrariness that comes from conventional forms of knowledge and discourses, but rather a deliberate incursion into the messy realm of chance, random connections and meaninglessness. What would happen if, instead of creating webs around a main author or even a topic, one accumulated links and documents in a way which is apparently haphazard, incomprehensible even to oneself (the screener-producer), let alone to the intended audience (the screener-consumer). Wouldn't such a web begin to resemble Hayles' video, and wouldn't the study of such hypertexts be more likely to focus on what is new about them from a literary point of view?

Hypertextual Wandersmänner

I propose randomness as a strategy here because it seems to promote a vision of the traveler that departs (if I may say so) from that of both the user of maps and the creator of maps, which I earlier equated with the reader and the writer. Travelers who do not go anywhere, apparently, do not need maps. They err—they subvert the idea of destination. Their wanderings are not trips, and we may feel that there is no meaning to their aimlessness. But this meaninglessness ceases as soon as the observer wants to make sense of the trajectory. Whoever observes the *flâneur* (and especially the urban flâneur, who is confronted with a tight network of streets) has to rethink the relationship between the traveler's body and the map, but also the status of the map as a metaphorical rendition of space: the flâneur's body, which does not follow a route or invent new paths toward an old destination, also subverts the vision of space as an empty vessel, a mere neutral receptacle of the network. On a map the roads make sense, the rest is background, wilderness; one cannot go there, but it is assumed that it is unnecessary, that no one would want to go there. If I try to observe the err-er, or follow him or her (or read and understand), I may be able to think of maps differently, adding new dimensions and accepting that other possible travels than the one which goes from one point of departure to a point of arrival are meaningful.

Michel de Certeau's *Practice of Everyday Life* is not a book about hypertext, and it may seem, at first, unrelated to the issue of maps and reading; but I have chosen his work as a meaningful theoretical guide because of the author's interest in spaces and his speculations about the way in which spatial and writing practices are related. Throughout the book, the same obsession recurs: our "everyday life" is dominated by the way in which our body relates to and imagines its surroundings. Writing and reading keep the trace of this constant process of negotiation. In *The Practice of Everyday Life,* space is the bottom line: the way in which we describe or use it conditions our definitions of history, of memory, of freedom and confinement, of difference: "The memorable is that which can be dreamed about a place" (109).

The part of the book entitled "Spatial Stories" seems to provide most of the theoretical distinctions needed to redefine our conception of space. The first point made in the chapter is that distinguishing between a travel metaphor and metaphor as travel is almost impossible: "In modern Athens, the vehicles of mass transportation are called *metaphorai.* To go to work or come home, one takes a "metaphor"—a bus or a train. Stories could also take this noble name: every day, they traverse and organize places; they select and link them together; they make sentences and itineraries out of them. They are spatial trajectories. . . . Every story is a travel story—a spatial practice" (115). Of course, one may argue that, in order to prove his point, de Certeau must rely on previously defined spatial categories: the word *Athens,* inserted in his narrative as a transparent example, is already a travel narrative, the dense residue of an immensely complex theory of space. For *Athens* to constitute a meaningful unit, we need to call upon our memory of texts which have taught us how to distinguish between "*espace*" (space) and "*lieu*" (place) (117), between narrative "tours" and narrative "maps" (119–21), between frontiers and bridges (126). In de Certeau's vision, not only are the story and the map so intricately interwoven that the subtlest theoretical distinctions are needed to separate them, but the story/travel/map is itself undistinguishable from the body of the storyteller/traveler/mapreader.

Perhaps the most relevant of de Certeau's analyses of the embodied travel narratives, the chapter "Walking in the City" inaugurates the third part of the book, entitled "Spatial Practices." Perched on the

110th floor of the World Trade Center, the author discovers that, when viewed from above, the city, "a wave of verticals" (91), can be seen as a map, a text to be read: "Elevation transfigures [the viewer] into a voyeur. It puts him at a distance. It transforms the bewitching world by which one was 'possessed' into a text that lies before one's eyes. It allows one to read it, to be a solar Eye, looking down like a god. The exaltation of a scopic and gnostic drive: the fiction of knowledge is related to this lust to be a viewpoint and nothing more" (92).

I suggest that the grand Icarian dream rests on an almost magical separation between the "transformed" viewer and the "possessed" viewed, and that this very distinction may be put in question if spaces are no longer imagined in terms of vertical and horizontal dimensions. But the advantage of such "viewpoint" reverie is to provide the earthly reader with an interesting model of how our own bodies are blended into the map by some imaginary god-like onlooker and interpreter.

De Certeau imagines the presence of the wanderer as a collective and virtual presence hovering above the real, a trace which modifies the thickness of the lines:

> It is true that the operation of walking on can be traced on city maps in such a way as to transcribe their paths (here well-trodden, there very faint) and their trajectories (going this way and not that). But these quick or thin curves only refer, like words, to the absence of what has passed by. Surveys of routes miss what was: the act itself of passing by. The operation of walking, wandering, or window shopping that is the activity of passers-by is transformed into points that draw a totalizing and reversible line on the map. (97)

Apparently, de Certeau's Wandersmänner have many points in common with what HyperCard language calls browsers, the most passive screener, the "lowest level" as the program puts it. The browser cannot change the text or the script but only navigate among already-configured trajectories. At first, using the term *wanderer* may appear to reinforce, rather than subvert, the distinction between the "real" traveler and some pale imitation, in the same way that the opposition between browser and screener seems to reproduce and refine the distinction between writer and reader. Like browsers, wanderers seem idle, passive. They passively consume what others have produced or written. The steps of the walker across the city are disembodied; like weightless information saturating a network, they are not embodied in a creation. In this vision the reality is the concrete structure of streets. Even recordings of the frequency or trajectories are rare; they belong to an abstract academic discipline and not to the "practice of everyday life." Not only are surveys of routes much less frequent than the printing of new city maps but, as de Certeau points out, they doubly miss their goal of representing the flâneurs' practice. Like a Derridean trace, such maps keep the memory of an absence. The recording itself metamorphoses the dynamic practice and paralyzes its creative potential, because it is still dependent on the pre-existing structure of the map: "The trace left behind is substituted for the practice" (97). "Surveys of routes miss . . . the act itself of passing by" as surely as one would miss hypertextuality by insisting on obtaining a hard copy of a web.

Yet, the virtualized bodies of the walkers, according to de Certeau, are also writing their own text, or rather, the interaction between their bodies and space constitutes a highly codified calligraphy, made of downstrokes and upstrokes, "*ces courbes en pleins et en déliés*" (180), and "the networks of these moving, intersecting writings compose a manifold story that has neither author nor spectator, shaped out of fragments of trajectories and alterations of spaces" (93). In the same way as he criticizes the opposition between the (always passive) reader-consumer and the (always active) reader-writer, de Certeau recognizes the browser-wanderer's ability to compose a text. The image of the idle flâneur changes: by superimposing a form of writing over the map, the browser now composes, like the musician adding notes to the staff.

Such a vision has the advantage of describing the browser as an agent capable of creation, but it belittles the browser's role as that of a marginal amateur whose text has no audience and no reader and who simply adorns the map with superficial reconstructions. The vision of the wanderer tracing letters with his or her body still relies on a series of oppositions which probably belong to an old paradigm (the distinction between the browser and the scripter, the reader and the composer), and it gives the impression that the map is a neutral space, a simple grid on which one can superimpose one's own meaning. But of course no map is neutral. When the wanderer roams around the tight network of city streets, his or her map makes sense—a different, more local sense—and this body reminds us that the supposedly anonymous and abstract map is not only a conduit for human information but also a political text. Comparing the map of Paris before 1853 (when Georges Eugène Haussmann became *préfet de Seine*) and after 1870 makes obvious the politics of geography implemented to push the working class farther away from the city (and to make sure that the notes added to the musical staff would not take the form of barricades). In the same manner, when I develop a hypertextual course for my students, I may rejoice in the feeling that I am allowing them to explore new territories and create their own meaningful connections, but the freedom is of course severely limited by my (perhaps unconscious) desire to avoid student intellectual barricades. If I spend one year creating the map of a hypertextual course, I may not be ready to let my students tamper with my beautifully rehabilitated cultural neighborhood. A barricade is a new destination, a place where people stop and hold their ground in the middle of what should be a street, a conduit, a link. How can I allow my students to alter the balance between links and documents?

In hypertextual space, the fear that the wanderer may, at any point, turn into a destructive rebel cannot disappear if we assume that there is such a thing as a reader and a writer in this environment. It seems to me that even as we are aware of redefining the borders of the text, the definition of the author, and the role of collaboration and authority, our hypertextual spaces are inhabited by the ghosts of old maps. Our fears and precautions, the way in which we protect stacks and organize our courses may well have little to do with new problems raised by hypertext. They may be a consequence of our inability to let the new appear in hypertexts.

Getting Lost in Hyperspace; Or, Losing the Screener?

If we cannot invent a screener who is not the heir to the writer-versus-reader paradigm, we may be afraid of what might eventually prove to be most liberating and productive of new knowledge in hypertexts. For example, if we remain screening readers, the absence of familiarity with the conventions of what we imagine as pre-existing hypertextual maps will cause frustration and the fear of being lost in hyperspace. If we think as screening writers, we shall anticipate this fear. Hypertextual space is not more complicated nor does it require an unusual level of spatial intelligence, but we are not used to visualizing or metaphorizing this form of spatiality.

As a result, when developing hypertextual spaces, screeners will be tempted to impose an even more rigid grid than the one we feel compelled to use when we write a book destined for publication. For example, when writing a twenty- or fifty-page chapter, nobody anticipates that the reader will want to come back exactly to a given passage, a given citation, a given word. The reader, however, does not feel lost. Even if finding a specific passage may indeed turn into an impossible, or at least frustrating task for whoever chooses to navigate that way, the large chunks of information accumulated in a twenty- or fifty-page chapter are not viewed as badly designed labyrinths. Yet, a long chapter is like an expressway with only one official on-ramp. Writers make no provision for their readers' desire to come back to a given point. Indexing is common in critical books, but not absolutely mandatory, and even the most elaborate system of indexing is not very rigorous. Linearity produces a degree of severe disorientation which readers accept very well. In hypertextual environments, the slightest impression that we are losing control of the overall structure may trigger a reaction of panic, a feeling that one can never get back to where one was. This panic is a tell-tale sign of an overwhelming desire for the spatial organization printed matter has forced us to be familiar with: the origin/beginning–versus–end/conclusion system.

I suggest that screeners' fear of disorientation may be a metaphorical anachronism, something like an unconscious and sacred fear of flying among early aviation pioneers. If we insist so much on guiding screeners when we invent hypertextual stories, the result may be boredom and uniformity. It seems to me that if we do not credit screeners with enough imagination to reinvent ways of navigating a story, we will end up with whole series of hypertextual experiments that will never be more interesting than the electronic information booths one encounters these days in public spaces.

If the fear of flying had been solved by desperately applying known systems of navigation to new configurations, planes would be driving up and down the Champs Elysées and would drop off their passengers in Dover, at the end of a road. In other words, hypertextual stories will be new but neither comfortable, nor aesthetically pleasing, nor even highly desirable, which, in turn, will make them outlandish and disorienting. And I wonder if it may not be desirable at this point to experiment widely with *dis*orientation rather than safety: for instance, I may want to experiment with the best ways of losing other screeners, as the hero of a detective story cleverly evades the official policemen who are tailing him. I have a feeling that the attempt may prove more difficult than I thought, simply because the reader may very well decide that hypertext makes the role of the detective or policeman a foolish one. In hypertext, the decision to be following another hero, another trail, may suddenly appear very desirable because the idea that one will find answers or a good story if one follows the hero until his or her final destination may eventually appear as an obsolete by-product of linearity.

If trying to lose other screeners became an active practice, we would also have to redefine the concepts of captive audience and followers, not only between speakers and listeners but also within a (supposedly single) text. Hypertexts could be a space where narrative seduction is reinvented as a result of the deterritorialization of stories. As George Landow forcefully demonstrates, "hypertext creates an open, open-bordered text" (61): "Hypertext blurs the end boundaries of the metatext, and conventional notions of completion and a finished product do not apply to hypertext, whose essential novelty makes difficult defining and describing it in older terms, since they derive from another educational and informational technology and have hidden assumptions inappropriate to hypertext" (59). The open-endedness of hypertexts (possibly of the lexias within hypertexts) changes not only the borders of the text but also the way in which we categorize portions of text and the way in which linearity affects storytelling activities.

Our printed texts are saturated with hierarchies that do not make much sense in hypertexts. I will take, as an example, the problem of what hypertextual spaces do to the idea of moving from the text to a quotation and vice versa, but the relationship between the "main" text and the quotation is a particular case of the hierarchies conventionally respected within a text. The quotation is a metaphor for the subsidiary, the secondary enclosed as minority discourse within the limits of a text. When linearity is dominant, quotations—like footnotes, or indexes, or table of contents, or even illustrations and intertextual references—tend to be considered as appendixes, whose supplementary function points both to the incompleteness of the main text and to its will for absolute power, separate identity, immediate presence. Texts within texts thus point to the different within the same and, consequently, to the same parading as different: in a printed text, a quotation follows or precedes a point which it supposedly illustrates; it serves both as alibi and authority; it presents itself as both the origin of the thought and its ultimate justification.

Imagine that I intend to write a scholarly article about *Lettres à une noire,* an epistolary novel by a Caribbean writer, Françoise Ega, and that I decide to screen it in a hypertextual environment. If you were, at present, screening this hypertext, not only the physical appearance of quotations, but also their function would be drastically modified: if I wanted to *quote* a passage *from Lettres à une noire,* I would not have to *import* a little passage *from* another document and paste in the *middle* of my own (main) text.[13] As a result, my critical text would look very different from what we are used to reading, and screeners (including myself later) would have to perform very different operations from those of readers. Instead of seamlessly moving from my critical argument to a quotation drawn from another self-contained and identifiable document, screeners would be "moved" "into" the other document and "find" themselves in the "middle" of another text. Or, to metaphorize it differently, the active screen would suddenly be occupied, not by my critical piece, but by another document probably called *Lettres à une noire*. Presumably, a specific passage or sentence or word would be temporarily highlighted or underlined or boxed as the result of the operation of following a link. Having moved or having been moved (whichever metaphor prevails) to the quoted text, the screener would most probably have the option of pressing a button to go back to the (by now) original article.

Metaphorically, text is not cut out and transported. Rather, the reader's gaze and attention shift as they are literally drawn from one (linear) unit to another. In other words, the screener takes a trip, and even if the operation remains mental (much in the same way as the navigation from one document to another is also a fiction used to describe the management of weightless and disembodied information), it raises at least two important theoretical and related problems: how are the conventions of authorial control and of narrative seduction modified by the dissociation between quotations and their appropriators.

At this point in the development of the technology, screening a quotation is more complex than quoting a passage, because the conventions governing the operation are not set. The effect of a quotation could be achieved in a number of ways over which both screeners (producer and consumer) could try to exert more or less control, limiting or increasing other screeners' freedom of movement. For example, suppose that, as a screener wandering in a hypertext, I encounter a little icon signaling the presence of a link (the fact that another screener or many other screeners wrote a downstroke or an upstroke at this particular point). In Intermedia, for example, a little arrow would tempt the screener to position the cursor over this invitation and to click one's approval of a deviation. Having responded to the conventional sign, the screener would be transported to the original text that another screener, at one point of his or her wandering, had found meaningful and related, had wanted to quote (of course, the idea of original text would probably have lost much of its ambiguous appeal by then).

The little arrow, a visible yet non-authoritarian sign would constitute a much more liberal way of guiding other screeners than the convention of forcing a quotation into the middle of a text, knowing that the reader has no choice but to read it and then return to the main argument. But one could also imagine more authoritarian (and potentially disturbing) ways of dealing with quotations: the transportation from one document to another could function transparently, not like an invitation to the reader but like an automated response over which screeners would have no power. For instance, if a screener at one point includes a little program or script and attaches it to one word, sentence, or screen, all the subsequent screeners would not encounter a little arrow or signal but be automatically transported to another text, to be later repatriated to the main text. All this would happen whether the screener wanted it or not, unless, of course, he or she knew how to bypass the textual mechanism (and the category of cheating screeners or subversive screeners is of course bound to reappear as the figure of the script overwriter who bypasses the most forceful links, or the blind navigator who falls in and out of loops without even knowing it).

The question of how much control is left to subsequent screeners is also linked to the problem of narrative seduction. Usually, a quotation is short (writers have been known to apologize for the length of a quotation) and does not constitute a powerful dis-traction or pull away from the main text, conceived as the argument to which the quoted text lends its support. We may imagine a way of reading which would consist of reading quotations only (the convention of indentation makes it at least practically feasible), but such an approach would be considered strange and would have to be justified. "Reading for quotations" as one "reads for the plot" as Peter Brooks puts it, is a strange form of intervention. Let us imagine that a professor of literature, when given a dissertation to read or evaluate, dismisses the student's writing and systematically scans the text for quotations.[14] If he admits to doing this, I will suspect that he is condescending and that he systematically assumes that the original writer is better than the critic. In a hypertext environment, there would be no way of keeping the attention of such a screener: given the slightest chance, he would move away from what he identifies as the critical text and spend the rest of his screening time within the original texts. Or rather, he would make every effort not to access one of the critical lexias and would make sure to remain within the territories of original texts. Of course, he would have to know exactly how he defines original in this case: when a quotation is indented, it is easy to pretend that there is the real poetry, or the real creative writing, or the real idea. It would be much more difficult to theorize this difference once the hierarchy between the quotation and the main text was reduced to bidimensional links connecting two documents.

The problem of seduction will remain as long as a given screener thinks like a short story writer and wants to be sure that other screeners follow him or her to the end. Assuming that I am in the middle of my argument and that I decide to quote Françoise Ega, I can use my hypertext program to link other screeners to the novel. But since both my own text and the other one would be linear, they would both tend to function like power magnets, since they are both configured to seduce the screener (the ex-reader) to finish the piece. When I quote in a printed article, I give the reader a little piece of another universe. In hypertext, nothing would stop the screener from forgetting about the first document. In print the fear of being interrupted by another text is alleviated by the fact that subsidiary texts often take the form of short fragments or lists (typically, one does not read lists, one consults them and then leaves them alone). Even if the reader is attracted by the footnote, he or she rarely starts reading "for the footnotes" and becomes fascinated with the nonlinearity and incompleteness of such a collection of fragments, just as one does not give up a novel to start reading the phone directory.

Not being afraid of losing one's reader translates as rhetorical devices or lack thereof: what would happen if every time I quoted I was afraid of losing my reader altogether? What would happen to the narrative contract of seduction if screeners could always count on others being distracted and not coming back? Would it be the end of storytelling as we know it (as E. M. Forster puts it, the king died and then the queen died of grief) or would hypertextual fiction function like nineteenth-century serialized writing, forever interrupted by news, commercials, weather reports, business columns, and all the different categories represented in a newspaper.[15] Would hypertextual fiction start looking like eighteenth-century novels, with their tendency toward self-reflexivity (the writer authorizing the reader to rest between chapters or commenting on the length of a given description or on the uselessness of a specific point)? As interruptions become the convention, the anticipated structure of texts, new pick-up lines or rather keep-up lines may become standard narratological categories: we may start imagining links comparable to the discourse produced by TV talk-show hosts who try to ensure that the viewers will not zap out of the program because they are bored by the content or distracted by the inevitable commercials. On the one hand, the commercials are a necessary distraction. They are analogous to quotations because they belong to another category of discourse, another text, which the system as a whole does want to impose on the viewer since, after all, commercials pay for the show. Like quotations, they are both secondary (they do not belong in the story) and crucial (they are a form of authority, of origin, of currency). "We'll be back after this" should soon have a more or less sophisticated hypertextual equivalent. Unless of course it becomes totally irrelevant to each screener what another does with a web. But this will not happen until the writer-reader totally disappears, which will probably never happen.

Consequently, the relationship between hypertext and authorship may never be radically reconfigured. In the same way that the old definition of context is often reinforced by a new medium which could potentially destroy it (and the same could be said about the canon), the dream of collaborative writing and participatory reading often falls short of the theoretically infinite possibilities offered by hypertexts.

(The Fear of) Collaboration and (the Uselessness of) Passwords

Collaboration raises the problem of borders between documents. If screeners are not yet willing to renounce their status as writers, hypertext may be more of a nuisance than a practical new medium: if I develop my own material for a course (and the problem probably lies in this very conception), my first concern will be to protect it from dangerous initiatives on the part of my student readers.

At present, a student or a browser, any relatively powerless screener, will probably see his or her collaborative efforts limited to minor corrections or additions. This is already much more than what happens when students read books, although the activity of scribbling in the margins is not really analyzed as an appropriative genre of discourse. Although it is theoretically possible to think of a student as just another screener, this may not happen until the corpus of hypertext grows to the point where it becomes a collective and anonymous giant web. As long as we feel responsible for one particular territory of links and documents, the ideal of collaboration will be severely limited by the principle of access privileges and electronic passwords. Only those screeners who are granted permission by more powerful screeners will have access to the authoring level of the hypertext. I am not saying that the system of protection is undesirable, but once again I am struck by the fact that the ideal represented by hypertexts (collaboration, participation, equalitarianism) (see Landow, 137–38) is often betrayed by the fact that old norms are still dictating our behavior. Right now, it is much easier to subvert the rigidity of the print medium (by quoting portions or reproducing pages or scribbling in the margins) than it is to have access to a locked stack. And when a screener is made powerless by a hypertext, the lack of power is even more absolute than when we are confronted with printed matter, which is a familiar domain where "poaching," as de Certeau puts it, is possible (165–76).

The norm of accuracy, exact reproduction and consequently the value of original edition or exact quotation, are taken for granted when one writes or reads books. But focusing on exact replication is both a cause and a consequence of the limitations of the print technology: perhaps books are fixed and unchangeable and authentic because the identity of the text is almost sacrosanct, even if opposed and often subverted. We are not about to do away with authorship, and with the figure of the writer as original thinker, with copyright issues and the assumption that knowledge is transmitted or inherited. But I wonder if the production of books as a long-mastered skill is not reinforcing the pattern: if it takes money, energy, skill, knowledge, and power to produce a book, the quality of the end-product will be measured by the difference between a professional and an amateurish work. If thousands of copies of one book have to be produced in order to ensure its commercial success and circulation, then the fact that each book is the same is crucial. Even if such requirements perpetuate undesirable forms of the printed status quo, we tend to cling to certain values.

The Gutenberg Project is thus under fire: Michael Hart, who takes care of a collective enterprise aiming to "distribute a trillion electronic copies from a collection of 10,000 books by 2001" is accused of "polluting the network with garbage" by a librarian who apparently chose to remain anonymous (Wilson, "Electronic Versions of Public-Domain Texts"). The Gutenberg Project is intended for a public of nonacademic screeners and purports to make material "available to everyone, all the time" (A16). As a result, certain features were considered unimportant and not included in the on-line version of the books (the version, the typeface, the edition, and so on). These supposedly less-than-perfect reproductions (but Hart points out that errors abound in printed books too and are far more difficult to correct) will not be trusted by academics. A Mr. Seaman, one of Hart's critics, is quick to point out that "there's not a whole lot of little old ladies reading these on laptops on the beach" (A16). But such an argument does not address the problem of academics' intense need for the missing attributes: it does not explain why, in the last decade of the twentieth century, we like to work on texts only if we are reassured that we know where they come from, that their origin is legitimate.

A mistake in a book is catastrophic, because it will be infinitely reproduced; on the other hand, we can trust a book to have been read and re-read and proofread and to represent exactly what the author meant. The Gutenberg Project is not investing so much in the productions of copies, and the resulting texts are not as fixed, partly because the producers of such electronic spaces have no stake in defending the frontiers or legitimacy of their copies. Let us assume for a minute that a degree of variation is accepted as the necessary by-product of making millions of unchecked copies. Of course, we will end up with adulterated texts. Garbled citations would become the norm rather than the exception. But this may also be described as a valuable difference from our present situation: perhaps literature would start functioning like gossip. It would be very difficult to claim that one has read *Madame Bovary* if vastly different texts were in circulation. It might become more productive to compare versions. Books might be replaced by dynamic versions of hypertexts, which might function like the games "Chinese whispers" or "telephone," in which someone whispers a sentence to his or her neighbor who passes on the information and so on until the end of a chain or circle. The point of the game is to marvel at the distortion or amount of noise (or poetry or wisdom) produced by what should be a simple reproductive device and which is, in fact, the arch collaborative creative process.

Of course, the idea that Baudelaire's *Fleurs du Mal* could dissolve into noise leaves me saddened and impoverished. If I were asked what book I would want to have on a desert island, I would immediately answer, with a degree of spontaneity calculated to impress the (hopefully important) interlocutor with my wisdom and organizational skills, "*Les Fleurs du Mal,* of course." Now, wouldn't it be tragic if I wanted a copy of *Les Fleurs du Mal* and had to be content with some approximation because the very notion of a single work would have fallen into disuse? Would it not be disturbing to know that, if my memory failed me, I would not be able to refresh it by glancing at a reliable copy of "Harmonie du Soir"? On the other hand, like all other geometrical parameters, desert islands may well be redefined by the fax machine.[16] And my definition of a poem may be changed and start resembling a system of thought based on orality. As Paul Delany and George P. Landow put it in their introduction to *Hypermedia and Literary Studies:*

> Computers may re-create certain qualities of pre-literate culture more pervasively than even Walter J. Ong has been willing to admit. In *Orality and Literacy,* Ong argues that computers have brought us into what he terms an age of "secondary orality" that has "striking resemblances to the old [oral, preliterate culture] in its participatory mystique, its fostering of a communal sense, its concentration on the present moment, and even its use of formulas." Nonetheless, although Ong finds interesting parallels between a computer culture and a purely oral one, he still insists: "The sequential processing and spatializing of the word, initiated by writing and raised to a new order of intensity by print, is further intensified by the computer, which maximizes commitment of the word to space and to (electronic) local motion and optimizes analytic sequentiality by making it virtually instantaneous." (12)

Paradoxically, a medium that allows me to store millions of bytes of information and instantaneously retrieve portions of texts that my human memory could never hope to manage efficiently might end up turning literature into a variation of oral performance.

Perhaps hypertextuality is closer than I imagine to Celtic bards' forms of knowledge (assuming it is true that they memorized millions of lines). It conjures up the vision of these human books living on the margins of a world destroyed by autos-da-fé and totalitarian powers in Bradbury's *Fahrenheit 451*. Theoretically, hypertexts may foreground the abstract principle according to which there is always a significant distinction between a unit of creation and the way in which it is performed (read or interpreted, or danced, and so on). As readers of post-structuralist theories, we know that author and reader are co-creators, but how does this knowledge really influence our definition of the work? In hypertextual spaces, each so-called copying, with its voluntary and involuntary distortion, carries with it the uncontrollable potential of added value and defacement, both excess and lack. As J. Yellowlees Douglas points out, in hypertexts, the problem of authorial intentionality is even more central and problematic than it is in conventional writing (see Moulthrop 132, footnote 10). Paradoxically, the medium which scares me most, because it relies so much on technology, and which disempowers me most as a reader used to accuracy is also the environment most sensitive to what specialists of chaos theories would call "initial conditions." The same specialists would probably argue that hypertexts' being theoretically infinite, open-ended, variable, and disorderly does not make them inherently liberatory. Perhaps hypertexts should be visualized, not as street maps imposed upon some empty meaningless space, not as a tidy network of little lines and squares symbolizing links and documents, but rather as the extraordinary complex mixture of randomness and organization, unpredictability and meaningfulness displayed by fractal images.[17]

O-W-E

If we let randomness function like a paradoxical organizing principle, we may be capable of hearing new and intriguing songs. Instead of thinking of myself as a writer or a reader, I would like to imagine hypertext as a medium which allows me to become de Certeau's wanderer: screeners would have to forget what they know about maps and invent new spaces and new meanings. The screeners' act of navigation would not be compared to the real map upon which the downstrokes and upstrokes of their writing would inscribe their supplementary mark. Their virtual itineraries would have as much (or as little) meaning as the supposedly real map which seems to serve as a channel for their creative energy. In fact, the reference to the real map may then appear as an obsolete reflex, the desire to go back to the time when wanderers had to orient themselves in a space divided between the network and the rest. A screener's navigation would not have to be the manifold story that has neither author nor spectator. It would be both read and written at the same time, but meaning would become fragile, easily destroyed, impossible to record.

I would like to propose Paul Auster's *City of Glass* as a possible example of what happens when two screeners follow each other in the hypertextual space constituted by the street maps of New York. *City of Glass* is a sort of detective story in the sense of one character following another, hoping to discover a secret, a story, an explanation that will allow him to predict the protagonist's behavior (or further travels). As Stillman walks all day through New York, following apparently meaningless itineraries, Quinn, the detective, refuses to consider this street wanderer as one of the anonymous bodies whose movements will be recorded but whose practice will be lost. What I find interesting in this short story is the passage from one form of map to another as Quinn realizes that he does not know what criteria to adopt to make sense of the other character's long walks. Since Stillman seems to lack a destination (which would be one justification for tailing a suspect), Quinn must concentrate on the way in which Stillman travels and hope to find meaning within the navigation process itself. Frustrated by the principle of linear narrative (where is Stillman going?), he turns to the practice itself. For once, the street wanderer's steps are elevated to the dignity of a signifying practice.

Once Quinn discovers that Stillman (and his embodied story) is not going anywhere, he starts keeping a trace of the suspect's (and thus his own) wanderings, to draw a map of the neighborhood within which Stillman confines his daily walks. As in hypertext fictions, or as if to parody the treasure hunt structure of adventure novels, a map suddenly appears in the middle of the story.

Then, in an impulse which appears mysterious and unmotivated even to himself, Quinn gradually switches from one map to another, from one theory of navigation to another: "For no particular reason that he was aware of, Quinn turned to a clean page of the red notebook and sketched a little map of the area Stillman had wandered in. Then, looking carefully through his notes, he began to trace the movements Stillman had made on a single day–the first day he had kept a full record of the old man's wanderings." The resulting map no longer represents New York, or a neighborhood. As Quinn dissociates Stillman from the map and accepts the idea that the old man's wanderings must be addressed on their own terms, new possibilities emerge.

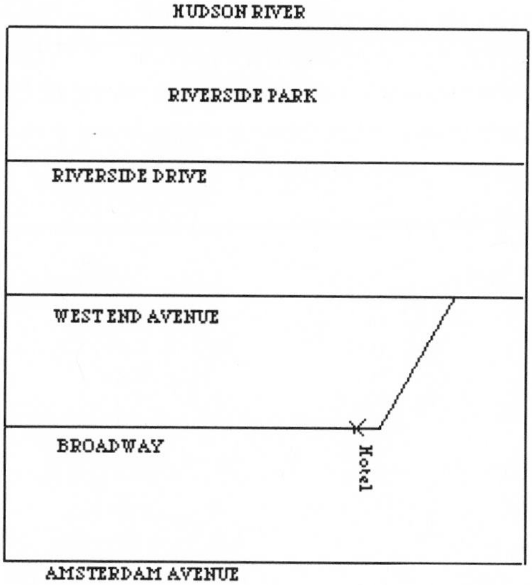

Studying the maps created by the flâneur, Quinn starts suspecting, even though uncertainty never disappears, that the old man is a walking word. The territory covered by his apparently random promenades form letters, first an *O*, then a *W*, then an *E*:

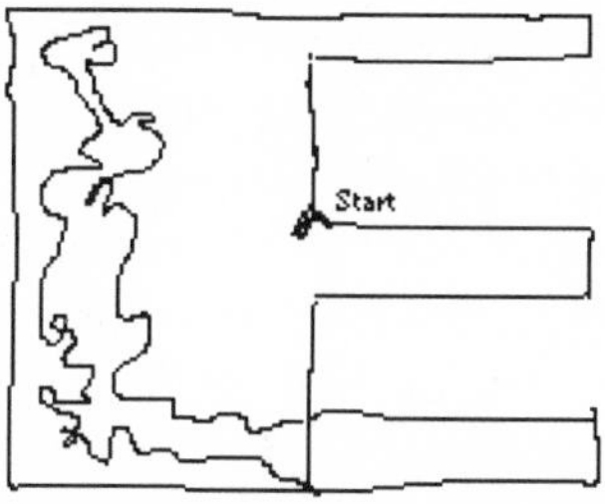

After "discounting the squiggles" (84), that is, after redefining noise and information, the detective slowly accepts the hypothesis according to which each daily excursion represents, or rather inscribes, a letter into the space and time of the old man's lonely screening activity. Stillman is indeed writing with his body, screening space according to a system which no street map can elucidate. And as more letters are recognized day after day, it becomes obvious that it is impossible to dismiss the possibility that a sort of message is being inscribed by Stillman's meticulous choices, and that the message in question is not immediately accessible, even once one has understood how it is produced. Like a literary text, Stillman's navigation remains mysterious once it has been deciphered: the new configuration is not the key to an encoded secret that could be revealed by Quinn's intelligent manipulations. Instead, he is left with a string of letters, "OWEROFBAB" (85), which may, or may not, signify "The Tower of Babel," he finally decides, and which remain, even if the "answer seemed inescapable," an uncompleted phrase, a hypothesis the immediate usefulness of which is not very apparent.

> Quinn paused for a moment to ponder what he was doing. Was he scribbling nonsense? Was he feeble-mindedly frittering away the evening, or was he trying to find something? Either response, he realized, was unacceptable. If he was simply killing time, why had he chosen such a painstaking way to do it? Was he so muddled that he no longer had the courage to think; on the other hand, if he was not merely diverting himself, what was he actually up to? It seemed to him that he was looking for a sign. He was ransacking the chaos of Stillman's movements for some glimmer of cogency. This implied one thing: that he continued to disbelieve the arbitrariness of Stillman's actions. He wanted there to be a sense to them, no matter how obscure. (83)

The quest for meaning does not disappear or miraculously result in crystal clear discovery. Paul Auster's originality may lie in this oscillation between the feeling of being lost and the intuition that new configurations are needed. The new map, which combines the two men's bodies and their wanderings, is an answer to the inadequacy of old stories of streets linking buildings, trips leading to destinations. When such structures become unproductive, new experiments are tried; but Auster's novel does not imply that meaning, the kind of comfortable, predictable meaning provided by old stories, will reward the bold screener who agrees to modify his point of view. In fact, Quinn does not find a new way of orienting himself. Rather, he discovers that the questions he used to ask are no longer meaningful. He starts writing differently (he "scribbles nonsense"), and his ways of dealing with a text are modified. As Quinn starts "fiddling" with the letters OWEROFBAB, "switching them around, pulling them apart, rearranging the sequence" (85), he begins to resemble the theoretical screener whose writing and reading activity are indistinguishable.

This poetics of randomness requires an enormous imaginary displacement. Quinn has to convince himself, not only that destination is secondary, if it exists at all, but also that meaning has not been displaced onto the trip itself (the old man's wanderings are not like one of those Caribbean cruises advertised on TV, where the trip is both the end and the means, where the ship is not a means of transportation but the actualization of elsewhere and of how to get there at the same time). Quinn never knows what Stillman meant, but he discovers that his previous systems of orientation were ineffective and that some system is at work even if he is not equipped to deal with it as a specific problem demanding a specific solution.

Like the old man's message, Quinn's story remains incomplete, fragmentary, unsatisfactory, because no one in the novel starts following him around into meaninglessness. His case (Stillman's and his own are now indistinguishable) is never resolved: his own adventure as a detective following a suspect does seem to end on an infinite open-endedness that resembles what a realistic narrator would call madness. As Quinn starts imagining Stillman's whole life as one long practice of street wandering (and therefore his own life as a mirror screener), he wonders "what the map would look like of all the steps he had taken in his life and what word it would spell" (155). Quinn dreams of a form of knowledge which he cannot put into practice. His own life, his wanderings, do inscribe a meaningless story: at the end of the book, Quinn is lost in hyperspace, because no other screener is prepared to follow in his footsteps. There is an omniscient narrator who intervenes at the end of the story. He claims that he has "followed the red notebook as closely as" he could, but he does not go all the way. When the red notebook loses its reader, the narrator, less patient and less imaginative than his hero, gives up: "At this point the story grows obscure. The information has run out, and the events that follow this last sentence will never be known. It would be foolish even to hazard a guess" (157). Because the narrator does not like guessing or nonsense or obscurity, because randomness does not appeal to him, Quinn literally disappears out of a space which is excluded from the text's logic: "As for Quinn, it is impossible for me to say where he is now" (158). The narrator's decision not to read the notebook is also a failure to screen Quinn's hypertext. The fiction of the walking word remains a wild hypothesis, an unrewarded attempt.

For a long time, I suspect, the activity of reading hypertexts (rather than screening them) will be considered acceptable and normal. The delay in the emergence of new knowledge may also be the condition of its future growth. Rather than imagining our period of transition to hypertext as a point when something old is replaced by something new, I would be content to see it described as a moment when two ways of reading or writing, and two ways of using maps, are plausible at the same time. At this point, I cannot tell if hypertexts will become so dominant that it will be considered silly to ignore them (my rejection of typewriters was not interpreted as intellectual originality). If and when hypertext comes to dominate the cultural scene, then those who refuse it will be called eccentric and their arguments will sound both very familiar and very useless. I don't know if the hypertext era will materialize and I don't know if it will be desirable. In the meantime, like Quinn, I would rather learn how to become a screener. If hypertexts never become commonly accepted, then screeners will have wasted their time and space, or failed, like Quinn, to tell a detective story. But it will be even worse if hypertexts become dominant and one realizes that one has lost the opportunity to contribute to the growing hypertextual corpus, the unfinished or unbegun "Tower of Babel."

I would rather make sure that my own random scribblings will contribute to what may become my own street map and writing, even if I am convinced that for a long time hypertexts will function like Ong's wheel-less horses, or perhaps like horseless horse-drawn carriages. The Ford Museum, located in Detroit, is a slightly quaint and nostalgic mirror image of the once-booming automobile industry. During my last visit, I was struck by its extremely non-hypertextual organization.[18] In the middle of one immense room, objects are displayed chronologically, each invention supposedly adding to the ever-growing sum of human realizations. One display attracted my attention because of its intentionally linear character. For a long time, I looked at what seemed to me like a traffic jam in history: in a long line vehicles were parked one right behind the other, as if the important factor was the lack of distance between each item. I was witnessing an account of the birth of the automobile. The series started with a few four-wheeled covered vehicles which were meant to represent the "last" horse-drawn vehicles followed by the "first" cars. The exhibit spans a relatively short period, from the turn of the century to the end of the Second World War. I understood this narrative to be a representation of Difference and Progress. There was some absolute difference between the last model of a category and the first prototype of another. Of course, a change had indeed occurred: engines had replaced the (invisible) horses. But what struck me in the exhibit was not Difference but a failed transition. I could not help seeing the first automobiles as rather silly-looking hybrids that had inherited very unnecessary features from the horse-drawn carriages. The latter give the impression of extreme adaption (another way of putting it is that they had reached the end of their evolution). The first automobiles, on the other hand, look amateurish and naive, because their shape, so obviously inspired by horse-drawn vehicles, lacks imagination. Even though their engine made them revolutionary, they have an obvious sameness rather than difference, especially as compared to the slick, aerodynamically improved models of the post–World War II period, which had gradually shed unnecessary features. Yet, it is only from the vantage point of elapsed time that the sameness can be seen as having been foregrounded at the expense of difference. Is it really important that we are now only capable of creating hypertexts which look like unnecessary and rather amateurish replications of great books?

NOTES

The research for this project has been made possible by a large interdisciplinary team to which I am deeply indebted. First of all, I want to thank Robert Hart and Nina Garrett for their help, encouragement, and support. They made me understand that I could reinvent computers instead of understanding them. Robert Jones was my hypertextual and technical guide. I want to thank Jim Gothard, Rex Clark, and Ulric Chung for their help in various hypertextual ventures, and the students who enrolled in the hypertextual Introduction to French Literature class for their conviction that their frustration with a less-than-perfect course could count as a fruitful theoretical experience. Without the released time granted by the University of Illinois Faculty Program in a Second Discipline, I would never have been able to do enough research on the subject to use it in my teaching. And finally, thank you to Rachael Criso for reading the draft of this manuscript.

1. The other side of the science fiction or fiction-of-science coin is nostalgia. See Michael Joyce's "Notes Toward an Unwritten Non-Linear Electronic Text, 'The End of Print Culture'" (*Postmodern Culture* 2.1 [Sept. 1991]) for a humorous account of how readers fight hypertexts because the book as physical object is endowed with sentimental properties: "The reader struggles against the electronic book. 'But you can't read it in bed,' she says, everyone's last ditch argument. Fully a year after Sony first showed Discman, a portable CD player the size of a Walkman, capable of holding 100,000 pages of text, a discussion on the Gutenberg computer network wanted to move the last ditch a little further. The smell of ink, one writer suggested; the crinkle of pages, suggests another. Meanwhile, in far-off laboratories of the Military-Infotainment-Complex . . . at Warner, Disney or IBApple and MicroLotus, some scientists work in synchronous smell-o-vision with real time simulated fragrance degradation shifting from fresh ink to old mold; while others build raised-text touch screens with laterally facing windows that look and turn like pages, crinkling and sighing as they turn. 'But the dog can't eat it,' someone protests, and—smiling, silently—the scientists go back to their laboratories, bags of silicone quibbles over their shoulders. What we whiff is not the smell of ink but the smell of loss."

2. As Walter Ong might put it (one of his chapter subtitles reads "Did you say 'oral literature'?") (*Orality and Literacy: The Technologizing of the Word* [London: Routledge, 1990], 10–15). Convinced that *oral* and *literature* should not be part of the same transparently set phrase, Ong points out, "Thinking of oral tradition or a heritage of oral performance, genres and styles as 'oral literature' is rather like thinking of horses as automobiles without wheels" (12).

3. Pat Aufderheide, in "Be All You Can Buy" (*Boston Review* [Feb. 1992], 18),

fulminates against music television (MTV) on the grounds that every item shown on the channel is really a commercial. The author points out that reporters and producers (and possibly all of us) forget that the "music videos themselves [are] commercials" and laments that some students "have trouble grasping why it's even an issue that a program should be nonstop commercials." But if MTV can be both "nonstop commercial" and culturally acceptable to a large audience, should we not reconsider the apparently irreducible difference between "commercials" and "programs"? The same blurring of logic is at work (but from the opposite ideological pole) when *MacWorld*'s usually brightly colored front page turns threateningly black and white to emphasize its accusing and inflammatory message: "America's Shame: The Creation of the Technological Underclass in America's Public Schools—How We Abandoned Our Children's Future" (Sept. 1992). The cover is a strange plunging perspective into a computer lab where one student is asleep in front of a machine, its screen obscured by a sign: "Broken computer. Do not use." I have to admit that I had trouble accepting that this was a typical view of a (typical?) public school student. I do not believe that the picture of a broken computer is really the best way of shaming America, even if the appeal to "education" is obviously a powerful buzzword. Here, as in MTV (but perhaps also in book "reviews" published by literary journals), the very distinction between advertising and disinterested prose is blurred by the existence of a magazine the purpose of which seems to be to give us enough information to urge us to buy. *MacWorld*'s issue title makes us responsible for failing to provide "our children" with technological knowledge and power, implying that each one of us is already convinced that "Technology" is indeed what is missing from "our" schools, that we should all remember that fighting for technology is a selfless endeavor and that if we do not participate in the "technological" future we are somehow morally and socially irresponsible. There are reasons for objecting to the cynicism of the rhetoric, but I wonder if readers who have grown up in a discursive era of weightless information do not have even much more powerful strategies (than the awareness of cultural criticism) against this new dominant discourse.

4. One may wonder, incidentally, why it took so long to proclaim the death of the book when the death of man, the death of the author, and the death of history generated such tiny ripples in the theoretical pool.

5. The word is used by Edward Jennings at the beginning of his review article on Landow's *Hypertext: The Convergence of Contemporary Literary Theory and Technology* (Jennings, "The Text Is Dead; Long Live the Techst" [*Postmodern Culture* 2.3 (1992)]). It is an interesting adjective for the purpose of my own reflection because it suggests an inside and an outside, the presence of a "land" defined by obvious if metaphorical frontiers. I suggest that hypertextuality will also exist as a politics of geography which may redefine and rename reading.

6. The literature about hypertext tends to consider Ted Nelson's definition as some kind of origin (Theodor Holm Nelson, *Literary Machines* [Swarthmore, Pa.: Published by the author, 1981]). Hypertext is itself often described as the offspring of Vannevar Bush's "memex" ("As We May Think," *Atlantic Monthly* 176

[1945]: 101–8). I am not sure that we absolutely need founding fathers, but I will adopt the idea that hypertext can be provisionally defined as an on-line form of "nonsequential writing" constituted of a "series of text chunks connected by links which offer the reader different pathways" (Nelson, 5). Nelson's *Literary Machines,* which one might describe as a printed draft or version of a hypertext project, is a good example of how hypertextual imagination can alter the way in which we think about books at the same time as our print culture shapes the future of hypertexts. Publishing *Literary Machines* implied a conviction that there is no absolutely linear evolution, and a little more than ten years later, Gregory Ulmer makes the same point: "It is perfectly possible to compose an essayistic equivalent of a hypermedia program, and to think electronically with paper and pencil" ("Grammatology Hypermedia," *Postmodern Culture* [Jan. 1991] 1.2).

7. For a review of available software and hypertextual creations see Robert Coover's "Finding Your Way in Hypertext: A Guide to the Software," (*New York Review of Books* [June 1992], 24) and Joseph Feustle's "Hypertext for the PC: The Ruben Darío Project" (in *Hypermedia and Literary Studies*, ed. Paul Delany and George Landow [Cambridge: MIT Press, 1991], 301). *The* Book is one of the most obvious sites for hypertextual experiments (see for example *MacBible* [Zonverdan Electronic Publishing] or *HyperBible* [Beacon Technology], which offers "study material, electronic atlases, pronunciation guides, search modes, the possibility of opening several windows," and so on).

8. Paulson does not use the word *hypertextuality*, but his vision of the end of the book is quite similar to that of hypertext experts. (I take this opportunity to thank him for sharing his material on the subject.)

9. In his review of Constance Penley and Andrew Ross's *Technoculture,* Joseph Dumit suggests that cultural studies provides the "most obvious" angle from which to study what he calls this "terrain," although the discipline "has often shied away from emphasizing machines." He adds that "by refusing to posit monstrous enemies in control of technology (especially of communications technologies)," he "provides models for rethinking intellectual technophobia."

10. For a study of the relationship between oppositionality and space, see Ross Chambers' *Room for Maneuver: Reading (the) Oppositional (in) Narrative* (Chicago: University of Chicago Press, 1991) (the title is another spatial metaphor). In it he says, "I am a non-driver who lives, perforce, in a city whose street-grid serves the needs of the automobile; I don't agitate for 'pedestrian rights,' but I do construct itineraries that are *mine,* adopting in particular a widespread student practice—students, too, are largely pedestrians in this college town—called 'cutting through' (i.e., using buildings and allotments as thoroughfares)" (6).

11. In Richard McGuire's illustration for Robert Coover's "The End of Books" in the *New York Times Book Review*, a cartoon character gazes intently at a book-shaped terminal, seemingly unaware that all around him, space is entirely occupied by an infinite number of free floating links and nodes (little white

squares adorned with pictures, symbols, letters, etc.) and to which he is potentially connected. The artist's rendition is really not that different from the "overviews" and "global maps" provided by hypertext programs like Storyspace (see the reproduction of the "global map" in Stuart Moulthrop's electronic version of Borges's "Forking Paths" in Landow, 111).

12. It is probably no coincidence that the survey course of English literature developed at Brown on Intermedia should be called "Context32." A hypertext may foster interdisciplinarity if developers already believe that interdisciplinarity is desirable and if they agree not to exert control over what other collaborators are likely to provide. But there again, the trust we put in other authors is often a question of hierarchical presumption: we assume that scientists will do a good job of patching up our own scientific deficiencies and that sociologists will not lower the standard of a web on nineteenth-century literature. I am not sure that potential conflicts about the "value" of each document are resolved in this multidisciplinary endeavor.

13. As the proliferation of italics in the previous sentence indicates, I am having trouble reconceptualizing my move without resorting to the spatial metaphors of the printed universe.

14. The only example I can summon of a reader insisting that he takes only quotations into account is a vaguely remembered literary reference which I experienced as a moment of frustration and anger: I associate (link) the memory with Philippe Sollers's *Femmes,* but I have not been able to locate the exact reference. I do not believe that I could have invented the passage, because my anger at the narrator's patronizing attitude is a much more vivid memory than the page number. The fact that I dare introduce a reference which might be inexact is also a self-reflexive comment in an article on hypertext: as I was trying to "screen" the 667 pages of Sollers's book in a desperate attempt to "find" the reference, I started having doubts about the intellectual value of the attempt. It struck me that it would be so simple to retrieve the passage electronically, searching for the word "citations" or "Faulkner." (My paratactic memory, unlike the computer, works metonymically, and such an apparently vague search would have brought a linear passage to my attention). When I started wondering if perhaps I was confusing Sollers with another author, I thought about how I could have "enlarged" my search to include either conventional categories such as "authors from the Tel Quel group" or more autobiographical groupings such as "documents I have screened between 1982 and 1992." Even to myself, this whole footnote is tainted with the guilt of resorting to "facile" tricks, but in the end I wonder what it is exactly that I want to privilege when I insist on correct citations.

15. It would be interesting to find out if the systematic interruption shortens or lengthens the reader's attention span. It is usually taken for granted that the modern zapper "no longer" knows how to read, because he or she cannot concentrate on a given text for more that two seconds. But I wonder if the zapper is not a reader who knows how to cultivate the memory of all the fragments he or she has just watched or read. Capable not only of going back

and forth among several stories (linearists might say abandoning each scenario sooner than he or she should have) but also of remembering many unfinished plots and of supplying what has been "missed," screeners would deploy more energy co-creating a work, collaborating in a fragmentary and irregular way.

16. See Katherine Hayles' "Postmodern Parataxis: Embodied Texts, Weightless Information" (*American Literary History* 2.3 [Fall 1990]: 394–421). Her subtle analysis opens on a comparison between two published images. She calls our attention to a Punch cartoon showing "two men, on a desert island, gazing gratefully down at the machine at their feet. The caption reads, 'God knows where we'd be without the fax machine'" (394).

17. In the same way as there is no outside language, there may be no outside the map. Often, the "background" of a map symbolizes either the uncivilized, the undiscovered, the wilderness or a space which does not have any significant attribute. I wonder if the distinction between the meaningfulness of links and nodes (roads and crossroads, or itinerary and destination) does not invent the convenience of a vacuum upon which roads are traced, like words on the blank page.

18. As opposed, for example, to the Museum of Science and Industry in Chicago, which is organized by themes or lexias and relies on a vast array of presentation techniques (dynamic animations, hands-on experiments, video tapes, cartoons, animated films, movies, traditional galleries of displayed static objects and various combinations of all media).

BIBLIOGRAPHY

Anderson, Benedict. *Imagined Communities: Reflections on the Origin and Spread of Nationalism*, 2nd ed., revised and augmented. London: Verso, 1991.

Anzaldúa, Gloria. *Borderlands: La Frontera, the New Mestiza*. San Francisco: Spinsters, Aunt Lute, 1987.

Aufderheide, Pat. "Be All You Can Buy." *Boston Review* (Feb. 1992): 18.

Auster, Paul. *City of Glass*. In *The New York Trilogy*. New York: Penguin, 1990.

Birkets, Sven. "Into the Electronic Millennium." *Boston Review* (Oct. 1991): 14–18.

Bolter, J. David. "Topographic Writing: Hypertext and the Electronic Writing Space." In *Hypermedia and Literary Studies*. Ed. Paul Delany and George Landow. Cambridge: MIT Press, 1991.

Bush, Vannevar. "As We May Think." *Atlantic Monthly* 176 (1945): 101–8.

Butler, Judith. *Gender Trouble*. New York: Routledge, 1990.

Chambers, Ross. *Room for Maneuver: Reading (the) Oppositional (in) Narrative*. Chicago: University of Chicago Press, 1991.

Conklin, Jeff. "Hypertext: An Introduction and Survey." *IEEE Computer* 20 (1987): 17–41.

Coover, Robert. "Finding Your Way in Hypertext: A Guide to the Software." *New York Review of Books* (June 1992): 24.

De Certeau, Michel. *The Practice of Everyday Life*. Trans. Steven Randall. Berkeley: University of California Press, 1983 (originally published as *L'invention du quotidien*. Paris: UGE 10/18, 1980).

Delany, Paul, and George Landow, eds. *Hypermedia and Literary Studies*. Cambridge: MIT Press, 1991.

Douglas, J. Yellowlees. "Beyond Orality and Literacy: Toward Articulating a Paradigm for the Electronic Age." *Computers and Composition* (Aug. 1989).

Dumit, Joseph. "Technoculture: Another, More Material, Name for Postmodern Culture?" *Postmodern Culture* 2.2 (Jan. 1992).

Feustle, Joseph. "Hypertext for the PC: The Ruben Darío Project." In *Hypermedia and Literary Studies*. Ed. Paul Delany and George P. Landow. Cambridge: MIT Press, 1991.

Glissant, Edouard. *Poétique de la Relation*. Paris: Gallimard, 1990.

Haraway, Donna. *Primate Visions: Gender, Race, and Nature in the World of Modern Science*. London: Routledge, 1989.

Hayles, Katherine. *Chaos Bound: Orderly Disorder in Contemporary Literature and Science*. Ithaca: Cornell University Press, 1990.

———. "Postmodern Parataxis: Embodied Texts, Weightless Information." *American Literary History* 2.3 (Fall 1990): 394–421.

Jennings, Edward. "The Text Is Dead; Long Live the Techst." *Postmodern Culture* 2.3 (1992).

Joyce, Michael. *Afternoon, a story*. Cambridge, Mass.: Eastgate Systems, 1990.

———. "Notes toward an Unwritten Non-linear Electronic Text, 'The End of Print Culture.'" *Postmodern Culture* 2.1 (Sept. 1991).

Landow, George. *Hypertext: The Convergence of Contemporary Critical Theory and Technology*. Baltimore: Johns Hopkins University Press, 1992.

Miller, Nancy. *Getting Personal: Feminist Occasions and Other Autobiographical Acts*. New York: Routledge, 1991.

Moulthrop, Stuart. "Reading from the Map: Metonymy and Metaphor in the Fiction of Forking Paths." In *Hypermedia and Literary Studies*. Ed. Paul Delany and George P. Landow. Cambridge: MIT Press, 1991.

———. *Victory Garden*. Cambridge, Mass.: Eastgate Systems, 1991.

Nelson, Theodor Holm. *Literary Machines*. Swarthmore, Pa.: Published by the author, 1981.

Ong, Walter. *Orality and Literacy: The Technologizing of the Word*. London: Routledge, 1990.

Paulson, William. "Computers, Minds and Texts: Preliminary Reflections." *New Literary History* 20 (1988–89): 291–303.

Penley, Constance, and Andrew Ross, eds. *Technoculture*. Minneapolis: University of Minnesota Press, 1991.

Piller, Charles. "The Creation of the Technological Underclass in America's Public Schools." *MacWorld* (Sept. 1992): 218–31.

Pratt, Mary Louise. "Arts of the Contact Zone." *Profession* 91: 33–40.

Scialabba, George. "Extra-Sensory." *Boston Review* (Feb. 1992): 16–17.

Ulmer, Gregory. "Grammatology Hypermedia." *Postmodern Culture* 1.2 (Jan. 1991).

Wilson, David. "Electronic Versions of Public-Domain Texts Draw Praise and Fire." *Chronicle of Higher Education* (Aug. 12, 1992): A15-16.

"How Do I Stop This Thing?": Closure and Indeterminacy in Interactive Narratives

J. Yellowlees Douglas

5

[Conventional novelistic] solutions are legitimate inasmuch as they satisfy the desire for finality, for which our hearts yearn, with a longing greater than the longing for the loaves and the fishes of this earth. Perhaps the only true desire of mankind, coming thus to light in its hours of leisure, is to be set at rest.

—Joseph Conrad, "Henry James"

Death is the sanction of everything the storyteller can tell. He has borrowed his authority from death. In other words, it is the natural history to which his stories refer back.

—Walter Benjamin, "The Storyteller"

Just how essential is closure to our readings of narratives? Do we read narratives to satisfy our need for the closure denied to us in our everyday lives, as both Conrad and Benjamin have argued? Is closure essential to the pleasure we take in reading narratives? Is it integral to both narrative aesthetics and poetics, as Peter Brooks has insisted? Using the sentence as a paradigm of narrative structure, Brooks argues that in narratives "the revelation of meaning . . . occurs when the narrative sentence reaches full predication".[1] Just as sentences are incomplete without their predicates, narratives without closure are like sentences which include only the subject and not the "action" of a sentence. Closure, in this view, completes the meaning of a story: "Only the end can finally determine meaning, close the sentence as a signifying totality" (22). It is the anticipation of this closure, Brooks argues, that enables us to interpret the narrative as we read through it. Although Brooks bases his poetics primarily on readings of nineteenth-century fiction and not on existing models of reading, his theory parallels psycholinguist Frank Smith's concept of prediction as the keystone to the act of reading. The act of prediction, which enables us to move forward in our reading, causes us continually to modify our responses to the text based on our predictions. It also causes us to turn pages, because, as Brooks notes, "the anticipation of retrospection [is] our chief tool in making sense of the narrative" (23).

As the experiences of readers engaged in reading interactive narratives for the first time have revealed, "strong" or "inner-directed" readers can substitute the metaphor of the map for the metaphor or trope of the text, which we understand, Brooks claims, through the chain of metonymies stretching through the narrative, binding beginning and middle alike to the ending.[2] Inner-directed readers may base their interpretations on the significance of the spaces occupied by narrative segments as they navigate through the structure of a text like Stuart Moulthrop's "Forking Paths," an interactive fantasy on Jorge Luis Borges's short story "The Garden of Forking Paths." They can even decide when their readings of the narrative are complete, based on their reconstructions of the narrative as a virtual, three-dimensional structure. But this, nonetheless, does not resolve the issue of how the suspension of closure affects reading at a local level. Do we read for closure anyway, even though the structure of hypertext narratives may displace it? Can we read entirely without a sense of closure, and, if we do, can the displacement of closure affect our reasons for reading narratives?

Classical Closure and Twentieth-Century Print Narratives

Really, universally, relations stop nowhere, and the exquisite problem of the artist is eternally but to draw, by a geometry of his own, the circle within which they shall happily *appear* to do so.

—Henry James, preface to *Roderick Hudson*

It is no coincidence that critics such as Brooks, Frank Kermode, and Walter Benjamin insist on closure as an essential component—perhaps *the* essential component—in narrative poetics. Contemporary concepts of ending and closure derive some of their authority from the earliest written example of poetics, Aristotle's simple definition of story as an aggregate of beginning, middle, and ending. For Aristotle, the definition of plot, or what we might call "story," is "a whole . . . [with] a beginning, a middle, and an end," where the beginning "does not itself follow anything by causal necessity" and the ending "itself naturally follows some other thing, either by necessity, or as a rule, but has nothing following it."[3] In the same vein, Kermode argues that the provision of an ending "make[s] possible a satisfying consonance with the origins and with the middle," thereby giving "meaning to lives and to poems."[4] But the ending need not necessarily be physically provided by the text itself (or announced by a lengthy newspaper obituary) in order to bestow meaning on the life or narrative that has preceded it, because, as readers of texts and of lives, we create "our own sense of an ending" by making "considerable imaginative investments in coherent patterns" (17). Endings, in other words, either confirm or invalidate the predictions we have made about resolutions to conflicts and probable outcomes as we read stories, watch films, or speculate about the lives of others. While the "coherent patterns" articulated by Kermode dimly echo Brooks's flow of metonymies, they also suggest Smith's concept of readerly predictions as the action that enables comprehension.[5]

For Smith, readers use hypotheses to limit ambiguity or uncertainty in their understanding of the text, and it is these inferences that enable readers to assemble the meaning of a text. For Kermode, however, readers form hypotheses about the present in order to anticipate the ending that will, in turn, confer meaning and significance on the hypotheses. Like Brooks's "anticipation of retrospection" (23), Kermode's act of reading is endlessly recursive, continually building a structure that presupposes an ending that, in turn, modifies the building of the structure. Brooks takes this still further, making closure the limitation on narrative that defines its shape and significance: "Any narrative plot, in the sense of a significant organization of the life story, necessarily espouses in some form the problematic of the talisman: the realization of the desire for narrative encounters the limits of narrative, that is, the fact that one can tell a life only in terms of its limits or margins. The telling is always *in terms* of the impending end" (52). Significantly, Brooks, Kermode, and Benjamin use closure as the single entity that confers cohesion and significance on narratives in a way that strongly suggests that the experience of narrative closure numbers among the principal pleasures of reading narratives—at once showing us how closure both prompts and enables us to read.

It is, perhaps, no coincidence that all three writers also typically concern themselves with what we might define as classical narratives, texts that all predate the modern and postmodern eras. Although Kermode touches briefly on Robbe-Grillet, acknowledging that readers of Robbe-Grillet are "not offered easy satisfactions, but a challenge to creative co-operation" (19), he concerns himself chiefly with fictions that have determinate closure—endings that are paradigms of an apocalyptic and definitive end. Discussing Robbe-Grillet's *In the Labyrinth,* he is only with difficulty able to grapple with the concept of the novel's representing a conceptual labyrinth that continually violates our expectations of narratives, a text that provides none of the continuity, coherent patterns, or closure endemic to works from which (and upon which) Kermode bases his textual aesthetics. "There is no temporality, no successiveness. . . . This is certainly a shrewd blow at paradigmatic expectations," Kermode writes, then dismisses Robbe-Grillet's work as simply "very modern and therefore very extreme" (21).

But neither Kermode, nor Benjamin, nor Brooks can explain how readers make their way through Robert Coover's "The Babysitter," Julio Cortàzar's *Hopscotch*, or John Fowles's *The French Lieutenant's Woman*—all of which contain multiple and therefore highly indeterminate endings—or even Thomas Pynchon's *The Crying of Lot 49*, which concludes abruptly immediately before the solution of the central mystery around which the narrative revolves. Further, all three critics deal with nineteenth-century narratives in which story and narrative are conventionally bound inextricably together. But in twentieth-century fiction stories may "end" long before the narrative finishes on the last page of a book, making it difficult for us to perceive to which ending Brooks, Benjamin, and Kermode refer. Although readers of Jane Austen's *Northanger Abbey* proceed through the novel wondering if Catherine will ever be united with her beloved Henry, I can work my way forward through Ford Madox Ford's *The Good Soldier* already knowing, perhaps not the end of the narrative itself, but certainly the "end" of the story, the events that take place at the very limits of its chronology.

With more than one-third of the narrative's bulk remaining, I learn that both Edward Ashburnham and Florence are already dead and that Nancy, mad and vacant, has been entrusted to Dowell's care. In a series of flashbacks that direct the action of the novel, Leonora and the novel's narrator, Dowell, meditate on the successions of deceptions practised by their two dead spouses, with Leonora's revelations informing Dowell's gradually evolving sense of the events he relates. In *The Good Soldier*, we do not discover closure in the "ending" of the story—which we learn less than two-thirds of the way through the narrative. Instead, we find closure in the way in which the narrative gradually confirms our conjectures, in the way that Leonora's fully informed viewpoint eventually endows Dowell's blissfully ignorant perspective with a complete knowledge of the events he has witnessed.

Similarly, what are readers to make of Robbe-Grillet's *In the Labyrinth*, which continually reverses our expectations from sequence to sequence, and from paragraph to paragraph—and even, occasionally, from sentence to sentence? A soldier walks through the streets of an unnamed town, carrying a box. He is lost; he is in his barracks dormitory. He is merely tired; he is mortally wounded. He is a figure in a photograph; he is a figure in an engraving; he is a soldier trudging through snowy streets. The engravings and photographs come to life; the sequences we read may or may not have happened—in fact they may not even be probable. At the end of the narrative, a doctor identifies the contents of the dead soldier's box; at the end of the narrative, the soldier and his box appear in an engraving and the narrative takes up again where it first began, with descriptions of the interiors of dusty rooms and the snow falling silently outside.

In Robbe-Grillet's novel, as well as in *The Good Soldier,* closure in the conventional sense has been displaced. The novel's end, like a labyrinth, simply draws us back to its beginning without confirming, negating, or resolving any of the tensions, questions, or hypotheses we may bring to our reading of the narrative. Whatever the narrative offers in the way of goal-seeking—the soldier's attempt to orient himself in a strange location, or the mission behind the box he clutches to him—is never resolved in the narrative. In narratives such as Robbe-Grillet's, where the referents for pronouns may change within the space of a paragraph, it is difficult for readers to establish any sense of causal relationship between characters' actions or narrative episodes. Contrary to the view of the relationship between expectation and causal relationships in reading expressed by some psycholinguists, our sense of causal reasoning in the narrative is not simply driven by expectations.[6] Instead, our perceptual proclivity for connections and causal relationships prompts us to form expectations that, in turn, help us comprehend what we read.

When these expectations are violated at every turn, as they are in *In the Labyrinth,* we call upon our knowledge of narrative conventions to hold our reading of the text together. As readers, we expect characters to remain constant throughout the narrative: we do not, for example, expect the soldier we follow through the streets to metamorphose into someone else as we follow him—as he does in Robbe-Grillet's novel. We expect that shifts in time and place will be signaled by transitions or descriptions that physically pursue characters as they move from one setting to another. We expect to learn about the most important events in the story through the narrative. But in Robbe-Grillet's narrative, we discover that the soldier is wounded without having learned just how or when this happened. The ending of the novel prompts me to recognize its structure as a textual labyrinth, but it is the continual subversion of my narrative expectations throughout the novel that gradually induces me to see this narrative as a form of anti-narrative. *In the Labyrinth* does not unfold a plot so much as it reveals to me the nature of the unseen elements for which I unconsciously search as I read—without delivering any of the actions, consequences, or resolutions I overtly seek. The ending, to use Barbara Herrnstein-Smith's definition of closure, simply removes any "residual expectations" I may have concerning the narrative: I know that the narrative physically has nothing left to reveal after I have finished my reading of it and that I am free to begin to make sense of the work as a whole.[7]

Many twentieth-century print narratives, as we have seen, have rendered problematic the traditional definition of closure. Only their physical endings ensure that their readers can hold no further expectations that something else will happen in the narrative, or that they will need to revise their concept of the narrative as a whole as a result of some as yet unexperienced narrative episode. Nonetheless, we can argue that this still confers upon the narrative the quality of Brooks's "anticipation of retrospection," promising readers that they will soon be able to see their inferences about the narrative action either affirmed or disproved when they finish reading the text. But what happens to readers of hypertext narratives, who can face in Michael Joyce's *Afternoon* as many as 539 places or narrative segments, accessed by way of 950 links, or, in Stuart Moulthrop's *Victory Garden,* as many as 991 places, read by way of 2800 links? Even a reader navigating through Joyce's *WOE,* which contains a relatively modest 63 places and only 221 links, has no comforting sense of having exhausted the narrative's array of possibilities in two, three, or even four readings.

What triggers the ending of a reading? Where print readers encounter texts already supplied with closure and endings, readers of interactive fiction generally must supply their own sense of an ending. This affords us a new understanding of the relationship between the structures integral to the act of reading and the concept of closure. What prompts readers to decide they are "finished" with a particular interactive narrative and to discontinue their readings of it? And can readings, cumulatively, approximate a sense of closure for readers, a sense that they have experienced the full range of the narrative's possibilities or have grasped the narrative as what media theorist J. David Bolter has dubbed a "structure of possible structures," even though their readings may not have explored every narrative space and link?[8]

One of the chief difficulties with discussing readings of interactive narratives is our inability to provide readings of print narratives as an index against which we can measure the time and effort involved. Reading hypertext narratives can take up to six times as long as reading print narratives.[9] A single reading of an interactive narrative such as *Afternoon* can thus occupy the same amount of time as a reading of an entire novel such as *The Good Soldier*. Or, conversely, depending on the paths readers take through the hypertext, one reading can correspond to the reading of a single chapter of *Lord Jim.* Finding no clear-cut divisions such as chapters between episodes or narrative strands, readers of interactive narratives encounter few cues as to when they can temporarily interrupt their reading, or when they can decide that they have completed the reading of a single version among many possible versions of the narrative.

In Search of Closure: Four Readings of *Afternoon*

Defaults in hypertext narratives like *Afternoon* connect segments more or less seamlessly: to move from one to the other, readers simply strike the return key. In my first reading of *Afternoon,* I pursued a strategy of navigating through the narrative primarily through its defaults. By answering simply yes or no at a single decision point—for instance, where the text of the place "Begin" asks, "Do you want to hear about it?"—it is possible to realize two completely different readings of *Afternoon,* even if the rest of the narrative is read by default only. In fact, it is possible, when reading through the narrative by way of default, to experience wildly different versions simply by altering a single response, as I discovered in two other, lengthy readings of the text. This strategy enabled my reading experience to somewhat approximate a reading of a print narrative, in that I did not need to deliberate about my options for movement at the end of each hypertext node. More important, this way of reading also provided me with physical cues—an absence of any default connections, signaled by a Macintosh "beep"—that prompted me to conclude each reading session as a complete version of the narrative.

As I completed each reading, however, I remained painfully aware that my reading represented only one among many actualizations of the narrative's constellation of possibilities. The most "straightforward" reading of *Afternoon,* significantly, is the most accessible: a reader can proceed through the entire narrative by striking the return key and activating defaults. This method of reading most closely resembles our experience of reading conventional print narratives. In this version of the narrative, the narrator, Peter, fears that he has seen the bodies of his estranged wife, Lisa, and son, Andrew, lying by the roadside at the scene of an accident as he drives to work. The narrative then follows his frenetic search for his ex-wife and son and his pursuit of evidence which will either confirm or disprove his fears about what he believes he has seen. This reading, however, ends abruptly 36 places later in the narrative, with the narrator deciding not to begin telephoning the local hospitals but, instead, to call someone named Lolly. Since Lolly has not yet appeared in the narrative, her significance to the narrator and the possibility that she may hold the key to the whereabouts of Lisa and Andrew combine to make this reading of the narrative seem particularly inconclusive. I feel prompted to return to the narrative, but the text will not default and I can physically proceed no further without altering my reading strategy.

On my second reading, while I encounter no places that refuse to default, I do, however, run into a relentless loop that pushes me repeatedly through the same sequence of places without offering any chance of escaping it—thus spelling the end of my second reading. At the point when the text refuses to default on my third reading of *Afternoon,* I have accumulated more ambiguities and tensions I wish to resolve than I did in the first reading. Peter's quest for the whereabouts of his ex-wife and son is still unfinished. Also, I want to confirm whether he is having an affair with a fellow-employee named Nausicaa and to assess the nature of his involvement with Lolly, a sometime therapist who also happens to be the wife of his employer. Instead of narrowing the margins of the narrative the further I read, *Afternoon* considerably broadens them. Where the number of probable and plausible outcomes in print narratives conventionally dwindles the nearer we approach their endings, the more of an interactive narrative we read the more these seem to multiply. My third reading of *Afternoon* has provided me with still more inferences to verify, and I cannot begin to form a sense of the narrative as a more or less complete structure of possibilities. My first three readings have satisfied none of the requirements for closure stipulated by psycholinguists like Trabasso, Secco, and Van Den Broek, by Herrnstein-Smith, or even by Kermode and Brooks. There seems to be no final, concluding metaphor here that organizes patterns in the text into a coherent, tangible whole.

By my fourth reading of *Afternoon,* I become uncomfortably aware of the mutually exclusive representations of events cropping up in each reading—most notably of a lunchtime exchange between Peter and his employer, Wert. In one version, the conversation gives no indication that the accident has occurred; in another, Wert distracts the worried Peter from his fears about the fates of ex-wife and child by making bawdy suggestions. In another scenario, only Peter is having an affair with Nausicaa; in yet another, Wert knows that both he and Peter are having an affair with Nausicaa and that Peter is blissfully ignorant of Nausicaa's involvement with him. In one version of the scene, Wert idly wonders aloud how Peter would react if he, Wert, were sleeping with Peter's ex-wife; in another, Wert is testing the extent of

Peter's ignorance of his involvement with Peter's ex-wife. While my readings of all these versions are logically possible, I cannot accept all of them simultaneously in my final understanding of the events described in *Afternoon.*

On my fourth reading of *Afternoon,* my uncertainty about Nausicaa's involvement with both Wert and Peter is confirmed by a sequence of places narrated by Nausicaa. Most significantly, however, this particular version of the narrative rearranges the sequence in which Peter first sees the bodies of the woman and child stretched out on the green lawn. In this instance, Peter cannot track down either Lisa or Andrew prior to his driving to work and has become distracted by his anxieties when he spots Lisa and Andrew riding in Wert's truck. The possibility that Lisa may be sleeping with Wert—and possibly, his recognition that Wert's lunchtime query may have been a real question—shocks him. Peter's feeling out of control is, in this version of *Afternoon,* accompanied by a physical loss of control of his car. In an ironic twist, Peter himself causes the accident that injures or kills his wife and son—and it may be his feelings of guilt that prompt an amnesiac search for their whereabouts that both follows this sequence and began my first, default-only reading of *Afternoon.* This reading ends, as did the first reading, on the place named "I call," with the narrator relating his actions to us: "I take a pill and call Lolly"—only this time, he calls Lolly to assuage his guilt. And it is his calling Lolly which has enabled her to reveal, in the places "1/," "2/," and "white afternoon," that Peter has caused the accident.

To penetrate the narrative to its furthest extent, to realize most of its possibilities, I need, in a sense, to experience the place "I call" in each of the readings. The beginning of the therapy, introduced in my first reading of *Afternoon* by the narrator's electing to call Lolly to stem his fears, becomes, through several encounters with the place "I call," an on-going process of realization and discovery that culminates in Lolly's intercession, encountered in my last reading. It is this gesture of calling Lolly, in the end, that enables Peter to face the fact that he is culpable for the deaths or injuries of his ex-wife and son. Joyce himself has noted: "In order to physically get to 'white afternoon,' you have to go through therapy with Lolly, the way Peter does," and it is only in the first and last readings that readers cannot move beyond "I call" by default—or by making navigational choices. The hypertext, quite unexpectedly, "ends," by leaving readers without the means to move further through the narrative.[10] In all other readings, this place defaults and also provides access to numerous other narrative strands. Of all the places in *Afternoon,* "I call" has the largest number of paths branching out from it—ten—making it, significantly, a place both physically and literally central to the structure of the narrative.

What, precisely, triggered my sense of having come to some sort of closure? My sense that I did not need to continue reading *Afternoon*? Most obviously, I became conscious of my readings having satisfied one of the primary quests outlined in the narrative: what has happened to Peter's ex-wife and child? Although my discovery that Peter caused the accident is not entirely congruent with his desire to learn of their condition, it does short-circuit Peter's quest. Since Peter himself caused the accident, clearly, he knows whether the pair is unharmed, fatally injured, or already dead. The language in the place "white afternoon" suggests the last possibility may be the most valid: "The investigator finds him to be at fault. He is shocked to see the body . . . on the wide green lawn. The boy is nearby."[11] The word *body* may signify that the woman Peter sees is lifeless, but it could also mean she is unconscious, inert, quantifiable as an accident victim. Although he does not identify the bodies he sees in this segment, elsewhere in the narrative the absence of Lisa and Andrew from home, office, and school suggests that they might be the accident victims Peter sees. Further, when Peter revisits the scene of the accident, he comes upon crumpled school papers written by his son, which may have fallen out of one of the vehicles on impact, and is moved to tears—again strongly suggesting that he has caused a fatal accident.

In building up to this particular reading of *Afternoon,* I become aware of an indeterminacy at work in the text that is peculiar, in its extent and character, to interactive narratives. I cannot really be certain that Peter did not simply see his ex-wife keeping company with his employer, swerve and strike another car, carrying an unknown woman and child in it. This scenario leaves Peter's quest for information about Lisa and Andrew as open-ended as it was when I first began reading the narrative. What leads me, then, to accept this reading as the reading of *Afternoon* that brings the narrative to some approximate, albeit stylized, version of closure?

First, *the text does not default, requiring that I physically alter my reading strategy or stop reading.* Since the place "I call" also refused to default the first time I encountered it, what distinguishes my first and last experiences of this physical cue? Why does it prompt me, the first time I come across it, to read the narrative again from the beginning, pursuing different connections, yet prompt me to stop reading the second time its "no-default" condition freezes me in place? The decision to continue reading after my first encounter with "I call" reflected my awareness that my first reading of *Afternoon* visited only forty places out of a total of 539, leaving the bulk of the narrative places still to be discovered on subsequent readings. Further, on the first reading I perceived the text's initial failure to default from the place "I call" as an invitation to return to the narrative. This recalls the same sort of re-direction of textual energies which Brooks mentions in his analysis of Freud's narrative of the Wolf Man:

> Causation can work backward as well as forward since the effect of an event . . . often comes only when it takes on meaning. . . . Chronological sequence may not settle the issue of cause: events may gain traumatic significance by deferred action or retroaction, action working in reverse sequence to create a meaning that did not previously exist. Thus the way a story is ordered does not necessarily correspond to the way it *works*. Indeed, narrative order, sequence as a logical enchainment of actions and outcomes, must be considered less a solution than part of the problem of narrative explanation. (280–81)

That is, this physical "conclusion" to the narrative sends me back into its midst to discover the cause of Peter's anxiety and to resolve additional questions that my journey through the narrative has already raised. Readers of Freud's narrative about the Wolf Man may have to page back through the narrative to assemble their own versions of the causation and motivation behind the occurrences they have discovered in the narrative. But on the other hand, as a reader of an interactive narrative, I am fairly certain that further readings of *Afternoon* will yield a different chronology, different apparent motivations, and even a different set of events leading to a conclusion totally dissimilar to that of the narrator gulping a pill and reaching for the phone to call his therapist friend.

Second, *this particular conclusion represents a resolution of the tensions which initially gave rise to the narrative. Afternoon* begins with two quests: Peter's search for the whereabouts of his ex-wife and son, to confirm whether they might have been the accident victims he glimpsed that morning, and our seeking a better sense of exactly what it is that Peter saw on his way to work. When we look at the accident through Peter's eyes, we see only the scene of the accident revisited by him several hours later—and we cannot begin to account for his nearly paralyzing fear that the bodies he saw so briefly might belong to those closest to him. The mere proximity of the accident to his son's school does not completely account for it, nor does the nature of the conversations he conducts later on that day with people who cannot recall whether they have seen Lisa and Andrew unharmed and going about their regular business.

My sense of the significance of "white afternoon" lies partially in its ability to account for the undertone of hysteria edging Peter's fear. If Peter has caused the accident that has injured them but has blocked this horrifying bit of knowledge from his consciousness, his inquiries would probably have this particular character of concern mixed with panic. Put another way, Peter's panic-stricken inquiries and fearful conclusions do not match any script I can recall from either experience or from other narratives that describe a search for the whereabouts of missing family members or friends. It does match, however, scripts familiar to me from narratives where characters attempt to forestall acknowledgment of a particularly painful or destructive event by proceeding about their business as if they were not already certain of what has happened.

Third, *this conclusion represents the resolution which accounts for the greatest number of ambiguities in the narrative.* In other words, this place represents the most *plausible* conclusion to the narrative's network of mysteries and tensions. Psycholinguistic models of reading posit plausibility and referentiality as the glue that holds texts together at the level of sentences and paragraphs.[12] Plausibility and reference in the larger narrative structure, likewise, direct the focus of my attention to the interpretation that refers to the largest number of narrative episodes and constructs the model of causation that seems, according to my knowledge of human behavior, to be the most likely, the most plausible. Wert's romance with Lisa accounts for the peculiar tenor of some of his comments to Peter, but it also accounts for testimony by Lisa, Lolly, and Nausicaa, throughout the narrative, to Peter's inability to see himself as anything but the center of everyone else's narrative. Without this reading of "white afternoon" representing the key to what really happened to Peter that morning, what am I to make of Lolly and Nausicaa discussing the accident and concluding that they should not blame "either of them"? This reading of "white afternoon" also accounts for the otherwise puzzling places "1/" and "2/" in Lolly's monologue:

> Let's agree that it is shocking, unexpected, to see this particular woman with [Wert]. Yes, I know that, for anyone else this should not be unexpected, that Peter should, at least, have suspected; but we nonetheless ought to grant him his truth. It is all he has, and so it is authentic. Let's agree he must feel abandoned—even, literally, out of control. . . . ("1/")
>
> Wert knows Peter takes this road.
>
> Peter knows we women are free. . . .
>
> The world is a world of properties and physical objects, of entropy. . . . Even coincidence is a free-will decision. ("2/")

Having discovered a series of places, culminating in "white afternoon" and "I call," that cumulatively satisfy my inferences about ambiguities and occurrences in the narrative, I find this reading also invites me to grasp the narrative as a whole, as a structure of possibilities representing one man's simultaneous drive to learn the fates of his ex-wife and son and mad dash away from his own culpability in an accident that may have caused their violent ends.

If the thrust of the narrative moves toward revealing the fates of Lisa and Andrew, it also works to reveal truths that Peter himself is too self-absorbed, insecure, or out-and-out terrified to admit. Lolly's monologue, ending in the revelation that Peter has caused the accident, represents the farthest reaches of this narrative movement. Once I have reached it, I am able to look back over the entire narrative and perceive it as a chronicle of Peter's denial of everything from his feelings for his ex-wife to his role in the car accident. In other words, I reach a point where I perceive the "structure of the work as, at once, both dynamic and whole"—satisfying Herrnstein-Smith's definition of conventional narrative closure (36).

Fourth, *my interpretation of the significance of "white afternoon" is tied to my perception of "I call" as a central "junction" in the structure of the text and of "white afternoon" as a peripheral, deeply embedded, and relatively inaccessible place in this narrative.* At least one media theorist and Joyce himself have pointed out that the cognitive map of *Afternoon* reflects his organization of the narrative as he wrote it and not the structure of readers' potential encounters with it.[13] But this does not prevent me from discovering some striking concurrences between my perception of the virtual space occupied by places such as "I call," and "white afternoon," and the spaces they occupy in the cognitive map of *Afternoon.*

The narrative's network of guard fields requires readers to have visited a particular space or selected a certain word or phrase from the text of a place. Together with a tracking device that keeps a record of places readers have visited, the mechanical set up of *Afternoon* appears to track readers based on whether they have visited "I call." The sequence of places visited determines which paths are accessible and which defaults tangible, causing my experience of the text to somewhat resemble Dante's penetration of the rings of Hell in *The Inferno*. The more I read the narrative, the closer I approach its center—and, like Dante, I cannot suddenly emerge in the environs known to Judas Iscariot in the very pit of Hell without having first visited the more lofty realms populated by those who merely lived lives without the benefit of Christian baptism.

The place "I call" seems to exist as a central junction, where readers are switched onto certain narrative strands that spiral down further into the narrative with each successive encounter. Significantly, the place "white afternoon," along with the rest of the sequence revealed in Lolly's monologue, is embedded at the deepest structural level of *Afternoon,* five layers below the uppermost layer of the narrative, the one through which readers first enter the text. Only two connections lead into this narrative strand, and a succession of guard fields ensures that it is reached only after a lengthy visitation of fifty-seven narrative places. When I arrive at it, I sense I have arrived at the end of something because "white afternoon" physically represents the farthest reaches of the physical spaces within *Afternoon.*

My arrival at a sense of an ending for *Afternoon* is thus tied equally to reading strategies translated directly from reading print narratives and to strategies which embrace the text as an interactive narrative existing in virtual, three-dimensional space. As a reader familiar with print narratives, I find my desire for closure sated by the fourth reading, which satisfies the tensions that originally give rise to the story and also resolves or accounts for the greatest number of ambiguities in the narrative. Yet, my sense of an ending here is informed equally strongly by my recognition of the significance of the lack of physical defaults and by my awareness of the relative centrality of "I call" and relative inaccessibility of "white afternoon." By embracing both points in a single reading, I experience a sense of having both literally and figuratively plumbed the depths of the narrative spaces of *Afternoon.*

The Suspension of Closure: *WOE—Or a Memory of What Will Be*

It is a story of being at the edge of something. That is not authorial intention but discovery. If in doubt how to read, ask your teacher or your heart.

—Michael Joyce, *WOE—Or a Memory of What Will Be*

In one sense, the layers of *Afternoon* represent what we could call stratigraphic writing. Its narrative structure enables us to delve through layer upon layer of singular versions of narrative events until we reach the bottom band, which holds the tale of the origin of the story in the same way that the oldest strata in sedimentary rock tell geologists of the earliest days of our fossil records. The event that triggers the narrative is Peter's accident, which lies in the bottom layer of

Afternoon, and it is his denial of this event that sets the narrative in motion.

Although *Afternoon* is not a mystery in the conventional sense, its action nonetheless takes its central thrust from the narrative dialectic of discovery and concealment, which drives events in nearly every narrative strand. Therefore, it is not terribly surprising that the narrative should prompt and complete my quest for a rough equivalent of narrative closure—although my search is somewhat satisfied through avenues (such as the physical cues of defaults and my knowledge of the narrative structure) beyond the boundaries of print narratives.

How do we know that this sense of closure is not simply unique to *Afternoon*? What happens when we encounter interactive narratives without clear-cut narrative tensions, texts without a narrative that establishes itself, from the outset of its most accessible reading, as a quest? Is closure integral to our reading of these works? In the absence of narrative tensions, do we discard our search for resolutions, or do we impose or invent them, in order to confer purposiveness on our readings?

Like Robbe-Grillet's *In the Labyrinth* or James Joyce's *Ulysses* or Virginia Woolf's *Mrs Dalloway, WOE—Or a Memory of What Will Be* is a narrative "about" its own structure. Joyce's and Woolf's novels span a single day in the lives of, in one case, Leopold Bloom and Stephen Daedalus, in the other Clarissa Dalloway and Septimus Warren Smith, expressing a pattern of tensions, conflicts, and ambiguities that cannot be resolved simply by the closing of the day. Although the day that begins and ends *Mrs Dalloway* permanently dispatches with one of the narrative's most overt questions—namely, what will happen to Septimus Warren Smith—it merely traces the origins of regrets, ambitions, desires, and decisions that drift through the minds and memories of Clarissa, Hugh, Richard, Peter Walsh, and Lucrezia Warren Smith. We expect the two parallel narrative strands involving the days of Clarissa and Septimus Warren Smith to intersect in a manner that will alter the direction of both, but we discover instead that their lives run in perfectly parallel lines. Clarissa approaches the life of Septimus Warren Smith only in her nearness to the eddies cast out by his suicide. The ambulance wailing down Tottenham Court Road, on its way either to or from the place where the dying Septimus lies, interrupts Peter Walsh's thoughts of Clarissa; later Clarissa will herself learn of the suicide from Lady Bradshaw, in the midst of her dinner party.

Mrs Dalloway, like *In the Labyrinth* and *The Good Soldier,* lies in the realm of narratives structured around what Joseph Frank dubbed "spatial form."[14] Noting that modernist literary works attempted to convey simultaneity and patterns of thought through recurrent images, fragmented narrative sequences, and the division of plot from narrative, Frank argued that these patterns acquired significance when perceived as part of a whole in the minds of their readers. Interpreting these works, or making meaning from these texts, in this view, occurred only after readers had finished reading the entire text. Taking Frank's concept further, David Mickelsen has argued that novels employing spatial form "are far from resolved," and are, instead, open works formed largely as explorations: "The world portrayed is in a sense unfinished (unorganized), requiring the reader's collaboration and involvement, his interpretation. . . . the 'implied reader,' in Iser's phrase, in spatial form is more active, perhaps even more sophisticated, than that implied by most traditional fiction."[15] Obviously, the spatial form at work in these print narratives exists in the minds of readers grappling with their intricacies of time and place, with patterns of recursion, and with digressions that violate expectations based on readings of conventional narratives.

Wrestling with the static, unidimensional form of the printed page, Proust similarly strained to portray time in a dimension of space in his *Remembrance of Things Past,* and, at one point, toyed with the idea of giving the sections of the narrative titles corresponding to the architectural details of a cathedral, for example, "Porch," and "Stained Glass of the Apse."[16] In *WOE,* however, Michael Joyce creates a narrative that physically, visibly reflects the same characteristics that distinguish narratives exhibiting what Frank and a large number of critics recognize as spatial form.

The perception of spatial form occurs in readers of print narratives as they work their way through layers of narrative time, juxtaposed images, recurrent themes, multiple perspectives on events, and parallel lives. According to Ivo Vidan: "Verbal space acquires consistency as the stylistic rendering of the text becomes apparent: reiteration, allusion, parallelism, and contrast relate some parts of the narration to others, and the construction imposes itself on the reader through the action constituted by the reading."[17] In the treatise that first brought the concept of spatial form to the attention of critics, Frank claimed that readers exploring narratives using spatial form were required, by the very nature of this pattern of references, ellipses, recursions, and fluctuating points of view, to suspend "the process of individual reference temporarily" until completing the narrative, when "the entire pattern of internal references can be apprehended as a unity" (13). The apprehension of the narrative as a structure or pattern of references is hardly a novel concept, since, as we have seen, it is more or less an integral part of the act of perceiving narrative closure. But it is Frank's insistence that we suspend our need to discover meaning as we read, reflected in his proclamation that James Joyce "cannot be read—he can only be reread" (19), that is problematic. On one hand, Frank may be accurate in claiming that we can only grasp the full meaning of these narratives when we consider them retrospectively, as gestalts or bundles of relations. But his belief that readers can read without perceiving associations and references, or without making predictions or seeing the grouping of images as already meaningful, flies fully in the face of nearly every theory of reader-response. Like the theories of reading and closure elaborated by Brooks, Benjamin, and Kermode, Frank's concept of spatial form is essentially an examination of modernist textual aesthetics—not an accurate model for how readers approach the reading of narratives.

Even as they begin reading a narrative, readers are interpreting texts: integrating details, forming and developing hypotheses, modifying, confirming, and abandoning predictions. The glue that holds texts together is the readers' ability to perceive references and causal connections linking phrases, sentences, and paragraphs. According to Stanley Fish, the very act of reading requires us, albeit generally unconsciously, continually to perceive links, references, and contexts for the words we read, which come to us already endowed with meanings:

> Meanings come already calculated, not because of norms embedded in language but because language is always perceived, from the very first, within a structure of norms. That structure, however, is not abstract and independent but social; and therefore it is not a single structure with a privileged relationship to the process of communication as it occurs in any situation but a structure that changes when one situation, with its assumed background of practices, purposes, and goals has given way to another.[18]

As Fish argues in "How to Recognize a Poem When You See One," reading is as much an act of constructing as of construing (327). In narratives where both story and narrative grow from a complex network of recurrent themes, densely interwoven thickets of time, and clusters of multiple perspectives, we do not suspend the action of construing/constructing, as Frank insists. What seems more likely is that we are unable to form determinate predictions, as we tend to in our readings of narratives with clear-cut conflicts and tensions calling for tangible resolutions. Instead, our coming to closure on these spatial or exploratory narratives involves our ability to construct models of the narrative structure that assign a place, weight, and significance to the associations and themes we have encountered—an action that recalls my own efforts in reading *Afternoon.*

It can be argued that since the advent of the modern novel readers have been challenged with the task of reading something that approximates the virtual, three-dimensional space of hypertext narratives. From the perspective of a media theorist like Bolter, *Ulysses* can only be reread because James Joyce was wrestling with spatial or "topographic" writing in a unidimensional, static medium (136). The act of perceiving reference, layers in time, multiple perspectives, and many of the devices used by modern and postmodern writers is infinitely simplified in reading interactive narratives, particularly where a narrative provides its readers with access to cognitive maps of the hypertext structure.

When I begin reading *WOE,* I am immediately confronted by a place entitled "Mandala," which opens over a cognitive map of the narrative structure. Significantly, the map itself resembles a mandala, with the place "Mandala" representing the hub of a narrative wheel, connected through a series of paths to five other places that, in turn, contain other, subsidiary places (see map of narrative structure of *WOE*). From "Mandala," however, readers need not pass through the five places on the upper-most layer of the narrative in order to gain access to the levels of narrative within each of these five places: a series of links, paths, and defaults connects "Mandala" with some of the text's most embedded places. In Buddhist practice, the mandala pulls the eye from the center of the image to the periphery or vice versa. In *WOE* (its title is a pun on the acronym of the journal for which the piece was expressly written, *Writing on the Edge*) the map is also a visual pun and a metaphor for a form of writing on the edge: physically, the reading of all places except "Mandala" takes place at the periphery, or on the edge, of the narrative structure. Literally, the narrative itself represents a sort of writing on the margins of experience, an accumulation of the experiences, memories, and metaphors from which fiction grows.

Although my reading of "Mandala" is colored by my awareness of its central place in the *WOE* narrative structure, my knowledge of its placement at the hub of the narrative structure does little to relieve the ambiguities of the text in this place. Here the protagonists are identified solely by the pronouns *he* and *she,* and the pair seem to be driving somewhere, but I cannot be certain even whether their journey is actually a physical one or whether it is simply metaphoric. As I move through the narrative by way of defaults, I encounter more scenes that portray the actions of a "she" and "he." Generally, as I read print narratives, if I lose track of the pronoun referents, I can easily verify them and assign their actions or declarations a meaning relative to my per-

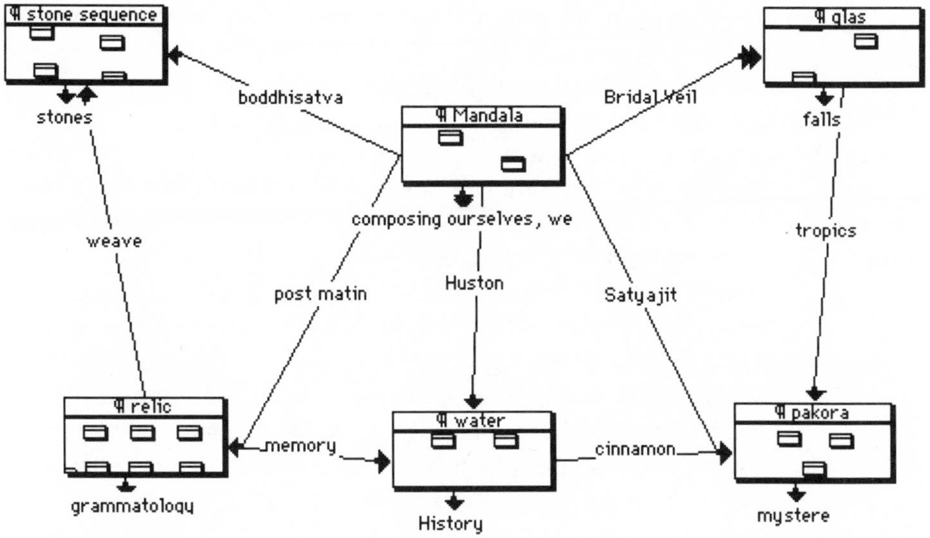

Cognitive map displaying the narrative structure of *WOE*

ception of the developing narrative. But because hypertexts can be read in a number of sequences, and interactive narratives such as *WOE* are clearly written to be read in a variety of orders, I cannot be certain, even if two places follow one another, that the pronoun referents in each are necessarily identical. When I encounter places that display physical continuity—places that are linked in a set sequence—I have no guarantee that the actions or actors depicted in them are the same across all of the places.

In print, I can safely assume that the "she" in *The Good Soldier* is the same Leonora I encountered in the preceding paragraph. In the interactive *WOE,* however, I find myself straining to minimize the indeterminacies that temporarily disrupt my reading of each place. There are four couples involved in the narrative strand entitled "Relic." Each of the places in this strand is easily distinguishable from places situated along other narrative strands by its pronoun title: "She," "They," "He," "It," "Your," "Their," "His," "Her," and "We." In a sense, the titles reflect my chief concern as a reader of these places—to establish just to whom each pronoun refers. Since the narrative of "Relic" involves adulterous liaisons between two married couples—as I discover four places into my reading of *WOE*—my need to establish who each "she" and "he" represents becomes essential to my making sense of the narrative. One couple, married with children, remain unnamed throughout the entire narrative of "Relic," making identification of pronoun referents particularly difficult. The others, however, are named "Filly" and "Steve," enabling me to identify when the "she" mentioned is *not* Filly by references to her made during conversations between the unnamed husband and wife.

When I read the place "Their," for example, I encounter a conversation between a man and a woman and manage to identify the woman as "not Filly," because the man here wonders if the woman wears this perfume because she knows he loves it on Filly. Who, then, is the man? I work back and forth in my reading of this passage, prospecting and retrospecting through the narrative in search of cues to his identity even as I continue reading. The fact that these people have packed the kids off to see the film *Dick Tracy* seems to indicate that they are married, a hypothesis reinforced by the man's shock when the woman tells him she believes that he is thinking of Filly. His reaction (wondering "Do you know?") seems motivated by guilt and I latch on to what we might call an "adultery" schema, familiar to me from my encounters with print and film narratives about married couples and affairs. Accordingly, I form the hypothesis that the man in this place is involved with his wife's friend Filly, although I cannot be certain just how much the wife does or does not know. Since the schema or script for adulterous relationships invariably involves a dialectic between deceit and discovery, however, I perceive the question of the wife's knowledge or ignorance of the affair as one of the tensions in the narrative that drives me to continue reading.

In the place "His" that follows "Their," I discover that the "she" lying in "his" arms is not the same "she" as in "Their," when Steve interrupts their post-coital musings by leaving a message on "his" answering machine. Since Steve is identified as "her husband," I realize that the woman must be Filly, Steve's wife. As no new characters have been introduced into the narrative—and my knowledge of print narrative conventions prompts me to assume that any new characters will be introduced in this narrative—and I know the man is not Steve, I conclude that the "he" here must be the unnamed husband and that what I have just read is a chronicle of an adulterous liaison. The physical juxtaposition of the places "His" and "Their" leads me to assume, as I would in print narratives, that the actors in both places will remain constant, making my shock at the switch in the identity of the woman more potent. Here the physical gaps separating narrative spaces approximate the space of cinematic cuts, making my reaction similar to the experience of a viewer watching two adjoining scenes in a film involving lovers, where in two separate scenes the slow pan of the camera moving up the intertwined bodies of a man and woman reveals two different women's faces topping seemingly identical sets of thighs, hips, and breasts.

As I read on through the narrative of *WOE,* however, the text does not become more determinate, as I had expected, based upon my knowledge of print conventions and believing that my predictions about the discovery/deceit dialectic would enable me to see the text of the places I encountered, as Fish argued, already in a determinate, meaningful context (309). Instead, I find myself seizing upon references and likely connections between smaller elements in the text in order to build a global structure of meaning, or a macrostructure. This process leads me to see a correspondence between an unnamed woman who murders her philandering husband and then kills herself and the relationship of the husband, wife, and best friend—and to use this correspondence to add incrementally to my hypothesis involving the adulterous couple. I modify my sense of the narrative structure of *WOE* and see this correspondence foreshadowing the violence that may ensue once the wife verifies her suspicions concerning the liaison between her husband and Filly. The murders are referred to in "Murders," "The Railroad," and "6/17 Father's Day," in an entirely different narrative strand at a different subsidiary level of the *WOE* narrative, but the connections I make between these places and the places along the "Relic" path bridge the gaps between these spaces easily, as other researchers in the reading of hypertext have discovered:

> Recent extensions of the concept of macrostructure suggest . . . that the macrostructural hierarchy is also "networked": the repetition in a text of a previously mentioned element may form a connection between the two related propositions, even if they are at different branches in the hierarchical macrostructure. . . . The macrostructures which readers build of texts allow them to organize and reduce complex information to a meaningful, manageable whole.[19]

Further, the familiar schema of adulterous liaisons that encouraged me to form certain predictions about the narrative of *WOE* as a macrostructure leads me to filter the information I receive elsewhere in the narrative according to whether it enables me to confirm or modify my hypothesis.

When I encounter a number of places that seem to have no bearing on the "Relic" narrative, I gloss over some of the same indeterminacies that excited my attention in the places "His," "Their," "It," and "We" in "Relic." I cannot find contexts in which to include what I read in those places, and sometimes I am not even certain, as a result of the ambiguous nature of the pronouns and the lack of a clear-cut context for the action within each place, who or what it is that I am reading about. Because my concept of the macrostructure of *WOE* has no context for these places, I simply place their contents in the background as I read. It

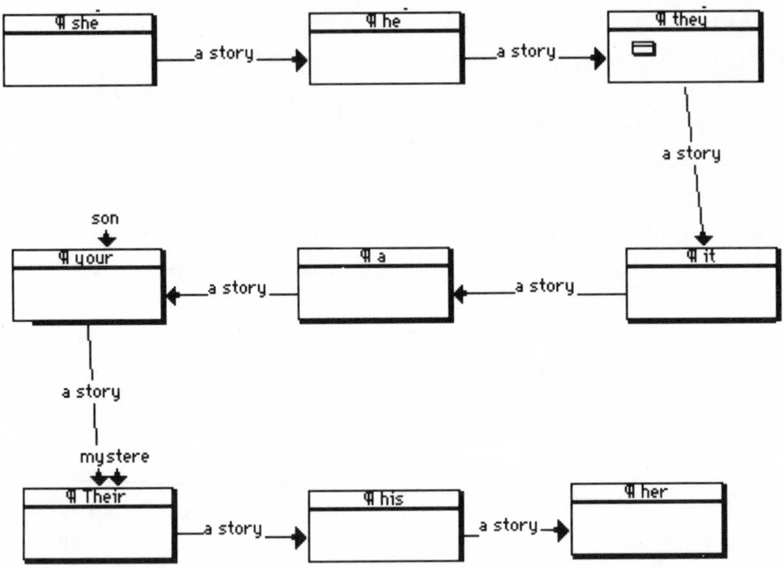

Cognitive map of part of the narrative "Relic" in *WOE*

is only when I grow frustrated at my inability to discover paths or links to more places on the "Relic" strand that I decide to consult the topographic map of *WOE* as a guide to navigation.

What I discover momentarily shocks me: instead of forming the principle narrative axis of *WOE,* with the other narrative strands feeding into and expanding on it, "Relic" is merely one of five places on the periphery of *WOE.* Although I had noticed the mandala-like shape of the narrative upon first opening the document to its topographic map, I had then lacked any context to make this particular bit of information meaningful to me, relevant to my reading the narrative. Now, however, my very purposive search obliges me to see in the structure of *WOE* a definitive negation of my suppositions about the text—particularly when I locate "Relic" as one of the five marginal places and peer at its structure within the confining space (see map of part of "Relic").

The words "a happy ending" close the text of the place "We," but when I first encounter them, I read the phrase as irony and attribute the words to the unidentified narrator, whom I believe to be the child of the unnamed married couple—a boy named Liam—since his is the only name excluded from the family list, which ends with "me." This clearly must be a child's eye view of the relationships shared by his parents and their friends, and, consequently, I perceive the inclusion of "a happy ending" in this place as an ironic counterpart to the problematic couplings I encountered elsewhere in "Relic."

Far from seeming an ending, these words originally appear to me as a narrative device employed strictly to heighten tension, to create a sense of suspenseful anticipation of the next developments in the "Relic" narrative. But my encounter with the topographic map reveals the "Relic" strand to be limited to the places I have already visited and, moreover, to end with the path also entitled "happy ending" that leads only to "We." The phrase, "a happy ending," it seems, truly does indicate a happy ending and nothing more. It seems that I have created the narrative tension myself in my reading, to prove or negate the hypothesis I have formed about "Relic" and *WOE* as a whole.

When I dip into the narrative of *WOE* again, I find myself still accumulating references to the characters first introduced in "Relic," who appear in different contexts. With their strongly sequential and causal links, narratives such as "Relic" act as a centrifugal force in a textual mosaic such as *WOE,* prompting me to read the other, disparate places in the narrative in light of their references to and consonances with the characters and events in "Relic." As I continue reading, I begin to rearrange my sense of *WOE* as a macrostructure and begin to see the references to a "doubled family," and the wife who murdered her husband and then killed herself as something other than portents of things yet to unfold in "Relic." This family tragedy seems to me to represent an echo from Joyce's own past, represented throughout *WOE* in the form of journal entries, a past that mirrors the unhappiness of the family in "Relic." Earlier, my reading incorporated the places "Murders," "The Railroad," and "Directions?" into a sequence that somewhat mirrored the tensions between the husband and wife in "Relic," and served as a device to heighten the suspense inherent in that narrative's dialectic of discovery/deceit. But, because the topographic map of *WOE* has negated this hypothesis, I am obliged to read these places differently. Accordingly, I form the hypothesis that Joyce's own past gave rise to his writing "Relic"—a hypothesis that thus accounts for the presence of the fragments of diaries and metatextual commentary on the act of writing *WOE* that Joyce includes elsewhere in the narrative.

Eventually, I evolve a sense of the narrative as an amalgam of fragments of experience gleaned from Joyce's own past in diary-like, dated extracts or places titled with numbers, snippets of news items and poetry, and metatextual commentary on the act of creating *WOE* itself—each representing one of the places ringing "Mandala." This revised sense of the narrative structure of *WOE* grows slowly as I create a network of references and connections between places—much as do readers engaging modernist narratives—reinforced by careful explorations of the topographic map of *WOE*. I arrive at a sense of the narrative as a complete structure long before I resolve any of the ambiguities I encounter in the text, without having ascertained anything approaching an answer to my many questions about the narrative and the events it describes. (Who, for example, is "M"? Did the murders really take place? What is the significance of the paths in the "Glas" strand that are named after directors: "Huston," "Ray," "Satyajit"?)

I feel a sense of having completed my reading of the work, of having arrived at a reading that encompasses the text, its narrative structure, and at least some of its imagery and thematic references and plausibly accounts for a majority of its places. This sense of closure is, perhaps, akin to that which enables us to distinguish a sense of an ending in our readings of *Ulysses* or *Finnegans Wake,* that approaches a sense of having arrived at one plausible reading of the narrative without having exhausted the many other readings of the narrative still possible. But I find my reading enabled less by my knowledge of the structure of *WOE* and its narrative contents than by my knowledge of schemata for other narratives that are also "about" their own narrative structure. In this instance, I rely on previous encounters with texts such as John Barth's "Lost in the Funhouse," in which the Funhouse was both a physical place visited by Ambrose, the protagonist, and a metaphor for the structure of the story—and of fiction itself. I also recall that when I first read "Lost in the Funhouse," in an undergraduate writing course to which I came already equipped with three years of studying modern and postmodern narratives, I was, not coincidentally, the only student in the class able to read the Funhouse as a metaphor for the experience of navigating through a fictional narrative, a reflection of the powerful role of schemata in enabling and shaping our readings of narratives.

In reading *WOE,* however, I also recognize deviations from the schema of narrative-as-structure, informed by my awareness of three conditions. First, my version of *WOE* could not reconcile all of the disparate texts I encountered under a single rubric, a single signifying metaphor which bestowed significance on each. The concept of *WOE* as a narrative about the production of coherent, tidy narratives from the inconclusive, fragmentary flotsam of everyday life could not also encompass, for example, the places along the paths named for directors. Second, my reading of the indeterminacies in *WOE* relied heavily upon the context in which I encountered each place. Since the sixty narrative places are connected by 221 links, the order in which I navigated through my reading of *WOE* was only one actualization among many possibilities. Finally, the schema that provided a script for my perceiving the disparate texts in *WOE* as part of a single, organic whole was reinforced by a schema not usually applicable to narratives—at least not to print narratives—that of the open work. As Umberto Eco points out:

> Multi-value logics are now gaining currency, and these are quite capable of incorporating *indeterminacy* as a valid stepping-stone in the cognitive process. In this general intellectual atmosphere, the poetics of the open work is peculiarly relevant: it posits the work of art stripped of necessary and foreseeable conclusions, works in which the performer's freedom functions as part of the discontinuity. . . . Every performance *explains* the composition but does not *exhaust* it. Every performance makes the work an actuality, but is itself only complementary to all possible other performances of the work. In short, we can say that every performance offers us a complete and satisfying version of the work, but at the same time makes it incomplete for us, because it cannot simultaneously give all the other artistic solutions which the work may admit.[20]

Inspired by the appearance of what he perceived to be a notable shift in aesthetics across an entire spectrum of art, informing the works of artists from Jean Dubuffet and Pierre Boulez to James Joyce, Umberto Eco in *Opera Aperta* (*The Open Work*) explores the radical differences in the aesthetics informing traditional and modern art.

Like the interactive narratives *Forking Paths, Afternoon,* and *WOE,* the works of modernists such as Henri Posseur, Alexander Calder, and Mallarmé leave their sequence or arrangement either to chance or to their audiences, providing them with a multiplicity of possible versions in which they can be experienced. Where traditional works appear to possess singular, determinate meanings, these modern "works in motion" seem consciously constructed to provide their audiences with "a field of possibilities . . . a configuration of possible events, a complete dynamism of structure . . . and a corresponding devolution of intellectual authority to personal decision, choice, and social context" (*Open Work,* 15–16). My version of the structure of *WOE* as a network of snippets of personal history, a chronicle of creation, and invented narrative is thus both reinforced and modified by my knowledge of Eco's aesthetics of the open work. On the one hand, my awareness of this aesthetic prompts me to see *WOE* as the paradigm of the open work, one which can embrace divisions normally insuperable in print narratives: commentary on the act of creation, the mechanics of production, the convergence of voices, past and present, the snatches of experience that become the grain that irritates, the core that we pearl over to become the stuff of fiction. *The Open Work,* however, also provides me with a schema for recognizing the discontinuities in *WOE* as endemic to the open work, its indeterminacies the source of the narrative's rich field of possibilities. I have, in a sense, a meta-script which also enables me to be comfortable with the very inconclusiveness of my reading, with its inability to account for everything I have discovered in *WOE.*

Reading for the Ending: Closure in Print and Interactive Narratives

Even though in interactive narratives, we as readers never encounter anything quite so definitive as the words "The End," or the last page of a story or novel, our experience of the text is not only guided but enabled by our sense of the "ending" awaiting us. We truly do read, as Brooks argues, in "anticipation of retrospection" (23). Our predictions enable us to minimize ambiguities, as Smith has argued (61), and to perceive words in an already largely determinate context, as Fish observes in "Is There a Text in This Class?" (318)—even when we read with an awareness of the possibility that these words can and may crop up in an entirely different context or contexts. The anticipation of endings is, in this sense, integral to the act of reading, even when there is no such thing as a physical "ending." Ultimately, we cannot separate the desire for an ending—which might resemble either the longing described by Conrad or the "sanction" seen by Benjamin in the epigraphs beginning this article—with our need to create contexts for the perception of what we encounter as we read in the immediate sense by anticipating what may follow in the future. When we read, prediction enables us to create contexts for the words and phrases we encounter that guide our interpretation of their meaning in an action that appears to unfold simultaneously rather than in discrete stages in time.

So when we navigate through interactive narratives, we are pursuing the same sorts of goals we do as readers of print narratives—even when we know that the text will not bestow upon us the final sanction of a singular ending that either authorizes or invalidates our interpretations of the text. Because our sense of an ending does not derive explicitly from the text itself in the case of hypertexts such as *Afternoon* and *WOE,* reading these interactive narratives sheds light on what—other than the physical ending of a story—satisfies our need for endings or closure. We rely on a sense of the text as a physical entity in reading both interactive and print narratives, on a sense of having finished reading all of the book's pages or having visited most of a narrative's places, of having grasped the spatial form of *Mrs Dalloway* or *The Good Soldier,* of having arrived at a space which does not default in *Afternoon,* or of having incorporated the contents of the periphery with the hub in *WOE*. Our sense of arriving at closure is satisfied when we manage to resolve narrative tensions and to minimize ambiguities, to explain puzzles, and to incorporate as many of the narrative elements as possible into a coherent pattern—preferably one for which we have a script gleaned from either life experience or encounters with other narratives. Unlike most print narratives, however, interactive narratives invite us to return to them again and again, their openness and indeterminacy making our sense of closure inevitably simply one "ending" among many. It is often impossible to distinguish between explaining a work and exhausting its possibilities in the sense of an ending we experience when we finish reading *The Good Soldier*. My readings of *Afternoon* and *WOE,* however, explain the versions of the texts I have experienced without exhausting the number of other versions and explanations I might experience on other readings. If we as readers truly do long for a sense of an ending as we might for loaves and fishes, it is not necessarily the definitive, death-like ending foreseen by Benjamin—it seems that merely a plausible version or versions of the story among many will suffice equally well.

NOTES

1. Peter Brooks, *Reading for the Plot: Design and Intention in Narrative* (New York: Vintage, 1985), 20.

2. For a full-fledged discussion of this issue, see Stuart Moulthrop's "Reading from the Map: Metonymy and Metaphor in the Fiction of Forking Paths," in *Hypermedia and Literary Studies*, ed. Paul Delany and George P. Landow (Cambridge: MIT Press, 1991), 119–32, and my "Gaps, Maps, and Perception: What Hypertext Narratives (Don't) Do," *Perforations* 3.1 (Spring/Summer 1992).

3. Aristotle, *Poetics,* trans. S. H. Butcher, in *Aristotle's Theory of Poetry and Fine Art,* 4th ed. (New York: Dover, 1955), 52.

4. Frank Kermode, *The Sense of an Ending: Studies in the Theory of Narrative Fiction* (New York: Oxford University Press, 1966), 17.

5. Frank Smith, *Understanding Reading: A Psycholinguistic Analysis of Reading and Learning to Read,* 3rd ed. (New York: Holt, Rinehart and Winston, 1982), 77.

6. See, for example, Tom Trabasso, Tom Vecco, and Paul Van Den Broek, "Causal Cohesion and Story Coherence," in *Learning and Comprehension of Text,* ed. Heinz Mandl, Nancy L. Stein, and Tom Trabasso (Hillsdale, N.J.: Lawrence Erlbaum, 1984), 87.

7. Barbara Herrnstein-Smith, *Poetic Closure: A Study of How Poems End* (Chicago: University of Chicago Press, 1987), 30.

8. J. David Bolter, *Writing Space: The Computer, Hypertext and the History of Writing* (Hillsdale, N.J.: Lawrence Erlbaum, 1991), 144.

9. Richard Ziegfeld, "Interactive Fiction: A New Literary Genre?" *New Literary History* 20 (1989): 363.

10. Personal communication with author, October 1991.

11. Michael Joyce, *Afternoon: a story* (Cambridge, Mass.: Eastgate Systems, 1990), "white afternoon."

12. Arguments for the primacy of causality, plausibility and referentiality in readers' comprehensions of texts are noted, for example, in Alison Black, Paul Freeman, and P. N. Johnson-Laird, "Plausibility and the Comprehension of Text," *British Journal of Psychology* 77 (1986): 51–62, and in John Black and Gordon H. Bower, "Episodes as Chunks in Narrative Memory," *Journal of Verbal Learning and Verbal Behavior* 18 (1979): 309–18.

13. Mark Bernstein, personal communication with author, November 1991; Michael Joyce, personal communication with author, October 1991.

14. Joseph Frank, "Spatial Form in Modern Literature," *Sewanee Review* 53 (1945): 221–40, 433–56, 643–53.

15. David Mickelson, "Types of Spatial Structure in Narrative," in *Spatial Form in Narrative,* ed. Jeffrey R. Smitten and Ann Daghistany (Ithaca: Cornell University Press, 1981), 74.

16. Joseph Kestner, "The Novel and the Spatial Arts," in *Spatial Form in Narrative,* 128.

17. Ivo Vidan, "Time Sequence in Spatial Fiction," in *Spatial Form in Narrative,* 133.

18. Stanley Fish, *Is There a Text in This Class? The Authority of Interpretive Communities* (Cambridge: Harvard University Press, 1980), 318.

19. Johndan Johnson-Eilola, "'Trying to See the Garden': Interdisciplinary Perspectives on Hypertext Use in Composition Instruction." *Writing on the Edge* 2.2 (Spring 1989): 104–5.

20. Umberto Eco, *The Open Work,* trans. Anna Cancogni (Cambridge: Harvard University Press, 1989), 15.

BIBLIOGRAPHY

Aristotle. *Poetics*. Trans. S. H. Butcher. *Aristotle's Theory of Poetry and Fine Art*. 4th ed. New York: Dover, 1955.

Barth, John. "Lost in the Funhouse." *Lost in the Funhouse: Fiction for Print, Tape, Live Voice*. Garden City, N.Y.: Doubleday, 1968.

Benjamin, Walter. "The Storyteller." *Illuminations*. Trans. Harry Zohn, ed. Hannah Arendt. New York: Schocken Books, 1969.

Black, Alison, Paul Freeman, and P. N. Johnson-Laird. "Plausibility and the Comprehension of Text." *British Journal of Psychology* 77 (1986): 51–62.

Black, John, and Gordon H. Bower. "Episodes as Chunks in Narrative Memory." *Journal of Verbal Learning and Verbal Behavior* 18 (1979): 309–18.

Bolter, J. David. *Writing Space: The Computer, Hypertext, and the History of Writing*. Hillsdale, N.J.: Lawrence Erlbaum, 1991.

Borges, Jorge Luis. "The Garden of Forking Paths." *Ficciones*. Trans. Anthony Kerrigan. London: John Calder, 1985.

Brooks, Peter. *Reading for the Plot: Design and Intention in Narrative*. New York: Vintage, 1985.

Coover, Robert. *Pricksongs and Descants*. New York: Plume, 1969.

Cortàzar, Julio. *Hopscotch*. Trans. Gregory Rabassa. New York: Random House, 1966.

Davis, R., and G. de Jong. "Prediction and Substantiation: Two Processes that Comprise Understanding." *Proceedings of the International Joint Conference on Artificial Intelligence* 5 (1979): 217–22.

Douglas, J. Yellowlees. "Gaps, Maps, and Perceptions: What Hypertext Narratives (Don't) Do," *Perforations* 3.1 (Spring/Summer 1992).

Eco, Umberto. *The Open Work*. Trans. Anna Cancogni. Cambridge: Harvard University Press, 1989.

Fish, Stanley. *Is There a Text in This Class? The Authority of Interpretive Communities*. Cambridge: Harvard University Press, 1980.

Ford, Ford Madox. *The Good Soldier: A Tale of Passion*. Oxford: Oxford University Press, 1990.

Fowles, John. *The French Lieutenant's Woman*. New York: Signet, 1969.

Frank, Joseph. "Spatial Form in Modern Literature." *Sewanee Review* 53 (1945): 221–40, 433–56, 643–53.

Garnham, Alan, Jane Oakhill, and P. N. Johnson-Laird. "Referential Continuity and the Coherence of Discourse." *Cognition* 11 (1982): 29–46.

Herrnstein-Smith, Barbara. *Poetic Closure: A Study of How Poems End*. Chicago: University of Chicago Press, 1987.

Johnson-Eilola, Johndan. "'Trying to See the Garden': Interdisciplinary Perspectives on Hypertext Use in Composition Instruction." *Writing on the Edge* 2.2 (Spring 1989): 92–111.

Joyce, Michael. *Afternoon: a story*. Cambridge, Mass.: Eastgate Systems, 1990.

———. *WOE—Or a Memory of What Will Be*. *Writing on the Edge* 2.2 (Spring 1991).

Kermode, Frank. *The Sense of an Ending: Studies in the Theory of Narrative Fiction*. New York: Oxford University Press, 1966.

Kestner, Joseph. "The Novel and the Spatial Arts." In *Spatial Form in Narrative*. Ed. Jeffrey R. Smitten and Ann Daghistany. Ithaca: Cornell University Press, 1981.

Mickelsen, David. "Types of Spatial Structure in Narrative." In *Spatial Form in Narrative*. Ed. Jeffrey R. Smitten and Ann Daghistany. Ithaca: Cornell University Press, 1981.

Mitchell, W. J. T., ed. *On Narrative*. Chicago: University of Chicago Press, 1981.

———. "Spatial Form in Literature: Toward a General Theory." *The Language of Images*. Ed. W. J. T. Mitchell. Chicago: University of Chicago Press, 1980.

Moulthrop, Stuart. "Containing the Multitudes: The Problem of Closure in Interactive Fiction." *Association for Computers in the Humanities Newsletter* 10 (Summer 1988): 29–46.

———. *Forking Paths: An Interaction after Jorge Luis Borges*. Unpublished hypertext, 1986.

———. "Reading from the Map: Metonymy and Metaphor in the Fiction of Forking Paths." In *Hypermedia and Literary Studies*. Ed. Paul Delany and George P. Landow. Cambridge: MIT Press, 1991.

———. *Victory Garden*. Cambridge, Mass.: Eastgate Systems, 1991.

Orasanu, Judith, ed. *Reading Comprehension: From Research to Practice*. Hillsdale, N.J.: Lawrence Erlbaum, 1986.

Plato. "Phaedrus." *Phaedrus*. Trans. Walter Hamilton. London: Penguin, 1973.

Pynchon, Thomas. *The Crying of Lot 49*. London: Picador, 1979.

Rimmon-Kenan, Shlomith. *Narrative Fiction: Contemporary Poetics*. New York: Methuen, 1983.

Robbe-Grillet, Alain. *In the Labyrinth*. Trans. Christine Brooke-Rose. London: John Calder, 1980.

Schank, Roger C., and Robert P. Abelson. *Scripts, Plans, Goals, and Understanding: An Inquiry into Human Knowledge Structures*. Hillsdale, N.J.: Lawrence Erlbaum, 1977.

Smith, Frank. *Understanding Reading: A Psycholinguistic Analysis of Reading and Learning to Read*. 3rd ed. New York: Holt, Rinehart and Winston, 1982.

Smitten, Jeffrey R., and Ann Daghistany, eds. *Spatial Form in Narrative,* Ithaca: Cornell University Press, 1981.

Spiro, Rand J., Bertram C. Bruce, and William F. Brewer, eds. *Theoretical Issues in Reading Comprehension: Perspectives from Cognitive Psychology, Linguistics, Artificial Intelligence, and Education*. Hillsdale, N.J.: Lawrence Erlbaum, 1980.

Trabasso, Tom, Tom Secco, and Paul Van Den Broek. "Causal Cohesion and Story Coherence." *Learning and Comprehension of Text*. Ed. Heinz Mandl, Nancy L. Stein, and Tom Trabasso. Hillsdale, N.J.: Lawrence Erlbaum, 1984.

van Dijk, Teun. *Macrostructures: An Interdisciplinary Study of Global Structures in Discourse, Interaction, and Cognition*. Hillsdale, N.J.: Lawrence Erlbaum, 1980.

Vidan, Ivo. "Time Sequence in Spatial Fiction." In *Spatial Form in Narrative*. Ed. Jeffrey R. Smitten and Ann Daghistany. Ithaca: Cornell University Press, 1981.

Waugh, Patricia. *Metafiction: The Theory and Practice of Self-Conscious Fiction*. London: Methuen, 1984.

Woolf, Virginia. *Mrs Dalloway*. 1925. London: Grafton, 1976.

Ziegfeld, Richard. "Interactive Fiction: A New Literary Genre?" *New Literary History* 20 (1989): 340–73.

Conclusions

Terence Harpold

6

In Conclusion (1)

"I want to say," says a character named Peter, somewhere in the course of Michael Joyce's hypertext fiction, *Afternoon, a story,* "I want to say I may have seen my son die this morning."[1] The problem is, he isn't sure; he doesn't want to be sure; he can't be sure. Like many hypertexts, *Afternoon* seems to begin *in medias res,* sometime after a pivotal encounter. On his way to work, Peter has witnessed a fatal automobile accident that might have involved his former wife and their son. But the apparent false start is a trick of the genre: *Afternoon* is a hypertext, bound to a different paradigm of narrative closure than the epic mode from which it borrows the cast of its opening lines.[2] Starting in the middle of a hypertext does not mean that there is an earlier beginning to which you will be able to return, even if making sense of everything else in the narrative depends upon it. The 539 lexias[3] in *Afternoon* include no description of the accident or of Peter's reaction as he drives by it. We have only his troubled memory of the scene that might have been and the complex trajectory of his efforts to discover—or avoid—what it is that he has seen, what it is that he remembers. When he returns to the site of the accident sometime later (when, exactly, is not clear, as the "before" and "after" of the moment are entangled by his inability to recall now what it was that he saw then), there are only the skid marks of a crashing car, the cigarette butts and footprints left by onlookers, and a shifting pile of newspapers, candy wrappers, and children's homework.

> Most of the papers are old and waterstained, dried by the sun into yellowing things. There is a fresh white paper with my son's name upon it, and red markings from a teacher. It is a report on Louis Quattorze [*sic*], and his looping handwriting makes me weep. It begins: "I am the Sun King," said Louis the Fourteenth of France. (*Afternoon,* "Fenceline")

The school report might be evidence that Peter's son was in the accident, or it might simply have been dropped, with the other flotsam and jetsam trailed by his classmates as they walked along the road on their journey home. You can work your way through *Afternoon* a half-dozen times without learning any more. There *is* more than this to say about the accident (we will return to this scene of failed memory), but the thing that impresses you on the second or third reading of *Afternoon* is that coming to a conclusion about what might have happened, while still appearing to be *possible,* seems as unlikely as it did on the first reading. What you make of what you read is confined to the interval in Peter's recollection that divides his account of what he has seen from his desire to make it actual, present, *real.* You have only scraps of paper, the traces of departed observers, the evidence of lexias reviewed repeatedly, the familiar shapes of darkened pixels against the blank field of the screen, suggesting with each recurrence that there is something more to be said. You could spend a long time deciphering the looping traces of this misremembered history.

Saying this, I concede, is not saying much more than that *Afternoon* is a narrative, albeit a very fragmentary and unruly one (at least by the standards of printed texts), and narratives are always things that are *told,* after the fact. We can only conjecture the existence of things before they were folded into the shroud of language: speech divides us from its objects, even as it makes them known to us. Saying that our readings of *Afternoon* are divided in this way is saying that it thus resembles other artifacts of language, diverted from their objective (the re-presentation of the thing so spoken) by the insufficiencies of the instrument (language) used to attain that goal—though this disjunction between the thing and the sign will be constituted or sustained differently within different species of discourse. *Afternoon* is a *digital* narrative and thus disposed to formulate this missed encounter in ways that would be impossible or unlikely in printed texts.

Afternoon was published as a Readingspace, a read-only format for Storyspace, the hypertext application in which the text was composed.[4] A Readingspace hypertext displays one lexia on the screen at a time, in a single, fixed window. The user switches between lexias by clicking on icons in a "toolbar" that floats over the window, or by double-clicking on words within a lexia or typing the same words in a text entry field, or by pressing the Return key. There are four buttons on the toolbar: a left arrow, which takes you to the previously viewed lexia; a "Browse" button, resembling a book, that opens a dialogue listing available "paths" (collections of links with shared labels) from the current lexia; and "Y" (yes) and "N" (no) buttons. The

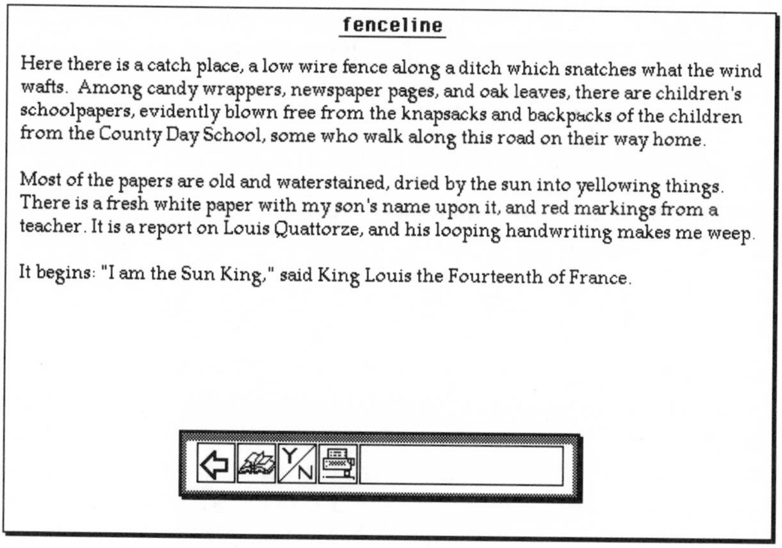

fenceline
Here there is a catch place, a low wire fence along a ditch which snatches what the wind wafts. Among candy wrappers, newspaper pages, and oak leaves, there are children's schoolpapers, evidently blown free from the knapsacks and backpacks of the children from the County Day School, some who walk along this road on their way home.
Most of the papers are old and waterstained, dried by the sun into yellowing things. There is a fresh white paper with my son's name upon it, and red markings from a teacher. It is a report on Louis Quattorze, and his looping handwriting makes me weep.
It begins: "I am the Sun King," said King Louis the Fourteenth of France.
Y
N

The "Fenceline" lexia from Michael Joyce's *Afternoon, a story*

Y and N buttons are used to respond to questions ("Do you want to hear about it?" asks the first lexia of the text, called "Begin") or to change the current lexia, though no indication is given of where one or the other response will lead. Pressing the Return key is the same as clicking on the Y button. The list of paths displayed by clicking on the Browse button is less informative than it might at first appear, as only the names of paths and the lexias they connect are listed. These are often cryptic or repetitive and seldom suggest much about the content of the target lexia.[5] Words within lexias that lead to other lexias (Joyce calls them "words that yield") are not identified by any distinguishing style or symbol.[6] There may be more than one such word in a lexia, and different yield words in the same lexia sometimes lead to only one target lexia. In some cases, where a yield word leads depends on the sequence of lexias that have previously been visited. The text makes heavy use of Storyspace's "guard" function, which places hidden restrictions on the reader's movements, making it impossible to visit some lexias until a specified sequence of other lexias has been followed. J. Yellowlees Douglas has calculated that *Afternoon*'s use of guards makes it unlikely that most readers will, in only one or two readings, visit more than 10 percent of the lexias in the text ("Print Pathways," ch. 3).

Superficially, *Afternoon* resembles the sword-and-sorcery, gumshoe detective, Star Trekking recreations that have heretofore dominated the field of interactive gaming.[7] What distinguishes Joyce's novel from that crowd is its sly resistance to readers' efforts to draw inferences from what they have read before. As Stuart Moulthrop observes, the suppleness of the yield mechanism makes all the difference:

> With this system in operation, *Afternoon* resembles an automated railway in which the points keep switching of their own accord. Since the story is heavily recursive, readers may find themselves frequently returning to the same textual locales; but a yield word that took them from "son" to "Sun King" on the first iteration may now lead somewhere else entirely. The text can seem to have a mind of its own and readers may easily feel lost within its shifting circuitry—an outcome consistent with the nondeterminist principles of the text.[8]

Reading the text, you move between episodes along paths that are not always marked. You make decisions, you choose directions and form conclusions, finding the next time through that they may lead you somewhere else; you may, very nearly, read differently every time you open the document. The cunning of a text like *Afternoon* lies in the limit of that "very nearly": each reading *cannot* be unique—the 539 lexias and the 950-odd links define a finite domain—except in a "citable" or "iterable" sense (to invoke Derrida's use of those terms) that has less to do with singularity than with a loss of originality.[9] Very nearly: it is possible to saturate the field of readings, at least in a serviceable, quotidian sense; and so you may repeat a reading, hoping to find the path between lexias that will close a question left open by a prior reading. But the possibilities need not be endless to be exhausting; your patience or your curiosity may not be a match for the text's erratic calculus, and the principle of contingent repeatability is sufficient in and of itself to block some conclusions. Douglas has, for example, identified four independent constellations of lexias in *Afternoon*; it is possible to read the fiction from within each of these constellations and not be aware of the position or significance of a given lexia in the other constellations ("Print Pathways," ch. 5). Moulthrop's *Victory Garden* includes nearly a thousand lexias and two thousand eight hundred links; it is possible to follow paths in that fiction for dozens of lexias, to independent closures, without coming across evidence that the text supports completely different paths joining the same lexias.[10] That you might *not* discover what you are looking for means that familiar strategies of discovery may always prove unreliable, and you might have to try again. "*Afternoon* is a 'mystery,'" says Moulthrop, "only in the older sense of that word, the sense of ritual or hieratic procedure" ("Hypertext and the 'Hyperreal,'" 262).

In other words, in a text like *Afternoon* it is possible only to arrive at a *contingent* conclusion. Any ending will be marked by the punctuality of interruption. (Thus the purest paradigm of a hypertext ending: you can just stop reading, decide that you've had enough, get up from the computer, and walk away.) But you cannot come to a definitive ending *within the docuverse.* "Closure is, as in any fiction, a suspect quality," says an unnamed voice in a lexia of *Afternoon* entitled "Work in Progress,"

> although here it is made manifest. When the story no longer progresses, or when it cycles, or when you tire of the paths, the experience of reading it ends. Even so, there are likely to be more opportunities than you think there are at first. A word which doesn't yield the first time you read a section may take you elsewhere if you choose it when you encounter the section again; and sometimes what seems a loop, like memory, heads off again in another direction.

The excess of possible trajectories means that you cannot quite be sure of where you are going, just as you may never be sure of where you have been. Readings of hypertexts are thus always subject to misadventure: the possibility that you might end up at a different destination from the one you intended overdetermines every turn you take. The presumed directionality of a link—instrument, signpost, and phylactery of the reading-as-navigation model that has dominated hypertext design and scholarship—is always supplemented by the link's potential for misdirection; the chance encounters of reading always may redefine the route you thought you were following. Which means (as I argue in "Contingencies," 136–37) that you have to take your chances. Taking them may mean making something of the accidents of reading. The reading of a hypertext (any kind of text) is guided by a will to make sense of the text, no matter what confusing or contradictory turn it may appear to take. In other words, it is guided by a determination to make all the chance encounters of the reading meaningful. Reading, then, relies on a duplicitous faith in the principle of chance, because chance is always assumed to be meaningful, which is the same thing as assuming that there is no real chance.

We measure the meaningful turns of a reading against a kind of superstitious limit-case: while it is *possible* (this equivocal faith in the absolutism of context proposes) that every element in the manifold within which a reading is situated may influence its course and resolution, some traits of the manifold—and, by consequence, *some* accidents of the reading—are more significant, more meaningful, than others. That some traits are favored over others no less significant on their own terms, this line of reasoning continues, is a matter for ideological or biographical inquiry, but not a challenge to the notion that, at a given moment or within a given critical or disciplinary context, a selected constellation of traits carries the day. The interesting flaw of this limited faith in context (one might argue that it constitutes the repressed kernel sustaining the concept of context) is not that a particular alternative constellation of meaningful traits (meaningful conclusions) may be constructed, *but that the general possibility of an alternative is always operative.*[11] This is not to suggest that there is no relation of causality, no instance of connectedness in reading a hypertext that could undo the effects of what we are accustomed to calling "chance," but rather that there is a principle of indeterminability (a generalized "chance") operating between the gaps in the reading that may sometimes turn you back on your path. The link *may not* join the threads you would navigate. It may not, in the end, get you to where (you thought) you were going.

Our equivocal faith in the limits of chance is supported by the insistence of the interface (it is the reason for, the Reason of, the interface) that the terrain we are covering can be mapped, can be modeled by the software or hardware and reformulated as a repeatable scenario, replayed each time in our memories of where we have been. Hypertexts are, as Jakob Nielsen has observed, "belief networks": if two lexias are linked, then we believe that they are related in some way.[12] Our readings are founded on an implicit guarantee that our engagement with the text will lead to an end, a resolution that repeats and informs the beginning, the place where we came in: a memorable conclusion. Navigation in a hypertext is, in other words, sustained by the promise of the end of a dialogue—the dialogue imagined to take place between the hypertext's author(s) and its reader(s), the dialogue among its lexias (Harpold, "Grotesque Corpus"), and, in a third case that unites characteristics of the other two, the dialogue between the reader as a *subject* of language and the hypertext as an *artifact* of language, to which the reader is subordinated (subjected) the moment she elects to enter it. Like readings of other kinds of texts, readings of hypertexts will always be sustained by a pledge of meaningful resolution that appears to be anchored in the artifact (in its reference) or in its commerce (the conversation between author and reader). Both cases are versions of the same structure: the founding of a promise of revelation in a scene of exchange between the reading subject and an Other who possesses an object guaranteeing the value and consistency of the exchange. This is the contractual obligation presupposed by (digital) narrative: a question from the reader is directed to the scene of an encounter, now missed. That inquiry is, *even before it is made,* presumed to be answerable by a voice from within that scene, one that will fulfill the dream of a convergence of the text's substance and signification. Reading is thus sustained by the relation Paul de Man identifies in the rhetorical figure of *prosopopoeia:* speech directed *to* the grave will elicit speech *from* the grave, a conversation with the absent interlocutor, the voice of one who exists only in the memory of his voice.[13] Moving onward, we have faith that we will return to a conclusion, guided by the voice of one who remembers where we have been and where we are going. And, by recognizing ourselves as the potential addressees of the reply from the absent Other who would spell out the text's truth, we seal our subordination to the Other's demand that we engage it in the conversation upon which its authority rests. The question "Do you want to hear about it?" will always elicit a response; whether we elect to answer yes or no, we must recognize the Other's authority in the first place to demand that we respond. In *Afternoon,* choosing "yes" to the first query takes us to a lexia entitled "Yes"; choosing "no" takes us to one entitled "No." Neither choice frees us from the burden of deciding what to do next or from the consequences of our enforced response.[14]

In any case, we have to come to a conclusion, even though the text's possible productivity, its memory of events that might have happened or might yet occur, will not be exhausted by our decision to get out.

> In my mind, the story, as it has formed, takes on margins. Each margin will yield to the impatient, or wary reader. You can answer yes at the beginning and page through on a wave of Returns, or page through directly—again using Returns—without that first interaction.
>
> There are not versions, but the story itself in long lines. Otherwise, however, the center is all—Thoreau or Brer Rabbit, each preferred the bramble. I've discovered more there too, and the real interaction, if that is possible, is in the pursuit of texture. (Joyce, *Afternoon,* "In my mind")

The conclusions of hypertext narrative—the ends we are coming to—are eccentric and recursive. Striking the Return key to move forward also returns us to a longer, albeit irregular path, back to an earlier encounter.

Going No-place

One of the most conspicuous traits of hypertextual form is founded on the absence of a class of structures that are common in other kinds of texts. Hypertexts lack cues marking clear divisions between the "primary" text and what Gérard Genette has called the "paratextual": the footnote, the chapter title, the marginal scribble—the array of printed matter on the periphery of the book.[15] In a hypertext these elements are perceptually as "close" to the trajectory of a reading as any element within the reading's "primary" path, and the same may be said of linked lexias from "other" documents, outside a text's formal limits. (That it is necessary when speaking of hypertexts to set off these words with quotation marks is evidence that the categories they presuppose are already liable to a deconstructive turn: adjectives of textual proximity and alterity in digital texts should always be read under erasure.) Most hypertext applications allow one to open multiple windows on different sections of a document, or on different documents. Though typically only one window reacts to the keyboard or mouse at any one time, all or part of every window is visible at the same time.[16] Moreover, most hypertexts use a browser or a similar navigational tool to display document structure in an outline, "overview," or *map* format; one can use the browser to switch between lexias that otherwise lack common navigational links or cues. The increased flexibility and transparency of movement within hypertexts, in comparison to printed texts, introduces a qualitative as well as quantitative change in the perceptual plane of reading: interrupting a sequence of lexias with the click of a mouse or the press of a key does not *feel* the same as flipping to the table of contents or to the back of a volume to find a note or check an index entry. The immediacy of the transition erases the sensation that you have moved between blocks of text that would on paper be inches, pages, or shelves apart, as opposed to, say, only a paragraph or a turned page away. The possibility in many hypertexts of interactive shuffling of lexias within a narrative forces you to change another expectation learned from printed texts: the order of the lexias (which in a hypertext may be subject to unpredictable variety) is no longer a reliable indicator of hierarchies of argument or plot development.

In a hypertext, the distinctions between textual registers collapse into a single measure—the pause between lexias, which is more a function of software design or microprocessor speed than of the "distance" between destinations. To be more precise, the spatial field dividing the textual from the paratextual—concrete in the printed volume, figural in the digital volume (though perhaps no less inevitably a component of how we conceptualize the form of these texts)—is contaminated by, subordinated to, the detour's temporality.[17] The pause may be measured by ever-smaller fractions of a microsecond, but it is ultimately irreducible, because *it has priority over the spatiality of the lexias it joins,* punctuating the periods upon which the narrative depends in order to anchor meaning among the sliding tokens of its re-presentation. The link (the place or moment of the detour) operates on two planes: In the metadiscourse of the interface, it is the signature of the pause, something you encounter and manipulate in hypertext applications all the time; it is as really "there" as the letters on the screen "really" describe the textual fields they represent. Phenomenologically, it traces a pure interval, spatiality deferred in time, displacement as dis-place-ment. Reading across the link—that is, reading more than one lexia in a hypertext—introduces a discontinuity that cannot be accounted for in a spatial model of the text's narrative structure, a point of singularity where everything that came "before" is changed in ways that cannot be predicted prior to that rupture. The passage between lexias resembles, in its irreducible punctuality (and, we will see in a moment, in its effect on the reading subject), what Slavoj Zizek calls the "pure act":

> The act differs from an active intervention (action) in that it radically transforms its bearer (agent): the act is not simply something I "accomplish"—after the act I'm literally "not the same as before." . . . The act is defined by the irreducible *risk:* in its most fundamental dimension, it is always *negative,* i.e., an act of annihilation, of wiping out—we not only don't know what will come out of it, its final outcome is ultimately even insignificant, strictly secondary in relation to the NO! of the pure act. . . . With an act, *stricto sensu,* we can therefore never fully foresee its consequences, i.e., the way it will transform the existing symbolic space: the act is a rupture after which "nothing remains the same." Which is why, although History can always be explained, accounted for, afterward, we can never, as its agents, caught in its flow, foresee its course in advance: we cannot do it insofar as it is not an "objective process" but a process continuously interrupted by the scansion of acts.[18]

The link is able to assume its conventional function as a marker of the lexial intersection only insofar as it concretizes (fixes, petrifies) the disjunctions between lexias, becoming thereby the measure of their retrospective interpretation and the anchor of the reader's position in relation to the promise of closure—naming the memorable "where" of the irreducible "when" of the break. A lexia in Joyce's *WOE—Or a Memory of What Will Be* begins,

> Here is the truth, though you will never know this for certain: all day long this window you now read stood empty (open for a while with the [Macintosh II]cx on, then sleeping in some data structure when it seemed there would be thunderstorms, before the haze burned off and the jungle heat of Michigan overcame me—it is Sunday June 17, 1990, Father's Day as we've already noted, yesterday the second number of the first volume of *Writing on the Edge* arrived in the mail, I do not own issue one, though I have cited Stuart's article from it, and this story itself somehow grows from that commissioned work which, if all goes well, you read now in some future number (there was talk of 5) of *WOE* [that last the name I've given this document temporarily on the cx] ⟨History is hard to bracket at the depth it requires⟩)}].[19]

Shandean digressions of this sort are very common in hypertext writing. You cannot write or read in this environment without ending up writing or reading to the moment. And the more you consider the temporality of the moment, the tighter the recursion of your memory of it. Closure, like versioning, is always fixed after-ward, *après-coup, Nachträglichkeit.* The historicity of digital narrative is hard to bracket because the disjunctive rhythms of its signifiers can so easily mislead you about the when of writing and reading. And the irreducible slices of deferral between the lexias, stretching in a series of cuts from a beginning (after the fact) to an ending (possibly before you get to a conclusion) will always claim their portion from you, always demand a certainty that you may never possess.

A Hypertextual Sophism

This reminds me of a story.

> A prison warden has three select prisoners summoned and announces to them the following: "For reasons I need not make known now, gentlemen, I must set one of you free. In order to decide *whom,* I will entrust the outcome to a test which you will kindly undergo.
>
> "There are three of you present. I have here five discs differing only in color: three white and two black. Without letting you know which I have chosen, I shall fasten one of them to each of you between his shoulders; outside, that is, of your direct visual field—any indirect ways of getting a look at the disc being excluded by the absence here of any means of mirroring.
>
> "At that point, you will be left at your leisure to consider your companions and their respective discs, without being allowed, of course, to communicate amongst yourselves the results of your inspection. Your own interest would, in any case, proscribe such communication, for the first to be able to deduce his own color will be the one to benefit from the dispensatory measure at our disposal.
>
> "His conclusion, moreover, must be founded upon logical and not simply probabilistic reasons. Keeping this in mind, it is to be understood that as soon as one of you is ready to formulate such a conclusion, he should pass through this door so that he may be judged individually on the basis of his response."
>
> This having been made clear, each of the three subjects is adorned with a white disc, no use being made of the black ones, of which there were, let us recall, but two.
>
> How can the subjects solve the problem?[20]

Game theorists call this kind of logic problem a "prisoner's dilemma." This example of the genre is the centerpiece of Lacan's 1945 essay,

"Logical Time and the Assertion of Anticipated Certainty: A New Sophism." It has, Lacan observes, no solution consistent with the methods of classical logic. Once the black/black/white combination has been excluded (each prisoner can see that both his companions wear white discs), there remain two possible combinations—black/white/white and white/white/white—and there is insufficient evidence to determine which is correct, at least if the problem is conceived "spatially" ("Logical Time," 9), that is, within each prisoner's field of vision the moment his companions' discs come into view. But Lacan has a story to tell here; the solution he proposes depends on the temporality of the telling, which is also the key to the significance of this improbable tale for a theory of hypertext narrative.

> After having contemplated one another for *a certain time,* the three subjects take *a few steps* together and pass side by side through the doorway. Each of them then separately furnishes a similar response which can be expressed thus:
>
> "I am white, and here is how I know it: as my companions were whites, I thought that, had I been a black, each of them would have been able to infer the following: 'If I too am a black, the other would have necessarily realized straight away that he was a white and would have left immediately; therefore I am not a black.' And both would have left together convinced that they were whites. As they did nothing of the kind, I must be a white like them. At that, I made for the door to make my conclusion known."
>
> All three exited simultaneously, armed with the same reasons for concluding. (5)

It is possible to move beyond the paralysis of the "spatial" reading of the evidence, says Lacan, on the condition that you take into account the value of the prisoners' *hesitation* to come to a conclusion as they head for the door. Let's call the prisoners A, B, and C and consider the problem from the vantage of prisoner A, remembering that B and C also occupy, from their point of view, the A position. (Lacan calls A the "real subject"—more on that in a moment—and B and C, the "reflected subjects" [6]). A wears a black or white disc, but he does not know which is his color; the absence of mirrors means that he can deduce his color only from what he is able to infer from the behavior of the other prisoners, neither of whom possesses any more information than he. Thus, as the explanation given by each as he leaves the room makes clear, each prisoner is compelled to assume (falsely, it turns out) what he cannot know, and to act as if he were already sure of the truth of his assumption. If any fails to act as though he already knows the answer to the warden's riddle, that is, fails to move in lock-step with the others, none of them can be sure of his conclusion.

A begins by assuming that he is black. If that were so, one of the others (B, for example) would leave *almost* immediately, after he had observed that the other (C) did *not* leave immediately, which would then mean that he (B) is not black. Because one of the others (C) does not leave immediately, with the second (B) in pursuit—because, in fact they begin to leave together—A concludes that he is white. There is no time here for second-guessing, at least not while the others are not also hesitating, so A must begin for the door as soon as he sees the others leaving, *after* a time required for each to observe that the other (each prisoner's B) has also hesitated to make his choice. The crucial detail here is that all three prisoners must hesitate *together, twice* in order for A to deduce that he is, indeed, not black (his original working assumption), because, if he were, the others would never have doubted the meaning of his initiative.

> If A, seeing B and C set off with him, wonders again whether they have not in fact seen that he is black, it suffices for him to stop and pose the question again in order to answer it. For he sees that they too have stopped: since each of them is really in the same situation as he, or more aptly stated *is* A insofar as real—i.e., insofar as he resolves or fails to resolve to conclude about himself—each encounters the same doubt at the same moment as he. Regardless of the reasoning A now imputes to B and C, he will have every right to conclude again that he is a white. For he supposes anew that, had he been a black, B and C would have had to *continue*; or at the very least, acknowledging their hesitation . . . that makes them wonder if they are not blacks themselves . . . they would have to *set off again before him*. . . . It is because they, seeing that he is in fact a white, do nothing of the kind, that he himself takes the initiative; which is to say that they all head for the door together to declare that they are whites. (7–8)

The prisoners' actions, says Lacan, are punctuated by two "suspensive scansions." These function as signifiers for the knowledge each does not possess (the color of the disc hidden from his view), insofar as they mark the temporality of the prisoners' efforts to reach a conclusion. "Their crucial value is not that of a binary choice between two inertly juxtaposed combinations [black/white/white and white/white/white]—rendered incomplete by the visual exclusion of the third—but rather of a verificatory movement instituted by a logical process in which a subject transforms the three possible combinations into three *times of possibility*" (9). He calls these three "times" of the sophism, "the instant of the glance" (*l'instant du regard*), "the time for comprehending" (*le temps pour comprendre*), and "the moment of concluding" (*le moment de conclure*) (10).[21]

The *instant du regard* is the moment of the prisoners' first view of their companions' discs. This is the time of the first, and only, logical exclusion that each prisoner is able to make, based purely on a synchronic reading of the evidence. "I am not confronted with two blacks, therefore I may be a white or a black." The certainty of this instant prepares the way for the contingent formulation to follow: "Because I don't see any blacks, I *may* be a black. If that were so . . ." The initial instant defines a margin of impossibility, founded on an exclusion, and converts a simple binary opposition ("I may be black or white") into an opposition between two distinct *series,* within which the subject must anchor himself to determine his identity: "I am one of either black/white/white or white/white/white; to determine my color, I must consider the response of another prisoner to (yet) another prisoner." As I noted before, Lacan calls prisoner A, from whose point of view the logical problem is constituted, the "real" subject. The instant of the glance is, of the three times of the sophism, the one most closely associated with the Lacanian Real. The initial moment is one of brute—Real—knowledge, logically prior to subjectivity. All the prisoner perceives is the *lack* of a signifier (from another vantage, he perceives the signifier of a lack) to which he must be attached in order to procure a place in a series of signifiers. To define his missing attribute, he must attend to its reflection in the actions of his companions.

In the *temps pour comprendre,* each prisoner observes the response of another subject to (yet) another subject. This is when the prisoner begins to draw a conclusion on the basis of his companions' delay in responding to the Real knowledge (the encounter with a lack) of the "instant of the gaze": "If I (A) am a black, then both of the others, seeing that the other is not a black, should waste no time in realizing that they are white." This second time is measured, says Lacan, by a "time of meditation" that each of the two whites (B and C) "must ascertain in the other" (11) and by which evidence the prisoner (A) "objectifies something more than the factual givens offered him by the sight of the two whites" (11). This period of meditation can be, says Lacan, as short as the instant of the glance; but it differs crucially from the first moment in that it inserts the subject into a reciprocal relation with the others, from which he is able to assume the certainty of his identity (12). The initial question, "What am I?" is thus converted to a different question, one that depends on the presumed response of an-other to the initial question: "*Which* am I?" The answer to the second question can be determined only from a *deferral* to or within the other's response (deferral in three senses of the word: a difference of attributes, a delay of decision, and a yielding of authority). As Robert Samuels has observed, the prisoner of the time for comprehending is caught in an obsessional circuit of possible identifications, from which he can escape only by affirming himself as a distinct subject, that is, by submitting himself to a particular signifier ("black" or "white") in a chain represented by the discs ("Logical Time," 71). The insertion of the subject into this game of specular rivalry prepares the way for the third moment of the sophism.

The *moment de conclure* is the time of the subject's hastening to bring the deductive process to an end, by assuming his identity (his mark, his sign, his resemblance to the attribute he cannot see) in the chain of signifiers. Each prisoner, observing the others hesitate twice, recognizes the full import of each prisoner's reflection on the others' inaction: "Because the others hesitate *with me,* as I move to conclude that I am black (from their lack of hesitation, after a period of meditation, on observing that the other is white), then I *must* be white." The force of the assertion ("I *must* be white") is, Lacan notes, what empowers the subject to exit the specular closure of the time for comprehending.

> If his hypothesis is correct—if, that is, the two whites actually see a black—they do not have to make an assumption about it, and will thus precede him by the beat [*temps de battement*] he misses in having to formulate this very hypothesis. It is thus *the moment of concluding* that he is a white; should he allow himself to be beaten to this conclusion by his counterparts, he *will no longer be able to determine* whether he is black or not. Having surpassed the *time for comprehending the moment of concluding,* it is *the moment of concluding the time for comprehending.* Otherwise this time would lose its meaning. It is not, therefore, because of some dramatic contingency, the seriousness of the stakes, or the competitiveness of the game that time presses; it is owing to the urgency of the logical movement that the subject *precipitates* both his judgment and his departure ("precipitates" in the etymological sense of the verb: headlong), establishing the modulation in which temporal tension is reversed in a move to action [*tendance à l'acte*] manifesting to the others that the subject has concluded. (12–13, Lacan's emphasis)

In the final moment of the sophism, there is no time to spare, no opportunity for hesitation. Of the three times of the sophism, the time for comprehending is situated most purely within the register of the *act,* in Zizek's sense of that term: a break, a rupture, changing everything that follows (hence its headlong, precipitate, no-turning-back quality). The only way out is to come to an end, to assert an identity by appropriating its mark, thus objectifying the response of the Other in the signifier. The closing assertion is, Lacan emphasizes, a subjective (subjecti*fy*ing) *act*: in saying, "I *must* be white," the prisoner is also saying "*I* must *be* (white)." In the moment of concluding, the prisoner emerges from the indeterminate reciprocity of the time for comprehending as a full-fledged subject, converted from what Lacan calls the "noetic subject"—"he can as easily be god, table, or washbasin," that is, a *thing*, a stupid, Real object—to an "'I,' [the] subject of the conclusive assertion" (14).[22]

The assertion that marks the moment for concluding is—and this is crucial for interpreting the significance of the "temporal tension" it "releases" (15)—a performative speech act that secures a place for the subject in the Symbolic insofar as he speaks his judgment and assumes thereby his attributive mark. "I hasten to say that I am white," says the prisoner, "because, if I do not (*hasten* to say, hasten to *say*), I may be convinced that I am not (that I am not white, that I am *not*)." The act of certitude that concludes the sophism constitutes at the same time an enforced ambiguity of the subject's status with regard to language. Taking on his mark, the subject defers to (is subject-ed to) the signifier he assumes; he gains a contingent kind of existence ("I *am* white/I am *not* black"), but he loses a portion of his being: the ineffable thing within himself, logically prior to his attachment to the signifier. What he loses, in other words, is his disc, the mark within the riddle's symbolic system of the object that he seeks to find within himself, *but can never actually locate within the terms of the riddle*. At the end of the second of the suspended motions, says Lacan, the sophism's assertion of certitude is "desubjectified to the utmost" (16), which is to say, observes Bruce Fink, that

> insofar as identification has taken place, the subject "identifying himself" or coming to be identified with a particular signifier (*viz.* white), the subject has become frozen, nailed down, objectified and thus de-subjecti*viz*ed. Subjecti*fi*cation—the making into subject (or into a full-fledged subject)—ties the subject to the signifier, killing him thereby as subject. We might say that a part of his being has been transformed into language/signifier(s), the "rest" being left to drift anew until a further identification/subjecti-*fi*cation takes place. . . . Part of his being has had to be sacrificed in the working out of the logical problem, and he has lost out on all counts. His being is now separated from language under which it had been slipping in the first moment, but that slippage returns with every new (forced) choice presented.[23]

You have to make a choice; you have to take your chances; you will always sacrifice a portion of your being in the moment of your conclusion. You may be able afterward to interpret that punctuation of the symbolic fabric—indeed, it would be more precise to say that the assertion of certainty can occur only if you posit as meaningful its pure contingency, if you define it as a free, rather than forced choice—but the punctual moment splits off a Real kernel that exceeds the capacity of language to account for meaning under any terms.

"Get set! Go! (—get lost!)" you can imagine the warden saying to the prisoners. His command to them has this ambiguous value precisely because of the identifications it compels them to assume. A distinction to keep in mind here is that between the *imaginary* and *symbolic* registers of identification in the sophism. Imaginary identification takes place on an axis joining the subject to another by means of a specular resemblance that the subject locates in the other. This is, in general terms, identification that sustains the transition from the first to the second time of the logical sophism, when the prisoner attempts to infer the color of his disc from the reflected responses of the other prisoners. Symbolic identification, on the other hand, is identification with a trait in the Symbolic order that confers a place for the subject in that order. It is, says Zizek, "identification with the very place *from where* we are being observed, *from where* we look at ourselves."[24] This is the identification that sustains the transition from the second to the third times of the logical sophism, when the prisoner recognizes that the true problem of the riddle is not "What color is my disc?" but "In which of the possible series of discs am I?" Finding a place in the series, however, means accepting the burden of the signifier, and the erasure of a portion of the subject's being. It means, in fact, identifying with a lack in the other that precludes the saturation of meaning that the subject was compelled to seek in the first place. "In imaginary identification," observes Zizek, "we imitate the other at the level of resemblance—we identify ourselves with the image of the other inasmuch as we are 'like him,' while in symbolic identification we identify ourselves with the other precisely at a point at which he is inimitable, at the point which eludes resemblance" (*Sublime Object,* 109).

This compulsion to imitate the inimitable touches on the ethical dimension of the logical sophism and brings its *story* full circle, back to the impossible promise of narrative. The voice calling on the reader to make sense of the text (the voice of prosopopoeia) is presumed to know—to enjoy—the Truth of the reading, that is, to reside in the place of the thing that will close it. But enjoyment (*jouissance,* the bliss of the thing in its immediacy) is forbidden, says Lacan, "to him that speaks as such, or else it can only be spoken between the lines."[25] Language divides us, as I began by saying, from the things of which it speaks. The subject can only approach *jouissance* obliquely, shifting between poles of prohibition and transgression. (1) The split within the subject instituted by symbolic identification is irreparable; enjoyment of the Real fragment thereby excised from reality is understood to be prohibited by the Other, whose authority rests on the assumption that it alone may possess the object-cause of desire. This is the negative register of what Lacan calls the "Law"; in its classic, Oedipal version, it is the paternal interdiction of sexual enjoyment of the mother. (2) The Symbolic must, however, be propped up by the promise that this impossible object *may* be recovered, for the subject can exist only within the field opened by its exclusion, circumscribed by its endless pursuit—the subject is compelled, in this sense, to help the Other disclose the object upon which its authority is founded, so as permanently to sustain closure and to saturate meaning. Thus the subject is compelled to transgress the Law, or, more properly, the Law and its transgression are two faces of the same principle at the origin of the subject's desire.[26]

This state of sustained disjunction is also the condition of the prosopopoeia presumed by an entry into narrative, the opening of a dialogue with an-Other. In demanding of you to take your mark—to begin—the voice promises a resolution, a real-impossible conclusion necessary for you to get out in time with a reasonable facsimile of your identity intact. Though not before you've paid a price for appearing to be sure about what you cannot know. And your relation to the point of closure from which the Other appears to speak—that is, your identity within the scene of narrative, your existence within its terms—is sustained only so long as you are unable to reach the promised end, only while you rehearse the punctuation of the exchange enforced by each detour.

In Conclusion (2)

What does this have to do with hypertext? Let's return for a moment to the *temps pour comprendre*. The "noetic subject," remember, is caught in a specular circuit. He can only determine his disc's color if he reflects upon (that is, if he acts as the reflection of) the responses of his companions. (Acting *as* the reflection of the others' responses objectifies the specular circuit, reducing it to a fixed point, subjecti*fy*ing the one who acts.) But the circuit of exchanges is closed until interrupted by an *act* (in Zizek's sense of the term) of *in*action. The prisoner is able to grasp the shift in the nature of his question (from "*What* is my color?" to "*Which* is my position?"), but he cannot decide between the two possible outcomes until all three prisoners move forward and then hesitate at least one more time. They need to hesitate only twice in order to determine the color of their discs, so long as they do not hesitate again, at which point each would have to (re)consider the others' motive for stopping.[27] In other words, they can hesitate any number of times, so long as they start and stop together. If they make it through the door before stopping a third (or fourth, etc.) time, they can come to a conclusion: they can respond to the Other's imperative ("Go! Stop! Be!"); they can fix the circuit of their *possible* identifications to a particular point in the series.[28] You have to make a choice in order to come to an end, or you have to keep going forward *as if you had made a choice,* believing that you can make a choice, just long enough to get out of the room. The resolution, the closure, that you obtain thereby is always equivocal, subtracting from you a penalty in exchange for the promise of its possibility.

In a 1991 essay ("Threnody"), I argued that the robust digressions of hypertext narrative replay the eccentric relation of the subject who inhabits the text (writer or reader) to signifiers that constitute the text's reservoir of meaning. I suggested that the hypertext link (in contradiction to its conventional definition: link as copula) is the mark of a *division* between lexias, and the index of an irreducible gap in the fabric of digital narrative. The detour of the link turns around "a place you can never get to, where something drops away between the multiple paths you might follow" ("Threnody," 172–73). This circuit traces, I concluded, the moment (Lacan's "temporal pulsation"[29]) of the subject's relation to the signifier that Lacan calls "fading," the occultation of a portion of the subject's being by the signifier as it concretizes her[30] position in the Symbolic.[31] The subject's fading is precisely what is at stake in the transition from the *temps pour comprendre* to the *moment de conclure*. The noetic subject is caught in a kind of suspension, measured by the two scansions that circumscribe the time for comprehending. Remaining inside the circuit of possible identifications means never getting to an end; it means never grasping the simulacrum of being (in the Symbolic) possible only by submitting to a signifier. But assuming the burden of a signifier—that is, in the sense of the logical sophism, coming to a conclusion—means also accepting the penalty of fading under the signifier.[32]

Either way, you lose, and the ambivalence of the sophism's solution is what prompts the obsessional reluctance to move forward that characterizes the time for comprehending. Much of my argument in "Threnody" turned on a summary description of the hypertext reader as a version of the obsessional neurotic, rehearsing the ritual circuit of his mortality in the endless turns of the text. A more elaborate formulation of that idea, in light of what I have been saying about the equivocality of closure and the occultation of the subject by the signifier in the *temps pour comprendre,* should help clarify what it is I take to be the specific significance of Lacan's sophism for a theory of hypertext narrative.

Obsessionals, I observed in "Threnody" (176), are fascinated by the spectre of death. "Their thoughts," says Freud, "are unceasingly occupied with other people's length of life and possibility of death; their superstitious propensities have had no other content to begin with, and have perhaps no other source whatever."[33] Beginning with Freud's analysis of the Rat Man, classical studies of obsessional neurosis have viewed the patient's overwhelming care for the welfare of others, usually members of his family or potential loved ones, as inverted aggressive wishes. The Rat Man's compulsion to count between the lightning flash and the thunderclap (to measure the distance of a possible strike from his "lady") or his removal of a stone from the road (so that her carriage might not strike it), and his subsequent return of the stone to its original place, bespeak, at best, an ambiguous concern for her well-being ("Notes upon a Case," 191). His constant preoccupation with the health of his father—who, we discover late in the analysis, has in fact already been dead for several years—is evidence, Freud concludes, of an alternating aggression and solicitude rooted in a murderous early defiance of the father's authority (204).

As Charles Melman and Stuart Schneiderman have pointed out, however, this reading of the obsessional's fascination with the safety of others interprets the ritual gestures directed toward the Other *as the neurotic understands them,* within the agonistic (classically Oedipal) theatre of a competition for a prize to which the patient imagines the Other has access.[34] "Another interpretation," says Schneiderman, "imposes itself and is closer to the truth. If the Rat Man thinks of his father as being alive when he is dead, why not hear this remark as signifying that his father, even when seeming to be alive, was dead?" (*Rat Man,* 25). In other words, the Rat Man's preoccupation with his father's mortality signifies his fixation on the problems of paternity and alterity in general, and on their relation to death—or, to be more precise, to the mortal effects of the paternal signifier: how the signifier of the father's desire introduces mortality into the experience of the *infans* and reflects mortality back into the place of the father. The obsessional is, as it were, captivated by the spectacle of fading in the Other, the occultation of the Other by the signifier of desire. More than any other neurotic, says Lacan, the obsessional is bound to the "dispossession and imaginary death" of the alienating other that is the original of his ego (a fellow prisoner, or, perhaps, as we shall see, the warden), bound to the irrevocable, lethal formulation that fading assumes when viewed from the neurotic's perspective.[35] In the language of the logical sophism, the obsessional subject prefers to remain suspended in the *temps pour comprendre,* where he may rehearse the moment when closure is precipitated but may refuse to follow it through, because doing so would reveal something he cannot bear to know: that closure within the field of the Other is also missing. The obsessional, says Schneiderman, "spends his time trying to arrange an encounter with the moment of truth, the moment when he will meet death, thereby hoping to make this encounter take place at a time convenient to him. He wants to master time and by implication to master death" (*Rat Man,* 8). His endless rituals are delaying tactics, locking in the contingent moment *prior* to closure.

The bind in which the obsessional finds himself is this: he seems to have every reason to believe that closure in the field of the Other is possible, because the Other appears to have promised it from the start. Melman asks, What did the young Rat Man see—or not see—under his governess's skirts that "fateful evening" of his fourth or fifth year? He proposes that what the boy saw was *nothing,* "the lack of the object as such, the lack itself" ("On Obsessional Neurosis," 131). As Schneiderman points out, the boy may have seen nothing, but he must have *expected* to find something, "he must have had the impression of having seen it there, of having seen or heard some *sign* which would have suggested as much" (*Rat Man,* 22). And he must have felt—something. "Let us imagine then," he says, "that Paul, the Rat Man, had been told something by his governess that led him to believe there was something under her skirt, something *for* him, to be communicated to him. The discovery of the lack of an object means that what the governess had said represented her as subject equivocally, thereby raising the question of why she was letting him do this, what she expected from him. So rather than being someone receiving a sign, the Rat Man was required to provide another signifier." (In an earlier passage, Schneiderman distinguishes between a *sign* and a *signifier* thus: the sign "has a single meaning, or refers to a single object. If a sign appears, then there must be an object behind it. If there is no object, the sign is not a sign, but becomes a signifier, defined as equivocal.") Schneiderman continues, "This is not always phonetic material; if the structure functions, other elements may take its place," in the same way that the "suspensive scansions" of the logical sophism function as signifiers for the prisoners' missing knowledge. "In the situation under study, the other signifier can only be the touch of his hands. (She did, after all, tell him to remain silent about the experience, thereby providing a sign of its forbidden quality.) But if the touch has the characteristic of the phonetic material of language, *it does not belong to or express the being of the one who uses it*" (*Rat Man,* 21–23, emphasis added).

The obsessional believes from the beginning the terms of the contract implied by the invitation of the Other to enter the scene of reading.[36] He believes in the promise of a discovery without penalty that language appears to make when it calls him to bind himself to its circuit. What the obsessional cannot bear is the realization that this resolution can only be provisional, that it is constantly and permanently divided, *because the Other ("big O", the Symbolic order) is also lacking,* is also split by a gap in the heart of speech. So the obsessional closes himself in a calculus that postpones that recognition. He collapses the circuit into a concrete formula (the missing signifier that the Rat Man is called upon to produce from beneath his governess's skirts, the missing disc that the prisoner in the *temps pour comprendre* is called upon to conjecture) that at once signifies the lack (the lack of an object) he fears, and compensates for the lack of being manipulable, utilitarian in the most technical sense of the word. Something he can use to get to where he is going (that is, to go through the motions of going there) but also to postpone a recognition that getting to a destination will subtract something from him and reveal that the Other is also subject to the penalties of (dis)closure. (Thus, the Rat Man's ritual prayers for his lady's safety, his fantasy of his father's ghost; and the passwords [*passworten*: Freud, "Notes on a Case," 318] that dominate his thinking: *rat, ratten, hieraten, dick, Glejisamen.*) In other words, the obsessional fixes (repairs, petrifies) the lack in the Other *by transforming his own occultation by the signifier into a positive term,* capable of guaranteeing the Other's consistency, and maintaining a promise that the Other can never keep.[37]

The hypertext reader reads the text as would an obsessional, insofar as he believes in the link, in its promise of a relation between lexias, and, ultimately, in the closure, saturation or saturability that founds the link as a navigational tool.[38] The ritual formulae that guide the deferrals of closure—the hypertextual *passworten,* Joyce's "words that yield," for example—extend the initial promise of a discovery of Truth in the place of the Other. Returning again and again to confirm the possibility of closure means refusing the gap in the field of the Other by replacing it with the positive term of the reader's own occultation within narrative. Like the obsessional, the hypertext reader is compelled by the double bind of a forced choice. He would seek to hold the Other accountable for the promise of discovery that language entails, but he also resists the recognition of the ultimate significance of that discovery, that the Other *can* be held accountable, that is, lacking. This double bind is, I think, the source of the unease on the part of many readers concerning the equivocal closure of hypertexts. It seems that you can never finish reading these documents, because you can never quite get from them what it is you seek. There is always more to read, more to uncover, without actually getting to the thing you're reading for. By comparison, opportunities in a printed text for returning to an encounter with the missing thing are limited; there are fewer ways in and out, and your options for prolonging your investigation are constrained by the material (if not to say, literal) resistance of the written artifact. The key to understanding the paradoxical significance of this discomfort is to recall the specifically Lacanian formulation of anxiety: "It is not," observes Zizek, "the lack of an object that gives rise to anxiety but, on the contrary, the danger of our getting too close to the object and thus losing the lack itself. Anxiety is brought on by the disappearance of desire" (*Looking Awry,* 8). Meaning (sustained by the gap of desire) and *jouissance* cannot coexist (Zizek, *Enjoy Your Symptom!,* 134); to approach the object-cause of desire too closely means losing the simulacrum of being that its pursuit guarantees you. In this sense, hypertextual (dis)closure evokes anxiety because it leads you to exactly what you were looking for, but not what you thought you wanted. And it is possible to continue reading only so long as you never quite find it.

I Want to Say

Let's finish by returning to *Afternoon.* As I noted earlier, you can move through the lexias of *Afternoon* by pressing the Return key at each new screen of text, that is, by responding with the default "yes" to the implicit question posed by the opening of each lexia, "Do you want to hear about it?" Doing this takes you through 36 lexias (and the beginning of Peter's efforts to remember what he saw on the way to work or to discover some evidence that will help him to remember), before dead-ending in a lexia entitled "I call," where Peter decides not to begin phoning local hospitals but rather to call someone named Lolly. You know that the path ends here because pressing the Return key does not take you anywhere else, and the computer stubbornly beeps at you every time you try to move onward.

You do not, however, know who Lolly is, and you do not know much about anyone else who has made an appearance in this, the most restricted sequence of lexias in the text. You could stop reading here, refusing after a single audience the text's promise that it has more to say.[39] Or, you could go back to the beginning and start again, perhaps several times, or until your patience or curiosity is exhausted, each time varying your responses—choosing "no" instead of "yes" or clicking on different words that seem likely to yield. (*Every* mouse click yields, so you cannot be sure that the word you clicked, rather than the lexia as a whole, was linked to the click's destination.) Subsequent readings will appear to reveal more about the characters of the fiction and the sequence of events. You may discover that Lolly is a sometime therapist married to Peter's boss. It is precisely because each reading *may* disclose some new particle of information that will appear to saturate the text with meaning, to guarantee the possibility of coming to a conclusion, that the reader feels compelled to return. Douglas's report of her experience of reading *Afternoon* is instructive in this regard:

> Instead of narrowing the margins of the narrative the further I read, *Afternoon* considerably broadens them. Where the number of probable and plausible narrative outcomes conventionally progressively dwindles in print narratives the nearer we approach their ending, the more of the narrative we read in interactive narratives the more these seem to multiply. . . . In one version [of *Afternoon*] the accident seems not to have occurred; in another, Wert [Peter's boss] distracts Peter from his fears about the fates of ex-wife and child with bawdy suggestions. In one scenario, only Peter is having an affair with Nausicaa [a co-worker]; in another, Wert knows both that he and Peter are having an affair with Nausicaa and that Peter is blissfully ignorant of Nausicaa's involvement with him. In one version of the scene, Wert idly wonders aloud how Peter would react if he, Wert, were sleeping with Peter's ex-wife; in another, Wert is testing the extent of Peter's ignorance of his involvement with Peter's ex-wife. While my readings of all these versions are physically possible, I cannot accept all of them simultaneously in my final understanding of the events described in *Afternoon*. ("Print Pathways," ch. 5)

Douglas, who may know *Afternoon* better than its author, has recorded spending three years reading and re-reading Joyce's text and coming to a conclusion about what has happened the morning of the afternoon of the phone call.[40] She extracts from her readings four unique versions of *Afternoon,* each supporting multiple minor variations. The fourth and conclusive version is anchored to her discovery of three lexias linked to "I call" (the dead end of the default reading), entitled "1/," "2/," and "white afternoon." These suggest that (1) Peter is concerned for the whereabouts of his ex-wife and son *before* he drives to work; (2) while driving to work, he may have seen them riding with Wert, and the shock of recognizing that his boss's offhand comment about having an affair with his ex-wife may not have been in jest causes Peter to briefly lose control of his car, resulting in another car's crashing to avoid his; (3) the car that crashes is the one in which his ex-wife and son were riding: Peter may have been responsible for the death of his ex-wife and son. Douglas asks,

> What, precisely, triggered my sense of having come to some sort of closure, my sense that I did not need to continue reading *Afternoon*? Most obviously, I became conscious of my readings having satisfied one of the primary quests outlined in the narrative: what has happened to Peter's ex-wife and child? Although my discovery that Peter has caused the accident is not entirely congruent with his desire to learn of their condition, it does short-circuit Peter's quest. Since Peter himself has caused the accident, clearly, he knows whether the pair is unharmed, fatally injured, or already dead. The language in the place "white afternoon" suggests the last possibility may be the most valid: "The investigator finds him to be at fault. He is shocked to see the body . . . on the wide green lawn. The boy is nearby." The word "body" may signify that the woman Peter sees is lifeless, but it could also refer to the fact that she is unconscious, inert, quantifiable as an accident victim. ("Print Pathways," ch. 5)

I would suggest that the key to the apparent conclusiveness of the "white afternoon" reading is not that it represents, to use Douglas's terms, "a resolution which accounts for the greatest number of ambiguities in the narrative" or "the most *plausible* conclusion to the narrative's network of mysteries and tensions" (ch. 5).[41] These readings, depending as they do on evidence (unambiguous markers of the Truth of the story) to establish their conclusiveness, interpret (the lack of) closure in the field of the Other as the neurotic would read it, sanctioned by the positive term of the reader's own sacrifice of her desire, in order to mask the desire of the Other. *It is rather the absolute inertness of the woman's body that establishes closure in the "white afternoon" reading.* The body and the discarded report on Louis Quatorze (which Douglas takes as evidence of the boy's death) represent simply the missing thing sought to bring the story to an end. They mark the literal dead end of the narrative, an appalling fragment broken off from its fabric: the position of the stupid, Real object at the focus of the reader's pursuit of closure. As such, they appear to confirm the promise of fullness and saturability (within the fiction of prosopopoeia) invoked by our first response to the opening question: "Do you want to hear about it?" With regard to this object, Peter's phone call to Lolly takes on a specific meaning. In the reading from evidence (the "neurotic" reading) the call can be interpreted, as Douglas suggests, as an effort to find someone who can help Peter remember and help relieve him of his feelings of guilt (Lolly is a therapist). Or, I would counter, it can be read more generally, as a call to the Other to recognize the value of the reader's (of Peter's) sacrifice, and thus to guarantee the closure for which that sacrifice is offered. Peter calls Lolly as if to ask, "Is this the thing I want to find? Is this the thing I want to say? *Is this the thing you want me to say?"*

The appeal to Lolly's guarantee can only lead nowhere, returning Peter (and the reader) to the immovable kernel of impossible closure. Could there be a more fitting signifier for the pure object-cause of desire than the idiotic beep of the computer that sounds every time you press the Return key? Is this not exactly what you were looking for when you replied "Yes, tell me about it" in the first place?

The secret of (hypertextual) dialogue with the Other is that the Other itself ("big O," the field of the Symbolic) is inconsistent, lacking, capable of being held accountable; the One who promises to know the Truth of the dialogue of narrative is, as Zizek says, purely an impostor (*Enjoy Your Symptom!,* 103). The link purports to represent the index of the Other's fullness (there is a story here, to be told to its conclusion), but it represents more correctly the blemish of the Other's lack (there is a story here, but no guarantee that you will ever be satisfied that you have come to its conclusion.) When the warden prefaces his demand of the sophistic prisoners by saying, "For reasons I need not make known now, gentlemen, I must set one of you free," he is revealing thereby the unbearable possibility that he himself may not be in charge, *that he may not know why the story must proceed according to the rules he is about to pronounce, that he may not know where it will end.*

I want to say . . . that I may have seen my son die this morning. That mine may have been a black disc. That I may have seen *nothing* under Miss Robert's skirts. *I want . . . to say.* A concealed copula joins the halves of the invocatory phrase that begins a story, soldering the irreducibility of lack to the divagation of narration, or, in another formulation, to the repeated act of beginning to read a narrative, of calling on it to fulfill its promise. Asking what it is you want to say is, in the end, asking the same of the Other, who always *may not* be able to give you the answer you are nonetheless compelled to pursue: "tell me a story," you say. "Tell me what *you* want. . . ." "Tell me the thing you are wanting. . . ."[42]

NOTES

1. Michael Joyce, *Afternoon, a story* (Cambridge, Mass.: Eastgate Systems, 1990). For extended discussions of *Afternoon,* see J. David Bolter, *Writing Space: The Computer, Hypertext, and the History of Writing* (Hillsdale, N.J.: Lawrence Erlbaum, 1990), 123–30; George P. Landow, *Hypertext: The Convergence of Contemporary Critical Theory and Technology* (Baltimore: Johns Hopkins University Press, 1992), 113–19; and J. Yellowlees Douglas, "Print Pathways and Interactive Labyrinths: How Hypertext Narratives Affect the Act of Reading," Ph.D. diss., New York University, 1992, ch. 5. I am indebted to Douglas for generously sharing her reading notes.

2. In the interest of avoiding confusion on the part of *my* readers, I should emphasize that *Afternoon* does not begin, in a conventional sense of the term, with Peter's hesitant declaration. The first lexias that one encounters after opening *Afternoon* make no mention of the accident, which enters the foreground of the narrative(s) only after about a dozen lexias have been viewed. My reasons for focusing on this "accidental" thread of *Afternoon* should become clearer as this essay progresses, but I do not mean to suggest that this is the "central," "most important," or even "symptomatic" thread of the text—it is, in fact, because *Afternoon* is a *hyper*text that such distinctions are highly problematic. There are other threads in *Afternoon* that are arguably as significant to the progress and conclusion of the reader's interaction with the text; "what makes [an] event important," observes Bolter, "is that it is a structural crossroads: the intersection of many narrative paths" (*Writing Space,* 125). That most readers of *Afternoon* (I offer this observation based on anecdotal evidence, the comments of those with whom I have discussed Joyce's work) are likely to conclude that it is mostly "about" the accident is, I suspect, a consequence of how *the accidental thread thematizes the disjunctions of its structure.* Other factors may of course come into play here: the affective value of the event (a father may have witnessed his son's death) or its mythic character (a *father,* his *son's* death, etc.). Much more work remains to be done on the subject of readers' predispositions to emphasize selected threads in robustly multiple narratives.

3. In this essay, I will follow a convention established by George Landow, who has used Roland Barthes's term *lexias* to describe the discrete textual chunks ("spaces," "nodes," etc.) linked in a hypertext. See Landow, *Hypertext,* 53; and Barthes, *S/Z,* trans. Richard Miller (New York: Hill and Wang, 1974), 13.

4. Storyspace was created by J. David Bolter, Michael Joyce, and John B. Smith. The Readingspace format is called Page Reader in the most recent releases of Storyspace. Design elements of the Readingspace and Page Reader formats have changed significantly over the course of Storyspace's development. The version illustrated here and described below is from the 1990 release of *Afternoon.*

5. In Storyspace's Page Reader, the Browse button is a structural lure, promising navigable cues and concrete form (note the *book* icon) but in fact returning information that fractures the spatiality of the cartographic metaphors it implies. See my discussion of this and related hypertext interface elements in "Ribbons," in Harpold, "Links and Their Vicissitudes," Ph.D. diss., University of Pennsylvania, 1994.

6. Storyspace is unusual among hypertext authoring systems in that it does not force authors to mark the presence of links with special symbols or typefaces. The user's manual for the program encourages the authors to choose their own approach as to the appearance of links (J. David Bolter, Michael Joyce, John B. Smith, and Mark Bernstein, *Getting Started with Storyspace* [Cambridge, Mass.: Eastgate Systems, 1993], 39), and Storyspace authors commonly leave links unmarked. Joyce's role in the development of Storyspace and his decision not to mark the links in *Afternoon,* the *Ur*-text of the hypertext fiction boom of

recent years, suggest that his preference for unmarked links has been decisive for the school of hypertext fiction that favors this method. The invisibility of links in *Afternoon* is a crucial element in the coerciveness of the text's yield mechanism, in that it implicitly founds the field of authority of Other to whom the links are *not* invisible. This is reinforced by the interface gesture that permits the Storyspace user to see very briefly the location of links in the current lexia by holding down the Command and Option keys simultaneously (links are framed in gray rectangles as long as the keys are held down). Thus peeking into the secret system of the text's narrative structure is, I would argue, another form of the petition to the Other to guarantee eventual closure. For a general discussion of the design of hypertext linking cues, see Shelley Evenson, John Rheinfrank, and Wendle Wulff, "Towards a Design Language for Representing Hypermedia Cues," in *Hypertext '89* (New York: Association for Computing Machinery, 1989), 83–92.

7. Bolter calls *Afternoon* an "interactive fiction" (*Writing Space,* 123). As I have noted elsewhere ("The Grotesque Corpus," *Perforations* 3 [1992], 3 n.4), I think this label has too often been applied to the Infocom-style adventure genre to be of much use in describing texts like *Afternoon.* Using it thus risks reducing the narrative undecidability of complex hypertexts to fit a model that they resemble only superficially. I would prefer the more evocative term *multiple fiction,* meant to describe a kind of limit-case of radical interactivity (the fiction is never the same in successive readings), first suggested by Joyce in his "Selfish Interaction or Subversive Texts and the Multiple Novel," in *Hypertext/Hypermedia Handbook,* ed. Emily Berk and Joseph Devlin (New York: McGraw-Hill/Intertext, 1991), 84.

8. "Hypertext and 'the Hyperreal,'" in *Hypertext '89* (New York: Association for Computing Machinery, 1989), 263.

9. See my discussion of hypertextual iterability in "The Contingencies of the Hypertext Link," *Writing on the Edge* 2.2 (1991): 126–38.

10. Stuart Moulthrop, *Victory Garden* (Cambridge, Mass.: Eastgate Systems, 1991).

11. A classic example of the "particular" alternative: Stanley Fish's spirited rejoinder to Norman Holland that an "Eskimo" reading of Faulkner's "A Rose for Emily" would, within the proper "interpretive community," be equally as acceptable as the Christological, sociological, psychoanalytic, and other readings that have been welcomed by the critical community. *Is There a Text in This Class? The Authority of Interpretive Communities* (Cambridge: Harvard University Press, 1980), 346–55.

12. *Hypertext and Hypermedia* (San Diego: Academic Press, 1990), 140.

13. *Prosopopoeia*: "the fiction of an apostrophe to an absent, deceased or voiceless entity, which posits the possibility of the latter's reply and confers upon it the power of speech. Voice assumes mouth, eye, and finally face, a chain that is manifest in the etymology of the trope's name, *prosopon poiein,* to confer a mask or a face (*prosopon*)" Paul de Man, "Autobiography as De-facement," *MLN* 94 (1979): 926. See Derrida's discussion of prosopopoeia in *Mémoires for*

Paul de Man, trans. Cecile Lindsay, Jonathan Culler, Eduardo Cadava (New York: Columbia University Press, 1986), where he explicitly situates it within the scene of narrative promise that I am evoking here: "Every reading finds itself caught, engaged precisely by the promise of saying the truth, by a promise which will have taken place with the very first word, within a scene of signature which is a scene of writing" (99).

14. You might, as I said, choose to stop reading. Or you might be forced to stop reading. A hazard of consuming digital texts that has, to my mind, been too little explored follows from the possibility that software can always crash, hardware can always fail, or these accidents may be made to appear to happen. Someone might trip over or intentionally pull the plug, a kind of fortuitous calamity unlikely to occur while you are reading a book. It is difficult to imagine a printed text that might, without warning, become catastrophically illegible. A text could be written with disappearing ink or on a fragile substrate that would crumble at the touch, but both of these accidental modifications of the artifact seem to me less cataclysmic than a thoroughly ill-mannered system crash.

15. Gérard Genette, *Seuils* (Paris: Editions du Seuil, 1987). See also Harpold, "Threnody: Psychoanalytic Digressions on the Subject of Hypertexts," in *Hypermedia and Literary Criticism,* ed. Paul Delany and George P. Landow (Cambridge: MIT Press, 1991), 172; Bolter, *Writing Space,* 160; Landow, *Hypertext,* 60.

16. *Afternoon*'s single-window interface is unusual. Joyce's choice of the Page Reader format may have been determined by a decision to push the limits of a familiar compositional model—in the typographic sense of the word—to their extremes. He began writing *Afternoon* as a test of the features of Storyspace when the program was in the first stages of development (Douglas, "Print Pathways," ch. 3), and the Readingspace format in which the text was published by Eastgate Press in 1987 used a late beta version of software. More recent complex fictions written in Storyspace (Joyce's *WOE,* Guyer and Petry's *Izme Pass,* Moulthrop's *Victory Garden*) have relied primarily on the program's multiple-window, topographically organized reading format.

17. See Moulthrop, "Reading from the Map: Metonymy and Metaphor in the Fiction of Forking Paths," in *Hypermedia and Literary Criticism,* 119–32; J. Yellowlees Douglas, "Gaps, Maps, and Perception: What Hypertext Narratives (Don't) Do," *Perforations* 3.1 (Spring/Summer 1992).

18. Slavoj Zizek, *Enjoy Your Symptom!* (New York: Routledge, 1992), 44–46.

19. *WOE—A Memory of What Will Be,* in *Writing on the Edge* 2.2 (1991). The bracketed "Macintosh II" is my editorial insertion. The nested series of brackets at the end of the citation is in the original.

20. Jacques Lacan, "Logical Time and the Assertion of Anticipated Certainty: A New Sophism," trans. Bruce Fink and Marc Silver. *Newsletter of the Freudian Field* 2.2 (1988): 4–5.

21. I prefer Bruce Fink and Marc Silver's translation of *temps pour comprendre,* "time for comprehending," to Robert Samuel's "time for understanding" ("Logical Time and *Jouissance,*" *Newsletter of the Freudian Field* 4.1–2 [1990]: 70). The second logical time of the sophism is not only one for discerning the meaning

of the other's response to a third subject's response to the chain of attributes but also one of integrating the observing subject's (prisoner A's) attribute within the series of attributes—that is, *comprehending* the series, in the sense of grasping the boundaries of its domain.

22. This emergence of the subject-ified "I" represents, says Lacan, the "essential logical form" of the "psychological birth" ("the existential form") of the subject as "I," a reference to the *je/moi* distinction that runs through much of Lacan's work in the 1940s and '50s. (*Je* = subject of the Symbolic, subject marked/divided by the signifier; *moi* = the alienated/alienating, "subjective" construct of the Imaginary, the "ego" of ego psychology. See, for example, "The Mirror Stage" and "Function and Field," 55.) Fink points out that Lacan's use of "precipitation" in this passage anticipates his later formulation of the subject as concurrently divided between two moments that correspond roughly to the *je/moi* distinction: "the subject as signified ('dead' meaning resulting from castration) and the subject as breach between two signifiers (as a spark jumping from one signifier to another, creating a connection between them)" ("The Subject as Metaphor," *Newsletter of the Freudian Field* 5.1/2 [1991]: 16).

23. "Notes on Temporal Tension," *Newsletter of the Freudian Field* 2.2 (1988): 25.

24. *The Sublime Object of Ideology* (London: Verso, 1989), 105.

25. "The Subversion of the Subject and the Dialectic of Desire in the Freudian Unconscious," trans. Alan Sheridan, in *Ecrits: A Selection* (New York: W. W. Norton, 1977), 319. Translation slightly modified.

26. This contradictory imperative explains Lacan's recasting of the superego/ego-ideal—conceived by Freud purely in terms of the Law's negative aspect—as the paradoxical figure of the Other insofar as it commands the subject to recover the lost object (by so naming the object, the Other prohibits its existence) and to *enjoy* it—an impossible task, bound to the impossibility of speech itself. "The Law," says Lacan, "appears to be giving the order, *'Jouis!'* ['Enjoy!'], to which the subject can only reply *'J'ouis'* (I hear), the *jouissance* being no more than understood" ("Subversion of the Subject," 319).

27. The minimum number of pauses needed to fix the color of a prisoner's disc is determined by the exclusion of at least one combination from the original set of discs, assuming that the number of black discs is always one less than the number of white discs. In a footnote ("Logical Time," 19 n.4), Lacan outlines the process by which one prisoner of four (four white discs, three black discs) determines his color after three suspensive scansions.

28. At the end of "Logical Time," Lacan emphasizes the *collective* character of the movement toward a conclusion, and the sociality of the constitution of the "I"—in this capacity, clearly linked to the social(izing) form of the ego-Ideal. In a footnote (20 n.6), he directs the reader to Freud's writings on collective psychology in *Group Psychology and the Analysis of the Ego* (*The Standard Edition of the Complete Psychological Works of Sigmund Freud,* ed. James Strachey, 24 vols. [London: Hogarth Press, 1953–74], vol. 18). I have written elsewhere on the collective fantasy of a suturing of the constitutive split of subjectivity that sustains

shared docuverses, exactly the function of equivocal closure that is formulated in the collective efforts of the subjective positions in Lacan's sophism. See my "Threnody: Psychoanalytic Digressions on the Subject of Hypertexts," in *Hypermedia and Literary Criticism,* 178. In that essay, I did not address what seems to me now a promising avenue of inquiry: how this communal effort to enclose the constitutive division of the speaking subject in a fantasy of conversing electronic personalities ("authors," "avatars," "actors," etc., each pretended to concretize an undivided, albeit openly "unreal" subject), works in the "consensual hallucination" of virtual reality.

29. *The Four Fundamental Concepts of Psycho-Analysis,* trans. Alan Sheridan (New York: W. W. Norton, 1981), 207.

30. I believe that a specifically Lacanian formula of the subject is far more flexible in regard to gender than is often asserted by critics of psychoanalysis. The most important elements of the final period of Lacan's teaching are expressly tied to formulas of the subject that exceed the classical Oedipal model, and to the recognition that this model is itself a *neurotic* understanding of the subject's relation to the Other and the Real. (I will return to this point later.) The use of gendered pronouns in discussions of specifically *digital* mimesis raises a more problematic subset of issues of gender within our models of the speaking subject. Most, if not all, of our prototypes of digital discourse are deeply infused with openly male/adolescent/"hacker" fascinations—a consequence of the social and sexual dynamics of professional and academic computing in the past five decades. As we develop and refine the theoretical discourses of digital practice, it will become increasingly important that we pay particular attention to functions of gender within the subject's relation to those practices.

31. *Fading* is Lacan's reworking of Ernest Jones's term, *aphanisis,* meaning a disappearance of all sexual desire, and (according to Jones) the general basis of castration anxiety in both sexes. Lacan rejects Jones's use of the term—the Lacanian ontology of the subject depends on the absolute primacy of castration—but retains the sense of "disappearance," now elevated to mean the "lethal" moment of the subject's manifestation under the signifier. Lacan introduces this use of the term in *The Four Fundamental Concepts,* 207–8. Jones introduced the term in its original sense in "Early Development of Female Sexuality," in *Papers on Psychoanalysis,* 5th ed. (London: Baillière, 1927), 438–51. Despite its English origins, *fading* is a common French word, dating from the early days of radio. Used to describe momentary disappearances of the audio signal, it seems an especially apt metaphor for the occultation of the subject in the digital field.

32. The penalty of fading is also a consequence of the irreversibility of Zizek's "act":

> We could say that the subject "undergoes" the act ("passes through" it) rather than "accomplishes" it: in it, the subject is annihilated and subsequently reborn (or not), i.e., the act involves a kind of temporary eclipse, *aphanisis,* of the subject. Which is why every act worthy of this name is "mad" in the sense of radical *unaccountability:* by means of it, I put at stake everything, including myself, my symbolic identity; the act is therefore always a "crime," a

"transgression," namely of the limit of the symbolic community to which I belong. (*Enjoy Your Symptom!*, 44)

33. "Notes upon a Case of Obsessional Neurosis," in *Standard Edition*, 10:151–318.

34. See Charles Melman, "On Obsessional Neurosis," trans. Stuart Schneiderman, in *Returning to Freud: Clinical Psychoanalysis in the School of Lacan*, ed. Stuart Schneiderman (New Haven: Yale University Press, 1980), 138; Stuart Schneiderman, *Rat Man* (New York: New York University Press, 1986), 25.

35. *The Seminar of Jacques Lacan, Book II: The Ego in Freud's Theory and in the Technique of Psychoanalysis (1954–1955)*, trans. John Forrester (New York: W. W. Norton, 1991), 268.

36. Serge Leclaire proposes that the obsessional's earliest experience of the constitutive division of language—the intervention of the (paternal) signifier of the mother's desire—is blocked by her unusually strong conviction that her child is sufficient, that her lack is filled by that substitute for the paternal phallus. The obsessional's desire is "precociously awakened and promptly satisfied"—his mother's satisfaction gives him every reason to believe the promise of the engagement with language, and the possibility of recovering the missed-remembered thing. ("Philo, or the Obsessional and His Desire," trans. Stuart Schneiderman, in *Returning to Freud*, 114–29.)

37. In this regard, fading serves a defensive function (against the spectre of lack in the Other) not unlike that envisaged by Jones in his first formulation of *aphanisis:* the positive value of occultation erases desire (in the Other, in the subject) by fixing the structure of lack at the moment of its precipitation. See Z. Lagrotta, "Le concept d'aphanisis dans la névrose obsessionelle," in *Hystérie et obsession: Les structures cliniques se la névrose et la direction de la cure* (Paris: Fourth International Encounter, 14–17 February 1986), 295.

38. In "Contingencies," I associated the instrumental function of the hypertext link with the fetish object, and an instrumental reading of the link ("doing stuff" with it) with perversion: "To read the link as purely a directional or associative structure is . . . to miss—to disavow [*Verleugnung:* Freud's term for mode of defense specific to perversion]—the divisions between the threads in a hypertext. 'Missing' the divisions is how the intentionality of hypertext navigation is realized: the directedness of the movement across the link constitutes a kind of defense against the spiraling turn that the link obscures. . . . What you see is the link as *link*, but what you miss is the link as *gap*" (134). The distinction between an obsessional faith in the possibility of narrative closure and a perverse fixation on the link as the instrument for movement toward closure is subtle and clearly demands a more detailed analysis than is possible here. Two provisional beginnings: (1) The distinction marks a shift in the character of the subject within each of the times of Lacan's sophism as applied to the problem of hypertext closure. The refusal to be fixed to a mark has an obsessional character; the willful, if not programmed, fixing to a mark has a perverse character. (2) Whereas the obsessional seeks to stop the gap in the Other with the positive term of his own lack, the pervert works entirely outside the economy of desire,

as the pure instrument of the Other's *jouissance,* with no concern for the gap in the Other, because its existence has been foreclosed.

39. You would thus be refusing the text's lure of possible closure *on its own terms.* Such a peremptory refusal of the logic of narrative (dis)closure constitutes, with regard to the transferential model I have been elaborating to this point, a *psychotic* response to the promise of closure. The psychotic subject refuses to engage in a dialogue with the Other and thus to shape his desire to the gap of the Other's desire. She gains, thereby, the exception to the penalty of the signifying split sought by the obsessional, but she loses any possibility of locating a position for herself within the Symbolic, that is, she loses the possibility of finding out how the story ends.

40. "Understanding the Act of Reading: The *WOE* Beginner's Guide to Dissection," *Writing on the Edge* 2.2 (1991): 117. See also chapter 5 in this volume.

41. For example: Peter fails to remember how the accident occurred because he can't face the knowledge of his responsibility for it. This repression accounts for the "undertone of hysteria" edging his fears (Douglas, "Print Pathways," ch. 5).

42. This echo of Lacan's famous *Che vuoi?*—the merciless question of the Other's desire ("Subversion of the Subject," 313)—is the opening of a sequel to this essay ("Ethics"), in Harpold, "Links and Their Vicissitudes."

BIBLIOGRAPHY

Barthes, Roland. *S/Z.* Trans. Richard Miller. New York: Hill and Wang, 1974.

Bolter, J. David. *Writing Space: The Computer, Hypertext, and the History of Writing.* Hillsdale, N.J.: Lawrence Erlbaum, 1991.

Bolter, J. David, Michael Joyce, John B. Smith, and Mark Bernstein. *Getting Started with Storyspace.* Cambridge, Mass.: Eastgate Systems, 1993.

De Man, Paul. "Autobiography as De-facement." *MLN* 94 (1979): 919–30.

Derrida, Jacques. *Mémoires for Paul de Man.* Trans. Cecile Lindsay, Jonathan Culler, and Eduardo Cadava. New York: Columbia University Press, 1986.

Douglas, J. Yellowlees. "Gaps, Maps, and Perception: What Hypertext Narratives (Don't) Do." *Perforations* 3.1 (Spring/Summer 1992).

———. "Print Pathways and Interactive Labyrinths: How Hypertext Narratives Affect the Act of Reading." Ph.D. diss., New York University, 1992.

———. "Understanding the Act of Reading: The *WOE* Beginner's Guide to Dissection." *Writing on the Edge* 2.2 (1991): 112–25.

Evenson, Shelley, John Rheinfrank, and Wendle Wulff. "Towards a Design Language for Representing Hypermedia Cues." *Hypertext '89.* New York: Association for Computing Machinery, 1989.

Fink, Bruce. "Notes on Temporal Tension." *Newsletter of the Freudian Field* 2.2 (1988): 23–28.

———. "The Subject as Metaphor." *Newsletter of the Freudian Field* 5.1/2 (1991): 16–20.

Fish, Stanley. *Is There a Text in This Class? The Authority of Interpretive Communities.* Cambridge: Harvard University Press, 1980.

Freud, Sigmund. *Group Psychology and the Analysis of the Ego*. Vol. 18 of *The Standard Edition of the Complete Psychological Works of Sigmund Freud*. Ed. James Strachey. London: Hogarth Press, 1953–74.

———. "Notes upon a Case of Obsessional Neurosis." In vol. 10 of *The Standard Edition of the Complete Psychological Works of Sigmund Freud*. Ed. James Strachey. London: Hogarth Press, 1953–74.

Genette, Gérard. *Seuils*. Paris: Editions du Seuil, 1987.

Guyer, Carolyn, and Martha Petry. *Izme Pass*. [Storyspace document.] *Writing on the Edge* 2.2 (1991).

Harpold, Terence. "The Contingencies of the Hypertext Link." *Writing on the Edge* 2.2 (1991): 126–38.

———. "The Grotesque Corpus." *Perforations* 3 (1992).

———. "Links and Their Vicissitudes." Ph.D. diss., University of Pennsylvania, 1994.

———. "Threnody: Psychoanalytic Digressions on the Subject of Hypertexts." In *Hypermedia and Literary Criticism*. Ed. Paul Delany and George P. Landow. Cambridge: MIT Press, 1991.

Jones, Ernest. "Early Development of Female Sexuality." In *Papers on Psychoanalysis*, 5th ed. London: Baillière, 1927.

Joyce, Michael. *Afternoon, a story*. [Storyspace document.] Cambridge, Mass.: Eastgate Systems, 1987.

———. "A Feel for Prose: Interstitial Links and the Contours of Hypertext." *Writing on the Edge* 4.1 (1992): 83–101.

———. "Selfish Interaction or Subversive Texts and the Multiple Novel." In *Hypertext/Hypermedia Handbook*. Ed. Emily Berk and Joseph Devlin. New York: McGraw-Hill/Intertext, 1991.

———. *WOE—A Memory of What Will Be*. [Storyspace document.] *Writing on the Edge* 2.2 (1991).

Lacan, Jacques. *The Four Fundamental Concepts of Psycho-Analysis*. Trans. Alan Sheridan. New York: W. W. Norton, 1981.

———. "The Function and Field of Speech and Language in Psychoanalysis." In *Ecrits: A Selection*. Trans. Alan Sheridan. New York: W. W. Norton, 1977.

———. "Logical Time and the Assertion of Anticipated Certainty: A New Sophism." Trans. Bruce Fink and Marc Silver. *Newsletter of the Freudian Field* 2.2 (1988): 4–22.

———. "The Mirror Stage as Formative of the I as Revealed in Psychoanalytic Experience." In *Ecrits: A Selection*. Trans. Alan Sheridan. New York: W. W. Norton, 1977.

———. *The Seminar of Jacques Lacan, Book II: The Ego in Freud's Theory and in the Technique of Psychoanalysis (1954–1955)*. Trans. John Forrester. New York: W. W. Norton, 1991.

———. "The Subversion of the Subject and the Dialectic of Desire in the Freudian Unconscious." In *Ecrits: A Selection*. Trans. Alan Sheridan. New York: W. W. Norton, 1977.

Lagrotta, Z. "Le concept d'aphanisis dans la névrose obsessionelle." In *Hystérie et Obsession: Les structures cliniques se la névrose et la direction de la cure*. Paris: Fourth International Encounter, 14–17 February 1986.

Landow, George P. *Hypertext: The Convergence of Contemporary Critical Theory and Technology*. Baltimore: Johns Hopkins University Press, 1992.

Leclaire, Serge. "Philo, or the Obsessional and His Desire." In *Returning to Freud: Clinical Psychoanalysis in the School of Lacan*. Ed. and trans. Stuart Schneiderman. New Haven: Yale University Press, 1980.

Melman, Charles. "On Obsessional Neurosis." In *Returning to Freud: Clinical Psychoanalysis in the School of Lacan*. Ed. and trans. Stuart Schneiderman. New Haven: Yale University Press, 1980.

Moulthrop, Stuart. "Hypertext and 'the Hyperreal.'" *Hypertext '89*. New York: Association for Computing Machinery, 1989.

———. "Reading from the Map: Metonymy and Metaphor in the Fiction of Forking Paths." In *Hypermedia and Literary Criticism*. Ed. Paul Delany and George P. Landow. Cambridge: MIT Press, 1991.

———. "Toward a Paradigm for Reading Hypertexts: Making Nothing Happen in Hypermedia Fiction." In *Hypertext/Hypermedia Handbook*. Ed. Emily Berk and Joseph Devlin. New York: McGraw-Hill/Intertext, 1991.

———. *Victory Garden*. [Storyspace document.] Cambridge, Mass.: Eastgate Systems, 1991.

Nielsen, Jakob. *Hypertext and Hypermedia*. San Diego: Academic Press, 1990.

Samuels, Robert. "Logical Time and *Jouissance*." *Newsletter of the Freudian Field* 4.1–2 (1990): 69–77.

Schneiderman, Stuart. *Rat Man*. New York: New York University Press, 1986.

Zizek, Slavoj. *Enjoy Your Symptom!* New York: Routledge, 1992.

———. *Looking Awry: An Introduction to Jacques Lacan through Popular Culture*. Cambridge: MIT Press, 1991.

———. *The Sublime Object of Ideology*. London: Verso, 1989.

THE POLITICS OF HYPERTEXT

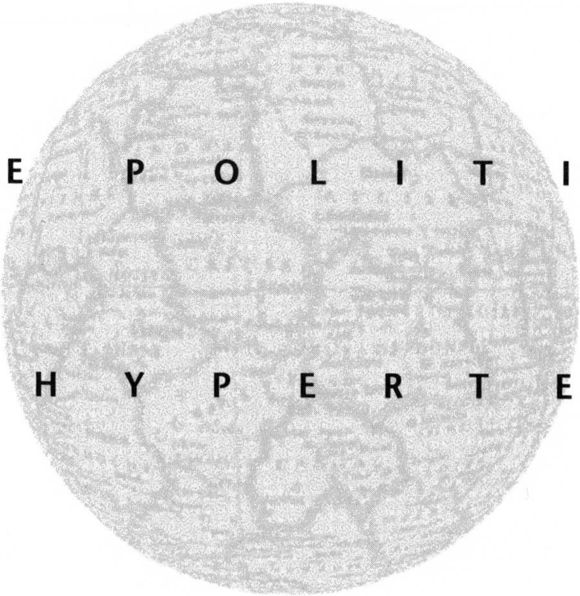

The Political Computer: Hypertext, Democracy, and Habermas

Charles Ess

7

A puzzling theoretical topography emerges from the literature on hypertext and computer communications: the claim that these technologies will democratize communication and society appears as a central justification, yet there is surprisingly little discussion of this claim, research on whether democratization occurs shows mixed results, and researchers even dispute if democratization is in fact desirable. This theoretical topography points initially to two central problems facing the democratization claim. First, its critics dismiss it as utopian or unworkable, and second, the claim threatens to become simply an ideology, an expression of personal or corporate preference. Without a more comprehensive theoretical foundation to counter these difficulties, the democratization claim can easily be dismissed by those who do not share the preference for democratic polity, and so it loses much of its justificatory power.

In light of these problems, I propose a turn to the Frankfurt School critical theory of Jürgen Habermas, who provides a comprehensive theory of democratic polity that avoids the initial criticisms of the democratization claim as utopian and ideological. Habermas's effort to defend modernity and modern technologies, including the computer technologies underlying hypertext, against critiques by both other members of the Frankfurt School and the postmodernist Jean-François Lyotard adds to the theory's ability to support the democratization claim in hypertext theory. And, by examining Habermas's theory of communicative action and his discourse ethic in greater detail, I show how this theory further articulates important theoretical connections between communication and democratic polity, providing still stronger theoretical justification for the democratization claim. Finally, I suggest what a hypertext system would look like if it were constructed according to the rules of Habermas's discourse ethic, so as to facilitate the kind of communication Habermas sees as a necessary condition of democratic polity. Such a system turns out to be consistent with previous claims and observations regarding democratization, but by incorporating Habermas's discourse ethic, it refines both the understanding of democracy and the technological and social conditions necessary for it to emerge. In these ways, Habermas's theory of communicative action provides a powerful theoretical framework in support of the democratization claim. At the same time, his discourse ethic offers important guidelines for hypertext practitioners who wish to redeem the promise of democratization.

Hypertext and Democracy: Theory and Practice

An Overview of Hypertext Theory

At first glance, hypertext and hypermedia systems appear to rest on the rather simple idea of the computer as an information manager that allows electronic recording and exploration of units of information and their relationships, the latter appearing in the form of links. In the now extensive literature on hypertext and hypermedia, there is apparent consensus regarding the origins of the idea of hypertext: it is usual to credit Vannevar Bush and his conception of the Memex machine, followed by the work of Douglas C. Engelbart and Theodor H. Nelson from the 1960s on.[1]

This consensus on origins quickly unravels, however, as we examine the theoretical issues surrounding hypertext and hypermedia. For example, Bush's original notion, reinforced and expanded by Nelson's various publications—that a hypermedia system would more adequately serve the researcher insofar as its nonlinear links more closely articulated what he took to be the natural function of the mind to associate ideas and information—is often contested, if not simply ignored (compare Barrett, xii–xviii). Similarly, hypertext and hypermedia are often defined in terms of their enabling a nonlinear style of writing and reading, one that represents a revolutionary change from the primarily linear mode of reading and writing associated with the book.[2] But here again, there is considerable dispute as to whether nonlinearity so clearly distinguishes hypermedia systems from printed text.[3]

Indeed, discussion of the most fundamental theoretical issues of hypermedia, including its basic definition, functions, and proposed educational and political implications, displays an equally fundamental diversity of views. To begin with, seeking a definition of hypertext or hypermedia reveals a spectrum of candidates. For example, although

Spiro and Jehng ("Cognitive Flexibility," 166) define hypertext in the familiar term of nonlinearity, their approach to hypertext appears to presume that such a text is largely limited to one reader on one machine. This conception of hypertext based on an isolated reader-learner dramatically contrasts with Bolter's more global understanding of hypertext, which includes computerized communications networks that enable both electronic mail and on-line group discussions in newsgroups or lists. For Bolter, "a communications network is . . . a hypertext in which no one writer or reader has substantial control, and because no one has control, no one has substantial responsibility" (*Writing Space,* 29). Somewhere between these two boundaries are definitions that insist on distinguishing between hypertext and the collaborative dimensions suggested by electronic networks, and definitions that join hypertext with collaboration and communication.[4]

Such definitional diversity suggests that, like the "fluid word" of electronic word processing, hypertext is itself a fluid concept.[5] Indeed, hypertext has been identified as resting on "fuzzy concepts" with regard to its epistemology; and as hypermedia further involves "fuzzy entities," should we, for instance, "include the user as a hypermedia entity"?[6] This lack of definitional clarity reflects not only the intrinsic fluidity of the electronic medium, as that medium is incessantly reshaped by on-going developments in hardware and software, but also what others have noted as the atheoretical character of much work on hypertext. So, for example, Spiro and Jehng observe that hypertext research in education is largely "driven by the power of the technology," rather than by, say, a theoretically grounded orientation, to the purposes and stages of learning and to the cognitive psychology of nonlinear learning (166). Similarly, Romiszowski describes the theory base of hypermedia in education as "at best patchy and inconsistent," such that, on balance, "we are still in the potential solution-seeks-compatible-problem stage of development" ("Hypertext/Hypermedia Solution," 340, 350). Indeed, it is not even clear that the "solution" of hypertext works: although networked hypertext systems appear to succeed in achieving important educational goals,[7] some research suggests that hypertext does not in fact enable more efficient access to information.[8]

The Claim of Democratization in Hypertext Theory

This diversity regarding basic definitions of hypertext, alongside the relative scarcity of theory in the educational domain, points to a set of central theoretical problems in the political domain. Perhaps the most compelling claim made for hypertext systems is that they will democratize access to information and thereby contribute to a greater democratization of society. This claim is thematic for hypertext visionary Nelson (*Dream Machines*) and is treated perhaps most extensively in those theories of hypertext rooted in literary critical theory, such as Landow's discussion of what he characterizes as "the generally democratic, even anarchic tendencies of hypertext" (*Hypertext,* 169–75, 185–90).

Apart from such critical theory approaches, however, the central claim of democratization has received strikingly little attention in either theoretical discussion or research regarding the impacts of applied systems.[9] Moreover, the small body of literature outside critical theory that discusses hypermedia and communication with regard to their potential for democratization is at best inconclusive and at worst distinctly skeptical and dismissive.

To begin with, if we look for empirical research to support or deny the democratization claim, the results appear to be mixed. For example, one of the best-known hypermedia systems, Intermedia, was intensively studied during its initial implementation at Brown University (Beeman et al., *Intermedia*). According to the study's principal author, however, democratization impacts of Intermedia are not clearly related to the hypermedia system as such and seem to be the result of larger social contexts in which the system is used.[10]

In addition to these mixed results in practice, theoretical discussion is divided. Romiszowski criticizes Bush's and Nelson's shared conception that hypertext will enable nearly universal access to a global network of electronic libraries as conjuring up a vision of a flood of information in which millions drown (330). Nor does everyone follow Landow, Bolter, and others who celebrate the "anarchic" or democratizing dimensions of hypertext that result from its blurring of the traditional boundaries of authority between author and reader, teacher and student. For example, McKnight, Dillon, and Richardson suggest that hypertext may support collaborative work—but only if traditional hierarchies between, say, a professor and a junior research assistant can be preserved in hypertextual annotations (136). Such an approach, which intends to preserve traditional hierarchies of authority, directly contrasts with the democratizing hypertext envisioned by Landow and others. Finally, Richartz and Rüdebusch ("Collaboration in Hypermedia Environments") take up the claims of democratization made by Bush and Nelson, only to dismiss what they characterize as a "fully democratic and anarchistic" hyperinformation environment for failing to "meet the needs of many commercial and public users, who do not want to rely on such a utopian society" (314).

The contrast between proponents and skeptics may be lessened somewhat if we distinguish between *degrees* of democratization. Writers such as Landow appear to have in mind democratization within a limited context—namely, the context of a class or computer lab. Democratization with regard to the traditional student-teacher relationship, however, is clearly different in degree from the democratization of a whole society or culture. This latter degree of democratization seems to be assumed by Richartz and Rüdebusch. The apparent debate thus dissolves insofar as proponent and skeptic use the term *democratization* in different senses. Even if such a distinction might serve to reduce the sharp contrast between proponents and critics, however, the need for such a distinction reiterates the central point: there is no agreement in hypertext theory regarding fundamental claims and definitions.

The literature of hypertext theory thus presents an odd theoretical topography. On the one hand, a crucial claim—the claim of democratization—is made for this technology. On the other hand, the literature in general is remarkable for its relative silence regarding this central claim. And among authors who explicitly address the democratization claim, there is a clear divide between proponents, such as Bush, Nelson, and Landow, and skeptics who see no essential connection between hypertext and democratization at all.

This theoretical topography also presents a series of philosophical difficulties, the most critical of which are the problems of ideology and utopianism. First, the criticism that such democratic societies are utopian means, simply, that the goals and values justifying these societies cannot be realized in the real world. Some representatives of Frankfurt School critical theory, for example, find the goals and ideals of democratic theory too far removed from the particularities and constraints of everyday praxis.[11] The rejection of democratic polity as utopian, moreover, is reinforced by a second criticism—that the choice of either democracy or hierarchy simply reflects personal or socially conditioned preferences, preferences or values that are *ideological* because no stronger reason or set of claims supports them.

Readers familiar with critical theory associated with the Frankfurt School will recognize here an instance of what Habermas in *Legitimation Crisis* and Lyotard in *Postmodern Condition* discuss as a legitimation crisis. Briefly, a legitimation crisis is a kind of social identity crisis experienced by the welfare state, as the primary values or beliefs that legitimate or support the authority of the state (and, by extension, other entities, such as political institutions, the natural sciences as a claim to knowledge, and so on) are discovered to be inconsistent or perhaps groundless. This discovery is problematic in modern societies because such societies, since their foundation in Enlightenment rationalism, in part claim that the legitimacy of their institutions no longer rests on tradition or religion but upon reason. Not only does such a discovery call into question the legitimacy of modern institutions, it also leads to a sense of lost freedom, meaning, and identity.[12] Lyotard expands this notion of crisis to apply it more generally to what he calls the metanarratives of the modern period, which include the metanarrative of Enlightenment rationalism as such (8).

This concern with legitimation, however, occasions a central dispute between Habermas and postmodernists such as Lyotard, and I shall return to that dispute in what follows. At this point, however, it is worth noting that the concern with legitimation is by no means restricted to critical theory and postmodernism. Several "crises of legitimacy" that have to do with difficulties in theories of property, for example, and in economic and political philosophy have aroused discussion in these domains (see Ess, "Technology, Huxley, and Hope," 34).

If the preference for democratic polity *is* simply ideological, then the dispute is irresoluble: some of us prefer democratization and some of us do not, and nothing more can or need be said. Accepting this charge therefore reduces a central justification of hypertext, crucial to Bush, Nelson, and Landow, to a mere ideological preference that can easily be brushed aside by those who do not share it.

These criticisms call for a theoretical framework that can demonstrate that the impulse towards democratization represents a value valid on more than ideological grounds—and that such democratization is in fact possible. This theoretical framework would powerfully reinforce the democratization thematic of Bush, Nelson, and Landow as a rationale supporting hypertext development. Such a theory, however, is traditionally more the concern of philosophers than of the educators, information scientists, education researchers, and other contributors to hypertext theory. Not surprisingly, then, as important as such a theory would be to support the democratization claim, current literature in hypertext theory does not provide it. Indeed, even if we shift our focus for a moment to larger but related domains beyond hypertext theory, we encounter the same theoretical topography and problem of ideology.

Democratization and Computers: The Larger Domain

The diversity of opinion regarding democratization within hypertext theory and praxis closely mirrors current scholarship in education, communications, and information science. Indeed, proponents of communications networks as such often make the claim of democratization, but a review of the literature pertinent to this claim provides further examples of theoretical deficits that a coherent theory of hypertext must overcome.

The extensive, if ambiguous, literature on the social and political effects of informatics includes both popular and scholarly research in communications and education and Jean-François Lyotard's analysis of postmodernism.[13] But in examining this literature, a first theoretical deficit immediately appears. As central as the notion of democracy is to these claims and this research, the literature has paid strikingly little attention to just what *democracy* might mean. For example, Michael Dertouzos understands democratic communications to prevail when "nearly everyone would be able to put his or her ideas, concerns and demands before all others."[14] Similarly, Sproull and Kiesler appear to use *democracy* as a synonym for the "open, free-ranging discourse" that often unfolds on computer networks—a discourse further associated with "broader access to information."[15] But recalling Romiszowski, how is such democracy to be distinguished from simple noise?[16]

This lack of definitional precision correlates with the considerable disagreement in the literature about whether communications networks in fact achieve such democracy and, on a fundamentally philosophical level, whether such democracy is in fact desirable. Research on electronic communications, including the use of communications in educational settings, reports mixed results regarding the degree to which such communications in fact achieve democratization.[17] Furthermore, some evidence indicates that, rather than democratizing communication by expanding access, electronic communications reflect and reinforce existing patterns of hierarchy and discrimination. For example, Susan Herring documents on-going patterns of sexism in the communications facilitated by a specific BITNET list.[18] Still more harshly, from a standpoint defined by Michel Foucault and Paulo Freire, Klaus Krippendorff finds that existing communication theory and technologies offer little in the way of what he calls "emancipatory discourse." Rather, he says, "information theory has created options and enabled a tremendous increase in the capacity for communication through technical channels but contributes little to the understanding of how such capacity may be used."[19] This work demonstrates in practice what others criticize as the failures of prevailing communications theories to endorse a genuinely inclusive and democratic ethic.

More generally, like those hypertext theorists critical of claims for hypertext democratization, not everyone agrees that the democratization of communications networks is a good thing. Proponents of democratization point to the French student strike in the spring of 1992, which took advantage of Minitel, a public telecommunications system, to organize demonstrations (*The Machine That Changed the World*, pt. 5), an example of computer communications contributing to democracy. Similar hopes for democratizing impacts are behind the installation of Public Electronic Network (PEN) in Santa Monica, California. But just as not all French government administrators may have greeted the students' use of Minitel as democratization, not every government representative is enthusiastic about the PEN version of electronic democracy ("Electronic Democracy: The PEN Is Mighty"). Similarly, some managers and administrators believe that such democracy threatens the hierarchy of modern organizations.[20]

We find here again, then, a theoretical topography that closely resembles the one we have seen emerge within the domain of hypertext theory. This topography—consisting of inadequate definitions of democracy, disagreement about the degree to which communications networks achieve such democracy, and, most fundamentally, mixed beliefs about whether democracy is desirable—only reinforces my initial conclusion regarding hypertext theory. Technology may be driven by dramatically contrasting values—say, democratic versus antidemocratic ones—but these values themselves are in dispute, and the literature offers no suggestion of how to resolve this dispute. We are thus again left with a technology possibly driven by dramatically contrasting values that may simply reflect preference and utopian ideology.

Critical Theory and a Turn to the Frankfurt School

Within the domain of hypertext theory, the democratization claim seems most fully endorsed in approaches to hypertext, such as Landow's, that explore the relationship between hypertext and hypermedia systems and significant concepts in structuralist, poststructuralist, and postmodern theory. These critical theories based in literary perspectives would hence seem to be the most attractive if we wish to pursue the promise of democratization.

I propose to examine another form of critical theory—namely, that of the Frankfurt School. Frankfurt School critical theory, specifically, the communicative action theory of Jürgen Habermas, offers a theoretical approach that articulates a more comprehensive hypertext theory, one that, first of all, defuses charges of ideology and utopianism. My turning to this school of theory is suggested by several observations. Literary critical theories (understood here primarily as those based especially in structuralist, poststructuralist, and postmodernist work) and Frankfurt School theory share a number of common origins and theoretical interests. Both, for example, make use of the work of Freud and Nietzsche; both frequently turn to the aesthetic and literary domains for theoretical insight. Both criticize modernity in various ways—especially what they see as the repressive structures of modern bureaucracies and social life. In particular, both Frankfurt School critical theorists and literary critical theorists have "a strong antipathy toward a modern culture dominated by technological rationality."[21] Since literary critical theories have supported a hypertext theory stressing democratization, these shared interests and themes stand as *prima facie* reasons for exploring Frankfurt School critical theory as well.

Moreover, because the critical theory of the Frankfurt School centers precisely on the philosophical issues surrounding the possibility and desirability of democratic polity, it presents itself capable of responding to the charge of ideology that attaches to the democratization claim. Frankfurt School critical theory confronts another problem hypertext theorists must face, namely, whether the technologies of hypertext (computers and communications networks) are intrinsically antidemocratic.[22]

Democracy, Ideology, and the Relationship between Theory and Practice

Frankfurt School critical theory began in Germany in response to the great political crises of the 1920s and 1930s—the emergence of fascism in the West (including, of course, Nazism in Germany itself) and the rise of Stalinism in the East. These failures in the quest for Enlightenment democracy force several questions, best stated in terms of the relationship between theory and practice. To begin with, they may support an argument for ethical relativism, or the claim that no universally valid beliefs or values exist. If such is the case, then the failure of Enlightenment democracy in some parts of the world simply reflects the diversity of cultural values: although Enlightenment theorists might have believed that the worth of the individual, freedom, and democratic polity applied to all human beings, the lack of universal acceptance of these values suggests instead that they are simply culturally determined.

In the face of such relativism, ethical and political philosophy have historically attempted to establish moral norms valid not simply within a given culture but within all. But the effort to establish universally valid norms raises a central problem regarding the relationship between theory and practice: any putatively universal claim runs the danger of excessive transcendence, in which the universal claim fails to represent or reflect precisely the individual and particular dimensions of specific people living in specific times and cultures. The effort to counter ethical relativism, in short, runs the risk of establishing universal norms that at the same time become too transcendent and too utopian to be realized in human praxis. The recognition of these allied problems of relativism and the theory-praxis relationship is at least as old as Plato and Aristotle, but Frankfurt School critical theory takes up this question especially in light of the work of Kant and Hegel.[23]

Habermas attempts to meet the problems of the theory-praxis relationship in part by what he calls "reconstruction" of the principal theoretical sources of democratic polity. At the same time, Frankfurt School theory responds to the theory-praxis issue by turning its attention to the nature of theory itself. In their efforts to establish a theory capable of generating universally valid norms (that could thus overcome the problems of relativism and the charge of ideology attaching to the democratic preference, and thereby sustain the validity of Enlightenment democracy), critical theorists, including Habermas, have attempted to join more traditional philosophical theories to more recent, empirically oriented psychological and sociological theories, most especially those of Max Weber and Sigmund Freud. In so doing, they hope to bring together the *normative* or *prescriptive* power of traditional ethics and politics (as these seek universal norms that prescribe what *ought* to be the case) and the *descriptive* accounts of empirical sciences (as these carefully attend to the particularities of human praxis in their descriptions of what *is* the case).

By thus refashioning the philosophical theories that undergird the ethical and political values of Enlightenment democracy, the Frankfurt School seeks to establish what Seyla Benhabib calls "quasi-transcendent" norms. Such norms remain compelling, since they may possess universal validity and thus overcome the problems of relativism and ideology. At the same time, they more fully incorporate descriptive accounts of the particularities and realities of human praxis and thus more successfully avoid the charge of utopianism (*Critique, Norm, and Utopia*, 263).

Modern Technology as Antidemocratic

Finally, I should note that Frankfurt School critical theorists developed a series of critiques of modernity and modern technology.[24] Enlightenment theorists, beginning with Descartes, held that modern science and technology contributed to the larger Enlightenment project of greater economic and political freedom in a democratic polity.

The paradigm of human rationality is defined for early modernity by Descartes, whose project of seeking absolute certainty by submitting all claims to knowledge to the acid bath of radical doubt resulted in the isolated self, aware only of its own existence, as the sole instance of certain knowledge. As a consequence, however, human reason emerges radically divorced from, and superior to, the senses and nature.

This divorce between human reason and the natural order provides the ideological justification for the human domination of nature by means of technology. Like human masters whose belief in the natural inferiority of the enslaved justifies their domination, radically divorcing human reason from nature allows us, in Descartes's phrase, "to render ourselves masters and possessors of nature."[25] This domination of nature supposedly brings freedom from labor and disease that in turn makes possible the greater human freedoms of a democratic polity.

Drawing upon the sociological insights of Max Weber,[26] the Frankfurt School argued that this dualistic conception of the relationship between self and nature led directly to various problems of modernity and modern technology, including the failure of Enlightenment democracy (see McCarthy, "Translator's Introduction," ix). More precisely, the project of modern technology as a primary expression of an isolated Cartesian reason is frequently characterized in the Frankfurt School as a project of domination and oppression of both nature and humanity.[27] For example, Max Horkheimer and Theodor W. Adorno argue about whether rationality in the West is intrinsically an instrument of domination (in which case, the Enlightenment endorsement of rationality could be expected to lead precisely to modern totalitarianisms), or whether reason as such may enjoy the autonomy and capacity for democratic polity assumed by Enlightenment theorists (in which case modern totalitarianisms reflect simply a distortion of such reason associated especially with modern technology).[28] Herbert Marcuse, in turn, argues in his *One-Dimensional Man* that the technological apparatus of contemporary society "tends to become totalitarian to the extent to which it determines not only the socially needed occupations, skills, and attitudes, but also individual needs and aspirations. It thus obliterates the opposition between the private and public existence, between individual and social needs. Technology serves to institute new, more effective, and more pleasant forms of social control and social cohesion" (xv). What Marcuse calls the totalitarian tendency of modern technology he further identifies with modern rationality itself.[29]

Following these Frankfurt School critiques of modern rationality and technology, Jürgen Habermas hence faces a two-fold project. To defend Enlightenment emphases on human freedom and democratic polity as more than ideological preferences and utopianism, he must develop a critical theory that can establish these emphases as universally valid, but he must avoid rendering them excessively transcendent and thus impractical and divorced from the particularities of human praxis. Moreover, he must develop a defense of democratic polity resting on a conception of human reason that also avoids the totalitarian dimensions of modern reason—and modern technology—identified by Frankfurt School critical theorists.

Again, such a theory clearly intersects the interests of a hypertext theory that endorses the democratization claim and yet is faced with charges of ideology and utopianism. If Habermas's theory can demonstrate that preference for democracy rests on universally valid claims, it will serve to defend hypertext theory. Moreover, Habermas's theory may work to counter charges raised by Frankfurt School critical theorists, as well as postmodernists, that the technologies of hypertext are themselves intrinsically antidemocratic.

In addition, as it focuses on the structures of communication, it provides a clear articulation of how communication, under specified conditions, is theoretically conjoined with democratic polity. This conjunction of communication and democracy supports hypertext theorists who claim that hypertext, especially as implemented by communications networks, contributes to democratic polity. Finally, Habermas's theory presents and defends rules defining the conditions of democratic communication, rules that will serve as powerful guidelines for hypertext systems that thus fulfill the democratization claim.

Habermas's Theory of Communicative Action
Modern Rationalism, Technology, and the Problem of Democracy

Adorno, Horkheimer, Marcuse, and other representatives of the Frankfurt School recognize that the Cartesian paradigm of reason is the source of both Enlightenment optimism regarding reason, and thus the possibility of democratic polity, and also the antidemocratic dimensions of modernity, including modern technology. They further recognize that modernity presents a dilemma: attempting to jettison the Cartesian paradigm because of its antidemocratic consequences rejects the foundation of democratic polity as such.

Habermas attempts to forge a middle ground between these two alternatives, one that acknowledges the critiques launched against modernity and modern rationalism in the Frankfurt School (and postmodernism) and at the same time preserves the modern commitment to human freedom and democratic polity. To do so, Habermas's theory of communicative action sets out to establish a notion of rationality—what he calls "communicative reason"—as an alternative to the Cartesian paradigm. According Habermas, communicative reason can be discerned in everyday experiences of communication, particularly in efforts to resolve conflict by dialogue rather than by force. By grounding communicative reason in this way, Habermas reformulates modern notions of freedom and democratic polity so as to defuse the various criticisms mounted against the Cartesian paradigm and its correlative problems, including the claim that modern technology is intrinsically oppressive and antidemocratic.

I examine Habermas's theory in four stages, first discussing how he grounds his understanding of communicative reason in what he identifies as the tacit assumptions of discourse. Second, I take up Habermas's effort to defend the universalizability of moral claims in specific kinds of discourse against the relativist position that denies the possibility of universally valid claims. These two points together provide a defense against the charge of ideology that attaches to the preference for democratic politics, especially since they provide a way of countering the relativism underlying this charge. Thirdly I discuss more extensively Habermas's notion of communicative rationality, with a specific focus on Habermas's discourse ethic, especially as it is grounded in carefully defined notions of freedom and community. Finally I examine what Habermas identifies as the ideal conditions of discourse—conditions that are at once conditions for democratic polity—and his proposed rules of reason as these structure the context of democratizing discourse. Taken together, these points outline a communicative reason that sidesteps the criticisms of the Cartesian paradigm, modern technology, and the computer technologies that underlie hypertext. Furthermore, these points are central to Habermas's effort to counter the criticisms that democratic polity is utopian or rests solely on mere ideology, and to make clear the theoretical relationships between communication and democratic polity.

Tacit Assumptions of Discourse

Habermas most extensively developed his theory of communicative action in the two volumes so titled (*Theorie des Kommunikativen Handelns*). In taking up a communicative ethic, he taps into a rich discussion among continental, especially German-speaking, philosophers that reaches back to the mid-1960s.[30] More recently, communicative ethics has been a theme of philosophical analysis and discussion by critical theorists such as Habermas, critical rationalists like K.-O. Apel and Hermann Lübbe, Kantians, and others like Seyla Benhabib and Fred Dallmayr. In addition, Habermas frequently makes use of the work of Stephen Toulmin (especially *The Uses of Argument*), who is well known for developing a "pragmatic account of argumentative validity" that replaces the focus of traditional logic on propositional inference with a focus on conversation or discourses (Ingram, *Critical Theory and Philosophy*, 147). Toulmin's more recent work, *Human Understanding,* also interests Habermas, precisely because it examines argument with a view towards the disputes between absolutist positions (that insist with dogmatic certainty on the universal validity of a given set of claims) and relativist claims (Habermas, *Theorie des Kommunikativen Handelns*, 24–28).

Specifically, Habermas draws on Robert Alexy, whose "Theory of Practical Discourse" ("Eine Theorie des praktischen Diskurses") articulates both assumptions and rules that Habermas has made central to his own communicative ethic. Alexy articulates as the starting point of a communicative ethic what he identifies as the basic assumption of conversation or discourse: "Whoever expresses a value judgment or an obligational judgment such as 'It is unjust if citizens in a state are discriminated against because of the color of their skin' or 'You should help your friend who has got into difficulty,' raises the claim that it is justifiable and hence correct or true" (151). Ingram summarizes Habermas's version of this crucial starting point this way: "Discourses typically arise whenever the justice of a norm, the sincerity of an expressed intention, or the truth of a cognitive belief is disputed. Claims to justice and truth are of special interest to him [Habermas], since, whenever we assert that something is true or right, we imply that all other persons should agree with us" (*Critical Theory*, 147). In this way, consensus replaces deductive and inductive validity as "the touchstone for truth and justice." And, presumably because persons in dialogue bring to their discourse their individual and particular backgrounds, interests, and so on, along with their skills in rational analysis, such consensus necessarily binds together "contingency and necessity, particularity and universality, factuality and normativity in discourse" (147).

In other words, Habermas sees in such consensus a conjunction between moral claims as ostensibly valid universally (the concern of traditional ethical and political theory) *and* the instantiation of these claims in ways that reflect and preserve the individual and particular interests of individuals in the domain of praxis. In this way, communicative action responds to the thematic concern of the Frankfurt School with the relationship between theory and practice—specifically, with the effort to avoid a "transcendental" set of moral norms so far removed from the particulars of human praxis that they become utopian in the sense of being unworkable. To put it another way, if communicative action works by consensus in this way, it grounds a set of quasi-transcendent, universally valid moral norms that are neither utopian (because they are too far removed from praxis) nor merely ideological (because they reflect only particular, culturally relative beliefs).[31]

Relativism and the Universalizability of Moral Claims

What Alexy and Habermas identify as the tacit assumption of discourse—that our claims are true or valid for others as well as for ourselves—can be restated as the universal, or potentially universalizable, validity of especially moral claims (that is, claims surrounding questions of truth and justice). Both Alexy and Habermas launch their communicative ethic with this claim of universal validity against the familiar arguments of contemporary naturalism and intuitionism that result in ethical relativism—the view that all claims, including moral ones, are at best valid only for the individual or the individual as situated in a culture.[32]

In addition to observing that discourse rests on a tacit assumption of such universally valid claims, Habermas attempts to defend the universalizability of claims in two ways. First, he offers an analysis of discourse in natural science that relies heavily on Toulmin. Second, he employs the phenomenological notion of the lifeworld as the larger context of discourse. These two points together, along with his critique of the arguments for relativism, work to argue that at least some forms of discourse, primarily in virtue of their *form,* may lead to universally valid claims.

To begin with, then, Habermas makes use of an analogy with the inductive process that allows scientists to come to agreement on causal relations as factual, necessary, and universal. It is to be emphasized that such agreement on causal relations involves a claim to universal validity: that is, scientists do *not* assert that their identification of causal relations as factual and necessary is simply a claim valid for individuals or individuals in a given culture. Such an identification of causal relations is not simply the result of personal preference or ideological conditioning.

In particular, according to Habermas, the *conditions* under which a scientist's discourse occurs are necessary conditions for arriving at universal or potentially universal claims. By analogy, and using a model of argument analysis established by Stephen Toulmin, Habermas argues that "under controlled conditions approximating complete impartiality and fairness, *the moral principle of universalizability (U)* enables us to agree factually on the consequences, favorable or otherwise, of norms, in a manner that is itself normatively binding."[33]

More generally, in *The Theory of Communicative Action,* volume 1, *Reason and the Rationalization of Society,* Habermas develops a phenomenological notion of a "lifeworld," one "bounded by the totality of interpretations presupposed by the members as background knowledge" (13). Such a lifeworld, with its background of shared assumptions, is then the context for the communicative practice Habermas takes as paradigmatic of rationality:

> Actions regulated by norms, expressive self-presentations, and also evaluative expressions, supplement constative speech acts in constituting a communicative practice which, against the background of a lifeworld, is oriented to achieving, sustaining, and renewing consensus—and indeed a consensus that rests on the intersubjective recognition of criticizable validity claims. The rationality inherent in this practice is seen in the fact that a communicatively achieved agreement must be based *in the end* on reasons. And the rationality of those who participate in this communicative practice is determined by whether, if necessary, they could, *under suitable circumstances,* provide reasons for their expressions. Thus the rationality proper to the communicative practice of everyday life points to the practice of argumentation as a court of appeal that makes it possible to continue communicative action with other means when disagreements can no longer be repaired with everyday routines and yet are not to be settled by the direct or strategic use of force. (17–18)

Habermas goes on to point out that what he calls communicative reason is centrally bound up with argumentation, defined as "that type of speech in which participants thematize contested validity claims and attempt to vindicate or criticize them through arguments" (18). Again following Toulmin, Habermas emphasizes that rational behavior includes openness to argument—that is, a willingness to recognize valid reasons, whether in order to accept or to criticize these, in contrast with the person "deaf to argument," the person who ignores reasons that run contrary to her or his views. Rational expressions are thus open to criticism and thus to improvement if mistakes of fact or logic are made. And, as Habermas points out, rationality and argumentation of this sort are further interwoven with learning: "We call a person rational who, in the cognitive-instrumental sphere, expresses reasonable opinions and acts efficiently; but this rationality remains accidental if it is not coupled with the ability to learn from mistakes, from the refutation of hypotheses and from the failure of interventions" (18).

Finally, notes McCarthy, given the ability to criticize claims within the context of the lifeworld and thus to identify and correct mistakes,

> forms of argumentation take shape which may be transmitted and developed within a cultural tradition and even embodied in specific cultural institutions. Thus, for instance, the scientific enterprise, the legal system, and the institutions for producing, disseminating, and criticizing art represent enduring possibilities of hypothetically examining the truth of statements, the rightness of actions and norms, or the authenticity of expressions, and of productively assimilating our negative experiences in these dimensions. ("Translator's Introduction," xiii)

In short, communicative action, the process of giving and criticizing reasons for holding or rejecting particular claims, is seen to operate in argumentation in the sciences, law, and criticism. Insofar as one grants that such argumentation leads to universally valid claims—an admission one is most likely to make with regard to the sciences—one then concedes Habermas's central point: communicative action defines a rationality capable, through discourse, of arriving at universal norms.

Of course, Habermas recognizes the facts of cultural relativism, that putatively universal norms agreed upon by all members of a culture are not agreed upon by members of other cultures. Such cultural relativism, however, does not necessarily force us to accept ethical relativism, the stronger claim that no universally valid claims or beliefs, especially moral norms, exist. In the first volume of *The Theory of Communicative Action,* Habermas takes up this issue in part as he makes use of Toulmin and others to develop what he calls a "formal-pragmatic" account of communicative action, one fully informed by the recognition of cultural relativism.[34] In addition, he directly faces the arguments for ethical relativism based on cultural relativism by way of reconstructing debates about rationality among English anthropologists and philosophers. Habermas finds that the case for relativism is not conclusive, which means that "while the universalistic claim of formal pragmatics cannot be conclusively redeemed . . . it can be rendered plausible" (138). At the same time, however, in keeping with the Frankfurt School's thematic interest in avoiding a theory too far removed from the domain of praxis, the claim of universal validity for communicative reason must be tested, and thus verified by praxis.[35]

Freedom and the Ethics of Discourse

In general, Habermas argues that universally valid claims may emerge from discourse, insofar as such discourse meets certain necessary (but not sufficient) conditions, the first of which is freedom and equality for participants. Referring to Habermas's more recent essay "Justice and Solidarity," Ingram describes Habermas's summary of "the basic intuition embodied in a discourse ethic" with the statement that "under the moral point of view, one must be able to test whether a norm or a mode of action could be generally accepted by those affected by it, such that their acceptance of it would be rationally motivated and hence uncoerced" (6; Ingram, *Critical Theory and Philosophy,* 145). In "Discourse Ethics" ("Diskursethik") Habermas identifies these conditions more precisely in the context of establishing his principle of universalization—a principle that intends to set the conditions for impartial judgment insofar as it "constrains *all* affected to adopt the perspectives of *all others* in the balancing of interests" (65). The principle of universalization itself states: "*All* affected can accept the consequences and the side effects" that a proposed moral norm's "*general* observance can be anticipated to have for the satisfaction of *everyone's* interests (and these consequences are preferred to those of known alternative possibilities for regulation)" (65).

In addition, Habermas articulates a second principle that, as he says, "already contains the distinctive idea of an ethics of discourse": "Only those [moral] norms can claim to be valid that meet (or could meet) with the approval of all affected in their capacity *as participants in a practical* discourse" (66). In short, the conditions for the practical discourse out of which universally valid norms may emerge include the participation and acceptance of *all* who are affected by such norms, as such norms meet their interests. Finally, Habermas stresses that such discourse requires freedom as a condition. We cannot expect the consent of all participants to follow "unless all affected can *freely* accept the consequences and the side effects that the *general* observance of a controversial norm can be expected to have for the satisfaction of the interests of *each individual*" (93). This means that consent and consensus achieved under constraint are not genuine consent and consensus. Only those norms to which individuals freely assent through such discourse can have universal validity. In this way, Habermas preserves the central legitimation argument of the Enlightenment philosopher Rousseau, who points out that we do not recognize the legitimacy of agreements made under duress. According to Rousseau, *might* (the ability to coerce agreement through force or intimidation) does *not* make moral *right* (an agreement legitimate between rational human beings that thus obliges them to observe the conditions of the agreement).[36] So, Habermas retains the Enlightenment focus on human freedom and rationality, but he does so by reformulating the notion of freedom as one that is necessarily intertwined with others in the community of communicative rationalities.[37]

Justice, Solidarity, and Democratic Polity: The "Rules of Reason"

To circumscribe such discourse more carefully, Habermas takes up rules first proposed by Robert Alexy as "the Rules of Reason" (Alexy, 165–67). In Habermas's formulation in "Discourse Ethics," these are:

> 1. Every subject with the competence to speak and act is allowed to take part in a discourse.
> 2a. Everyone is allowed to question any assertion whatever.
> 2b. Everyone is allowed to introduce any assertion whatever into the discourse.
> 2c. Everyone is allowed to express his attitudes, desires, and needs.
> 3. No speaker may be prevented, by internal or external coercion, from exercising his rights as laid down in (1) and (2). ("Diskursethik," 86)

As Ingram points out, the *ideal speech situation* constructed by these rules stresses first of all equality and freedom for each participant, but freedom here has a tightly defined meaning. The participants in the ideal speech situation are first free *to* participate in the discourse in critical ways so as to express their attitudes, desires, and needs. In addition, the ideal speech situation must establish a context in which participants are further free *from* coercion of several sorts. Their participation in discourse will be "unobstructed by ideological prejudices, temporal limitations, and external domination be it cultural, social, political, or economic" (*Critical Theory and Philosophy,* 148).

These rules mark out the requirements for a *just,* if ideal, speech situation. In addition, Habermas later argues that the ideal speech situation further requires a sense of *solidarity* between participants. Such solidarity involves concern for the well-being of both one's fellow human beings and of the community at large. As Habermas puts it in "Justice and Solidarity," *justice* concerns the equal freedoms of unique and self-determining individuals, while *solidarity* concerns the welfare of consociates who are intimately linked in an intersubjectively shared form of life and thus also to the maintenance of the integrity of this form of life itself" (47, quoted in Ingram, 149).

This insistence on both justice and solidarity is important from the standpoint of the theory-practice problem. If justice, even defined in terms of the discourse ethic, threatens to become too abstract, too ideal, or too theoretical and thus removed from the particularities of praxis, the stress on solidarity, as an emotive concern for one's neighbor and his or her concrete needs, balances a general notion of justice with attention to the particular interests and needs of individuals in concrete situations. Furthermore, this thematic effort fully to inform theoretical norms with the particularities of praxis also involves recognizing the legitimacy of a *diversity* or plurality of norms that reflects a diversity of communities and participants.[38]

The ideal speech situation, finally, is not simply the environment out of which universally valid norms may emerge. The ideal speech situation, with its requirements for freedom, equality, and solidarity, also provides a definition of justice "in terms of *formal rules of democratic fairplay*" (Ingram, *Critical Theory and Philosophy,* 149). This is to say, the rules and conditions of the ideal speech situation describe the necessary conditions of democratic polity.

True to their Kantian heritage, these rules and conditions point towards a crucial, but difficult, middle ground between two more familiar philosophical positions. On the one hand, to claim that there are truths and values with universal validity frequently leads to a position of intolerant dogmatism. This position asserts that a particular set of truths and values are the only universally valid ones and that alternative ones are by definition false. (In Habermas's terms, this is the absolutist position.) On the other hand, one may claim with the ethical relativists, and by extension with at least some postmodernists and poststructuralists, that no universally valid truths and values exist. Such relativism allows for a tolerance and acceptance of individual and culturally diverse claims to truth and value, but it does so at the cost of being forced to accept *all* claims to truth and value, such as "the earth is flat" and "mass murder is an acceptable lifestyle."

By circumscribing the *form,* in contrast with the *content,* of ideal discourse and democratic interchange, Habermas's discourse ethic articulates a standard or criterion that, he claims, is universally valid. That is, the rules and conditions of the ideal speech situation are necessary conditions for achieving legitimate moral norms, norms that legitimately hold for all participants. At the same time, however, the *content* of this discourse is to be filled in by particular participants at particular times, representing the particular needs and interests of particular communities. In this way, two different communities may hold to the same rules of discourse and so meet the universally valid standard for discourse and democratic interchange. Nonetheless, reflecting precisely the intention of the rules to preserve the free expression of individual interests, two such communities may achieve consensus on quite different moral norms.[39] In this way, the discourse ethic attempts to establish a universally valid standard—more precisely, "a procedure for hypothetically testing whether existing norms and institutions correspond to the rational needs of those affected" (Ingram, 154). The discourse ethic thereby avoids the absolute tolerance of a consistent ethical relativism. Whereas an ethical relativist would be forced to accept the legitimacy of moral norms achieved, for example, through the threat of force against a community, the discourse ethic condemns such norms as illegitimate, precisely because they fail to reflect the freedom, reciprocity, and solidarity it requires. However, by articulating a form that may issue in a *plurality* of norms for a diversity of communities that reflect the particular interests of particular participants, the discourse ethic avoids the absolute intolerance of dogmatism.[40]

The discourse ethic thus articulates the communicative conditions of democratic polity in such a way as to strike a theoretical middle ground that preserves both universally valid forms and a pluralism of diverse communities. Such an ethic, which intentionally avoids the totalitarian threat of monolithic universals imposed without regard for individual and cultural differences, points instead to what Ingram sees as the primary arena for the discourse ethic—grass-roots democracy:

> Habermas's discourse ethic is best seen as a recommendation to institute participatory democratic discourses at a grass-roots level, however imperfect they may be. Only under these conditions can people define their needs rationally, develop their reflective competencies collectively, regulate their property relations freely, and choose with full consciousness those very specific rights and duties that conform to their sense of justice, given their peculiar historical circumstances. (*Critical Theory and Philosophy,* 155)

Habermas is seeking to meet one aspect of the theory-practice problem. Again, the discourse ethic intends to establish universally valid norms as these emerge from such discourse. But precisely because this is the unconstrained discourse of free individuals, these norms will reflect those individuals' particular interests, needs, and specific historical context.

In addition, the discourse ethic represents not only the conditions for legitimating putative moral norms and for democratic polity; it further represents a specific form of rationality, one that, in contrast with the paradigmatic notion of the isolated reason in Descartes, includes rather than excludes the emotive, the expression of individual needs, and so on. This form of rationality, which Habermas calls communicative reason, is distinct from what earlier critical theorists attacked as a calculative or instrumental rationality. As we have seen, Marcuse especially argues that modern technology, as such, is the direct expression of a reason that seeks to "master and possess nature." It can thereby only serve in the domination and oppression of both nature and humanity, in direct contradiction with the initial emancipatory hopes of the Enlightenment.

In contrast with the dualistic logic that defines the Cartesian subject solely within a hierarchical relation of domination and subordination, communicative reason begins in relationship with others, allowing for the possibility of equality as it simultaneously preserves the intractable difference between free selves. Similarly, communicative reason does not issue in theoretical norms radically divorced from the particular needs and interests of individuals. Rather, the discourse ethic intends precisely to preserve the particularities of praxis in the universally valid norms that are to emerge from consensus.

Accordingly, Habermas's notion of communicative rationality allows for the possibility that modern institutions—notably science, law, and aesthetic criticism—may in fact become genuinely democratic insofar as they incorporate communicative reason and the discourse ethic. By implication, modern technologies, specifically computers and computer communication networks, would appear to avoid critiques such as Marcuse's, insofar as these technologies likewise enable the unconstrained discourse of communicative reason.[41]

Communicative Reason, Hypertext, and Postmodernism

Summary: Habermas's Defense of Democratic Polity

What I have called the democratization claim—the belief that hypertext technologies, especially as these technologies include computer communications networks, may lead to a democratization of society—appears to find extensive support in Habermas's communicative action theory in several ways.

First, as Habermas's theory seeks to defend universally valid norms including the preference for democratic polity, it provides an initial defense against the charge that this preference is simply ideological in character. As Habermas shows, the preference for democratic polity in fact lies implicit within the structure of everyday discourse as such.

Second, Habermas makes clear the theoretical connections between communication and democratization. The rules and conditions of the ideal speech situation describe the necessary conditions of democratic polity. Insofar as this analysis and definition of democratic polity is sound, hypertext theorists who can show that hypertext systems facilitate communications that meet these conditions will thereby demonstrate that such systems in fact contribute to democratization. In fact, such systems would serve to test in praxis the validity of Habermas's theory, thus providing an instance of the sort of empirical verification that he calls for as part of his effort to resolve the tension between theory and practice.

Third, Habermas's notion of communicative rationality rescues modern technologies, including those underlying hypertext systems, from criticisms raised against them as antidemocratic. Again, insofar as hypertext theorists can demonstrate that hypertext systems facilitate the unconstrained discourse of communicative reason, a discourse that leads to consensus on important norms, such systems would both fulfill the democratization claim and clearly avoid the totalitarian tendency alleged by Marcuse.

Fourth, we have seen that the democratization claim can be dismissed not only as resting on mere ideological preference; it has also been attacked as utopian. But as Habermas takes up the theory-practice problem thematic of Frankfurt School critical theory, he further provides a way of meeting this criticism as well. Frankfurt School critical theory begins precisely with the question of whether, in the face of the failures of Enlightenment democracy in both East and West, such democracy should be dismissed as utopian, as representing a theoretical ideal so far removed from human praxis as to be unworkable.

Several aspects of Frankfurt School critical theory and Habermas's communicative action theory defuse this criticism of democratic theory. As we have seen, Frankfurt School critical theory in general seeks to bridge traditional philosophical theories with such empirically informed theories as sociology, psychology, and so forth. In particular, Habermas's communicative action theory rests in part on empirical analyses of communication. Furthermore, insofar as communicative rationality is to be informed by both the particularities of individual need and desire and by the specific context of given communities, the theoretical norms emerging from this sort of discourse promise to be more closely shaped by the realities of praxis from the outset. Finally, because communicative rationality is always open to further discussion, these norms are always open to revision in light of the failures of such norms to be fully realized in praxis. Communicative rationality thus intends to avoid the critique of utopianism attaching to theoretical norms more at odds with the particularities of praxis. Indeed, if Habermas's analysis of communicative action is correct, the democratic thrust, though not perfectly realizable perhaps, is nonetheless already partially realized in everyday discourse. To reject this democratic thrust as utopian would succeed only if one chose to ignore this thrust in everyday communication.

Habermas's Critique of Postmodernism

Finally, Habermas's theory supports a democratizing hypertext more consistently than do poststructuralist and postmodern theories previously explored by theorists who endorse the democratization claim. In fact, Habermas and literary critical theory part ways precisely on the question of the viability of democratic politics. In particular, Habermas points out a series of crucial theoretical problems in literary critical theories, problems of central importance precisely to hypertext theorists who take up the claim of democratization. Specifically, he argues that poststructuralist theories may have antidemocratic consequences. If his criticism holds, it points out the danger that a hypertext theory restricted to such theories might not only be suspected of a commitment to democratic politics that emerges as utopian and ideological: more fundamentally, such a hypertext theory would threaten to run aground on several internal contradictions between its commitment to democratic politics and the implicitly antidemocratic consequences of poststructuralist literary critical theories.

In contrast with Habermas's critical theory, which intends to defend the legitimacy of democratic politics against a variety of criticisms, both poststructuralists and postmodernists appear to lead in two apolitical, if not antipolitical directions (Ingram, *Critical Theory and Philosophy*, 197–204). First, as Habermas contends, poststructuralists and postmodernists undermine the possibility of opposing totalitarianism by rejecting Enlightenment notions of freedom, individual autonomy, communal solidarity, and democratic self-determination.[42]

Second, poststructuralists and postmodernists reject these modernist notions as they more generally reject the modernist project of attempting to found a universally valid system of beliefs and values. As we have already seen, however, correlative with this rejection is the endorsement of ethical relativism—the position that argues that values and beliefs are valid only within a specific context. Hence, the preference for democracy is relative or valid only for those individuals and cultures that affirm such a value: alternative political forms are equally valid in alternative contexts.

Philosophers commonly note that such relativism tends to undermine itself as it presents an obvious paradox: if there are no universally valid claims, then the relativists' claim that there are no universally valid claims cannot be universally valid. Similarly, Habermas argues that these accounts are internally contradictory and self-defeating. According to Ingram, "the poststructuralist dissolution of the acting subject into a plurality of language games (Lyotard), a force-field of power relations (Foucault), or an open system of linguistic signifiers (Derrida) relativizes all rational distinctions and identities to the point where political resistance becomes meaningless. Why be political if there is no ideal to be fought over, no subject to be emancipated?" (1990, 205). Moreover, such relativism simply reinforces the original charge of ideology attaching to the claim of democratization in hypertext theory. If the ethical relativism enjoined by poststructuralists and postmodernists holds, then the preference for democratic polity is in fact ideological, rather than reflecting a value holding greater validity.

A hypertext theory endorsing the democratization claim would thus face not only the original problem of addressing the charge of ideology; if restricted to poststructuralism and postmodernism, such a theory would in addition encounter two internal contradictions, for it would endorse a relativism that only reiterates the charge of ideology and would entail antidemocratic consequences directly at odds with its claim to democratization. Such a theory would not only run the risk of being exposed as ideological in its commitment to democratization but would further risk contradicting itself with regard to this basic commitment.

A third contradiction may emerge regarding the very technologies of hypertext—namely, their underlying technologies of computers and computer-based communications networks. One can examine this point in the example of Lyotard's critique of modernism, since he develops an extensive critique of computerized society inclined towards using computers and computer-based technology in ways that support the power of the state, especially as these technologies function as a "terror" that threatens to silence any dissent.

One of the motives for a shift from modern to postmodern views is the critique launched by Lyotard against modern technology as supporting a form of terror. Lyotard argues that modern technology—specifically in the form of "a generalized computerization of society" (*The Postmodern Condition,* 47)—by no means serves what he characterizes as the humanistic and idealist "narratives of legitimation" characteristic of the modern period. (These themes, notice, are precisely the modernist themes underlying the commitment to democratic polity—namely, the humanistic Enlightenment theme of political liberation towards a democratic society by means of scientific advance [31–32, 34] and the subsequent stress in German Idealism on achieving a systematic unity of all knowledge [32–35].) Rather, he argues that such technologies serve instead the interests of states and companies in the pursuit of power, not truth, especially as such technologies help define and reinforce what a computerized society accepts as reality (46–47). Computers in a computerized society, he concludes, "could then become the 'dream' instrument for controlling and regulating" not simply the market system but the society itself—a use of the computer that would further entail terror (67), defined as "the efficiency gained by eliminating, or threatening to eliminate" a participant in the "language game" of society (63).

To be sure, in contrast with this devastating critique of the computerized society, Lyotard finally claims that "justice," as an alternative to terror, would require the public to have "free access to the memory and data banks" of computerized society (67). This, coupled with his analysis of the self as a "nodal point" in the communication circuits that constitute much of social relations (15), implies that he agrees that increased access to information across computer networks is a good thing. Nonetheless, how are we to reconcile Lyotard's critique of technology as the dream instrument of totalitarianism with his vision of this same technology as facilitating the free play of language games he calls "paralogy"? More importantly, how are we to justify the preference for the justice of paralogy over the totalitarian use of computer communications?

Lyotard in fact echoes Habermas's turn towards communication, in that he bases his notion of paralogy on an analysis of narration as communication (see especially Lyotard's ch. 5). But as he rejects the Enlightenment narrative of emancipation and democratization—a narrative that would support a democratizing use of technologies over their totalitarian uses—he thereby falls prey to Habermas's critique that postmodernism undermines the grounds for opposition to totalitarianism. More generally, in light of the relativism associated with postmodernism, it is by no means clear how the "justice" of paralogy is to be argued for against totalitarianism.

Lyotard's critique of computers and computer-based communication networks thus threatens hypertext theory with a third contradiction. Simply, this critique directly contradicts the claim that hypertext systems promise a democratization effect—especially as these systems are understood to involve precisely the computer-based networks attacked by Lyotard. A hypertext theory that takes up the democratization claim, but is overly reliant on postmodernism of this sort, faces a striking contradiction between its fundamental endorsement of democratic polity as a justifying value of hypertext and the attack in postmodernism on the very technologies underlying hypertext as terrorist.

Of course, a hypertext theory associated with literary critical theories can avoid the threat of these internal contradictions by following Landow's strategy of noting from the outset that he does not assume a simple isomorphism between computer hypertext and such theories (*Hypertext*, 2, 205 n. 1). At the same time, further complementing the theoretical base of hypermedia with Habermas's theory of communicative action offers hypertext theorists interested in the promise of democratization a number of theoretical advantages. These advantages begin with his defense of the democratic preference against charges of ideology and utopianism. He further defends modern technologies against charges of a totalitarian or antidemocratic bias, as he develops an alternative conception of the rationality thought to be at work in these technologies. We can also now see how Habermas's theory of communicative action also avoids the internal inconsistencies threatening literary critical theory, as Habermas attempts to ground the preference for democratic polity as a universally valid norm, thus avoiding the relativism of literary critical theory that reinforces the ideology critique and the potentially antidemocratic consequences of this relativism.

Hypertext and Habermas: The Realization of Democratic Communication

What would a democratizing hypertext system based on Habermas's communicative ethics look like? To begin with, the first rule of reason—"every subject with the competence to speak and act is allowed to take part in a discourse"—would seem to require the conjunction of hypertext systems and computer networks we have seen endorsed in Nelson's *Dream Machines* (33) and Bolter's *Writing Space* (29–30). Although such a system would thus be open to many participants, it would not necessarily become the expansive system envisioned by Nelson in *Dream Machines,* of "a hundred million simultaneous users, adding a hundred million documents an hour to the system" (144). Rather, such a system would facilitate discourse among a diversity of grass-roots communities that might agree, by way of the same form of discourse, upon different norms, and thereby preserve individual and cultural differences.

Further, the hypertext linking and organization of such a system would need to facilitate the critical aspects of this discourse. In particular, it would have to enable the ability to question any assertion whatsoever and to introduce any assertion whatever (rules 2a and 2b). Such a system would record and track any claim, its supporting claims, and the questions raised regarding these claims—where all claims and questions would exist as individual hypertext nodes linked to each other.

Such systems already exist in some measure. But Habermas's discourse ethic further makes clear that the democratization claim of hypertext depends not only on the hardware and software design but also on the larger social context of use. Rules 2c and 3 in particular make the point that democratizing discourse cannot be constrained by censorship regarding what texts may be introduced. More broadly, this discourse must further be free from other forms of social coercion—the subtle but powerful cues of hierarchy, status, gender, and so on.

In these ways, Habermas's theory provides a powerful theoretical framework, centered on the effort to ground the preference for democratic polity as more than ideological and as consistent with modern technologies. At the same time, this framework further reinforces and refines conceptions and observations we have noted in the literature. Again, the stress on communicative action as the arena of democratizing discourse reinforces the conceptions we have seen of hypertext as both networked and as a read-write system which allows users to actively modify existing texts. It further undergirds the commitment to democratic polity and refines the conception of democratic discourse and the conditions of such discourse. In particular, Habermas's conception of unconstrained discourse supports something like the notions of "open, free-ranging discourse" (Sproull and Kiesler, 116) that would ostensibly allow "nearly everyone . . . to put his or her ideas, concerns and demands before all others" (Dertouzos, 69). But it refines and supports these conceptions as it articulates the rules of reason that must be observed to make such discourse possible—and by clearly showing how this discourse is theoretically tied to democratic norms, which are further defended as universally valid. Furthermore, Habermas's theory would endorse a more democratic form of communication—specifically, a nonsexist one—as against both documented failures of communications networks to achieve such democratization and correlative criticisms that existing communications theories fail adequately to endorse emancipatory and non-sexist discourse (Krippendorff, 194; Steiner, 168). Similarly, Habermas's theory reiterates the point that the character of the social contexts in which a system is used are equally critical to its success at democratization (Beeman; Riel). But his rules of reason help define these contexts more carefully—as they, again, make clear the theoretical connection between contexts structured in these ways and the democratization sought for in these contexts and through these technologies.

In these ways, the incorporation of Habermas's discourse ethic in a hypertext system promises to result in the democratization claimed for both hypertext and computer networks, since it provides a framework that both endorses and refines existing conceptions and observations regarding hypertext, networks, and democratic communications. In grounding the democratic preference (as a quasi-transcendental norm) in a communicative action consistent with the computer technologies of hypertext, Habermas also avoids the potential contradictions of poststructuralist literary critical theories as he further provides a powerful theoretical defense of the democratization claim against charges of ideology and utopianism.

NOTES

I wish to thank many people who have generously shared suggestions and the results of their work : Trent Batson (Gallaudet University), William Beeman (Brown University), Michael Day (University of California, Berkeley), Thomas Duffy (Indiana University), Susan C. Herring (University of Texas, Arlington), Paul Kahn (IRIS, Brown University), Karla Kitalong (Michigan Technological University), Kalle Lyytinen (University of Jyväskylä), Robert Alun Jones (University of Illinois, Urbana/Champaign), Victoria Nasman, James O'Donnell (University of Pennsylvania), Margaret Riel (AT&T Learning Network), Benjamin Singer (University of Western Ontario), and Karla Tonella (University of Iowa). I would also like to thank George P. Landow (Brown University) for his encouragement to pursue Habermas in relation to hypertext theory—and my colleagues Peter Browning, Don Moss, and Sharon Nell whose careful reading and suggestions contributed substantially to greater clarity.

1. Perhaps the best introduction to hypertext is given in three collected essays—J. David Bolter, "Literature in the Electronic Writing Space," Theodor Holm Nelson, "Opening Hypertext: A Memoir," and George P. Landow, "Hypertext, Metatext, and the Electronic Canon," in *Literacy Online: The Promise (and Peril) of Reading and Writing with Computers*, ed. Myron C. Tuman (Pittsburgh: University of Pittsburgh Press, 1992). See also Edward Barrett, ed., *The Society of Text: Hypertext, Hypermedia, and the Social Construction of Information* (Cambridge: MIT Press, 1989), xii; John J. Leggett, John L. Schnase, and Charles J. Kacmar, "Hypertext for Learning," in *Designing Hypermedia for Learning,* ed. David H. Jonassen and Heinz Mandl (New York: Springer-Verlag, 1990), 27; George P. Landow and Paul Delany, "Hypermedia and Literary Studies: The State of the Art" in *Hypermedia and Literary Studies*, ed. Paul Delany and George P. Landow (Cambridge: MIT Press, 1991), 4; J. David Bolter, *Writing Space: The Computer, Hypertext, and the History of Writing* (Hillsdale, N.J.: Lawrence Erlbaum, 1991), 23; Andrew Pollack, "Two Men, Two Visions of One Computer World, Indivisible," *New York Times*, Dec. 8, 1991: sec. 3, p. 13; George P. Landow, *Hypertext: The Convergence of Contemporary Critical Theory and Technology* (Baltimore: Johns Hopkins University Press, 1992), 14. For a more complete

bibliography of Bush, Englebart, and Nelson, see Terence Harpold's bibliography in *The Hypertext/Hypermedia Handbook,* ed. Emily Berk and Joe Devlin (New York: McGraw-Hill, 1991).

2. Compare Theodor H. Nelson, *Dream Machines: New Freedoms through Computer Screens—A Minority Report. Computer-Lib: You Can and Must Understand Computers Now* (Chicago: Hugo's Book Service, 1974; rev. ed., Redmond, Wash.: Microsoft Press, 1987) 1, 29; Landow, *Hypertext,* 4, 57, 101; J. David Bolter, *Turing's Man: Western Culture in the Computer Age* (Chapel Hill: University of North Carolina Press, 1984), 163, and *Writing Space,* 22–23; Rand J. Spiro and Jihn-Chang Jehng, "Cognitive Flexibility and Hypertext: Theory and Technology for the Nonlinear and Multidimensional Traversal of Complex Subject Matter," in *Cognition, Education, and Multimedia: Exploring Ideas in High Technology,* ed. Don Nix and Rand J. Spiro (Hillsdale, N.J.: Lawrence Erlbaum, 1990), 166.

3. Cliff McKnight, Andrew Dillon, and John Richardson, eds., *Hypertext in Context* (New York: Cambridge University Press, 1991), esp. chs. 1 and 2; James O'Donnell, "St. Augustine to NREN: The Tree of Knowledge and How It Grows," *Serials Librarian* 22 (1992): 3–4.

4. For example, Leggett et al. (31) distinguish sharply between collaborative and other forms of hypertext. By contrast, Delany and Landow (14–15, 32–33) take up hypertext as essentially tied to collaboration and communication, as do all of the following: Nicole Yankelovich, Norman Meyrowitz, and Andries van Dam, "Reading and Writing the Electronic Book," reprinted in *Hypermedia and Literary Studies,* 59; Thomas M. Duffy and Randy A. Knuth, "Hypermedia and Instruction: Where Is the Match?" in *Designing Hypermedia,* 212–13; David H. Jonassen and R. Scott Grabinger, "Problems and Issues in Designing Hypertext/Hypermedia for Learning," in *Designing Hypermedia,* 8; and Peggy M. Irish and Randall H. Trigg, "Supporting Collaboration in Hypermedia: Issues and Experiences," in *The Society of Text,* 90–106. An additional definitional question concerns whether a hypertext system is a "read-only" system, such as a reference manual or information kiosk, or a "read-write" system, which allows users to modify hypertexts. Bolter's inclusion of communications networks in hypertext clearly assumes a read-write system.

5. Phil Mullins, "The Fluid Word: Word Processing and Its Mental Habits," *Thought* 63, no. 251 (1988): 413–28.

6. Peter Michael Fischer and Heinz Mandl, "Toward a Psychophysics of Hypermedia" in Jonassen and Mandl, xiv.

7. See George P. Landow, "Hypertext in Literary Education, Criticism, and Scholarship," *Computers and the Humanities* 23 (1989): 173–98; Charles Ess, "The Pedagogy of Computing: Hypermedia in the Classroom," *Hypertext '91* (New York: Association for Computing Machinery, 1991), 277–89; Robert A. Jones, "The Hypermedia Lab/Civitas Evaluation (Fall Semester 1991)," (Urbana-Champaign: University of Illinois).

8. See, for example, Philip Rubens, "Reading and Employing Technical Information in Hypertext," *Technical Communication* 38, no. 1 (Feb. 1991). Rubens's study of twenty-six subjects compared their abilities to retrieve infor-

mation from printed materials and from a hypertext system, in conjunction with performing specified tasks. The subjects were significantly more efficient in finding information in the paper document. See also Patricia Wright, "Cognitive Overheads and Prostheses: Some Issues in Evaluating Hypertexts," *Hypertext '91* (New York: Association for Computing Machinery, 1991).

More fundamentally, Joseph T. Jaynes's "Limited Freedom: Linear Reflections on Nonlinear Texts" criticizes the nonlinearity and lack of structure in hypertext environments, calling them "by their very nature antithetical to the motivations and requirements" of writers and readers (*The Society of the Text,* 158). Indeed, Duffy and Knuth directly dispute the claims made by William Beeman et al. in *Intermedia: A Case Study of Innovation in Higher Education,* (Providence, R.I.: Brown University, IRIS, 1988) and reiterated by Landow ("Hypertext in Literary Education") that hypermedia systems in general, and the Intermedia system used at Brown in particular, succeed in promoting nonlinear thinking.

9. In preparation for this article I consulted three data bases: various indices in philosophy, psychology, sociology, and so on available through DIALOGUE; the "Periodical Abstracts Ondisc" for Jan. 1989–Apr. 1992 of *ProQuest* (Ann Arbor, Mich.: UMI); and the journals index residing on the BITNET list COMSERVE, supported by the Communication Institute for Online Scholarship (CIOS) and indexing more than sixteen thousand journal articles on communications. I used standard Boolean searches to find articles indexed according to some combination of *hyper* (as a wildcard for *hypermedia* or *hypertext*), *democra* (as a wildcard for *democracy, democratic,* etc.), *computer*, and *network*. The number of "hits" in these searches ranged from the vanishingly small (e.g., four articles in the "Periodicals Abstracts") to zero (*no* articles in the COMSERVE data base for hypertext or hypermedia in conjunction with the other descriptors). A similar search using Nexis, undertaken by Karla Tonella (1992), was equally disappointing: nine articles on e-mail and computer communications turned up for the entirety of 1989–91.

Kalle Lyytinen's "Information Systems and Critical Theory—A Critical Assessment" (*Critical Management Studies,* ed. M. Alvesson and H. Wilmott [Beverly Hills, Calif.: SAGE, forthcoming]) represents the only line of research I have encountered that attempts rigorously to develop and apply what Lyytinen calls a social action perspective to office information systems, under the more general category of information systems theory. This work includes considerable use of Habermas's theory of communicative action, supplemented with other sources. Unfortunately, while his results are certainly suggestive for hypertext theorists, Lyytinen does not specifically address the implementation of hypertext or hypermedia systems.

10. William Beeman, personal communication to author, Jan. 23, 1992. Similarly, Margaret Riel, with regard to teaching writing by way of networks, points out that technology alone does not lead to improved learning ("Computer-Mediated Communication: A Tool for Reconnecting Kids with Society," *Interactive Learning Environments* 1, no. 4 [1990]: 255–63). What is critical

to the remarkable improvements she has documented is rather the social context of learning (262). See as well Riel, "Approaching the Study of Networks," *The Computing Teacher* (Dec.–Jan. 1991–92), 5–7, 52.

11. See note 23 for an explanation of the term *praxis*.

12. See Thomas McCarthy, *The Critical Theory of Jürgen Habermas* (Cambridge: MIT Press, 1978), 37–38, and ch. 5; and David Ingram, *Critical Theory and Philosophy* (New York: Paragon House, 1990), 160–63.

13. For a general overview, see Lee Sproull and Sara Kiesler (1991) and Thomas W. Malone and John F. Rockart (1991). Arnold S. Kahn and Robert G. Brookshire (1991) provide an overview of pertinent research in education regarding the communications impacts of computer networks. In particular, they point to a series of articles that suggest that computer networks contribute to more democratic discussion: Norman Coombs and A. Friedman (1987); B. W. Hesse, C. M. Werner, and I. Altman (1988); S. Kiesler, J. Siegel, and T. W. McGuire (1984); R. E. Rice and G. Love (1987). As well, see Margaret Riel (1990, 1991–92) for additional bibliographic sources on networking in education.

In the domain of communication theory proper, Joseph B. Walther (1992) summarizes research and theories regarding both negative and positive relational behavior on communications networks.

14. Michael L. Dertouzos, "Communications, Computers and Networks," *Scientific American* 265, no. 3 (Sept. 1991): 69.

15. Lee Sproull and Sara Kiesler, "Computers, Networks, and Work," *Scientific American* 265, no. 3 (Sept. 1991): 116, 119.

16. While not directly addressing the question of democratization via computer-based communications, Jeffrey Abramson, Christopher Arterton, and Gary Orren evaluate the democratization potential of mass media technologies such as television, cable TV, and radio in *The Electronic Commonwealth: The Impact of New Media Technologies on Democratic Politics* (New York: Basic Books, 1988). In sharp contrast with the lack of conceptual clarity we have seen in hypertext and computer literature regarding the basic definition of democracy, Abramson, Arterton, and Orren are careful to begin their analyses by distinguishing among three conflicting understandings of what democratic governance has meant in American political history: plebiscitary, emphasizing individual autonomy and maximizing the number of persons directly involved in government; communitarian, stressing service in the common good and the importance of "participation in public space" (23); and pluralist, stressing free competition among diverse interest groups (see 19–28). Briefly, these authors find that the plebiscitary approach (represented in polls, public opinion surveys, and "electronic town halls") runs the danger of fostering majoritarian systems, in which individual and minority rights may be crushed by majority rule (23ff.).

Assessed in these terms, most of the writers we have examined appear to assume a plebiscitary form of democracy—the weakest form, according to Abramson et al., who argue for a communitarian-pluralist form, which may be enhanced by mass media technology, to offset the dangers of the plebiscitary form. Interestingly, we will see Habermas's discourse ethic endorse a strikingly similar emphasis on communicative participation in achieving consensus regarding the common good (intersecting with Abramson et al.'s notion of communitarian democracy) for a particular community (intersecting with their notion of pluralist democracy). See Abramson, Arterton, and Orren, 30, 276ff.; and Jürgen Habermas, "Justice and Solidarity: On the Discussion Concerning 'Stage 6,'" *Philosophical Forum* 21, nos. 1–2 (Fall–Winter 1989–90): 38–39.

17. Arnold S. Kahn and Robert G. Brookshire, in "Using a Computer Bulletin Board in a Social Psychology Course" (*Teaching of Psychology* 18, no. 4 [Dec. 1991]: 245–49) cite S. R. Hiltz, "The Virtual Classroom: Using Computer-Mediated Communication for University Teaching" (*Journal of Communication* 36, no. 2 [1986]: 95–104) as an example of a study in which a networked environment made students feel awkward about communication. While several studies they reviewed support the notion that computer-mediated communications systems work to increase communication, two other studies (C. N. Quinn et al., 1983; C. S. Saunders and J. E. Heyl, 1988) report students complaining that they did not enjoy the "disjointed" character of communication by way of the computer. For discussion of how modern technologies—specifically, computers and computer-based communications networks—appear to have disruptive and alienating impacts upon users, see as well: Borgmann (1984); Turkle (1984), esp. ch. 6; and Westrum (1991), ch. 14, "The Distancing Effects of Technology."

More generally, a number of studies support the claim that computer networks indeed facilitate communication and learning. In addition to those cited by Riel and by Kahn and Brookshire, see, for example, Day (1992), Bateson et al. (n.d.), and, with specific reference to scholarly communication, Harrison and Stephen (1992).

18. By contrast, a government employee with access to e-mail reported to me the relatively spontaneous development of an e-mail network—using military computers—to organize support for abortion rights.

19. Klaus Krippendorff, "The Power of Communication and the Communication of Power: Toward an Emancipatory Theory of Communication," *Communication* 12 (1989): 194. Krippendorff continues, "Unfortunately much of communication technology has developed in the service of power. Communication theories that help sell products, improve productivity or adjust individuals to the realities of others produce inequalities they are unable to overcome. Research . . . reifies if not legitimizes existing paths of influence and domination. Positivism in the social sciences is predicated on maintaining the gap between the intelligently communicating theorists (who are largely a-theoretical about their own communication practices) and the 'cultural dopes' their theories of communication claim to describe."

Linda Steiner proposes a feminist ethic that will "invent means of extending and broadening who gets to communicate," as against existing theory that remains hierarchical and exclusive ("Feminist Theorizing and Communication Ethics," *Communication* 12 [1989]): 168).

20. See Benjamin D. Singer, "The New Media and Electronic Anomie," *Communications in Canadian Society,* ed. B. Singer (Scarborough, Ont.: Nelson Canada, 1991); and Sproull and Kiesler, 118, 119.

21. Ingram, *Critical Theory and Philosophy,* 196. Compare Jean-François Lyotard, *The Postmodern Condition: A Report on Knowledge,* trans. Geoff Bennington and Brian Massumi (Minneapolis: University of Minnesota Press, 1984). Lyotard concludes his critique of Habermas by noting that their dispute is not over the goal or cause of their respective theories—namely, "justice" in some form; rather, it is over whether such justice is better achieved through the consensus-oriented approach we will examine in Habermas or through an endorsement of what Lyotard calls "paralogy" (66).

22. The literature on Habermas is extensive: a 1990 bibliography lists over 3,000 publications (Rasmussen, 1990). Fortunately, several good introductions to Frankfurt School critical theory exist. McCarthy (1978) is a standard, if somewhat dated, introduction by perhaps the foremost Habermas translator and interpreter; his "Translator's Introduction" to the first volume of Habermas's *Theorie des Kommunikativen Handelns* [*Theory of Communicative Action*] is also useful, if compact. David Ingram has written both specifically about Habermas (*Habermas and the Dialectic of Reason* [New Haven: Yale University Press, 1987]) and more comprehensively about Habermas and the Frankfurt School (1990). Seyla Benhabib, in *Critique, Norm, and Utopia: A Study of the Foundations of Critical Theory* (New York: Columbia University Press, 1986), goes into much greater detail than Ingram does, and includes considerable discussion of the dispute we shall follow here between postmodernists and Habermas; like McCarthy, however, she writes for a philosophically literate audience.

Three especially helpful anthologies of Frankfurt School critical theory are those edited by Andrew Arato and Eike Gebhardt (*The Essential Frankfurt School Reader* [New York: Continuum, 1982]), Stephen Eric Bronner and Douglas MacKay Kellner (*Critical Theory and Society: A Reader* [New York: Routledge, Chapman, and Hall, 1989]: 345–78), and David Ingram and Julia Simon-Ingram (*Critical Theory: The Essential Readings* [New York: Paragon Press, 1991]). Similarly, Gerry D. Ewert's "Habermas and Education: A Comprehensive Overview of the Influence of Habermas in Educational Literature" (*Review of Educational Research* 61, no. 3 [Fall 1991]) provides a compact introduction to Habermas and his reception in educational theory.

23. Compare Benhabib: "Aristotelian practical philosophy was a unified teaching of ethics and politics that investigated the specificity and the conditions of human praxis. By 'praxis' Aristotle meant the most *human* [emphasis mine] activity, the realization of which was only possible in the *polis,* in the human community where speech and action were not only acquired, but most significant, could be best actualized" (5).

24. These critiques also foreshadow similar critiques launched by postmodernists. See Ingram's *Critical Theory and Philosophy* (198–99) for a discussion of how Adorno's *Negative Dialectic* employs a form of deconstruction similar to that associated with Derrida. Likewise, Ingram points out Habermas's

recognition of Foucault's critique of western rationalism as close to the themes of the Frankfurt School (200–202). In addition to his extensive overview of the complex theoretical disputes between Frankfurt School critical theories and literary critical theories, Ingram also discusses recent critical theory vis-à-vis feminist theories (ch. 7). Again, Benhabib (1986) is more complete, if more demanding, in this regard. See as well Marie Fleming, "Women's Place in Communicative Reason" (1992).

25. *Discourse on the Method of Rightly Conducting the Reason and Seeking for Truth in the Sciences*, trans. E. S. Haldane and G. R. T. Ross, (Cambridge: Cambridge University Press, 1972), 119.

26. See Ingram (1990), 50–54, and Benhabib, esp. 182–85, 255–60.

27. Ingram puts it this way: "The progressive domination of an objectified nature by a sovereign humanity was regarded by Hegel and Marx as the key to emancipation. For Adorno and other critical theorists, however, it is implicitly totalitarian. The domination of nature, they argued, extends to humanity itself, in the form of psychological repression and social engineering. So long as subject and object are seen as opposed terms, enlightenment can but serve only to increase domination" (*Critical Theory and Philosophy*, 77).

28. Max Horkheimer and Theodor W. Adorno, *Dialektik der Aufklärung* (Amsterdam, 1947). Translated as *Dialectic of Enlightenment*, trans. John Cumming (New York: Herder & Herder, 1972). See Benhabib, *Critique, Norm, and Utopia*, 163–71; and Ingram, *Critical Theory and Philosophy*, 60–67.

29. See especially Marcuse's chapter 6, "Technological Rationality and the Logic of Domination," and Ingram, *Critical Theory and Philosophy*, 80. As Ingram puts it, the analyses of Adorno, Horkheimer, and Marcuse point to just this dilemma: "Either scientific or moral rationality may be realized—but not both" (74). Briefly, the pessimism towards the possibility of Enlightenment rationality's achieving democratic polity brought to the forefront by Adorno and Horkheimer in the *Dialectic of Enlightenment* is deepened by Adorno's later analyses, especially *The Authoritarian Personality* (1950), *Negative Dialectics* (1966, 1973), and *Aesthetic Theory* (1970, 1984). In this direction, anticipating postmodernist critiques, Adorno argues that the dialectical-practical reason of Enlightenment rationality fails to offset the totalitarian dimension of technological-instrumental reason—because its own category of totality cancels out the requirement that freedom be preserved in nonidentity, in the autonomy of "the other." At this juncture, Adorno retreats from the political to the aesthetic—resurrecting the aesthetic turn of German Idealists who claimed that imagination and the aesthetic promise to resolve the oppositions between subject and object, individual and society, freedom and nature, universal and particular. (See Ingram's discussion in *Critical Theory and Philosophy*, 74–79.)

Marcuse will likewise turn to the aesthetic, in hopes that it will transform what we have seen him identify as the otherwise totalitarian tendency of modern reason, science, and technology. He does so primarily by appropriating Freud in his *Eros and Civilization*. (See Ingram, 79–91, 93–103.)

Karla Kitalong's "Hard Sell/Soft Sell: Computer Commercials and the Contesting of the Hegemonic Technological Elite" powerfully exploits these critiques of modern technology to criticize the claims to Enlightenment democratization through computers made in a recent television commercial produced by a major computer manufacturer. Her bibliography includes additional useful references for those wishing to explore the repressive dimensions of computer technology, especially from feminist perspectives.

30. Walther Zimmerli, for example ("Ist die kommunikationstheoretische Wende ein Ausweg aus dem 'Hermeneutikstreit'?" in *Theorie zwischen Kritik und Praxis: Jürgen Habermas und die Frankfurter Schule*, ed. Roland Simon-Schaefer and Walther Ch. Zimmerli [Stuttgart: Friedrich Frommann, 1975]), examines the roots of Habermas's turn in 1969 towards a theory of communicative competence, beginning with Habermas's dispute with Hans-Georg Gadamer, referring to a series of exchanges among Habermas, Gadamer, and the so-called Critical Rationalists, later collected under the title *Hermeneutik und Ideologiekritik* (1971).

31. Habermas took up these questions of theory, practice, and the legitimation of moral norms very early in his work—most notably in *Erkenntnis und Interesse* (1968), translated into English as *Knowledge and Human Interests* in 1971, and in *Theorie und Praxis* (1971), translated into English as *Theory and Practice* in 1973. For a discussion of these, see McCarthy, *Critical Theory of Habermas*, 40–60, and Ingram, *Critical Theory and Philosophy*, 113–19.

32. As we shall see, postmodernism and poststructuralism also endorse such a relativism. This means, however, that they thereby reinforce the charge of ideology made against the claim of democratization in hypertext theory, and thereby rob the democratization claim of much of its justificatory power. The following comments will hence directly bear on the issue as to whether a communicative ethic, by countering relativism, may offer an important theoretical addition to such hypertext theory.

33. Ingram, *Critical Theory and Philosophy*, 147–48, referring to Habermas's "Wahrheitstheorien" ["Theories of Truth"].

34. As the title "formal-pragmatic" suggests, such an account reflects the Frankfurt School interest in resolving the theory-praxis problem by combining both formal and empirically oriented theories. Specifically, Habermas undertakes the ambitious project of conjoining formal semantics, speech-act theory, and other approaches to the "pragmatics" of language as "an attempt at rationally reconstructing universal rules and necessary presuppositions of speech actions oriented to reaching understanding" (*Reason and the Rationalization of Society*, 138).

35. So McCarthy notes: "In the end, the claim that the concept of communicative rationality has universal significance can be decided only by the empirical-theoretical fruitfulness of the research programs based on it—in different domains from the construction of a formal pragmatics of language and the reconstruction of the ontogenesis of communicative competence to the development of theories of anthropogenesis and social evolution" ("Translator's Introduction," xiv).

36. See especially his argument in the opening book of *The Social Contract,* especially chapters 3–6.

37. Ingram discusses these reformulations in greater detail (though he omits the reference to Rousseau), especially in relation to Kant's conception of the human being as a moral autonomy and the correlative ethics (*Critical Theory and Philosophy,* 145–46).

38. At the same time, however, Benhabib criticizes Habermas on just this point. She argues that Habermas's ethic remains too abstract, as it is rooted in a rational notion of a "generalized other,"—one that ultimately fails to include the particular and concrete desires and needs that are more fully lifted up as a central dimension of ethical decision making by Carol Gilligan, *In a Different Voice: Psychological Theory and Women's Development* (1982), and in her "ethic of care" (Benhabib, 340–41).

39. So Habermas is careful to point out that "the universalist position does not have to deny the pluralism and the incompatibility of historical versions of 'civilized humanity'; but it regards this multiplicity of forms of life as limited to *cultural contents,* and it asserts that every culture must share certain *formal properties* of the modern understanding of the world, if it is at all to attain a certain degree of 'conscious awareness' or 'sublimation'" (*Reason and the Rationalization of Society,* 180).

40. On this point, see *Reason and the Rationalization of Society,* 135, 180. For a brief explanation of this issue in Kant's ethics, see Lewis White Beck, "Translator's Introduction," xix–xx.

41. In point of fact, Habermas lays the groundwork for this redemption of modern technology by way of realigning it with a communicative reason as early as 1968, in his "Technik und Wissenschaft als 'Ideologie,'" translated as "Technology and Science as 'Ideology.'" Here he introduces a distinction between communicative action, on the one hand, as involving symbolic interaction and consensus, and a "purposive-rational" action associated with technology, empirical science, and an instrumental reason that seeks to control reality (91–93, in McCarthy, *Critical Theory of Habermas,* 23–24; see Benhabib, 228–29).

42. See Habermas, "Modernity: An Unfinished Project" (based on a lecture given in 1980; English translation, 1991). As Ingram points out, poststructuralists and postmodernists reject these Enlightenment conceptions because, on their analysis, they likewise are seen to lead to totalitarianism (*Critical Theory and Philosophy,* 204). Habermas seeks to meet these critiques—already anticipated in some measure by critiques developed within the Frankfurt School—by responding that the poststructuralist and postmodernist analyses assume a conception of reason (identified in Frankfurt School critical theory in terms of instrumental or technological rationality) that fails to account for all of rationality. On this view, in fact, Habermas sees the poststructuralists and postmodernists as repeating the analysis—and finally the error—of earlier Frankfurt School critical theorists.

As we have seen, Habermas intends to avoid the antimodern and thus antidemocratic consequences of both sorts of critical theory by developing an alternative conception of rationality—a "nonobjectifying emancipatory rationality inherent in communication," to which attaches the tolerance of difference and pluralism sought by both sorts of critical theory (Ingram, 204) and which provides a justification for democratic polity.

BIBLIOGRAPHY

Abramson, Jeffrey, Christopher Arterton, and Gary Orren. *The Electronic Commonwealth: The Impact of New Media Technologies on Democratic Politics*. New York: Basic Books, 1988.

Adorno, T. W. *Aesthetische Theorie*. Frankfurt: Suhrkamp, 1970 (published posthumously). Translated as *Aesthetic Theory,* Trans. Christian Lenhardt. London: Routledge & Kegan Paul, 1984.

———. *Negative Dialectics*. New York: Seabury Press, 1973.

Adorno, T. W. et al. *The Authoritarian Personality*. New York: Harper & Row, 1950.

Alexy, Robert. "Eine Theorie des praktischen Diskurses." In *Normenbegründung-Normendurchsetzung*. Ed. Willi Oelmüller. Paderborn: Schöningh, 1978. Translated as "A Theory of Practical Discourse." Trans. David Frisby. In Benhabib and Dallmayr (1990).

Arato, Andrew, and Eike Gebhardt. *The Essential Frankfurt School Reader*. New York: Continuum, 1982.

Barrett, Edward, ed. *The Society of Text: Hypertext, Hypermedia, and the Social Construction of Information*. Cambridge: MIT Press, 1989.

Bateson, Trent, Joy Peyton, Terence Collins, Michael Spitzer, Christine Neuwrith, and Diane Thompson. *Final Report: The ENFI Project* (n.p., n.d.).

Beck, Lewis White. "Translator's Introduction." In Immanual Kant, *Foundations of the Metaphysics of Morals* and *What Is Enlightenment?* Indianapolis: Bobbs-Merrill, 1959.

Beeman, William O. Personal communication to the author. Jan. 23, 1992.

Beeman, William O., Kenneth T. Anderson, Gail Bader, James Larkin, Anne P. McClard, Patrick McQuillan, and Mark Shields. *Intermedia: A Case Study of Innovation in Higher Education* (a final report to the Annenberg/CPB Project). Providence, R.I.: Brown University, IRIS, 1988.

Benhabib, Seyla. *Critique, Norm, and Utopia: A Study of the Foundations of Critical Theory*. New York: Columbia University Press, 1986.

Benhabib, Seyla, and Fred Dallmayr, eds. *The Communicative Ethics Controversy*. Cambridge: MIT Press, 1990.

Berk, Emily, and Joe Devlin, eds. *The Hypertext/Hypermedia Handbook*. New York: McGraw-Hill, 1991.

Bolter, J. David. "Literature in the Electronic Writing Space." In Tuman (1992).

———. *Turing's Man: Western Culture in the Computer Age*. Chapel Hill: University of North Carolina Press, 1984.

———. *Writing Space: The Computer, Hypertext, and the History of Writing*. Hillsdale, N.J.: Lawrence Erlbaum, 1991.

Borgmann, Albert. *Technology and the Character of Contemporary Life*. Chicago: University of Chicago Press, 1984.

Bronner, Stephen Eric, and Douglas MacKay Kellner. *Critical Theory and Society: A Reader*. New York: Routledge, Chapman & Hall, 1989.

Bush, Vannevar. "As We May Think." *Atlantic Monthly* 176 (July 1945): 101–8.

Coombs, N., and Friedman, A. "Computer Conferencing and Electronic Mail as 'Classroom Communication.'" Paper presented at the third annual Conference on Computers and the Handicapped, Oct. 1987, Northridge, Calif.

Day, Michael. "Networking: The Rhetoric of the New Writing Classroom." Conference presentation, EDUCOM. Oct. 16–19, 1991, San Diego, Calif.

Delany, Paul, and George P. Landow, eds. *Hypermedia and Literary Studies*. Cambridge: MIT Press, 1991.

Dertouzos, Michael L. "Communications, Computers, and Networks." *Scientific American* 265, no. 3 (Sept. 1991): 62–69.

Descartes, René. *Discours de la méthode*. Leiden: Jan Maire. Translated as *Discourse on the Method of Rightly Conducting the Reason and Seeking for Truth in the Sciences*. Trans. E. S. Haldane and G. R. T. Ross. Cambridge: Cambridge University Press, 1972.

Duffy, Thomas M., and Randy A. Knuth. "Hypermedia and Instruction: Where Is the Match?" In Jonassen and Mandl (1990).

"Electronic Democracy: The PEN Is Mighty." *Economist*, Feb. 1, 1992: 96.

Ess, Charles. "The Pedagogy of Computing: Hypermedia in the Classroom." In *Hypertext '91*. New York: Association for Computing Machinery, 1991.

———. "Technology, Huxley, and Hope." In *Technology and Human Productivity: Challenges for the Future*. Ed. John W. Murphy and John T. Pardeck. New York: Quorum Books, 1984.

Ewert, Gerry D. "Habermas and Education: A Comprehensive Overview of the Influence of Habermas in Educational Literature." *Review of Educational Research* 61, no. 3 (Fall 1991): 345–78.

Fischer, Peter Michael, and Heinz Mandl. "Toward a Psychophysics of Hypermedia." In Jonassen and Mandl (1990).

Fleming, Marie. "Women's Place in Communicative Reason." In Harvey and Okruhlik (1992).

Gilligan, Carol. *In a Different Voice: Psychological Theory and Women's Development*. Cambridge: Harvard University Press, 1982.

Habermas, Jürgen. "Diskursethik: Notizen zu einem Begrüngungsprogram." In *Moralbewusstsein und kommunikatives Handeln* (Frankfurt: Suhrkamp, 1983). Translated as "Discourse Ethics: Notes on Philosophical Justification." In *Moral Consciousness and Communicative Action*. Trans. Christian Lenhardt and Shierry Weber Nicholsen. Cambridge: MIT Press, 1990.

———. *Erkenntnis und Interesse*. Frankfurt: Suhrkamp, 1968. Translated as *Knowledge and Human Interests*. Trans. Jeremy J. Shapiro. Boston: Beacon Press, 1971.

———. "Justice and Solidarity: On the Discussion Concerning 'Stage 6.'" *Philo-*

sophical Forum 21, nos. 1–2 (Fall–Winter 1989–90): 32–52.

———. *Legitimationsprobleme im Spätkapitalismus*. Frankfurt: Suhrkamp, 1973. Translated as *Legitimation Crisis*. Trans. Thomas McCarthy. Boston: Beacon Press, 1975.

———. "Modernity: An Unfinished Project." In Ingram and Simon-Ingram (1991).

———. "Technik und Wissenschaft als 'Ideologie.'" Frankfurt: Suhrkamp, 1968. Translated as "Technology and Science as 'Ideology.'" Trans. Jeremy Shapiro. In *Toward a Rational Society*. Boston: Beacon Press, 1970.

———. *Theorie des Kommunikativen Handelns*, 2 vols. Frankfurt: Suhrkamp, 1981. Vol. 1 translated as *Reason and the Rationalization of Society*. Trans. Thomas McCarthy. Boston: Beacon Press, 1984a. Vol. 2 translated as *Lifeworld and System: A Critique of Functionalist Reason*. Trans. Thomas McCarthy. Boston: Beacon Press, 1987.

———. *Theorie und Praxis*. 4th ed. Frankfurt: Suhrkamp, 1971. Translated as *Theory and Practice*. Trans. John Viertel. Boston: Beacon Press, 1973.

———. "Wahrheitstheorien" ["Theories of Truth"]. In *Vorstudien und Ergänzungen zur Theorie des kommunikativen Handelns*. Frankfurt: Suhrkamp, 1984b.

Harrison, Teresa M., and Timothy Stephen. "On-Line Disciplines: Computer-Mediated Scholarship in the Humanities and Social Sciences." *Computers and the Humanities* 26 (1992): 181–93.

Harvey, Elizabeth D., and Kathleen Okruhlik, eds. *Women and Reason*. Ann Arbor: University of Michigan Press, 1992.

Hermeneutik und Ideologiekritik: Mit Beiträgen von K.-O. Apel, C. v. Bormann, R. Bubner, H.-G. Gadamer, H. J. Giegel, J. Habermas. Frankfurt: Suhrkamp, 1971.

Herring, Susan C. "Gender and Participation in Computer-Mediated Linguistic Discourse." Paper presented at the annual meeting of the Linguistic Society of America, Jan. 12, 1992, Philadelphia.

Hesse, B. W., C. M. Werner, and I. Altman. "Temporal Aspects of Computer-Mediated Communication." *Computers in Human Behavior* 4 (1988): 147–65.

Hiltz, S. R. "The Virtual Classroom: Using Computer-Mediated Communication for University Teaching." *Journal of Communication* 36, no. 2 (1986): 95–104.

Horkheimer, Max, and Theodor W. Adorno. *Dialektik der Aufklärung*. Amsterdam, 1947. Translated as *Dialectic of Enlightenment*. Trans. John Cumming. New York: Herder & Herder, 1972.

Ingram, David. *Critical Theory and Philosophy*. New York: Paragon House, 1990.

———. *Habermas and the Dialectic of Reason*. New Haven: Yale University Press, 1987.

Ingram, David, and Julia Simon-Ingram. *Critical Theory: The Essential Readings*. New York: Paragon Press, 1991.

Irish, Peggy M., and Randall H. Trigg. "Supporting Collaboration in Hypermedia: Issues and Experiences." In Barrett (1989).

Jaynes, Joseph T. "Limited Freedom: Linear Reflections on Nonlinear Texts." In Barrett (1989).

Jonassen, David H., and R. Scott Grabinger. "Problems and Issues in Designing Hypertext/Hypermedia for Learning." In Jonassen and Mandl (1990).

Jonassen, David H., and Heinz Mandl, eds. *Designing Hypermedia for Learning* (Proceedings of the NATO Advanced Research Workshop on Designing Hypertext/Hypermedia for Learning, July 3–8, 1989, Rottenburg/Necker, FRG.) Berlin: Springer-Verlag, 1990.

Jones, Robert A. "The Hypermedia Lab/Civitas Evaluation (Fall Semester 1991)." University of Illinois, Urbana-Champaign. Photocopy.

Kahn, Arnold S., and Robert G. Brookshire. "Using a Computer Bulletin Board in a Social Psychology Course." *Teaching of Psychology* 18, no. 4 (Dec. 1991): 245–49.

Kiesler, S., J. Siegel, and T. W. McGuire. "Social Psychological Aspects of Computer-Mediated Communication." *American Psychologist* 39 (1984): 1123–34.

Kitalong, Karla Saari. "Hard Sell / Soft Sell: Computer Commercials and the Contesting of the Hegemonic Technological Elite." Conference of Commission on Semiotics and Communication, Speech Communication Association, Oct. 29–Nov. 2, 1992, Chicago.

Krippendorff, Klaus. "The Power of Communication and the Communication of Power: Toward an Emancipatory Theory of Communication." *Communication* 12 (1989): 175–96.

Landow, George P. *Hypertext: The Convergence of Contemporary Critical Theory and Technology*. Baltimore: Johns Hopkins University Press, 1992.

———. "Hypertext in Literary Education, Criticism, and Scholarship." *Computers and the Humanities* 23 (1989): 173–98.

———. "Hypertext, Metatext, and the Electronic Canon." In Tuman (1992).

Leggett, John J., John L. Schnase, and Charles J. Kacmar. "Hypertext for Learning." In Jonassen and Mandl (1990).

Lyotard, Jean-François. *The Postmodern Condition: A Report on Knowledge*. Trans. Geoff Bennington and Brian Massumi. Minneapolis: University of Minnesota Press, 1984.

Lyytinen, Kalle. "Information Systems and Critical Theory—A Critical Assessment." In *Critical Management Studies*. Ed. M. Alvesson and H. Wilmott. Beverly Hills: SAGE, forthcoming.

The Machine That Changed the World. Pt. 5, *The World at Your Fingertips*. Written, prod., and dir. Robert Hone. Exec. prod., Jon Palfreman. A WGBH Boston/BBC TV coproduction in association with NDR/Hamburg: 1992.

Malone, Thomas W., and John F. Rockart. "Computers, Networks, and the Corporation." *Scientific American* 265, no. 3 (Sept. 1991): 128–36.

Marcuse, Herbert. *Eros and Civilization. A Philosophical Inquiry into Freud*. Boston: Beacon, 1955.

———. *One-Dimensional Man: Studies in the Ideology of Advanced Industrial Society*. Boston: Beacon, 1964.

McCarthy, Thomas. *The Critical Theory of Jürgen Habermas*. Cambridge: MIT Press, 1978.

———. "Translator's Introduction." In Habermas (1984a).

McKnight, Cliff, Andrew Dillon, and John Richardson, eds. *Hypertext in Context*. New York: Cambridge University Press, 1991.

Mullins, Phil. "The Fluid Word: Word Processing and Its Mental Habits." *Thought* 63, no. 251 (1988): 413–28.

Nelson, Theodor H. *Dream Machines: New Freedoms through Computer Screens—A Minority Report. Computer-Lib: You Can and Must Understand Computers Now.* Chicago: Hugo's Book Service, 1974. Rev. ed., Redmond, Wash.: Microsoft Press, 1987.

———. *Literary Machines,* ed. 87.1. Fredericksburg, Tex.: Theodor H. Nelson, 1987.

———. "Opening Hypertext: A Memoir." In Tuman (1992).

———. "Replacing the Printed Word: A Complete Literary System." *IFIP Proceedings* (Oct. 1980): 1013–23.

O'Donnell, James. "St. Augustine to NREN: The Tree of Knowledge and How It Grows." *Serials Librarian* 23, nos. 3–4 (1992): 21–41.

Pollack, Andrew. "Two Men, Two Visions of One Computer World, Indivisible." *New York Times*, Dec. 8, 1991, sec. 3, p. 13.

Quinn, C. N., H. Mehan, J. A. Lewin, and S. D. Black. "Real Education in Real Time: The Use of Electronic Message Systems for Instruction." *Instructional Science* 11 (1983): 313–27.

Rasmussen, David M. *Reading Habermas*. Cambridge: Basil Blackwell, 1990.

Rice, R. E., and G. Love. "Electronic Emotion: Socioemotional Content in a Computer-Mediated Communication Network." *Communication Research* 14 (1987): 85–108.

Richartz, Martin, and Tom D. Rüdebusch. "Collaboration in Hypermedia Environments." In Jonassen and Mandl (1990).

Riel, Margaret. "Approaching the Study of Networks." *Computing Teacher* (Dec. 1991–Jan. 1992): 5–7, 52.

———. "Computer-Mediated Communication: A Tool for Reconnecting Kids with Society." *Interactive Learning Environments* 1, no. 4 (1990): 255–63.

Romiszowski, Alexander J. "The Hypertext/Hypermedia Solution—But What Exactly Is the Problem?" In Jonassen and Mandl (1990).

Rousseau, Jean Jacques. *The Social Contract and Discourses*. Trans. G. D. H. Cole. New York: Dutton, 1950.

Rubens, Philip. "Reading and Employing Technical Information in Hypertext." *Technical Communication* 38, no. 1 (Feb. 1991): 36–40.

Saunders, C. S., and J. E. Heyl. "Evaluating Educational Computer Conferencing." *Journal of Systems Management* 39 (1988): 33–38.

Singer, Benjamin D. "The New Media and Electronic Anomie." In *Communications in Canadian Society*. Ed. B. Singer. Scarborough, Ont.: Nelson Canada, 1991.

Spiro, Rand J., and Jihn-Chang Jehng. "Cognitive Flexibility and Hypertext:

Theory and Technology for the Nonlinear and Multidimensional Traversal of Complex Subject Matter." In *Cognition, Education, and Multimedia: Exploring Ideas in High Technology*. Ed. Don Nix and Spiro Rand. Hillsdale, N.J.: Lawrence Erlbaum, 1990.

Sproull, Lee, and Sara Kiesler. "Computers, Networks, and Work." *Scientific American* 265, no. 3 (Sept. 1991): 116–23.

Steiner, Linda. "Feminist Theorizing and Communication Ethics." *Communication* 12 (1989): 157–73.

Tonella, Karla. Personal communication. Jan. 19, 1992.

Toulmin, Stephen. *Human Understanding*. Princeton: Princeton University Press, 1972.

———. *The Uses of Argument*. Cambridge: Cambridge University Press, 1958.

Tuman, Myron C., ed. *Literacy Online: The Promise (and Peril) of Reading and Writing with Computers*. Pittsburgh: University of Pittsburgh Press, 1992.

Walther, Joseph B. "Interpersonal Effects in Computer-Mediated Interaction: A Relational Perspective." *Communication Research* 19, no. 1 (Feb. 1992): 52–90.

Westrum, Ron. *Technologies and Society: The Shaping of People and Things*. Belmont, Calif.: Wadsworth, 1991.

Wright, Patricia. "Cognitive Overheads and Prostheses: Some Issues in Evaluating Hypertexts." In *Hypertext '91*. New York: Association for Computing Machinery, 1991.

Yankelovich, Nicole, Norman Meyrowitz, and Andries van Dam. "Reading and Writing the Electronic Book." Originally published in *IEEE Computer* 18 (Oct. 1985), reprinted in Delany and Landow (1990).

Zimmerli, Walther Ch. "Ist die kommunikationstheoretische Wende ein Ausweg aus dem 'Hermeneutikstreit'?" In *Theorie zwischen Kritik und Praxis: Jürgen Habermas und die Frankfurter Schule*. Ed. Roland Simon-Schaefer and Walther Ch. Zimmerli. Stuttgart: Friedrich Frommann, 1975.

Physics and Hypertext: Liberation and Complicity in Art and Pedagogy

Martin E. Rosenberg

8

Everything habitual draws an ever tighter net of spiderwebs around us; then we notice that the fibres have become traps, and that we ourselves are sitting in the middle, like a spider that got caught there and must feed on its own blood. That is why the free spirit hates all habits and rules, everything enduring and definitive; that is why, again and again, he painfully tears apart the net around him, even though he will suffer as a consequence from countless large and small wounds—for he must tear those fibres *away from himself,* from his body, his soul.

—Friedrich Nietzsche, *Human, All Too Human*

All the operations of our intellect tend to geometry.

—Henri Bergson, *Creative Evolution*

Everything is a machine.

—Gilles Deleuze and Félix Guattari, *Anti-Oedipus*

In her influential "Cyborg Manifesto," Donna J. Haraway identifies a new site for gender-based political struggle in the transformed social matrix she calls "the informatics of domination."[1] She defines this matrix as an interface between the binary discourse of computers and the rhythms of the body, and then tropes both resistance to domination, and complicity with it, in the figure of the cyborg, the subject resulting from this merging of artificial and biological intelligences.[2] For Haraway, the trope of the half-human, half–artificially intelligent cyborg articulates the condition of internal domination felt by women in a cultural matrix controlled by men, a matrix that extends to the forms of technology available within that culture.

Taking Haraway's approach one step further, it will be useful to make visible the ideological warfare implicit in this trope of the cyborg-as-matrix, for the terms of the struggle as Haraway describes it reflect in part struggles within and among disciplinary territories (in both the social and the academic meaning of the word *disciplinary*), struggles which in part are dependent upon another set of tropical oppositions.

Haraway's dependence upon the opposition of determined mechanism and contingent organism in describing female subjectivity, and her attempts to conflate that opposition, is typical of the avant-garde thrust beyond and not simply between two competing discourses. For example, Haraway's initial opposition may be explained strictly in terms of competing theories of noise as entropic threat or negentropic possibility, or in terms of the competing computational and the emergent-properties paradigms in cognitive science.[3] In terms of entropy, she states: "Cyborg politics is the struggle for language and the struggle against perfect communication, against the one code that translates all meaning perfectly, the central dogma of phallogocentrism. That is why cyborg politics insists on noise and advocates pollution, rejoicing in the illegitimate fusions of animal and machine."[4]

It is helpful to remember that Boltzmann's mathematical formula for computing the amount of entropy in a system parallels rather precisely Shannon's mathematical formula for computing the amount of noise in any given message.[5] In this passage, Haraway's celebration of noise, contingently present in an otherwise determined channel of communication, plays directly on the doubled condition of threat and promise associated with entropic processes.[6] She employs these tropes ideologically in order to align tactics of resistance with the laws of thermodynamics, in opposition to tropes of precise causality associated with the laws of dynamics and aligned with the conditions of domination.

This ideological warfare between deterministic and contingent representations of both physical and cultural phenomena has its rhetorical origins in physics. That is, the opposition between determinism and contingency, which helps to articulate differing perspectives on noise in information theory or on the properties of human intelligence in cognitive science, depends upon the distinction between the epistemological assumptions underlying the precise, deterministic, and reversible laws characteristic of geometric representations of reality, exemplified by the term *dynamics,* and those underlying the irreversible laws characteristic of statistical approximations that govern complex events, exemplified by *thermodynamics*.

While Haraway associates this ideological conflict strictly with the problematics of female subjectivity, we must now see the tropical oppositions framing this conflict as problematic for analyses of human subjectivity beyond the scope of gender. We should keep in mind the epistemological and political enactments played out by these tropical oppositions, as well as their genealogical context, as we investigate the properties of hypertext.

Hypertext, as theorists describe it, seems to function as a site for two mutually exclusive yet fundamentally complicitous human impulses: a struggle for liberation and a surrender to domination. By examining the physics tropes that hypertext theorists resort to in order to polemicize the capacity of hypertext to liberate its users, we may witness these exclusive yet complicitous impulses and thus render problematic those polemics. Like Nietzsche's spider, these theorists have become entrapped by the very tropes used to describe the condition of systemic imprisonment in the first place. Yet, this is not to condemn these polemics but to demonstrate that hypertext theorists, consciously or unconsciously, are part of a sustained genealogy of avant-garde philosophers and artists drawing on these same tropical oppositions to ground their polemics.

It will be useful, at least from a historical perspective, to situate the claims of hypertext theorists in terms of an avant-garde "tradition," as we demystify them. These theorists claim that hypertext systems function as vehicles for avant-garde artistic and pedagogical purposes; they claim that hypertext can "liberate" its users. Enthusiasts construe hypertext as offering its consumers radically different and rewarding aesthetic and educational experiences: works of fiction and poetry in the arts and information-retrieval and text-generation systems in the classroom. Examples of the former include the fictions *Afternoon,* by Michael Joyce, and *Victory Garden*, by Stuart Moulthrop. Examples of the latter are *The Dickens Web* and *In Memoriam Web;* Storyspace, created by J. David Bolter and Michael Joyce; Mindwriter (part of the Daedalus System), by Hugh Burns, Fred Kemp, and the Daedalus Group; and RHIZOME, by the five members of the RHIZOME Project.[7]

I wish, in particular, to respond skeptically to the way that proponents of hypertext systems depend on tropes from physics and mathematics to describe how hypertext may offer resistance to and liberation from the constraints of the habitual patterns governing the consumption of more pedestrian forms of art and education. (As a founder and the director of the RHIZOME Project, I include myself among them.) What follows, then, is a critique of the posited correspondence implied by these tropes between specific laws of physics, associated with the terms *geometry, nonlinearity, nodes, contingency, indeterminacy*, and *entropy,* and specific properties of hypertext that would validate its use as a medium for artistic expression and pedagogy. These correspondences become foregrounded whenever tropes imply, as they must, an essential connection between language and the things and ideas to which they refer.

According to Hayden White, a trope is a turn of phrase linking an abstract concept to the physical world, thus establishing a correspondence between the physical world and human ideation. Tropes are "inexpungeable from discourse in the human sciences."[8] For Jacques Derrida, tropes reflect a tolerance for a "provisional loss of meaning" to arrive at "what is proper."[9] Tropes, then, demonstrate their truth only by assuming some essential connection between word and thing: "Like *mimesis,* metaphor comes back to *physis,* to its own truth and its presence. Nature always finds in it its own analogy, its own resemblance to itself, and finds increase there only of itself" (45). But this implied self-evidence becomes problematic when the fiction of essential language no longer disguises how tropes allow for "an inevitable detour," a "horizon of circular appropriation of the proper sense" (73), and this problem becomes especially acute in trans-disciplinary borrowings. Every trope, therefore, becomes a fiction, the authorship of which all writers must deny in order to preserve the referentiality or truth-content of their discourse.

Scientists resort to tropes from cultural phenomena to make their descriptions of physical phenomena accessible; similarly artists and social philosophers resort to tropes from physical phenomena to explain phenomena in their domains. These borrowings become complicated further by the relative status of each discipline. For example, the borrowing of tropes from physical phenomena by the arts and social philosophy marks their marginalized position, while the borrowing of cultural tropes by scientists marks their cosmological reach, reflecting the domination of the sciences across the range of social discourses. Any physics trope will be more true than any cultural trope. As Michel Serres writes of the poverty of the arts, "science is on the side of power, on the side of effectiveness; it has and will have more and more credit, more intellectual and social legitimacy, and the best positions in government; it will attract strong minds strong in reason and ambition; it will take up space."[10]

Here Serres emphasizes the legitimating power as well as the fictiveness of tropes from science. Before we proceed, it is important to recognize that the motive for constructing such correspondences lies with the will to power—a power that the avant-garde cannot wield without recourse to the tropes that possess it: after all, it was Nietzsche who defined truth as a mobile army of metaphors. Furthermore, this motive depends upon a condition of language that Jean Baudrillard calls "seduction," a term congruent with the notion that the tropical dimension of language is irreducible—"that which extracts meaning from discourse and detracts it from its truth."[11] In other words, by playing out the full implications of the physics tropes that these theorists use, we may observe how the desire for liberation implicit in the avant-garde moment becomes seduced by the will to tropical power that enacts merely a simulation of the desired moment of perfect freedom, which by definition, exists in infinite regression but which, as the opening quotation implies, remains the omega of every Nietzschean Free Spirit.

First, it will help to situate this struggle within the discourse of hypertext theorists more precisely in political terms. Most discussions of politics and hypertext concern the ways in which the technology of hypertext alters the realm of information and its modes, as well as the ways in which institutions, as forms of technology, circumscribe the usefulness of hypertext itself.[12] George P. Landow underscores the naivety of those embracing this new technology when he notes: "Writers on hypertext almost always continue to associate it with individual freedom and empowerment" (169), and he goes on to show how the political impinges upon hypertextual space in any number of ways.

But I am concerned with freedom and power as issues at the more subtle level of epistemology. While Haraway's concept of the cyborg obviously applies here, I would like to shift to a system of tropes operant in the writings of Gilles Deleuze and Félix Guattari in order to make the problematic tropics of liberation and complicity in hypertext more visible. I am speaking specifically of the micropolitical field of struggle that Deleuze and Guattari locate between the "zone of indiscernibility," which represents the ways in which the mind and body of a subject may be "dominated" (Haraway's term) or determined by systems of cultural signification that remain invisible to that subject, and the "zone of impotence," where the subject, unconstrained by those systems, can thrive in a space where the three forms of creative resistance to determination, or "becoming" (intense, animal, imperceptible), may emerge.[13]

I have argued elsewhere that Deleuze and Guattari draw explicitly from tropes that play out the distinction between time-reversible dynamic forces and time-irreversible thermodynamic processes in order to articulate the distinction between the concept of the "war machine" as functioning in both macro- and micropolitical zones of domination, and the nomad and rhizome as concepts articulating the contingent condition of "becoming" that enables resistance to domination.[14] Hypertext theorists draw on these same tropical oppositions to conceptualize this fuzzy micropolitical realm between determination and freedom, particularly those theorists who associate the technology of hypertext with the avant-garde thrust—the "leading edge" in art and education. This investigation requires first locating and observing the function of physics tropes in discourse on hypertext and then examining more closely the physics behind the tropes in order to make explicit and then demystify the claims implied by those tropes.

Hypertext and Physics Tropes

An environment for software design with pedagogical as well as aesthetic implications, hypertext has attracted numerous enthusiasts seeking to transform education and art. Tactics made possible by hypertext include its inherent capability to alter writing and reading in ways barely imaginable—except by certain recent critical theorists, particularly poststructuralists.

For example, many premise these claims for hypertext on its remarkable capacity, as discussed by Landow and Bolter, to "literalize" the poststructuralist notion of intertextuality.[15] *Literalize* refers to the capacity of hypertext to offer "nonlinear" access to units, or "lexias" (a term from Barthes), of text or information.[16] This nonlinearity enables the dispersal of the logic(s) of narration and argumentation by offering divergent reading and writing trajectories: nodes that lead to the actual texts rather than footnotes that only hint at further research; or, the possibility of multiple alternative plottings for fiction or the explicit exploration of metaphoric echoes for poetry.

Most important, these patterns explode the relationship between writer and reader by making the role of the reader more participatory, even subversive, and it is this subversion that proponents have cited as an example of how transformative the experience of hypertextual art and pedagogy might become. Here, the consumer of the hypertext becomes empowered through the contingencies of choice made possible by this nonlinear relationship among multiple blocks of lexias or texts. According to Bolter: "The reader may well become the author's adversary, seeking to make the text over in a direction that the author did not anticipate. . . . The computer therefore makes visible the contest between author and reader that in previous technologies has gone on out of sight, 'behind' the page."[17]

One dimension to this contest lies with the condition of contingency that these choices create for the reader. As Terence Harpold writes, "contingency is . . . a foundational principle in our relations with the texture of these [hypertextual] artifacts."[18]

Yet, part of the charm associated with this new "writing space" also has to do with the capacity of "wreaders" to jump through links from lexia to lexia, forwards, backwards at will—a wreader in control of the cursor, a wreader who can freeze the text, who is aware of a Home button, as in HyperCard, or of the mapping features of Storyspace, a wreader who can gain an instant, transcendent perspective of the wreading trajectory. This control over experience, exemplified by the "function" of transcendence to detach the observer from the phenomena being observed, reminds one of the control over the natural environment enabled by the calculus of Leibnitz and Newton,[19] a control that enables astronomers to track the motions of the planets or comets forwards and backwards in time and gunnery officers to estimate the trajectory of shells in order to maximize their "effect." So, all contingencies available to the wreader become domesticated by his or her complete control of the process of choosing direction.

The problem with this claim, and its valorization of the wreader's control over the multiple trajectories possible through hypertext documents or writing spaces, lies with the explicitly geometrical dimension of hypertext. Lexia and links—the connections possible between cards, buttons, and fields (as in HyperCard), or the "container-and-spaces mapping of Storyspace"[20]—together create rhetorics entrapped in the necessarily logocentric geometry of regulated time and space. (We might note that rhetoric, in its classical sense as a science of structuring relationships among units of information according to the needs of a persuasive situation, depends much on geometrical tropes such as "stasis" and that the four master tropes, as well as the concept of schema, are premised upon spatial relationships.)[21] In other words, we need to confront the geometrical nature of hypertext systems *and* their rhetorics by noticing: first, the imprecision with which hypertext theorists are using the terms *nonlinear* and *multilinear*; second, that these terms are being used as functional equivalents; and third, that these supposedly equivalent terms, as they apply to the dimensions of print medium and the reading process within hypertext systems, correspond to the indifference toward the direction of time's flow that calculus and other geometries exemplify and render problematic by their spatialization of duration (and its implicit linearity) into discrete units.

Now, *nonlinear* has a quite different significance in nonlinear dynamics and nonequilibrium thermodynamics, two forms of "chaos theory."[22] In the context of chaos theory, the term *nonlinear* refers to kinds of mathematical equations that have to do with accounting for complexities in the causality of a system in phase space. This has some relationship with the notion of contingency, and we will address the promise of a correspondence of hypertext with the nonlinearity associated with the science of complexity, from a skeptical perspective, later on. Yet, it would be useful to point out that in nonlinear dynamics, the purpose of nonlinear equations is to demonstrate with as much precision as possible a deterministic account of complex events.

It is safe to say that the uses of the trope *nonlinear* by hypertext theorists have more properly involved the sense of the determined or practically contingent direction of words, as they are written or read. In this sense, what hypertext theorists mean by "nonlinearity" is more properly analogous to what physicists call "symmetry," or "reversibility." Since the focus in hypertext theory is on the functional direction of signification, the correspondence with symmetry and reversibility works more precisely, because these terms refer to the direction of the flow of duration or time. Words must be read one after another, and cannot be read backwards; we might say that the reading process is linear in the sense that its trajectory remains irreversible. If, however, the irreversible reading process could be interrupted through the intrusion of technology in the form of hypertextual nodes, which would then offer optional significatory trajectories (what might be called "multilinear" directional flows), then we might call hypertext environments symmetrical or reversible. That is, the technological environment of hypertext remains (as much as possible) functionally indifferent to the chosen trajectory of the wreader. Thus, at least as hypertext theorists use them, *nonlinear* and *multilinear* are equivalent.

First, though, let us address the aesthetic claims made for nonlinear, contingent hypertext systems, claims that link art produced in hypertextual environments with the avant-garde tradition, its continuity with postmodern modes of expression, and its agenda from a micropolitical perspective. One can read the history of the twentieth-century avant-garde as a genealogy of tactics of resistance to geometry, and, in this respect, the works of Deleuze and Guattari represent a logical extension of this genealogy. I argue that, simply put, the recourse to physics tropes by hypertext theorists constitutes a part of this genealogy as well. In order to proceed with this argument, it will be necessary to explore more precisely the ways in which tropes from physics become used to represent domination and resistance.

A crucial issue here, therefore, concerns the ways in which avant-garde polemics have confronted geometric representations of the physical world, including the spatialization of time, by which I mean the domination of the human experience of duration by mechanical clocks and by calculus, solidified during the First Industrial Revolution, a domination first diagnosed by Henri Bergson in *Matter and Memory* (1896).[23] Historically, the avant-garde derives much of its transgressive energies from its resistance to this hegemony through an obsessive celebration of contingency. The works of Marcel Duchamp, Max Ernst, Samuel Beckett, John Cage, Thomas Pynchon, the dance group Pilobolus, as well as jazz symptomize that resistance and its energies. If we consider hypertext seriously as an avant-garde medium, it should stand scrutiny in terms of this ideological struggle between the time-reversible assumptions governing geometry and the time-irreversible assumptions governing statistical accounts of contingency, as that struggle informs the history of the avant-garde in art as well as in social philosophy.[24] The many references to Deleuze and Guattari in this volume alone, for example, and Deleuze's debt to Nietzsche and Bergson in particular, make obvious the importance of this genealogy to an understanding of the discourse of hypertext theorists.

Theorists of hypertext hope that the contingencies of choice made available through the operation of lexias, nodes, and links to other lexias, as they are found along the otherwise stable linearity of a single primary text as a sequence of lexias, will liberate the users (the "wreaders" or "riters") from the confines of relentless narrative linearity (or from the linear mono-logic of academic discourse, for that matter). But, in theories of the avant-garde, the enemy is not linearity but the nonlinear perspective of geometry; not the prison house of time but the fiction of transcendence implied by the indifferent epistemological stance toward time. We need to confront the fact that, for *any* avant-garde moment, the problem lies with the capacity of geometry, as it constitutes the structure of any medium, including hypertext, to seduce, in Baudrillard's sense of the word, any particular strategy of resistance to its frame. Geometry can accomplish that seduction simply by *promising* to the observer functional transcendence.

Ilya Prigogine and Isabelle Stengers have analyzed rhetorically the ideological dimension of the opposition between reversible and irreversible perspectives within the physical sciences—between "Being" (premised on geometry as the precise, nonlinear representation of events, and associated with the field of dynamics) and "Becoming" (premised on statistical formulations of contingent events irreducible to certainty, irreversible with respect to duration, and associated with the field of thermodynamics).[25] By applying Prigogine and Stengers' ideological critique of epistemological assumptions in physics to the polemics of avant-garde discourse, including hypertext systems and their uses, we may observe how the possibilities for contingent movement within hypertext documents, valorized by recent proponents, merely enact simulations that remain complicitous with the logocentric structures that regulate our thoughts as well as our lives.

Reversible and Irreversible Time

To understand the distinction between reversible and irreversible systems, and the usefulness of that distinction for evaluating the claims made for hypertext, we must question the assumption that we have freedom to wander the topology of hypertext, to define our own positions in that hyper-territory, and to design the conditions for a rhetoric capable of guiding our journeys through its multiple realms. Yet, in confronting what kind of grounding hypertext systems may have, we must look at two things: (1) how the relations among cards, buttons, and fields (as in HyperCard) constrain the rules for any rhetoric by limiting its logic, construed in terms of spatial structures and temporal flows; and (2) how the structures of thought brought to this virtual environment constrain our ability to manipulate its supposedly distinct logic and rhetoric. (It is a virtual environment, yet it seems real because it brings structures of thought to the surface of a thinker's attention by projecting those thoughts onto a screen and allowing the thinker to "witness" them.) So, even the designers of hypertext must bear the same credulity toward its geometry as do the "interactive" wreaders.

I also participate in this credulity. It is what I call the naive lines of reasoning: (1) the properties of hypertext—lexias, links, and maps, or cards, buttons, and fields—enable nonlinear access to information and nonlinear autonomous construction of narrative forms from preexisting options; or (2) these properties enable nonlinear access to different questions and to options that aid in the generation of thought (Michael Joyce's distinction between "exploratory" and "constructive" systems).[26] Logic, which governs academic discourse, is linear; nonlinear thinking therefore becomes associated with creativity, as in associative leaps. Logic is hierarchical; nonlinear association is smooth. Here we may wish to resort to Deleuze and Guattari's distinction between striated, arboreal structures and smooth, rhizomatic structures, suggesting, as Johndan Johnson-Eilola, my colleague on the RHIZOME Project claims, that linear, hierarchical structures in hypertext are logocentric, smooth, nonlinear structures are nomadic, and so on.[27]

From this perspective then, linear thinking represents the prison house and nonlinear thinking offers liberation from that prison: freedom of thought becomes literalized in a virtual environment in which the programmer takes the initiative, and victory occurs when this virtual liberatory hypertextual realm wages war on the structures of thought brought to this virtual reality by the "naive" interactive consumer of hypertext, or so we would like to believe.

The valorizing of nonlinear thinking depends to a large extent on the distinction between what the popular understanding construes as *old* and *new* physics, and on the popular appropriation of tropes specific to that opposition. This distinction is a false one, and our popular culture's celebration of nonlinearity is unfortunate. The distinction depends on the incorrect premise that the so-called new physics constitutes a new and better knowledge than the old physics. In fact, if we accept the insights of Prigogine and Stengers, drawn as they are from the work of their predecessor Henri Bergson, no fundamental epistemological shift really occurred between classical and quantum physics, or between quantum mechanics and nonlinear dynamics (or chaos theory) and its most familiar manifestation, fractal geometry. Two underlying assumptions unite all these very different analyses of physical systems: time is as symmetrical as space, and geometry can represent, with certainty, the physical world.

As it is construed in physics, symmetry, or reversibility, is coextensive with a geometrical representation of physical reality. To anticipate my argument concerning the claims of hypertext theorists, *anything* produced out of a systemic relationship between lexias and links, cards, buttons, and fields also participates in the same geometrical episteme that produced Newton's laws and classical stasis theory, Feynman diagrams of subatomic particle interactions, formal logic, computer languages, and the fractal scaling of seacoasts, black holes, and chess.

All these systems of thinking assume that physical events are reversible with respect to time, so that the laws governing the motion of the solar system and the trajectory of subatomic particles make sense whether or not the events that we view move forward or backward in time. Further, in geometry it remains possible to reduce all events to simple immutable laws that are true for all time and that transcend the events that they describe. As Prigogine argues, serious problems exist with this perspective.[28] In order to understand why this abstract investigation of the geometrical conception of reality is important to hypertext, let's briefly examine Prigogine's critique of that conception.

Being and Becoming: Prigogine's Critique of the Physical Sciences

Prigogine's work (alone and with Stengers) is important, not just for his claim of locating the "becoming" of time's arrow even in the reversible worlds of quantum electrodynamics and low-temperature physics, but for his confrontation with the ideological dimension of certain epistemological assumptions concerning physical systems as well. These assumptions reveal an ideological bias toward a mechanistic model of physical events. This bias within the discipline of physics remains so dominant that Prigogine, though his research was in the physics of self-organizing systems, was awarded the Nobel Prize in chemistry.[29]

Irrespective of his reputation as a physicist, Prigogine's career has lasting value simply for having brought this issue (which really belongs to the philosophy of science) to the surface. Further, a long genealogy exists of attempts to construct relationships between physical and intellectual systems (Bergson's being one among many others), and I am referring to those attempts from a skeptical perspective (complicity theory) to explore the role that physics tropes play in the claims made for hypertext. Prigogine argues that there are two fundamental assumptions at work in physics, the first of which concerns the nature of being.

Assumption One: Being

According to this assumption, laws of nature are transcendent to nature and are reversible with respect to time. This means that time has no real existence with respect to physical laws; it remains a constant, a function but not a presence. The purpose of physics, therefore, is to discover the laws of nature in their simplest formulation as they govern the behavior of physical systems. The prime symptom of this assumption is the reduction of those physical systems to geometry: calculus, which spatializes time with respect to the history of a system; Feynman diagrams, which represent the symmetry and reversibility with respect to time of subatomic particle interactions; Einstein's general relativity, which, among other things, predicts the effect of gravity on time-space geometry and the effect on light's trajectory as it passes through that geometry; and John Wheeler's extension of relativistic physics, which theorizes how black holes in time-space geometry could actually become "worm-holes" into another quadrant of that same geometry (universe) or "white holes" into a potentially infinite number of parallel time-space geometries (universes). Classical stasis theory, the fractal scaling of seacoasts, quantum mechanics, relativity, and chess (a metaphor used both by Feynman to describe the laws governing quantum interactions and by de Saussure to describe the principles of langue-parole) all share the geometric frame.

The field of dynamics studies matter and its interactions with the aim of "reducing" those phenomena to the simplest formal description possible. The greatest proponent of this view, Albert Einstein, put it this way:

> In mechanics the future path of a moving body can be predicted and its past disclosed if its present condition and the forces acting upon it can be known. Thus, for example, the future paths of all planets can be foreseen. The active forces are Newton's gravitational forces depending on the distance alone. The great results of classical mechanics suggest that the mechanical view can be consistently applied to all branches of physics, that all phenomena can be explained by the action of forces representing either attraction or repulsion, depending only upon distance and acting between unchangeable particles.[30]

Leibniz and Newton developed infinitesimal calculus as a quantitative tool to freeze dynamic forces into a potentially infinite series of instant still frames. By providing a way to perform this operation, calculus enabled scientists to discover what Prigogine calls the lawful, deterministic, and reversible nature of those forces.[31] Calculus enabled a mastery over the natural world precisely by allowing scientists to deduce from an initial state the series of inertial or accelerating states that a planet, cannonball, or other object passes through, not only into the future, but into the past as well.

We have already noticed how the series of lexias in a hypertext system seems to possess the properties of calculus, by enabling users to leap forward or backward, lexia by lexia. Each lexia remains separate, virtually autonomous; the wreader's experience of the sequence of lexias remains discontinous, except as the author or reader establishes linkages among them. But this does not cover the profound dislocations made possible by leaps through nodes or links to other texts that embody other linearities. However, by referring to Einstein's *General Theory of Relativity* and Wheeler's *Geometrodynamics,* by constructing correspondences with those methodologies from physics sharing the geometrical assumptions of calculus, we will be able to demonstrate that the possibilities for transforming the processes of reading and writing, inherent to hypertext, are constrained by those very assumptions. The shared dependence on the geometrical frame by these disparate theories provides a crucial hint at the limits for hypertextual expression.

Applications: Einstein, Wheeler, and the Docuverse. Einstein's special theory of relativity demonstrates mathematically that observers are not stable with reference to objects of perception. For example, the Lorentz transformation computes, with reference to an observer in an inertial (geometric) frame, how objects shrink or human beings (as in the Twins Paradox) may "age" less quickly as they accelerate to the speed of light.[32] The general theory of relativity demonstrates that space, as represented by the geometry of Newton, also lacks stability: given certain gravitational conditions, time-space geometry may curve, as revealed when light appears to bend in the gravitational field surrounding a local star, such as our sun.[33]

But so far, these "revolutionary" discoveries do not in any sense invalidate geometry as *the* premise for the dynamic perspective in physics. Einstein's (and Hermann Minkowski's) innovations simply adapted geometry to account for these distortions by encompassing them in a four-dimensional, space-time geometry. As Nobel laureate Wheeler puts it: "Space is different for different observers. Time is different for different observers. Space-Time is the same for everyone."[34]

What becomes invariant here is not time and space, as represented by a geometrical matrix, but pure geometry itself. Geometry represents differing events relative to particular observers in terms of a postulated stable field. As Lawrence Sklar discusses in his works on the philosophy of space-time, three possible interpretations of the status of geometry emerge from this problematic: first, a substantial "ether" underlies geometry, energy, and matter; second, geometry and therefore gravity only emerge heuristically in the extended space between distant bodies and their relative observers; and third, in a cosmological sense, there is only geometry, gravity, and radiation, and not only bodies but their relations and transformations are products of pure space-time geometry itself.[35] Bergson demonstrates other possible formulations of the experience of duration that cannot be represented even by fourth-dimensional geometry.[36] Some seventy years later, Prigogine adopts this angle of attack in his critique of time-reversible and time-irreversible systems. But the third option spelled out by Sklar becomes of special interest to our discussion of hypertext, because it situates Wheeler's theory of geometrodynamics, especially his work on the cosmology of black holes, which provides the most precise analogy to Ted Nelson's concept of the *docuverse* as an infinite number of texts linked by nodes.[37]

Wheeler addresses black holes, which are anomalies in the time-space geometry of Einstein and Minkowski.[38] Most conceptions of black holes see them as points of infinite density, as singularities with an infinite gravitational pull that distorts the time-space geometry in their environs. Wheeler theorizes that these black holes may also indicate not just a point of singularity but a *portal,* a vortex that may serve as a node through which matter may enter and, in some mysterious way, exit. This portal enables two possibilities: first, a black hole might become a "wormhole" that would allow jumps from one place, through a "hyperspace," to another location in the same geometrical grid; the second and more interesting possibility is that a black hole might have a reverse function, and mathematical representations of "white holes" have been developed to describe how matter might emerge from a node in space-time geometry. This theory evolved even to the point of postulating that a black hole might function like a white hole emerging in a parallel universe. In this extension of general relativity, there could be any number of parallel universes connected by any number of gravitational anomalies in their respective time-space geometries.

Wheeler took this concept further by attempting to explain matter itself as densely curved time-space geometry that traps radiation in a standing wave: nothing exists except energy and geometry. One implication of Wheeler's attempt to subsume everything extant into geometry is that geometrodynamics constitutes a theory that represents all forces and processes in terms of an invariant, ontologically stable frame that dissolves the distinction between form and essence. At its moment in the history of field theories, geometrodynamics was thought of as the ultimate hegemony, the beginnings of Einstein's dream: a grand unified theory of everything (geometrical). It has had, however, no experimental verification, and therefore constitutes a dead end in theoretical physics. Still, Wheeler's theory provides an excellent model for Nelson's "docuverse" and its rhetoric of texts and links, as Landow has discussed.[39]

Recent theorists of hypertext, and of the rhetorics possible from observing reading and writing within its environs, distinguish between text and hypertext. Text is a field of words, paragraphs, and pages, while hypertext includes these as well as nodes and links among texts. As Moulthrop, one of the most sophisticated hypertext theorists, puts it: "Hypertext rhetoric must take into account more than just the ordering of language into structures and genres inherited from orality or print literacy. It must also address a more complicated meta-management in which the user modifies ordering processes themselves . . . a secondary literacy."[40] The movement through a link or node from one text, arranged as a sequence of lexias, to another part of that text or to a completely different text, also a sequence of lexias, corresponds with the movement or trajectory of particles through a black hole that could serve as a worm hole or as a white hole to another time-space geometry. Therefore, if we follow this correspondence to its logical conclusion, the laws governing properties of Wheeler's multi-universe and Nelson's docuverse must account for those laws governing black holes as local disruptions of the geometrical field as well as the "normal" operations of the field itself, and those governing nodes as local disruptions of the linearity of an individual lexia as well as the operations within a particular lexia.

We have mentioned that an adequate description of those disruptions in discourse can be found in poststructuralist investigations into the perpetual instability of all systems of signification. But what critical theorists have done by emphasizing those dislocations, and what hypertext theorists have done by emphasizing links and nodes as part of the rhetoric of a new hyper-literacy, is to ignore how, once the dislocation occurs, a normalcy emerges as the space-time black-hole adventurer, or the hypertext reader, acclimates to the new geometry or new sequence of lexias. Like the characters in Proust's *A la recherche du temps perdu,* hypertext users cannot sustain the experience of dislocation once it has occurred; unless, of course, as in the case of the unfortunate black-hole jockey who accidentally picks a black-hole singularity, never to be seen again, the hypertext user gets lost by passing, irreversibly, through one particular link.

The potential terror of that moment has resonance with the claims for hypertext as an avant-garde medium. It would be the goal of any avant-garde use of hypertext to find a way to sustain that experience of dislocation that would indicate the prolonged liberation from the hegemony of geometry and the constraints that its rhetoric places on the user's awareness. Yet, we should postpone that observation in order to more fully exfoliate the tropics of physics and hypertext. In order to do this, let us return, through Bergson's notion of contingent duration, to Prigogine's theories of self-organization as exemplary of the time-irreversible perspective.

Assumption Two: Becoming

According to this assumption, time is irreducible and irreversible; that is, because it remains inconstant, the laws governing its behavior cannot be simplified to simple, immutable laws. The prime symptom of this assumption about physical events with respect to the contingency of time's arrow is the recourse to statistical analysis in predicting the behavior of macroscopic systems like Brownian motion or heat in engines. Approximations become necessary, since certainty, with respect to determining cause and effect in complex systems, remains a pipe dream. As is exemplified by equilibrium and nonequilibrium thermodynamics, one can never, for instance, locate with certainty where on a new Ferrari rusting will begin, or when; one can never know precisely when, and according to what configuration, slime mold cells will spontaneously aggregate (Prigogine, *From Being to Becoming,* 103–30).

In addition to making this ideological critique, Prigogine's work has focused on locating to what extent physical systems heretofore privileged for assumption 1 are vulnerable to questions confronted by assumption 2, such as finding time's arrow in low-temperature quantum states, or even in subatomic particle interactions. Let me be more specific. The search for certainty according to assumption 1 was challenged decisively by the second law of thermodynamics (given any isolated system, that system will move in the direction of greater entropy or disorder, ultimately reaching stasis, or equilibrium). Articulated further by Ludwig Boltzmann's order principle (given a closed system, that system will always choose the direction of greatest probability), the second law forces observers to recognize the roles that randomness and the *irreversibility* of time play in physical processes: it is far more likely that a Ferrari will turn into a pile of rust than that a pile of rust will turn into a Ferrari (Prigogine and Stengers, *Order out of Chaos,* 122–26). According to Boltzmann, then, the state of any system will remain perpetually contingent until it arrives at its state of stasis or equilibrium, when systemic fluctuation becomes no longer possible. Thus, Prigogine argues, came the birth of not the science of simplicity and certainty but the "science of complexity" (104).

Prigogine won the Nobel Prize in chemistry (1977) for demonstrating how the theory of nonequilibrium thermodynamics can explain processes that seem related formally to entropic processes yet which generate order out of chaos. Although randomness often seems a "threat," as when either a change in the "boundary conditions" or the "macroscopic parameters" (*Order out of Chaos,* 106) of the Ferrari previously mentioned brings it to maximum entropy, for Prigogine, randomness also signals the moment when a physical, chemical, or biological *bifurcation point* projects alternative futures or histories for that system. These futures may in turn indicate increasing orderliness rather than disorderly chaos (Prigogine, *From Being to Becoming,* 103–22).

That moment of bifurcation in the history of the system can never be observable with any certainty, and therefore the specific pattern of self-organization can never be predicted, because the statistical nature of phenomena can never be explained with the precision expected of dynamic systems. It is the contingency of a system that enables alternative histories, alternative temporal linearities, to emerge. A textual system with the aid of nodes can not only project for the writer or reader the choice of alternative textual linearities but can also literalize them. Theorists of hypertext point to this choice as the essential property that enables avant-garde appropriations of the hypertext environment. To confront the claims made for the victory of contingency over the properties of geometry within the environs of hypertext, we need to explore how the oppositional tropes of "being" and "becoming" from physics inform the polemical struggle of the subject from hegemonic dominance at the micropolitical level of thought—a struggle first articulated by Henri Bergson and then enacted in the modern and postmodern avant-garde.

Applications: The Battlefield of Art. In a posting on the electronic mail discussion list Technoculture, Stuart Moulthrop constructed an opposition between the author-designers of hypertext fiction and the hypertext readers they wished to influence, to initiate.[41] Such an opposition suggests that hypertextual environments may constitute a virtual battleground, the site of a struggle not unlike that of the free spirit in the opening quotation of this essay.

Following this conceit, one might say that the avant-garde moment enabled by that warfare represents some kind of victory, a victory not over the user but over the structures of cognition that determine the habitual trajectories of the user's thoughts. To what extent can the battlefield be designed by the combatants? To what extent are the combatants already inscribed before they even design the field and begin the struggle? The savvy programmers may inscript the hypertext; the naive consumers may be inscribed by the hypertext. Yet, whether scripting or inscribed, both the programmers and the consumers of their products remain, without doubt, determined by fundamental structures of thought that have the time-reversible perspective of geometry as one origin. Because of the contingent bifurcations enabled by the ability to choose among trajectories from the geometric frame of one lexia, hypertext theorists claim, as Terence Harpold has, that it might be possible for hypertext fictions to "carnivalize" or otherwise disrupt the habituated reading and thinking patterns of its consumers.[42]

My rhetorical thrust here is to bring the war back home, to demonstrate how, so far, proponents of hypertext as a transformative medium have yet to frame their discussions in terms of the past debate over the "status" of the avant-garde moment. Further, I wish to demonstrate how hypertext, as an avant-garde medium, remains an inadequate vehicle for that transgressive and liberating moment. I am limiting my focus here to the micropolitical concern with how hypertext may influence the cognitive processes of the subject.

We can see how critics have found it inherently difficult even to identify the forces contending in this warfare within hypertext, as in this telling passage from George Landow's superb investigation of the relationship between hypertext and recent (read: avant-garde) literary and cultural theories. Attempting to link the multidirectional nature of hypertext and its effect on narrative and on time itself, Landow draws on the literary criticism of Gérard Genette in order to compare this capacity for multidirectionalism to the reader's experience of the characters in Proust's meditation on time, *A la recherche du temps perdu:*

> Whereas Genette's characterization of the Stendhalian oeuvre captures the reader's experience of the interconnectedness of [Michael Joyce's] *Afternoon* and other hypertext fictions, his description of temporality in Proust conveys the experience of encountering the disjunctions and jumps of hypertextual narrative. Citing George Poulet's observation that in *A la recherche du temps perdu* time does not appear as Bergsonian duration but as a "succession of isolated moments," he points out that similarly "characters (and groups) do not evolve: one fine day, they find that they have changed, as if time confined itself to bringing forth a plurality that they contained *in potentia* from all eternity. Indeed, many of the characters assume the most contradictory roles *simultaneously*" ([Genette, *Figures of Literary Discourse,*] 216). In other words, in *A la recherche du temps perdu* readers find themselves taking leaps and jumping into a different time and different characters. In a hypertext narrative it is the author who provides multiple possibilities, by means of which the readers themselves construct temporal succession and choose characterization. (Landow, *Hypertext,* 114)

The problem with Genette's reading of Proust's *Recherche,* and with Landow's appropriation of that reading to make a claim for hypertext, arises from the way Proust's characters experience time as leaps, as a "succession of isolated moments." They move forward and backward from one singular moment to another precisely because the hegemony of clock time and of calculus causes them to fail to *sustain* the intuitive experience of what Bergson called contingent duration.[43] The immersion in pure and irreversible contingency, according to Bergson, constitutes the fundamental ground of human consciousness (and bears a genealogical relationship with Nietzsche's "Eternal Return"), the loss of which, according to Bergson, has had unfortunate psychological and sociocultural consequences: "In vain, therefore, does life evolve before our eyes as a continuous creation of unforseeable form: the idea always persists in that form, unforeseeability and continuity are mere appearance, the outward reflection of our own ignorance. What is presented to the senses as a continuous history would break up, we are told, into a series of states" (*Creative Evolution,* 30). Those consequences are the direct result of the mind's entrapment by a "latent geometry, immanent in our idea of space, which is the mainspring of our intellect and the cause of its working" (210).

For Bergson, Immanuel Kant's a priori categories (of time and space as "coordinated" in a relational, geometric grid) were not a priori at all, but ideological constructs superimposed upon the manifold of human consciousness to aid in the activity of that consciousness *in the world.* Irreversible, contingent duration, then, can occur only by disrupting this "latency," by demonstrating how the human mind can experience duration completely independently of the precisely uniform repetition governing the trajectories embedded in spatio-temporal geometry: "For the system of to-day actually to be superimposed on that of yesterday the latter must have waited for the former, time must have halted, and everything become simultaneous: that happens in geometry, but in geometry alone" (277). Liberated human consciousness, in this sense, means liberation from a geometric ideological construct that disguises the nature of human awareness in order for it better to plot industrial schedules, the trajectories of cannonballs, the circumnavigation of the globe.

In fact, one way to discuss the relationship between romanticism and the avant-garde is to point out the romantics' fascination with the fragment, and the energies released by the accompanying fragmentation and transcendent liberation of what Lacoue-Labarthe and Nancy call the "system-subject,"[44] a construct that resonates with Haraway's concept of the cyborg. For these theorists, the system-subject refers to the self subjugated by Kant's a priori categories—the sublime moment of its liberation; the fragment the vehicle for that liberation. As a system, the subject believes that there *is* a *cogito,* a transcendent *je* independent of objects of perception. From the perspective of Western epistemology, as Dalia Judowitz demonstrates, this *je* has had autonomous existence since Descartes and Newton and Leibniz's calculus.[45] In the energized moment of fragmentation, subject and object are no longer distinct and time takes on supple forms. If continuity exists between romanticism and the avant-garde, it lies with the polemical will to fragmentation. Therefore, our crucial question addresses whether the lexias of hypertext and the fragments symptomizing the romantic transgression of that system-subject (which would include Nietzsche's aphorisms) function in the same transgressive way.

In *Proust and Signs* (1977) and *Bergsonism* (1990), Gilles Deleuze demonstrates the centrality of Bergson's theories of contingent duration, and their extrapolation in his theory of creative evolution, to Proust's aesthetic. This centrality suggests that the translation of *A la recherche du temps perdu* should not be *Remembrance of Things Past* but *In Search of Lost Time.*[46] Accepting this reading, then, Proust's multinovel sequence becomes the search for momentary insurrections of an experientially contingent duration, subjugated by the regimes of modernity, enabled only by a precise sensory stimulation, and compromised inevitably when that moment (tea and cake) becomes associated with the regulated frames of memory and of the habitual rituals of daily life.

Bergson meant his theory of evolution—a dialectic of contingent duration and systemic memory propelled by a living force called *élan vital*—to apply to intellectual as well as physical systems. This theory informs Proust's critical concern with the symptoms for the "evolution" of the characters in *Recherche.*[47] I wish to hammer home this point of the role that contingency plays in transgression, defined here as this exploration of the desire for liberation and for evolution (broadly construed). Bergson's critique of duration had a seminal influence on a genealogy of the avant-garde that stretches from Proust and Duchamp in any number of directions, and in particular to Beckett, Cage, and Pynchon as well as to performance artists. Bergson's ideological critique of time and space had similar impact on the hegemony theories of Gramsci, and therefore on Althusser, and thus as well on Foucault's notion of discursive formations and Deleuze and Guattari's notion of a war machine and of the nomad and rhizome as articulated tactics of resistance to domination by that machine.

Perhaps equally important for this discussion, Bergson's critique of the human cognition of duration became a crucial reference point for discussion of Prigogine's ideological critique of the distinction in the physical sciences between the reversible, geometrical frame identified as being and the irreversible, contingent perspective identified as becoming. It is no accident that Deleuze draws on the term *becoming* to articulate processes of resistance in that indistinct realm between the zone of indiscernibility and the zone of impotence.

To return briefly to the passage discussed by Landow, in *Recherche,* the characters experience time as discrete, discontinuous units, as jumps and leaps. The reader also experiences the units of narrative and of discrete representations of character. Landow refers to these as analogues of the discontinuous "lexias" of hypertext systems. I argue that, if he wishes to valorize these qualities of hypertext, then his own comments underscore precisely the failure of hypertext to serve as a medium for micropolitical liberation, as avant-garde artists and social philosophers have defined that struggle for liberation since the turn of the century. Now, it is only fair to point out that "liberation" is not the focus of Landow's discussion here, for he is attempting to illustrate how it is precisely the hypertextual regulation of narrative duration through lexias that enables the literalization (we might even say visualization) of the poststructuralist concept of intertexuality. But, given our insistence on the essentially geometrical nature of hypertextual space, we need now to look at the issue of duration or time, contingency, and the question of bifurcating systems, from the perspective of Prigogine.

Contingency, the Bifurcation Point, and Seduction by Geometry

Self-organization processes in far-from equilibrium conditions correspond to a delicate interplay between chance and necessity, between fluctuations and determinable laws. We expect that near a bifurcation, fluctuations or random elements would play an important role, while between bifurcations the deterministic aspects would become dominant.

—Ilya Prigogine and Isabelle Stengers,
Order out of Chaos

In the title of a groundbreaking essay, Moulthrop demonstrates how the physics tropes used to explain hypertext slip between the ideologies of being and becoming.[48] On the one hand, the reference to Roman Jakobson's structural linguistic model of the linear (metonymic) and nonlinear (metaphoric) dimensions of language becomes linked precisely to the geometrical trope of the map: a two-dimensional grid is implied, coordinating metonymy with reference to time and metaphor with reference to space, both of which are the essential constitutents of narrative and, as coordinates, remain fixed in their relationship. On the other hand, Moulthrop's reference to Borges's short story "The Garden of Forking Paths" alludes precisely to the capability of a given hypertext system to generate any number of Prigoginian bifurcation points, by offering the contingent possibilities of trajectory in the history of one text in that system, therefore projecting, through a node or nodes, alternative trajectories of narrative, for example. In fact, in another essay, Thomas Weissert has applied Prigogine's notion of bifurcations to explicate Borges's story.[49]

Yet, except for the dislocations made possible by the leaps through the nodes of a hypertext, what really occurs is that the attention of an observer simply becomes shifted from one geometry to another. Differences may exist between one geometry and another, but from the perspective of avant-garde polemic, no fundamental change can occur in the framing of human awareness by regulated space and time, as exemplified by the reading process, *except* in that brief moment of nodal dislocation.

Further, no claim for the experience of dislocation can be made simply by asserting that the docuverse of hypertext reveals the simultaneity of all linear texts. The only way that hypertext theorists might valorize such an experience would be to suggest that the *functional* transcendence enabled by assuming *any* geometrical frame itself constitutes a fundamental shift in human awareness. We have examined the reasons why, historically, this simply does not work as an avant-garde tactic; yet, William Dickey makes that very claim in his essay "Poem Descending a Staircase."[50] Dickey's misreading of Marcel Duchamp's painting *Nude Descending a Staircase* again demonstrates the slippage that occurs when physics terms used by hypertext theorists are caught between the ideologies of being and becoming. Duchamp read Bergson and other theories of duration carefully, and his work consistently assaulted the geometrical frame. Yet Dickey writes, "As in Duchamp's *Nude Descending a Staircase,* we understand our experience as process rather than product, and in that process are all steps and all stances of the staircase's descent at the same time" (144). This reading of Duchamp's representation of a series of still moments of the nude's descent in two-dimensional space misses the artist's scathing critique of the hold that geometry has on the two schools of avant-garde art of his day, cubism and futurism. Whereas Picasso's cubism represents an object's three dimensions in a two-dimensional plane independent of the flow of time, and whereas Marinetti's futurism attempts to capture time's acceleration in that same (necessarily geometric) plane, Duchamp spoofs them both by synthesizing them in a representation of the spatialization of time—an artistic calculus if you will.

Duchamp's scandalous work, which emphasizes geometry's complete hegemony over the modern Western subject, directly confronts the inadequacy of painting to disrupt that hegemony (he stopped painting after completing this work). We need to remind ourselves of that, even as we reflect on the trajectory of Duchamp's career as an avant-gardist attempting to disrupt geometry's grip: in his work *To stare at, with one eye closed, for over an hour*; in his chess treatise *Opposition et les cases conjugées sont reconciliées,* which attempts quixotically to isolate the precise moment when contingency, in the form of a mistake, creeps into the precise, causal formality of endgame moves; and in *Being Given: (1) the Fountain, (2) the Illuminating Gas,* which celebrates sexual energies and the linearity of a flowing fountain in a geometric space conscribed by a chessboard-like floor.[51]

So, despite the attention paid to hypertext with respect to contemporary avant-garde literary theory and to tropes from physics, we can see how the docuverse enacts—simulates, in fact—an intertextuality that demonstrates, through its nonlinear symmetries, how entrapped we remain within the geometry that determines the frames of our awareness.

I find it potentially more interesting that Deleuze and Guattari base their notion of a micro- and macropolitics of creativity (influenced by Nietzsche, Bergson, and Prigogine) on the premise that only tactics of subversion that remain indifferent to geometry can produce a liberatory state, a localized death.[52] The fork in the road, the bifurcation point in the history of a system, represents the moment when Nietzsche's eternal return acts upon a system, when Bergsonian duration acts upon memory, its always-already contingency destroying the sense of past and future enabled by the geometric regulation of time and space. Made possible by a superimposition of order onto the contingencies of life by recourse to geometry, the transcendent mastery of past and future enables the evaluation of exigency with respect to expediency, and this is the cornerstone of calculus, classical rhetoric, and logocentrism. The destruction of this sense through art constitutes the horror of the avant-garde moment, what might be a more precise rendering of the postmodern sublime. And, supposedly, with that horror comes the liberation implied by the (local) death of geometry.

Some critics hope that in education the same destruction through pedagogy will constitute an empowerment of the student through the adoption and mastery of new strategies of critical thought. To a certain extent, the pedagogy implied by the RHIZOME Project is guided by this intuition. Yet, the claims that I have made for the RHIZOME Project illustrate how completely illusory this empowerment becomes. What I have discovered is that these new strategies of thought, which model processes of contingency and which are enabled by the design of bifurcating patterns of lexias in hypertext, merely reenact the very logocentric, geometric patterns the software attempts to subvert.[53]

The Battlefield of Pedagogy: The RHIZOME Project and the Seduction of Logocentrism

The motives for the RHIZOME Project lie with Edward Barrett and John Slatin's speculation that hypertext environments have the capacity to *simulate* thought patterns in a pedagogically useful way.[54] The object of this hypertext system is simply to model performative (process) and analytic (static) heuristics on separate HyperCard stacks and to arrange them so that students may use them separately or in a dialectical sequence of performance and analysis that might be likened to the cycle of improvisation, taping, transcription, and arrangement necessary for sophisticated jazz composition, or the patterned interaction of contingent duration with structures of memory propelled by vital impetus described in Bergson's theory of creative evolution. The stacks, in the ordered sequence, are Jazz Writing (improvisation), Brainstorming (selection, organization, and analysis), Arguprompt (performance of a formal argument), and Enthymemes (which "translates" truth claims first into enthymemes, then into formal syllogisms, of assertions made in Arguprompt), with ancillary stacks addressing transitions and problems of style.

More precisely, the patterns of thought sequenced in linear and recursive patterns, especially in the Jazz Writing stack, were designed to follow rather closely the patterns of self-organization that Prigogine attributes to linear and nonlinear catalytic processes in chemistry, or other stochastic processes in physics and in chaos theory (in these arenas, the term *nonlinear* refers to mathematical equations that account for the recursiveness, or a stability far from equilibrium, in the history of physical systems).

For example, in Jazz Writing, the student responds to a stimulus (in the form of a classical topic) introduced either randomly by the computer or by the student, at which point the student encounters instructions to perform freewriting in response to the stimulus. After this, a new stage occurs, during which the student can preserve sections of that performance on separate cards. In turn, since those cards are linked in a linear way, they enable the student to develop the preserved thought in a particular trajectory that follows a traditional rhetorical or logical tactic, such as narrative or definition, with each trajectory entering into a new and separate HyperCard stack. Or, the student may choose to highlight a crucial concept, and then, in a recursive way, export that concept back to the beginning of Jazz Writing, so to repeat the sequence. That sequence could loop endlessly or lead the student to choose any of five categories through which to develop that thought in separate trajectories, all of which lead to the precisely articulated trajectory of a linear argument in Arguprompt.

Of course, the problem with this well-intentioned pedagogy, based as it is on the principles of self-organization, is the way in which a truly spontaneous writing environment, such as that enabled by Jazz Writing, becomes domesticated by the strict linearity of logocentric argumentation, exemplified by the prompts within Arguprompt and Enthymemes stacks. There are two causes for that domestication, one technological and one pedagogical.

First, the spontaneity of process-oriented invention tactics becomes seduced by the geometry of hypertext, with its capacity to freeze the duration of a line of thought to a given lexia, and the spatialization as well as dispersed organization of thought in terms of hierarchies and categories, the very inhibiting structures from which process-oriented writing technologies are designed to liberate students. Second, no matter how self-conscious I may be in critiquing the social costs of logocentric thinking (which we cannot discuss adequately here), as a teacher I recognize that logocentric thought is precisely what my students need to master as a discourse that empowers them in the world.

My celebration of rhizomatic thinking as an enactment of principles derived from self-organizing systems remains naive, and I am very disturbed by the way "liberatory" pedagogy becomes seduced by the very structures from which it seeks to escape. What this essay has sought to examine is whether the resultant complicity is due to my design or to the geometrical nature of hypertextual space, no matter what the design. The next sequence of stacks to be designed is tentatively called "The Human Event" and employs similar linear and recursive patterns, modeled from the contingency of self-organizing systems, to simulate more sophisticated ideological analyses of human events across the curriculum. Perhaps it will solve this problem. Somehow, I doubt it.

In any case, whether employed for art or for pedagogy, the properties of nonlinearity that we have identified demonstrate that the "writing space" of hypertext cannot be considered a zone of liberation, because of its epistemological and ideological link with the geometric perspective in physics and with the stasis of logocentrism. Assuming that hypertext art and pedagogy should enact the avant-garde obsession with liberation, how to construct an environment in hypertext to liberate its consumers seems to be the task at hand. We have a long way to go before this will be possible. We can sense how Michael Joyce's and Stuart Moulthrop's notions of networked real-time hypertext, resulting from the link of Storyspace to *Interchange,* with its collective performances analogous to avant-garde jazz ensembles, or Donald Byrd's collaborationist Awopbopaloobop Groupuscle, and especially the dislocations inherent to virtual reality systems, may provide possible approaches. These approaches have yet to be accounted for theoretically,[55] with the exception of Moulthrop's "Rhizome and Resistance" (chapter 9, this volume), which, to my mind, offers a cogent answer to the challenge of this critique.

We may wish, in the end, to valorize contingency as Bergson, Whitehead, Fraser, Deleuze, Prigogine, and Deleuze and Guattari see it, as the initial condition for all creativity in intellectual systems and for life in physical systems. But this returns us to the valorization of creativity and freedom over geometry and system, with linearity and nonlinearity taking up positions directly reversed from where we began. Still, at least we have distanced ourselves from the rhetorical power of the physics tropes articulating the nonlinear model of hyper-freedom associated with Jung and the so-called new physics, a "liberation" that celebrates a bankrupt transcendence complicitous with the prison house of *logos*.

NOTES

1. Donna J. Haraway, *Simians, Cyborgs, and Women: The Reinvention of Nature* (New York: Routledge, 1991), 161–62.

2. By *resistance,* Haraway means the search by the Other for a state undetermined by mechanisms of signification generated by those dominant. By *complicity* I mean the sense that such an undetermined state remains beyond the horizon of possibility and that to dream beyond that horizon is to be seduced. Yet seduction constitutes an irreducible condition of language, which "extracts meaning from discourse and detracts it from its truth" (see Jean Baudrillard, "On Seduction," in *Jean Baudrillard: Selected Writings,* ed. Mark Poster [Stanford: Stanford University Press, 1988], 149). Here I suggest that Haraway's opposition of the binary discourse of machines and the discourse of even the organs of human bodies is itself a binary opposition, an opposition which is the result of Haraway becoming seduced by the tropical nature of discourse. Baudrillard's definition of seduction and Hayden White's definition of trope seem congruent (see discussion below). I merely observe that, given seduction as the irreducible condition of language, Haraway must allow herself to be seduced in order to communicate.

3. For excellent discussions of ideological warfare within cognitive science, see Daniel C. Dennett, *Consciousness Explained* (Boston: Little, Brown, 1991); Gerald M. Edelman, *Bright Air, Brilliant Fire: On the Matter of the Mind* (New York: Basic Books, 1992); Francisco J. Varela, Evan Thompson, and Eleanor Rosch, *The Embodied Mind: Cognitive Science and Human Experience* (Cambridge: MIT Press, 1991). In all three books, the ideological split over representing the functions of human consciousness seems to organize around a deterministic/statistical axis, despite differences in terminology among those representations. I am simply following Ilya Prigogine's argument that this axis has its rhetorical origins within the discipline of physics.

4. Haraway, 176.

5. See for example, William R. Paulson, *The Noise of Culture: Literary Texts in a World of Information* (Ithaca: Cornell University Press, 1988) on how this ideological split over the place of noise in acts of communication informs our understanding of literary texts as cultural artifacts, as well as on how it informs contemporary critical theory.

6. See Paulson, 54–66.

7. *Afternoon, Victory Garden, In Memoriam Web, The Dickens Web,* and the hypertext environment they use, Storyspace, are available from Eastgate Systems, 134 Main Street, Watertown, Mass. 02172. Landow's Storyspace version closely follows the Intermedia one created by him, Julie Launhart, and Paul Kahn. Landow, Kahn, and students at Brown University have created several dozen other large Storyspace webs containing instructional or resource materials, experimental fiction, and so on. The Daedalus System is available from the Daedelus Group, Inc., 1106 Clayton Lane, Suite 248W, Austin, Tex. 78723. RHIZOME is available from the RHIZOME Group (Martin E. Rosenberg, Johndan Johnson-Eilola, Stuart Selber, Thomas I. Ellis, and Marianne Phinney), c/o Department of English, Texas A&M University, College Station, Tex. 77843–4227.

8. Hayden White, *The Tropics of Discourse* (Baltimore: Johns Hopkins University Press, 1978), 1–2.

9. Jacques Derrida, "White Mythology: Metaphor in the Text of Philosophy," *New Literary History* 6 (Autumn 1974): 45.

10. Michel Serres, "Literature and the Exact Sciences," *Sub-Stance: A Review of Theory and Literary Criticism* 59, xviii, #2, 4.

11. Jean Baudrillard, *Selected Writings,* ed. Mark Poster (Stanford: Stanford University Press, 1988), 149.

12. See George P. Landow's excellent chapter on the politics of hypertext in *Hypertext: The Convergence of Contemporary Critical Theory and Technology* (Baltimore: Johns Hopkins University Press, 1992), 162–201. His survey may be augmented by referring to Stuart Moulthrop's earlier "Politics of Hypertext," in *Evolving Perspectives on Computers and Composition Studies: Questions for the 1990s,* ed. Gail Hawisher and Cynthia L. Selfe (Urbana-Champaign: NCTE Press/Computers and Composition Press, 1991).

13. Michel Foucault conceives of the reaches of control in terms of the metaphor "capillaries of power." See *Power/Knowledge: Selected Interviews and Other Writings,* ed. Colin Gordon (New York: Pantheon, 1980), especially the chapter "Truth and Power." See Gilles Deleuze and Félix Guattari, *A Thousand Plateaus: Capitalism and Schizophrenia,* trans. Brian Massumi (Minneapolis: University of Minnesota Press, 1987), 226. For a discussion of "Becoming Intense, Becoming Animal, Becoming Imperceptible," see 232–309.

14. See my "Dynamic and Thermodynamic Tropes of the Subject in Freud and in Deleuze and Guattari," in *Postmodern Culture,* forthcoming.

15. See Landow, *Hypertext,* 8; J. David Bolter, *Writing Space: The Computer, Hypertext, and the History of Writing* (Hillsdale, N.J.: Lawrence Erlbaum, 1991), 163.

16. Landow, 24–25. See Roland Barthes, *S/Z* (Paris: Editions du Seuil, 1970).

S/Z trans. Richard Miller (New York: Hill & Wang, 1974), 13.

17. Bolter, 154.

18. Terence Harpold, "Grotesque Corpus," *Perforations 3/After the Book: Writing Literature/Writing Technology* (Spring–Summer 1992): 6. See also Terence Harpold, "The Contingencies of the Hypertext Link," *Writing on the Edge* 2.2 (1991): 126–38.

19. For a discussion of this transcendent perspective implied by calculus, and its implied ideological perspective, see Ilya Prigogine and Isabelle Stengers, *Order out of Chaos: Man's New Dialogue with Nature* (New York: Bantam, 1984), especially chapter 2, "The Identification of the Real."

20. Michael Joyce, private communication, June 4, 1992.

21. See Mark Turner, *Reading Minds: The Study of English in the Age of Cognitive Science* (Princeton: Princeton University Press, 1991), 75.

22. We can follow this ideological split in scientific epistemology in the field of chaos theory as well. For a decidedly time-reversible geometric bias, see James Gleick, *Chaos: Making a New Science* (New York: Penguin, 1987), 241–72. For a time-irreversible bias, see Ilya Prigogine, *From Being to Becoming: Time and Complexity in the Physical Sciences* (New York: W. H. Freeman, 1980), 103–50.

23. Henri Bergson, *Matter and Memory,* trans. Nancy Margaret Paul (New York: Zone Books, 1988). As I explore in my book-length manuscript, "Fables of Self-Organization: The Cultural Work of Physics Tropes in the Discourses of the Avant-Garde," there is continuity between Bergson's critique and Nietzsche's notion of the eternal return; both look back to Boltzmann's formalization of contingency in his order principle; both Nietzsche and Bergson served as seminal influences on the works of Gilles Deleuze.

24. See the prominence of this issue in such recent collections as Frederick Burwick and Paul Douglass, eds., *The Crisis of Modernism: Bergson and the Vitalist Controversy* (Cambridge: Cambridge University Press, 1992).

25. Ilya Prigogine, *From Being to Becoming*; Prigogine and Stengers, *Order out of Chaos.*

26. Michael Joyce, "Siren Shapes: Exploratory and Constructive Hypertexts," *Academic Computing* 3 (1984): 14.

27. Johndan Johnson-Eilola, "Control and the Cyborg," forthcoming in *Journal of Advanced Composition.* Deleuze and Guattari, *A Thousand Plateaus,* 25.

28. Prigogine and Stengers, *Order out of Chaos,* 1–23.

29. Prigogine's marginalization has not been limited to physics. Although his work helped to frame discussions of chaos, Prigogine does not even appear in Gleick's popularization. See David Porush's insightful critique, "Making Chaos: Two Views of a New Science," *New England Review and Breadloaf Quarterly* 12, no. 4 (Summer 1990): 427–42.

30. Albert Einstein and Leopold Infeld, *The Evolution of Physics* (New York: Simon & Schuster, 1966), 62, 65.

31. Prigogine and Stengers, *Order out of Chaos,* 60.

32. Albert Einstein, *The Meaning of Relativity,* 5th ed. (Princeton: Princeton University Press, 1956), 24–54.

33. Einstein, *Meaning of Relativity,* 55–108.

34. In N. Katherine Hayles, *The Cosmic Web: Scientific Field Theories and Literary Strategies in the Twentieth Century* (Ithaca: Cornell University Press, 1984), 47.

35. See Lawrence Sklar, *Space, Time, and Space-Time* (Berkeley: University of California Press, 1974), and *The Philosophy of Space-Time* (Berkeley: University of California Press, 1985).

36. Einstein and Bergson debated each other directly on this subject: see Bergson's *Durée et simultaneité,* 1922; *Duration and Simultaneity,* trans. Leon Jacobsen (Indianapolis: Bobbs-Merrill, 1965).

37. Theodor H. Nelson, *Computer Lib/Dream Machines* (Seattle: Microsoft Press, 1987). Reference in Landow, *Hypertext,* 9.

38. John Archibald Wheeler, *Geometrodynamics* (New York: John Wiley, 1966). Charles W. Misner, Kip S. Thorne, and John Archibald Wheeler, *Gravitation* (San Francisco: W. H. Freeman, 1970; 1973), 819–915. B. Kent Harrison, Kip S. Thorne, Masami Wakano, and John Archibald Wheeler, *Gravitation Theory and Gravitational Collapse* (Chicago: University of Chicago Press, 1965), 69–82, 124–48.

39. George P. Landow, "The Rhetoric of Hypertext: Some Rules for Authors," in Paul Delany and George P. Landow, *Hypermedia and Literary Studies* (Cambridge: MIT Press, 1991), 81–104.

40. Stuart Moulthrop, "Beyond the Electronic Book: A Critique of Hypertext Rhetoric," *Hypertext '91* (New York: Association of Computing Machinery, 1991), 291–98.

41. Technoculture, an electronic forum (accessible on the Internet), April 4, 1992.

42. Harpold, "Grotesque Corpus."

43. Bergson, *Matter and Memory,* 186; *Creative Evolution,* trans. Arthur Mitchell (New York: Henry Holt, 1911), 96. See his explanation of the tyranny of geometry over duration, *Creative Evolution,* 36.

44. Phillip Lacoue-Labarthe and Jean-Luc Nancy, *L'Absolu littéraire: Théorie de la littérature du romantisme allemand* (Paris: Editions du Seuil, 1978). *The Literary Absolute,* trans. Phillip Barnard and Cheryl Lester (Albany: State University of New York Press, 1988), 34–35.

45. Dalia Judowitz, *Subjectivity and Representation in Descartes: The Origins of Modernity* (Cambridge: Cambridge University Press, 1988). See chapter 1.

46. Gilles Deleuze, *Bergsonism* (New York: Zone Books, 1988), 91–114. *Proust and Signs* (1977). This is Deleuze's central thesis. See also the gloss in Gilles Deleuze and Félix Guattari, *Anti-Oedipus: Capitalism and Schizophrenia,* trans. Robert Hurley, Mark Seem, and Helen R. Lane (Minneapolis: University of Minnesota Press, 1983), 318.

47. See Landow's gloss on Genette's reading, above.

48. Stuart Moulthrop, "Reading from the Map: Metonymy and Metaphor in the Fiction of 'Forking Paths,' " in Delany and Landow, *Hypermedia and Literary Studies,* 119–32.

49. Thomas Weissert, "Representation and Bifurcation: Borges's Garden of

Chaos Dynamics," in N. Katherine Hayles, ed., *Chaos and Order: Complex Dynamics in Literature and Science* (Chicago: University of Chicago Press, 1991), 223–43.

50. William Dickey, "Poem Descending a Staircase: Hypertext and the Simultaneity of Experience," in Delany and Landow, *Hypermedia and Literary Studies,* 143–52.

51. This piece, like most of the important works of Duchamp, can be found at the Philadelphia Museum of Art.

52. See the game theory of war passage in Deleuze and Guattari, *A Thousand Plateaus,* 352–53.

53. Martin Rosenberg, "Prigogine, HyperCard, and the Dialectic of Stasis and Process in the Teaching of Argument," in *Hypertext in the Classroom: Theory and Practice,* ed. William Condon (Houghton, Mich.: Computers and Composition Press, forthcoming).

54. Edward Barrett, "Introduction," xix, and John Slatin, "Reading Hypertext: Order and Coherence in a New Medium," in Delany and Landow, *Hypermedia and Literary Studies,* 161. Rosenberg, "Prigogine, HyperCard, and the Dialectic of Stasis and Process in the Teaching of Argument." The informing insight structuring the RHIZOME stacks is simulation of thinking patterns that match performative and analytic heuristics.

55. I organized a special format session for the Conference of College Composition and Communication (Nashville, 1994) to explore relations among hypermedia, cognitive science, nonlinear dynamics and nonequilibrium thermodynamics as they might inform traditional conceptions of rhetorical invention. The conference was chaired by Cynthia L. Selfe; papers included John Slatin, "Hypertext: Invention and Information"; Stuart Moulthrop, "Strange Attractors and the Rhetoric of Informating Texts"; Martin Rosenberg, "Fractals, Self-organization and Simulation: Hypertext and the Invention of Disciplines"; and Paul Taylor, "Synchronous Conferences as Dissipative Structures."

Rhizome and Resistance: Hypertext and the Dreams of a New Culture

Stuart Moulthrop

9

Long Dreams

In his novel *The War Outside of Ireland,* and more recently in his hypertext fiction *Afternoon,* Michael Joyce remarks on a shift in the postindustrial wind. We seem, he suggests, to be undergoing a change of identity, weaving a fresh social fabric. "I have argued elsewhere that Japan is now everywhere. It is the long dream of a new culture."[1] Like Roland Barthes before him (*Empire of Signs*) and William Gibson after (*Neuromancer*), Joyce registers the rising appeal of a dream-state characterized by headlong technological advancement and the groundless play of signifiers. There are many reasons to think of this state as Greater Nippon—not just the recent economic prominence of Japan, but also the example it offers of a hyperadaptive, *bricoleur* society rebuilding itself from its own ruins. As Joyce says, however, "Japan" is now everywhere, not a state but a state of mind, so the name seems somewhat arbitrary. We could as easily invoke other dreams of cultural revolution: George Bush's megalo-American "new world order"; Jean Baudrillard's nightmare of "total spatio-dynamic theatre"; Donna J. Haraway's vision of cyborg politics played out within "a polymorphous information system" that has become "a deadly game."[2]

All of these long dreams have something in common: the conviction that the transition from a mode of production to a "mode of information" has effects exceeding the traditional boundaries of economics and politics.[3] The transforming effect of rapidly evolving communication and information technologies appears first in the marketplace, but like Joyce's imaginary Japan, the marketplace of semiotic exchange is now everywhere: in our homes, in our bedrooms, in our minds. Changes in technology portend more than, in Mark Poster's phrase, "the end of the proletariat as Marx knew it" (129); they suggest possibilities for a reformulation of the subject, a truly radical revision of identity and social relations (111). The effects will touch us (so we dream) in our languages, our narratives, our domestic objects, our fashion systems, our games and entertainments. The changes will be felt throughout our culture.

"The long dream of a new culture" is in fact less a revolution or overturning of the old order than it is an ecstasy, an attempt to stand outside any stable order, old or new. As Jean-François Lyotard observes, the concept of revolution itself has become invalid (along with such models as evolution, enlightenment, and class struggle). Postmodernism begins for Lyotard with "incredulity toward metanarratives," a rejection of any mythology, explanatory fiction, or paradigm*atic* story.[4] In place of *paradigm* Lyotard submits *paralogy* (61), or language gaming, a strategy that advances the play of discourse by declaring the rules for commercial or intellectual performance continually negotiable. The dream of a new culture is a fantasy of immanent change, or as Gilles Deleuze and Félix Guattari put it, "smooth voyaging": "Voyaging smoothly is a becoming, and a difficult, uncertain becoming at that. It is not a question of returning to preastronomical navigation, nor to the ancient nomads. The confrontation between the smooth and the striated, the passages, alternations, and superpositions, are under way today, running in the most varied directions."[5] It is precisely this "confrontation between the smooth and the striated," between two fundamentally different cultural registers, on which I want to focus in order to explore the interface between information technology and culture. This interface is in many ways a site of resistance, for the smooth and the striated can at times manifest an almost dialectical opposition; but it is also a place where polemics predicated on this apparent dialectic necessarily break down. In examining the nature of this failure we may come to a better understanding of interactive media and how they are implicated in our neocultural dreams.

Hypertext and Rhizome

We begin on the *Thousand Plateaus*—which is appropriate for a commentary on hypertext and culture, since Deleuze and Guattari's rhizome-book may itself be considered an incunabular hypertext. Though the text arrives as a print artifact, it was designed as a matrix of independent but cross-referential discourses which the reader is invited to enter more or less at random (Deleuze and Guattari, xx). Having no defined sequence beyond a stipulation that the conclusion be saved for last, the book's sections or "plateaus" may be read in any order. The reader's implicit task is to build a network of virtual connections (which more than one reader of my acquaintance has suggested operationalizing as a web of hypertext links).

But *A Thousand Plateaus* serves in this discussion as more than an example of proto-hypertext. It has also been a major influence on social theories and polemics that have a strong bearing on the cultural integration of new media. In the entire poststructuralist pharmacopeia, Deleuze and Guattari's cultural critique seems the most potent of psychotropics. Their major work, *Capitalism and Schizophrenia,* sets in motion perhaps the most radical reinterpretation of Western culture attempted in the second half of this century. Geopolitics, psychoanalysis, neurobiology, sexuality, mathematics, linguistics, semiotics, and philosophy all fall within the purview of their encyclopedic project. Like other poststructuralist enterprises, its major efforts are directed against the order of the signified in favor of the signifier; but, especially in the second part of *A Thousand Plateaus,* Deleuze and Guattari do not simply uproot the old order, they go on to postulate a vividly conceived alternative.

As Brian Massumi points out in his introduction, Deleuze and Guattari's dreamed-of new culture proceeds not from *logos,* the law of substances, but rather from *nomos,* the designation of places or occasions (xiii). Hence their various co-resonating tropes of nomadism or nomadology, deterritorialization, lines of flight, smooth and striated spaces, double articulation, war machines, refrains, and rhizomes. The generating body for all these tropes (the arch-rhizome) is the concept of a social order defined by active traversal or encounter rather than objectification. Figures for this order include the ocean of the navigator or the desert of the nomad, as opposed to the Cartesian space of the engineer or the urban grid of the policeman. Or, to invoke organic metaphors, what Deleuze and Guattari have in mind is a chaotically distributed network (the rhizome) rather than a regular hierarchy of trunk and branches. "Many people have a tree growing in their heads," Deleuze and Guattari observe, "but the brain itself is much more a grass than a tree" (15). All these metaphors attempt to displace a language founded on logocentric, hierarchically grounded truth and replace it with an unfounded play of anarchistic, contingent paralogies.

Energized by opposition to the rightward political drift of the West and the demise of state socialism in the East, these ideas have spread rhizomatically among poststructuralists and postmodernists, especially those committed to social alternatives. Thomas Pynchon's nod to Deleuze and Guattari in *Vineland* may seem trivial (he credits them with "the indispensable Italian Wedding Fake Book," which saves the day at a gangster wedding), but it suggests deeper connections between their work and his own subversive fictions.[6] In a less oblique homage, the anarcho-theorist Hakim Bey invokes nomadology to justify his "temporary autonomous zone," a site of resistance designed for "an era in which the State is omnipresent and all-powerful and yet simultaneously riddled with cracks and vacancies."[7] The grammatologist Gregory Ulmer takes this line of thinking further in his introduction to *Teletheory,* acknowledging that "the challenge for us is to think nomadically from within the State apparatus."[8] Even the fundamentally traditional theorist Jay David Bolter, who does not invoke nomadology directly, seems more inclined to *nomos* than *logos* when he describes emerging writing systems as dynamic, spatial, and antihierarchical.[9]

Bolter's description of our historical moment as "the late age of print" (2) suggests that our dreams of a new culture are implicated in a specific *technologique:* the transition from a social order founded on the printing press to one in which discursive practices are redefined for newer technologies like hypertext. Likewise, Ulmer speculates on the cultural complex "TV/AI," the intersection of video and the digital processing of language (which may have less to do with artificial intelligence than it does with interactive media). We need to inquire more closely into the relationship between these conceptions and post-logocentric or nomadic thinking. What might Deleuze and Guattari's radical theories of information and culture mean for people concerned with practical informatics, especially in the areas of hypertext and hypermedia?

Smooth and Striated Writing Spaces

Certainly the idea of a discourse system founded on *nomos* as opposed to *logos* relates strongly to current thinking about hypertext systems, especially those which are not viewed simply as "electronic books," or print by another name. According to Michael Joyce, who has used hypertext extensively in the teaching of writing, the medium offers writers "a structure for what does not yet exist." This is a space for improvisation and discovery where users may pursue multiple lines of association or causation rather than having to fit assertions into an exclusive, singular logic.[10] Martin Rosenberg's RHIZOME writing software (discussed in his own contribution to this book), represents a similar overture toward multiple and explicitly recursive forms of expression. It is not hard to relate these conceptions of writing space, which Joyce calls "constructive hypertext," to the distinction Deleuze and Guattari draw between smooth and striated cultural spaces.

Striated space is the domain of routine, specification, sequence, and causality. Phenomenologically, it consists of the world of perception as processed by the coordinate grid or some other geometric structure into a set of specified identities. Socially, striated space manifests itself in hierarchical and rule-intensive cultures, like the military, the corporation, and the university. As Marshall McLuhan observed, the dominant medium of communication in such cultures—print—fosters an objectified and particularized view of knowledge.[11] Striated space is defined and supported by books, those totemic objects that Alvin Kernan celebrated as "ordered, controlled, teleological, referential, and autonomously meaningful."[12] The occupants of striated space are the champions of order, purpose, and control—defenders of logos, or the Law.

In smooth space, by contrast, "the points are subordinated to the trajectory" (Deleuze and Guattari, 478). Smooth space is defined dynamically, in terms of transformation instead of essence. Thus, one's momentary location is less important than one's continuing movement or line of flight; this space is by definition a structure for what does not yet exist. Smooth social structures include ad hoc or populist political movements, cooperatives, communes, and some small businesses, subcultures, fandoms, and undergrounds. Smooth societies favor invention and indeed entrepreneurship, consensual decision making as opposed to command, and holistic, parallel awareness over particular and serial analysis.

Interactive media do not represent the first technological expression of this social order. McLuhan's electronically mediated global village and Ulmer's age of video both operate in smooth space, which is best served not by the linearizing faculties of print but by the parataxis and bricolage of broadcasting. In spite of being a champion striathlete, the media critic Neil Postman reveals a fundamental truth about television when he links its basic grammar to the pseudotransition "Now . . . this."[13] Paradoxically, smooth social space is mediated by discontinuities. It propagates in a matrix of breaks, jumps, and implied or contingent connections which are enacted (Joyce would say, constructed) by the viewer or receiver. The textual model here is not the book, or, as Roland Barthes called it, "the work," but rather "the text," a dynamic network of discursive relations of which any material record can represent only a subset.[14] Smooth space is an occasion; Deleuze and Guattari call it a becoming.

Does hypertext represent a smooth space for discourse and, beyond that, for textually mediated social relations? After all, interactive media exhibit the same phenomenological structure as cinema and video. Hypertexts are composed of nodes and links, local coherences and linearities broken across the gap or synapse of transition, a space which the receiver must somehow fill with meaning.[15] In describing the rhizome as a model of discourse, Deleuze and Guattari invoke the "principle of asignifying rupture" (9), a fundamental tendency toward unpredictability and discontinuity. Perhaps, then, hypertext and hypermedia represent the expression of the rhizome in the social space of writing. If so, they might indeed belong in our dreams of a new culture. It might be attractive, especially if one wanted to make radical social claims, to argue that hypertext provides a laboratory or site of origin for a smoothly structured, nomadic alternative to the discursive space of late capitalism.

Hypertext and Culture

Claims along these lines have been advanced (carefully and with due reservation) by the hypertext theorists Ted Nelson, Jay David Bolter, and George Landow. Nelson suggests that interactive media will encourage "populitism," the dissemination of specialized knowledge within unconventional or unofficial networks.[16] Bolter notes the gradual erosion of absolute social hierarchies in the West and suggests that networks and hypermedia will administer the *coup de grâce*. He notes Elizabeth Eisenstein's thesis that print was an important factor in the consolidation of bourgeois culture. As Bolter sees it, however, "electronic writing has just the opposite effect. It opposes standardization and unification as well as hierarchy. It offers as a paradigm the text that changes to suit the reader rather than expecting the reader to conform to its standards" (233).

Landow is more cautious about such revolutionary claims. He considers the possibility that a decentered culture might overwhelm critical voices, yielding not a rainbow coalition but a majority blasted into silence by the explosion of electronic discourse. But though he raises concerns about the design of large-scale networks, Landow does not ultimately give this objection much credence. What reassures him is the importance of active reception in hypermedia. Landow maintains that the constantly repeated requirement of articulated choice in hypertext will produce an enlightened, self-empowered respondent: "In linking and following links lie responsibility—political responsibility—since each reader establishes his or her own line of reading."[17]

All of these conceptions (Landow's in particular) at least resemble operations in smooth social space. The hypertextual reader traces threads in any direction across the docuverse without regard to textual hierarchies. She is free (and as Landow insists, specifically licensed) to create linkages not sanctioned by the present divisions of culture and discipline—free to construct idiosyncratic networks of knowledge, or "mystories" (84) as Gregory Ulmer calls them. The genre of mystory is a way of thinking about the matrix of ideas that cuts across cultural registers, mixing the disciplinary with the personal or the ludic. Ulmer offers among his examples the (indeed plausible) linking of Ludwig Wittgenstein's *Philosophical Investigations* to the films of Carmen Miranda (62, and his chapter in this volume). Until now, this sort of intertextual play has been the preserve of poststructuralist critics like Hélène Cixous and Jacques Derrida, or postmodern novelists like Kathy Acker and Thomas Pynchon. Yet, this kind of textual promiscuity would be a regular feature of the cultural systems that Nelson, Bolter, and Landow describe and have undertaken to create.

Nor are these visions of smooth information systems limited to humanist concerns like literary criticism and philosophy. Nelson's Xanadu, which is still the grandest scheme for hypertext yet proposed, promises to network *all* the world's textual information. Nelson imagines a genre of information production something like the mystory, consisting almost entirely of connections between divergent texts and disciplines.[18] Presumably such a system would represent as important a resource for scientists as it would for humanists, as K. Eric Drexler has realized in his own forecasts for the future of scientific communication. Drexler proposes a hypertextual network for researchers engaged in nanotechnology, both as a medium for quicker dissemination of intellectual output and as a check on dangerous experimental practices.[19]

More recently, a group of information system designers from the Boeing Corporation have suggested something like smooth discursive space as a medium for large engineering projects: "Certainly hypermedia will continue to be an effective way of presenting static reference information," they note, "but a larger role for hypermedia requires eliminating the distinction between authors and readers. We assume that all members of engineering teams will be able to create and access information in a shared, distributed environment."[20] Though the idea of computer-supported collaborative work is hardly new, the Boeing proposal introduces a fairly radical element into the shared work environment: the notion of "eliminating the distinction between authors and readers." In general, the Boeing proposal seems about as far from Deleuze and Guattari as one could imagine, except for this one striking design specification. If the distinction between author and reader were indeed eliminated, one would also have to discard any sense of textual identity or hierarchy, at least in absolute terms. Since the hyperdocument would always be in flux, it could not be constituted as a series of discursive stabilities but would in actual fact represent a smooth space constantly reconfigured by lines of flight (a phrase which, in the case of Boeing, might be more than figurative).

This scenario calls to mind a somewhat unbelievable prospect. Nomad *engineering?* Surely the intellectual domain of the engineer is the epitome of striated consciousness, dedicated as it is to precision, causality, and method. Wittgenstein meets Carmen Miranda may be one thing, but we have just infiltrated Deleuze and Guattari into Boeing Information Systems—an insurgency that must give us pause. What is really likely to happen when the hierarchically organized, routinized space of the corporation meets the rhizomatic propensities of electronic media? Are such encounters conceivable as anything more than flights of fancy, or might the ostensible "smoothness" of the new writing systems be more delusion than Deleuzean? These questions are bound to disturb our dreams of a new culture.

Design Anything That Way . . .

Dreams, after all, correspond only obliquely to waking experience. Thomas Pynchon, who has a lot of interesting things to say about both dreams and technologies, has given us a parable that may be of use here. It is found in *Gravity's Rainbow,* a fiction that departs from the principles of realist narrative in ways that themselves suggest a smooth or nomadic mode of discourse. The central mysteries of the novel are never resolved, tailing off into arabesques of impossibility. The protagonist neither dies nor survives at the end but is "broken down . . . and scattered," his identity no longer definable in narrative terms.[21] Ostensibly unconnected characters and events participate in shadowy, irrational schemes of analogy and inversion, patterns that seem closer to intuition or dreamwork than to logical relations, yet the author of this rhizomatic text has his roots in the striated space of the military-industrial complex. Before turning to fiction, Pynchon studied applied physics at Cornell and worked as an engineering assistant for none other than the Boeing Corporation. Moreover, the great obsession of his novel is a weapons system, the German V-2 rocket, one of the direst instruments of striated *technologique.*

Pynchon articulates the convergence of the nomadic and the techno/logical throughout *Gravity's Rainbow,* but it surfaces most vividly in the stories of Leni and Franz Pökler, two of the more ideologically significant characters in the novel. They are a classic misalliance, Cancer and Aquarius, *nomos* and *logos* sharing the same unhappy bed. Franz is a young chemical engineer who is gradually drawn into the

Nazi secret weapons program. Leni is a somewhat naive socialist who travels the opposite route, joining street actions against the fascists. The marriage is doomed, but in its final days the conflict crystallizes in a way we may find instructive:

> He was the cause-and-effect man: he kept at her astrology without mercy, telling her what she was supposed to believe, then denying it. "Tides, radio interference, damned little else. There is no way for changes out there to produce changes here."
>
> "Not produce," she tried, "not cause. It all goes together. Parallel, not series. Metaphor. Signs and symptoms. Mapping on to different coordinate systems, I don't know . . ." She didn't know, all she was trying to do was reach.
>
> But he said: "Try to design anything that way and have it work." (159)

The domestic troubles of Franz and Leni Pökler illustrate the tension between smooth and striated cultures: the mystic and the engineer, the revolutionary and the obedient servant, the street fighter and the lab worker. In Leni's holistic or metaphoric world view, events relate semiotically, not as intersections of forces but as intertextual references among "different coordinate systems." This scheme itself maps rather neatly onto the idea of smooth space, since it describes the universe as a plenum of evocative possibilities ("signs and symptoms") rather than a hierarchy of necessary connections. We might also note that Leni becomes in the course of the novel a literal nomad. The end of the war finds her a camp survivor and a displaced person, haunted by nightmares of the deportation trains.

Franz, on the other hand, still believes that the striated culture of science will deliver transcendence in the form of interplanetary flight. "Cause-and-effect man," man of the Law, he derides his wife's mysticism in the name of the reality principle. For him the tangible, measurable world is all that can be the case. If information does not have direct physical consequence, if it is not *data* given over to some form of analysis, then he regards it as worthless. By the end of the novel, Franz will learn the horror of his ways—most brutally when he discovers the slave labor camp that adjoins the Nordhausen missile factory. But despite this conversion, his rebuke to Leni hangs over the remainder of the novel, which after all is itself the kind of rhizomatic enterprise that Franz so deeply mistrusts.

As an implicit critique of Deleuze and Guattari's radical vision, Franz's operationalizing challenge must resonate sharply against our dreams of a nomadic hypertextual culture. *Try to design anything that way*—as a parallelistic network of signifiers with no hierarchy of sequence and no constraint on future expansion—*and have it work.* This would seem an enormous undertaking. Perhaps Boeing will need to rehire Thomas Pynchon. More likely not, though. It seems improbable that any practical communications system can be conceived as a nomad space, a network of signs and symptoms, or perhaps even a structure for what does not yet exist. Novels, maybe; engineering systems, probably not.

For that matter, some critics insist that even hypertextual fiction must retain a degree of striation. Thinking about the application of interactive technologies to narrative, Robert Coover notes that we may be approaching a great reversal. If multilinear forms like hypertext have emerged partly from writers' dissatisfaction with the monology of print, then perhaps, Coover speculates, writers in the age of hypertext will have the opposite complaint: "One will feel the need, even while using these vast networks and principles of randomness and expansive story line, to struggle against them, just as one now struggles against the linear constraints of the printed book" (cited in Landow, 119). Writers of hypertext—even writers of hypertext fiction—may need to carry both the Pöklers in their minds: the anima of parallel consciousness as well as the animus who always insists that things be made to work.

The Perils of Geometry

What does it mean in practical terms to resist the "randomness and expansiveness" of hypertext? Coover suggests that we must reinvent conventions, modifying familiar fictional properties like plot and character to suit the multifarious context of hypermedia.[22] Anyone who actually tries to create a large-scale hyperdocument will recognize the wisdom of this counsel. Vastness and randomness are not particularly valuable per se. Some principles of regulation and constraint are essential. Thus various theorists have represented hypertextual discourse, not as a wholesale embrace of indeterminacy, but rather as the articulation of global variability in tension against local coherence.[23] In other words, hypertext may not be quite the smooth or rhizomatic structure some have made it out to be.

This concession to operational demands raises some distinctly disturbing questions about our dreams of a new culture. Deleuze and Guattari register a significant warning about the misleading possibilities of techniques for multiple discourse:

> To attain the multiple, one must have a method that effectively constructs it; no typographical cleverness, no lexical agility, no blending or creation of words, no

syntactical boldness, can substitute for it. In fact, these are more often than not merely mimetic procedures used to disseminate or disperse a unity that is retained in a different dimension for an image-book. Technonarcissism. Typographical, lexical, or syntactic creations are necessary only when they no longer belong to the form of expression of a hidden unity, becoming themselves dimensions of the multiplicity under consideration; we only know of rare successes in this. (22)

Though Deleuze and Guattari have print rather than electronic composition in mind here (most prominently *Finnegans Wake*), the seduction of "technonarcissism" is a very clear danger for hypertext. In designing a discursive practice dedicated to multiplicity and flexible articulation, we must always be aware of "hidden unity." That which purports to be a true multiple—a rhizome, a nomadology, a smooth space—may in fact be only a little world made cunningly, some deterministic system passing itself off as a structure for what does not yet exist. It may even be the case, as Martin Rosenberg argues in this volume, that we are hopelessly bound to determinism as a consequence of our engagement with technologies of writing.

With these possibilities in mind we may need to broaden the terms of Coover's prognosis. As interactive systems come into wider use, we are indeed likely to develop a resistance to their properties; but this resistance will probably involve at least two stages. The strictly operational resistance that Coover foresees is only the beginning. If hypermedia systems do become regular features of working life in organizations like Boeing, then this problem will no doubt find a range of solutions. The struggle against hypertextual vastness will generate rhetorical or generic strategies that limit the most problematic propensities of the medium. Landow's "rhetoric of arrivals and departures"[24] and Ulmer's mystory are both likely prototypes for this response. But these rhetorical compromises will not end the troubles that Coover predicts.

A second wave of critique or resistance is likely to follow once such strategies are in place: a resistance predicated not on practice but on ideology. An early indication of this emerging line of criticism can be found in Martin Rosenberg's skeptical assessment of current hypertext theory, laid out in his contribution to this book, "Physics and Hypertext: Liberation and Complicity in Art and Pedagogy." Rosenberg registers a crucial dissent from the generally celebratory treatment of hypertext and its cultural possibilities. His analysis of hypertext theory's reliance on tropes of reversible time and linear geometry brilliantly reveals the bad faith in which many of us (myself included) have been known to operate. But precisely because Rosenberg's critique is so devastating, it leaves us all (himself included) with very little in the way of an ideological standpoint. As the title of Landow's chapter asks, *What's a critic to do?* The prospects are daunting. Nonetheless, since Rosenberg is most assuredly right in his objections, we must give his attempt at theoretical resistance close attention.

Rosenberg has recognized the hazard of technonarcissism. Developers of interactive media, in his assessment, have been irresistibly seduced by a logocentric world-view. He points out that "*anything* produced out of a systemic relationship between lexias and links, cards, buttons, and fields also participates in the same geometrical episteme that produced Newton's laws and classical stasis theory, Feynman diagrams of subatomic particle interactions, formal logic, computer languages, and the fractal scaling of seacoasts, black holes, and chess."[25] Hypertext systems are entirely routinized, after all: they are contrivances composed of discrete rules and relationships, designed to be regular and reliable even in their "vastness and randomness." But despite this underlying allegiance to system, Rosenberg asserts, hypermedia theorists present their products as alternatives to striated discourse and its culture. He points out that this is pure delusion. Just as the lexical play of *Finnegans Wake* does not really liberate Joyce's text from the constraints of *logos,* so no amount of apparent multiplicity can exonerate hypertext of its complicity in military-entertainment-information culture. Claiming that hypertext effects a transition from reductive hierarchies to polyvalent networks will not do. As Rosenberg observes, linearity and multilinearity are identical from a topological perspective. Why should they be any different in terms of ideology? Lines are still lines, *logos* and not *nomos,* even when they are embedded in a hypertextual matrix. Such matrices are always edifices, never autonomous zones; they are structures that do not allow for deterritorialization. No technologically mediated link can ever constitute a genuine line of flight.

Rosenberg's critique is indeed chastening, and it should provoke theorists of interactive media to serious reconsideration of our more radical claims. But unlike Robert Coover, Rosenberg is unwilling to adopt an overt conservatism—as a result of which, his critique forces us to confront a crucial problem. Where Coover acknowledges that writing systems are indeed systematic, Rosenberg insists on the possibility of a true construction of the multiple, or, as he puts it, "liberation." "Liberated human consciousness," he argues, "means liberation from a geometric ideological construct that disguises the nature of human awareness in order for it better to plot industrial schedules, the trajectories of cannonballs, the circumnavigation of the globe." This is indeed a noble goal, and one that most hypertext theorists, as well as most liberal intellectuals, would probably espouse. But how are we to arrive at this goal? Freely (and courageously) confessing that he shares the "naivety" of most hypertext theorists, Rosenberg admits that his work on RHIZOME, a constructive hypertext system for writing pedagogy, betrays its own geometrical complicities. "As a teacher," Rosenberg notes, "I recognize that logocentric thought is precisely what my students need to master as a discourse that empowers them in the world." This is honesty. But it does leave us at the mercy of Franz Pökler's challenge: "try to design anything that way and have it work."

If we take Rosenberg's critique seriously, we come swiftly to the limit not just of our terms but of our communications technologies. Rosenberg has demonstrated how the concepts of *techne*, and indeed function itself, are at odds with our rhetoric of liberation. Our dream of a new culture requires us to abandon all operational thinking, so there is no point, really, in discussing implementations. Rosenberg's critique forces us to consider another Pynchonian fable, the fragment called "New Dope": "the minute you take it you are rendered incapable of ever telling anybody what it's like, or worse, where to get any" (*Gravity's Rainbow,* 745).

The allegorical possibilities of "New Dope" are numerous: it might stand for the ultimate *Steigerung* of gnostic enlightenment, or, more simply, for death, or it might represent the state of mind necessary to fully understand *Gravity's Rainbow* (once you do, you can't tell anybody about it). For our purposes, though, an economic or ideological interpretation seems more appropriate. The new dope is a commercial failure because it represents a true alternative to the capitalist order, a product which can never be advertised or effectively organized into a market—it may be significant that in Pynchon's novel "New Dope" is presented as an underground film conceived by the black marketeer and film director Gerhardt von Göll. This could be the arch-capitalist's worst nightmare. "Dealers are as in the dark as anybody," Pynchon explains. Connections can occur only by accident. "It is the dope that finds *you,* apparently" (745).

In acknowledging Rosenberg's critique of hypertextual geometries, we may have to admit that our visions of cultural revolution represent the same old new dope, a pure utopia of pure paralogia, beyond any requirements of design or rational implementation and thus absolutely unrealistic—a very long dream indeed. Though, of course, the reality principle cannot be kept at bay forever. If all we can do is wait for the change to find us, then what are we to do in the meantime? If engagement with hypertext and other technologies can only lead back into the logocentric matrix, then what action should we undertake instead? These questions open onto an even more salient issue: if the operational struggle against hypertext leads to rhetorical compromise, then where does an uncompromising ideological resistance lead?

One answer is, unsurprisingly, right back to the late age of print. Rosenberg alludes briefly to practical experiments in interactive media by figures like Michael Joyce and Donald Byrd, but most of his text is devoted to an admirably erudite commentary on theories of time and geometry, ranging from Bergson and Duchamp to Prigogine and Deleuze and Guattari. I want to criticize this stance, but I cannot do so justly without admitting that the very same objection could be made (with less credit for scholarship) against my own essay. Our various appeals to intellectual heritage are not without their ideological implications. *What's a critic to do?* Having failed to theorize interactive technologies as genuine avenues of change, we retreat into a battle of the books, appealing to the core of our bibliographic tradition. In this instance the strategy is the message, and the message concerns the medium. What do we do while waiting for the new dope to find us? We write yet more literary theory—which is arguably the most self-serving and self-involved form of logocentrism. Absent any truly transformative engagement with the pragmatics of new media, the ideological resistance to hypertext seems to lead Rosenberg and me and a fair number of our colleagues right back to the striated space of the library—where most humanists have always been most comfortable in the first place.

Resistance Is Futile

Suppose, however, that one were willing to leave the library and to develop an ideological critique of hypertext through a practical engagement with the medium. To echo Deleuze and Guattari, we know of only rare successes in this, though the ostensible failures may be much more interesting. Bolter raises the possibility of such an implicated critique of hypertext with his electronic version of *Writing Space,* available as a separate title from the publishers of the book. The two texts, print and hypertext, differ significantly. The copyright provisions for the hypertext, for instance, are designed to accommodate the temptations of electronic copying and redistribution. Bolter in effect grants reproduction rights to his readers with only a few conditions and cautions:

> As long as you keep [this] text in the electronic medium, you may also change it as you see fit and hand the changes on to others. You may want to indicate that you have changed the text. On the other hand, you may not, but then your readers will probably falsely assume that the original author was responsible for the text you wrote. All readers should be aware that anything in the text may have been added by someone other than the original author. But of course, this caveat applies in a Borgesian way to the previous sentence as well.[26]

Bolter's Borgesian copyright notice gestures toward a kind of textual smoothness, a writing space in which individual lines of authority or proprietorship may be blurred or rearranged. The recursive playfulness of the last sentence underscores this point: perhaps even the author-function who warns you about multiple authorship is other than the one countersigned "Jay David Bolter." Welcome to the text-as-rhizome, where every apparently stable or atomic division of expression can break down to reveal a subtext, some less-than-primal scene of writing.

The playfulness of this text is in no way disingenuous. The electronic version of *Writing Space* is published in an open, read-write format: its reader can actually intervene in the text. Suppose a writer were to attempt a critique of hypertext in just such a "constructive" context, within the terms of "a structure which does not yet exist" in any fixed or definitive form. We do know of one very interesting attempt at this. The writing in question was undertaken (and this may be indicative) not by a professional critic but by an undergraduate at Carnegie Mellon University, a school known for its emphasis on science and technology. This response to hypertext came out of a pedagogical experiment inspired by theories of resistant or "strong" interpretation, in which students were asked to use hypertext to interrogate the authority of authors and teachers.[27]

The task given to students in this experiment matched the terms of Coover's prediction: both as readers and writers, they were asked to struggle against the randomness and expansiveness of the hypertextual medium as expressed in a particular electronic text. The object of their attention was a pastiche of Borges's "The Garden of Forking Paths," a story that provides some of the conceptual groundwork for hypertext fiction. In the story, Borges deconstructs the linearity of detective fiction by presenting the reader with an alternative conception of narrative time: "In all fictional works, each time a man is confronted with several alternatives, he chooses one and eliminates the others; in the fiction of Ts'ui Pên, he chooses—simultaneously—all of them. *He creates,* in this way, diverse futures, diverse times which themselves also proliferate and fork. . . . Sometimes, the paths of this labyrinth converge: for example, you arrive at this house, but in one of the possible pasts you are my enemy, in another, my friend."[28] The electronic pastiche attempts to realize the model of narrative discourse outlined in this passage, adding to the original Borges text a number of related and tangential story lines, all of them connected by a series of hypertextual links. Students could explore (and expand if they wished) a fairly dense network of narrative. But the emphasis in the experiment lay on interpretive independence, which was defined as the ability both to recognize a text's basic procedures and to imagine alternatives. The implicit challenge for students, therefore, was to subvert the hypertextual structure of multiplicity and variation, more or less as Coover has specified.

The writer who responded to this challenge most ingeniously, Karl Crary, distanced himself from the hypertextual pastiche by proposing a taxonomy for this heterogeneous writing. He created categories for original, imitated, and added material, attempting to set the text in order by naming its parts and their origins. He would thus give back to Borges what was his and identify his teachers' incursions as something less than original. Crary included with this catalogue a thoughtful discussion of both the legal standing of the pastiche (dubious) and its aesthetic legitimacy (about which he was more generous). But the most crucial aspects of Crary's work lay in its material context. To begin with, he wrote not a conventional, linear essay but a hypertext, a network of places and links which can be traversed according to various sequences. Even more significant, Crary's commentary was attached to the structure of the pastiche as a subnetwork accessible at various points from the older text. Crary's submission was a composite electronic document comprising the text on which he had been asked to comment and his own discourse, both integrated into a single hypertextual network.

Because of this strategy of production, Crary's project represents a particularly clever and illuminating failure. Though his intervention makes a very bold attempt at resistant interpretation, it could not fulfill its subversive designs on the hypertextual pastiche. The reasons are fairly clear. Since Crary built his taxonomy within the hypertext on which it comments, he opened himself to a fatal recursion: his taxonomy includes itself within one of its own categories (material with no direct bearing on the Borgesian story). Because of this, although the taxonomy may comment on the pastiche, it cannot achieve any discursive separation from the original structure. It is, indeed, irresistibly joined to the object of its commentary not by a logical but by a nomadic relationship, a pathway laid out in writing space. The sort of resistance Crary sets out to practice depends upon the striated space of the humanist library, where the words in the books stay between their covers. In the promiscuous or rhizomatic environment of hypertext, this kind of resistance is futile.

The limits on Crary's resistance are easiest to appreciate if we consider his text from the perspective of a subsequent reader, one who knows nothing about its authors or the conditions of its creation. Since Crary merged his contribution into the existing hypertext, it may be perceived by a subsequent reader-constructor not as authoritative critical discourse but rather as another paralogical move in the game of pastiche. That game involves a complicated nesting of fictions within fictions. Borges's main narrative consists of the memoirs of an executed spy, framed by an unnamed editor who reminds us that the first two pages of the original text are missing. The spy's story mentions an ancestor, Ts'ui Pên, who has written a novel called (of course) "The Garden of Forking Paths." To make matters even more confusing, the pastiche adds several metafictional characters who comment on the narrative structure that contains them. Later readers have no reason to find Crary, author of the taxonomy, any less fictional than these characters, or Ts'ui Pên, or the nameless editor. Perhaps we made him up, or perhaps Borges did, or perhaps Borges invented the whole bunch of us. Or vice versa. As Bolter observes, *caveat lector.*

But in bringing this warning to our attention, Karl Crary's ostensible failure produces a very enlightening demonstration of hypertextual discourse in action. It is, clearly, a failure only by the narrow definition of one pedagogical language game. In fact what Crary has produced is an example of a metalepsis, or jump outside the game, a transforming (perhaps even liberating) move which allows us to perceive the constraints our writing systems impose on us. Having perceived and mapped these limits, we may be able to reconstitute our thinking about hypertext and rhizomatic discourse. Crary's paralogy might not lead us to the threshold of a new culture, but it might help us understand the changes that have come about in our old one.

In outcome at least, Crary's resistance to hypertext contrasts sharply with that of literary theorists. We who write theory tend to suffer from a surfeit of idealism and an antipathy to operational compromise. Confronted with the geometrical complicity of hypertext, some of us fail to acknowledge our naivety and fall back into the discursive space of print and an often unexamined nostalgia for the *logos*. Perhaps Crary fails for the opposite reason, because (at the beginning of his college career, after all) he is so solidly committed to the possibility of rational solutions. He sets out to save the text for the Law because he believes erroneously that he can design something that works, a scheme for sorting out the bewildering tangle of hypertextual relations.

This account gives Crary much less credit than he deserves. In fact, his problematic encounter with hypertext represents not just the complement of our critical errors but a model of erratic progress. For all his understandable logocentrism, Crary does not turn back to the library but instead takes his chances in the new medium. He could have hit the books and written a conventional paper, as many of his classmates did; but Crary chose to work in hypertext, which takes a certain intellectual boldness to begin with. Moreover, he elected to work *within the object text itself,* and this choice was definitive. Crary invades the nomadic space of hypertext in the name of the *logos*—and if he ends up planting his flag in a hall of mirrors, he has nonetheless made a very important discovery, both for himself and for his teachers.

That discovery is the practical proof of a principle expounded by Deleuze and Guattari, namely, that smooth and striated spaces "exist only in mixture: smooth space is constantly being translated, transversed into a striated space; striated space is constantly being reversed, returned to a smooth space" (474). The dyad of smooth/striated represents not a dialectic but a continuum—a conception that has considerable consequences for our understanding of hypertext and its possibilities for cultural change. To begin with, it suggests that Robert Coover is right to characterize the future of interactive media in terms of "struggle" (as Martin Rosenberg says in his article, cultural "war"). Our work in hypertext will involve a constant alternation between *nomos* and *logos*. We will create structures which we will then deconstruct or deterritorialize and which we will replace with new structures, passing again from smooth to striated space and starting the process anew.

Above all, Crary's lesson in the futility of resistance can teach us something about the nature of the new culture of which we dream when we venture into hypertext. It suggests that this culture may not resemble the liberated or autonomous zones which Hakim Bey and Thomas Pynchon have fantasized. Hypertext—and its as yet more distant cousins, virtual reality and cyberspace—will not produce anarchist enclaves or pirate utopias. Rosenberg is right: with apologies to all utopian theorists, hypertext will not liberate us from geometry, rationalist method, or the other routinizing side effects of alphanumeric thinking. Nor does hypertext represent Coover's "end of books," though the foundations of print culture are bound to be shaken a bit by the new media. Hypertext and other emerging technologies mark not a terminus but a transition. As Bolter has written, "the computer is simply the technology by which literacy will be carried into a new age" (237).

There will, of course, be nothing simple about the new age or its technologies. The transition seems likely to be both permanent and perpetual. If our destiny is indeed some version of Greater Japan, then we are in for more complexity, not less, more turbulent transversals of hierarchy into nomad space, more anxious reversals of chaos into new order. Such instability and complexity come with the deterritorialized territory. Think of Tokyo, an urban immensity without street names, where every house and building has its number in the striated grid, but where personal navigation is strictly nomadic, a matter of sketches and narratives. *What's a critic to do?* Head east till you come to the Ono-Sendai Building, hang a left at the statue of Colonel Sanders, third pachinko parlor on the right, you can't miss it.

If we can say anything at this point about interactive media and their possibilities for cultural change, it must be that any new culture will be as promiscuous as its texts, always seeking new relations, fresh paralogical permutations of order and chaos. This activity may not make us avant-garde, but it should keep us busy. We may discover that we are the children of Leni and Franz Pökler, inheritors of both a mother-right and a patrimony, a capacity for cosmic understanding and a knack for making things work. In Pynchon's novel, Franz and Leni's daughter, Ilse, is taken away by the SS and made into a kind of living movie, returned to her father once a year for brief glimpses. In our relationship to our dream parents we will need to circumvent such dire machinations. Our medium of expression will not be anything so linear and monologic as cinema, but rather the hybrid, smooth-striated domain of hypertext, the new writing space. "Writing is preeminently the technology of cyborgs," Donna Haraway reminds (176), and our encounter with these new media may well be a first step toward cyborganism, which is perhaps the ultimate transversal of rhizome and machine.

We may find ourselves one day arriving as the first nomads of cyberspace, voyaging smoothly across the grids of consensual hallucination. But such excursions are a few years off yet. For the moment, as we wait for century and millennium to play themselves out, we must be satisfied with less grandiose visions and more pragmatic insights. Here is one: in our long dreams of a new culture, we may be better served by an erroneous but venturesome conservatism than by the most radical strains of pure theory.

NOTES

1. Michael Joyce, *Afternoon, a story* (Cambridge, Mass.: Eastgate Systems, 1990). In hypertext documents, citations are most conveniently made by the title of the node or lexia from which the quotation comes, in this case, "Japan".

2. Jean Baudrillard, *Simulations*, trans. P. Foss, P. Patton, and P. Beitchmann (New York: Semiotext(e), 1983), 140; Donna Haraway, *Simians, Cyborgs, and Women: The Reinvention of Nature* (New York: Routledge, 1991), 161.

3. Mark Poster, *The Mode of Information: Poststructuralism and Social Context* (Chicago: University of Chicago Press, 1990), 16.

4. Jean-François Lyotard, *The Postmodern Condition: A Report on Knowledge,* trans. Geoff Bennington and Brian Massumi (Minneapolis: University of Minnesota Press, 1984), xxiv.

5. Gilles Deleuze and Félix Guattari, *A Thousand Plateaus: Capitalism and Schizophrenia,* trans. Brian Massumi (Minneapolis: University of Minnesota Press, 1987), 482. For further discussion of Deleuze and Guattari and electronic textuality, see Martin Rosenberg's essay in this collection, "Physics and Hypertext: Liberation and Complicity in Art and Pedagogy."

6. Thomas Pynchon, *Vineland* (New York: Little, Brown, 1990), 97. For more on the Pynchon-Deleuze connection, see Martin Rosenberg's "Invisibility, the War Machine, and Prigogine: Dissipative Structures and Aggregating Processes in the Zone of *Gravity's Rainbow," Pynchon Notes* 29 [forthcoming].

7. Hakim Bey, *T.A.Z.: The Temporary Autonomous Zone, Ontological Anarchy, Poetic Terrorism* (New York: Autonomedia, 1991), 101.

8. Gregory Ulmer, *Teletheory: Grammatology in the Age of Video* (New York: Routledge, 1990), 169.

9. Jay David Bolter, *Writing Space: The Computer, Hypertext, and the History of Writing* (Hillsdale, N.J.: Lawrence Erlbaum, 1991), 159, 231.

10. Michael Joyce, "Siren Shapes: Exploratory and Constructive Hypertext," *Academic Computing* 3 (Nov. 1988): 11 ff.

11. H. Marshall McLuhan, *The Gutenberg Galaxy: The Making of Typographic Man* (New York: Signet, 1969), 155.

12. Alvin Kernan, *The Death of Literature* (New Haven: Yale University Press, 1990), 144.

13. Neil Postman, *Amusing Ourselves to Death: Political Discourse in the Age of Show Business* (New York: Penguin, 1985), 99.

14. Roland Barthes, *The Rustle of Language,* trans. Richard Howard (New York: Hill & Wang, 1986), 61.

15. On the significance of gaps in the semiotics of hypertext, see Terence Harpold, "The Contingencies of the Hypertext Link," *Writing on the Edge* 2 (1991): 126–39; and his chapter in this volume.

16. Theodor Holm Nelson, "How Hypertext (Un)Does the Canon," (address to the Modern Language Association, Chicago, Dec. 28, 1990).

17. George P. Landow, *Hypertext: The Convergence of Contemporary Critical Theory and Technology* (Baltimore: Johns Hopkins University Press, 1992), 184.

18. Theodor Holm Nelson, *Literary Machines* (Sausalito: Mindful Press, 1990), 1/5.

19. K. Eric Drexler, *Engines of Creation: The Coming Era of Nanotechnology* (New York: Anchor, 1987), 230.

20. Kathryn Malcolm, Steven Poltrock, and Douglas Schuler, "Industrial-Strength Hypermedia: Requirements for a Large Engineering Enterprise," P. Stotts and R. Furuta, eds. *Hypertext '91* (New York: Association for Computing Machinery, 1991), 15. For more on the applications of hypertext in industry, see H. Van Dyke Parunak, "Toward Industrial-Strength Hypermedia," in *Hypertext/Hypermedia Handbook*, ed. E. Berk and J. Devlin (New York: McGraw-Hill, 1991), 381–89.

21. Thomas Pynchon, *Gravity's Rainbow* (New York: Viking, 1973), 737.

22. Robert Coover, "The End of Books," *New York Times Book Review*, June 21, 1992, p. 25.

23. See Bolter, Joyce, Harpold, Landow.

24. George P. Landow, "The Rhetoric of Hypermedia: Some Rules for Authors," in *Hypermedia and Literary Studies*, ed. Paul Delany and George P. Landow (Cambridge: MIT Press, 1991), 81–104.

25. Martin Rosenberg, "Physics and Hypertext: Liberation and Complicity in Art and Pedagogy," p. 278 in this volume.

26. Jay David Bolter, *Writing Space* (hypertext version), "Copyright III."

27. See Stuart Moulthrop and Nancy Kaplan, "They Became What They Beheld: The Futility of Resistance in the Space of Electronic Writing," in *Literacy and Computers*, ed. C. Selfe and S. Hilligoss (New York: Modern Language Association, forthcoming).

28. Jorge Luis Borges, *Labyrinths*, trans. Donald A. Yates (New York: New Directions, 1962), 26.

THE NEW WRITING

Socrates in the Labyrinth

David Kolb

10

Can we do philosophy using hypertext? What kind of work might a philosophical hypertext do? Could it do argumentative work, or would any linear argument be a subordinate part of some different hyper-work? But what is thinking if not linear? In the course of this discussion I shall bring such questions into the neighborhood of several philosophers for whom thinking is more than a linear process.

Authors of familiar linear text work hard to create a convincing sequence of narrative or exposition or argument. A hypertext by contrast comes as a web of text, like a landscape that cannot be seen all at once but can be explored along many different routes. The author cannot control which links the reader will pursue, and in some systems the reader can create new units and links, so that the web changes and grows. The roles of author and reader begin to shift as the being of the text changes.

Such multiply connected texts will be used in many ways. We do not know what those ways will be. There is no reason to think there is one essential or best way to use hypertext, any more than there is one essential or best way to use paper. Writing on paper can produce laundry lists, thank-you notes, scholarly treatises, disjointed jottings on the back of train schedules, love letters, instruction manuals for VCRs, romance novels, and countless other items whose points and criteria have little in common. We can imagine how hypertext might help or alter activities that we already perform with ordinary text, but it is harder to imagine what new forms of life or new uses might develop (although we already know one, a new form of cooperative writing).

Officially, according to Plato, philosophy's work involves the critical self-observant search for the truth. But is critical dialogue and reading a form of life or a part of other form(s) of life? In Plato, the activity of philosophy leads us to discover who and where we are and how we should live. In the process, Socrates tries to convince us that the search for the truth is not merely a means but is itself a component of any good human life that goes along with the grain of the universe. This larger work of self (and communal) discovery (and creation) is an activity to which we might imagine philosophical hypertext making a contribution.[1]

There are some quite traditional functions that hypertext could perform in philosophy:

1. It could be used to emphasize the structure and outline of standard argumentative essays (for instance, by equipping the essay with an overview or outline whose links would take you to the relevant parts of the essay).
2. It could present a reference collection of philosophical texts that included links from texts to commentaries, discussions, alternatives, refutations, bibliographies, and the like.
3. Its links could enhance editions of the collected writings of thinkers by making connections that could not be found with standard search routines.
4. A jointly composed active hypertext web could be a place where philosophical dialogue (multilogue?) could happen. Because hypertext allows any lexia to be "next to" any other, such a web would provide a very flexible medium of discussion. (A *lexia*—the word is adapted from Roland Barthes—is an individual unit of text in a hypertext.) Hypertext would allow topics to be connected without forcing the writer-reader to decide under which single heading the additional comment would be registered. It would also enhance possibilities for textual reuse: what I posted would not be erased but, besides arguing with me, you might make links that grafted my statements into new contexts that made "my" texts work very differently than I intended. This kind of philosophical hypertext could be a powerful method of contesting or supplementing my claims.

Such implementations of hypertext are worthwhile and would enrich the field of philosophy in many ways. Nonetheless, in these forms hypertext still functions as a presentation medium that remains subservient to the traditional goals and organization of philosophy. For the most part, links would embody the standard moves of argumentation—making claims, giving backing, contesting claims, raising questions, stating alternatives, and so on. The text would be multilinear but would remain organized around the familiar philosophical forms of linear argument.

There are more radical uses of hypertext. The most experimental so far have been in fiction. There the narrative line is under attack. Could there be a hypertext philosophy that departed from philosophy's argumentative moves and traditional linear form?

> The traditional novel— . . . which Hegel called "the epic of the middle-class world"—is perceived by its would-be executioners as the virulent carrier of the patriarchal, colonial, canonical, proprietary, hierarchical and authoritarian values of a past that is no longer with us. Much of the novel's power is embedded in the line, that compulsory author-directed movement from the beginning of a sentence to its period, from the top of the page to the bottom, from the first page to the last. Of course, through print's long history, there have been countless strategies to counter the line's power. . . . true freedom from the tyranny of the line is perceived as only really possible now at last with the advent of hypertext . . . where the line in fact does not exist unless one invents and implants it in the text.[2]

Could this also be true of philosophy? Is a nonlinear philosophical work possible, or is philosophy so committed to the line that hypertext must remain an expository device or an informational tool for philosophical texts, unable to offer a brave world of new philosophical textual strategies?

> No fixed centers, for starters—and no edges either, no ends or boundaries. The . . . line vanishes into a geographical landscape or exitless maze, with beginnings, middles, ends being no longer part of the immediate display. Instead: branching optional menus, link markers and mapped networks. There are no hierarchies in these topless (and bottomless) networks [of] evenly empowered and equally ephemeral window-sized blocks of text and graphics. (Coover, 23)

Would such a writing be desirable in philosophy?

On the one hand, philosophy, though it was born in the evenly empowered fragments of the pre-Socratics, became self-conscious in the forward movement of the Platonic dialogue. It declared its need of system and syllogism with Aristotle and grew through the combative summae of the medievals into the argumentative chains of Descartes and Spinoza, then it built the great nineteenth-century systems and today shows itself most precisely in the crafted linear form of the analytic article. It would seem that there is no way to deny the line and still do philosophy. Hypertext appears at best an informational convenience, but its shapeless depths must not be allowed to weaken argumentative linearity, or philosophy will be reduced to rhetoric.

On the other hand, the Platonic dialogues are elusively inconclusive, Aristotle's system is not intended to be deductively tight, there are the forests of medieval commentaries on commentaries, the nineteenth-century systems are disturbingly nonlinear, and there are counter-traditions attacking or perverting the line from at least Pascal and through Kierkegaard, Nietzsche, Wittgenstein, and today's deconstructionists. While current philosophy appears mostly as the essay or the anthology, there have also been the meditation, the aphorism, the pensée, the diary, the dialogue, and other forms. So perhaps hypertext will make a new kind of philosophical writing possible.

It is an odd question to ask: "What can hypertext do to and for philosophy?" It is like asking what print can do. But there are some generalities that were observed, as early as Plato, about the effect of writing on communication, memory, and thought. Writing is the first step in thought's losing control and gaining control of itself: losing control because, as Plato complains, writing removes the content from the living process of dialogue that should be fully present and responsible to itself; gaining control because the units of exchange can be frozen and inspected and structured more intricately, just as Plato wrote and rewrote his dialogues; yet again losing control, because even with that rewriting the words and structures take on lives of their own. They do so in oral discussion too, but in hypertext words and structures can find their way into more contexts and changes.

Philosophy is in many ways a child of writing. There are few if any oral texts that might be technical philosophy. (The Indian Vedanta sutras come to mind, with their lapidary conciseness fit for memorization, but they soon become embedded within a cloud of written commentary.) There are many oral texts that might do some of the things philosophy does, but the specific philosophical gesture seems to want writing, to preserve lines for future examination.

Philosophy has always exhibited some tension between writing and live performance. Socrates wrote nothing. Plato writes condemning writing. Medieval teaching consisted of oral commentaries and debates on written texts. Jewish and Tibetan philosophical practices weave an intricate interplay of written and oral performance. Even professionalized philosophy today usually judges contemporary thinkers on oral quickness as well as on written depth.

I have assembled here some considerations that urge against philosophy's using hypertext as more than an expository device. They are based on a classical conception of philosophy and make a strong case that philosophy cannot lose its line, which I almost believe is so. This argument is then subjected to qualifications derived from several thinkers who question or supplement the line.

The principal argument against web writing in philosophy is straightforward: philosophy essentially involves argument, and argument essentially involves a beginning, middle, and end, so that a truly philosophical text needs a line. This position claims more than that works of philosophy should include arguments within their texture; it says that any single work should be structured as a large argument. It is through the argumentative line of its overall structure that any piece of philosophical writing does its work.

An argument links premises and conclusion. To use the hackneyed example, from "All men are mortal" and "Socrates is a man" we must conclude that "Socrates is mortal." This is not reversible, since from "Socrates is mortal" and "Socrates is a man" we cannot conclude that "All men are mortal." There is a structure to the argument that must be respected. The three sentences could be linked in a hypertext web, but that is not enough to give the unidirectional dependence demanded by argumentative structure.

It is true that for expository convenience the parts of the argument may come in any order in the text, but the argument will be present only when the underlying linear abstract structure is indicated in some manner. It is also true that some arguments have multiple beginnings and branches that jointly support conclusions or diverge from premises, but these still arrange into a unidirectional abstract structure with beginnings, middles, and ends. A philosophical argument (or a mathematical proof) cannot be presented as a cloud of disjointed statements. The conclusion is that philosophy's line cannot be dissolved in the way some have dreamed of dissolving the narrative line. On this view hypertext would have to respect the line by making arguments the units of presentation and by maintaining some overall linear argumentative structure.

This amounts to a claim that philosophy loses its identity if it is not structured as an argument. This essentialist claim can be further developed: in a hypertext web without a line there would be no overall structure that would enable one to hold the text still and locate the claims being made, in order to have a clear object to criticize. In introductory philosophy courses students are often told that the first thing they should do is "find the conclusion." Then they are told to "outline the argument." Since an outline contains constant indications of its structure, one knows one's location at all times. One needs to know where one is in the larger structure, so that one can see what is being claimed and be able to criticize it. The line brings focus, and focused criticism is essential to philosophy, one of whose parents was Socrates's insistence on responsible, limited assent to carefully defined claims.

This emphasis upon linear argument contrasts with hypertext webs that may have no fixed beginnings or endings, are hard to explore, may have no conclusions, and may deliberately avoid being caught in any totalizing overview. So, to do hypertext philosophy without the line that leads to a conclusion would seem to denature philosophy into its traditional opposites, rhetoric or idle talk.

Rhetoric: the hypertext would perhaps be an accumulation of words and images and considerations that persuade the reader to adopt an attitude or a course of action, but this persuasive effect would not be controlled by a line that provides a route for criticism and rational evaluation in terms of the goal of truth rather than the goal of persuasion. (It is true that there are modes of philosophy that attack the distinction between philosophy and rhetoric, but these usually do so as the conclusion of an argument that does conventional philosophical work.)

Idle talk: the hypertext would just expand as conversation might, enjoying the act but not standing watch over itself by asking about conclusions and grounds. Socrates tried to convert his listeners and bring them into the position of constant responsibility for their own and others' discourse. Conversation can be its own pleasure and work within a complex network of changing goals and its own logic of response, but Socrates wants philosophy to be single-minded, subordinating discourse to the single search for grounds and truth. From Plato on, philosophy has insisted on the need for de-cision, in its root meaning of cutting off what it takes to be wandering excess and keeping to the narrow path. Socrates tends to picture our usual conversations as either goalless pleasurable exchange or manipulative rhetoric; he seeks to turn all conversations into occasions for teaching and responsibility. (We might suspect that a philosophical hypertext would have to find ways to let discourse overflow this strict goal-orientation while remaining self-critical and responsive.)

The previous consideration can be amplified in a more practical way. There is a danger that creating a philosophy hypertext web would be the functional equivalent of writing without self-discipline, publishing one's drafts and jottings, or self-indulgently exfoliating ideas without taking a position. This extravagance would infect the philosophical work with some well-known diseases: wandering commentary, endless qualifications, fruitless self-reflection, unnecessary contentiousness, the piling up of meta-level upon meta-level. This result could both stem from and itself promote intellectual laziness, or it could cater to a noncritical audience that wants to be titillated by the passage of ideas but not challenged in its own beliefs or values.

The obvious response to this third consideration is that bad writing is bad writing, whether it is in hypertext or linear text. But the consideration suggests that working up one's drafts and jottings into good philosophical writing is precisely a matter of critical mastery and judgment that demand and produce a line. What would *thinking* mean if it were not providing form and focus, definite claims, critical judgment, beginnings, middles, and ends, and so preventing an indefinite accumulation of words and images? This question remains open.

A classical answer to these classical considerations might be to grant that philosophy needs the argumentative line but to deny that a philosophical hypertext web need be limited to one single line. Hypertext philosophy should be considered not as a single author controlling a line into a text but as a net of linear texts confronting one another in a kind of endless expansion, as they have in fact done in the history of philosophy. But this response provides only a weak defense of philosophical hypertext, for we already have that open web of interacting texts—it is the library, and it contains its own links and internal maps in its commentaries, concordances, bibliographies, and footnotes. The links in a hypertext library would make possible many new types of commentaries and collections, but these new features might still allow individual units to remain structured in linear ways.

Can hypertext webs provide new possibilities for writing something that might be less linear or nonlinear and yet still do philosophical work? If the above considerations are accepted, it would appear that philosophy is constituted by the presence of the line. But even if the line is required, it may not necessarily be the single controlling element in philosophical writing. Not all paths follow the line.

Philosophy's line finds itself constantly surrounded by supplements which it both desires and rejects: marginalia (as in medieval manuscripts), parallel columns of text (as in Kant's antinomies), parenthetical (and footnote) remarks that provide self-critical comments, ampliative material, methodological reflections, objections and replies, ironic juxtapositions, historical precedents and deviations, references to other texts, quotations, and so on.

Footnotes are said to be a kind of primitive hypertext, but there is one important difference. At least in books where footnotes actually appear at the foot of the page, the note and the text it comments on are present together. The note and text form one visual gestalt. (In hypertext systems this gestalt can happen only if more than one window can be presented on screen simultaneously, but even then the windowing apparatus separates them.) Another example of the same problem is James Joyce's work. *Finnegans Wake* in particular is sometimes cited as a proto-hypertext. But this is misleading; Joyce's work depends on the simultaneity and the emerging together of the multilingual play of meanings and structures. Separated into discrete links, the combinations would lose much of their power.

Plato's dialogues are notorious for their sinuous movement and their pauses to talk about themselves, and Aristotle's texts are full of remarks that beg for links to other discussions. Writing philosophy, one feels a constant tension between the desire to reach out into the surrounding discourse that opens a place for the line, and the reverse desire for compactness and linearity. Philosophy wants to cover everything with its graffiti, to find itself always already arrived, but also to utter only the one first magic necessary word.

We can insist on the linear nature of argument, but in what is argument embedded? There is a knowing how to go on which is knowing how to read, how to continue the series, how to use the tool. This knowing is a matter of finding ourselves accepting descriptions, of knowing what sort of place "we" are in. This place is not established by argument; it is presupposed in being able to follow an argument.

The classical philosophical dream is that philosophy as a whole be one huge rigorous discourse, which usually means one huge chain of arguments. But where is the chain anchored (and how do we know what it is to follow it)? Aristotle said (in the *Posterior Analytics*) that either a chain of argument has to be anchored in premises that are evident in themselves and so do not need argument (the choice of Aristotle and Descartes and many today) or the chain must be circular (in complex ways, the choice of Hegel and of today's holists). Either way, the big argument should dominate the overall structure of any text in which it appears.

In fact, it is preparations for the big argument that often dominate the texts. Arguments, big or small, are surrounded by a more informal discourse that leads us to and from the argument. This discourse puts us in a position to follow the line. There are discourses that get us into position to accept the premises, to understand the situation, to follow the argument, to tie the line into life.

For many philosophers the austerity of the mathematical proof stands as the ideal, yet, as Kant pointed out, philosophy and mathematics are crucially different in that mathematics starts with definitions while philosophy ends with them.[3] Philosophy discusses alternative first principles and disputes definitions and modes of argument. It tries to find a rigorous way of disclosing the conditions that make rigorous lines possible.

Even the purest philosophical line in a technical article or book has vestigial or presupposed discourses of this type surrounding it. They furnish the understanding of what the piece is and what to do with it. The real structure of the philosophical work is not simply argumentative. To read philosophy as always embedded in such informal discourse demands that one pay attention to parts of the text students are encouraged to rush over in their eagerness to find the conclusion and outline the argument. A more circumspect mode of reading does not make such essentialist presuppositions.

On the other hand we have to be careful not to make the parallel mistake of saying that the fluid discourse is itself totally without argumentative structure. The point should be that argument and fluidity are always linked. Just as we cannot say that argument absorbs the fluid discourse, so we cannot say that the surrounding discourse is primary in the sense that it has some special nonargumentative structure of its own.

So, the argumentative line is surrounded by a fluid discourse in which there are no fixed primacies and no firm meta-levels, because in that discourse such things get established, though in an always discussable manner. Which is not to say that the fluid discourse never accomplishes anything; bearings are given. Hypertext seems to be a medium in which this fluid discourse could flourish.

I see two matching temptations here: the first, to dismiss the embedding discourse as preparation, a ladder to be thrown away once we have climbed it; the second, to make that discourse into a new kind of line. Hypertext is not likely to give in to the first temptation, but we can learn something about the possibilities of hypertext philosophy from someone who gave in to the second, Georg Wilhelm Friedrich Hegel. It may seem surprising to invoke the great systematizer here, but there is a lesson we can learn from him, and a caution.

The lesson is the possibility of two-dimensional philosophical discourse, where the links do multiple duty. Hegel's books appear to be resolutely linear treatments of a sequence of many detailed categories and historical periods. But that movement has a peculiar structure: the transition from one category to another turns out to be an aspect of a larger transition, which turns out to be a moment in a yet larger movement, and so on up to the major movement of the system, which takes the form of a circle, not of a line with a beginning and end.

For example, in Hegel's political philosophy a particular detailed transition, say, between two parts of property law or two aspects of the division of labor, also expresses part of a larger movement by which the bourgeois social structure defines itself, which in turn acts as a phase in still larger movements concerning the embodying of freedom, the relation of history and social identity, and the coming of self-understanding of our place in the world process. These larger movements do not just sum up a series of micro-movements; there are complex mutual influences among the levels. There is no single micro-transition to which one can point and say that there and nowhere else the larger movement is accomplished.

In pointing out relations between aspects of property law or kinds of religious symbols, Hegel means to show how they derive their identity from their relation to each other but also how that relation in turn depends for its identity and stability on its insertion in a larger exchange, and so on. The links found in Hegel's texts work on many levels at once, performing different movements at different paces.

Furthermore, at none of these levels do the links function as moves in standard arguments. Argumentation does occur, but it is subordinated to Hegel's attempt to capture and arrange into an interdependent whole the set of contexts and categories that are the preconditions of argument. Hegel's ambition is to show how all the situations (and directions and self-understandings and categories of thought) that set the place of argument can be grasped as moving towards a final communal self-understanding.

However one questions such grandiose ambition, Hegel's approach offers two lessons for our hypertext theme. The first is that philosophy can indeed be made out of a discussion of the place and preconditions of argument's line. Such philosophy need not itself proceed as a big linear argument, though it may use argument within its own movement. Secondly, links and transitions may have other forms than the standard argumentative moves, and they may be elements in many motions at the same time.

Here, however, is the caution. Hegel tries to show complex relations of mutual constitution and interdependence among the categories that structure thought. Those relations do not fit easily into linear arguments, but neither do they fit the relations usually said to connect units of a hypertext.[4]

Hypertext is often diagrammed as boxes connected by arrows. In *The Science of Logic,* Hegel complained about the geometric or numerical diagrams employed in his day to model the relations among thoughts. Such diagrams, he said, showed too few types of relations (inclusion, exclusion, and one- or two-way relation). Moreover, he objected, they presupposed that the items being related were distinct and already definite at either end of the diagram's lines. Such diagrams cannot easily show the mutual dependencies and co-constitution among our categories of thought; they tend to reduce these relations to inclusion-exclusion or whole-and-part. The caution, then, is that hypertext may make its lexias too independent and its relations too geometric to allow the complex interdependencies that nonlinear philosophy might want to explore.[5]

Peter Whalley discusses this issue in connection with the standard comparison of linear text and hypertext:

> It is a mistake to think of conventional texts, and particularly expository teaching texts, as being purely linear. Text linguists . . . have shown how, under a superficially linear form, authors may create rich, complex relational structures. It could even be argued that the simple pointer and hierarchical structures provided in hypertext are semantically more limiting than the implicit relationships created in conventional materials . . . [in which] cycles of ideas are repeated and overlaid upon each other. For example a central idea may be repeated within progressively more complex contexts. The skillful author may use the linear text form to weave an entirely nonlinear pattern of associations in the reader's mind.[6]

Can hypertext display the process of first expounding an idea as independent or immediately given then showing it to be involved in complex relations that qualify its independence and constitute a larger unity? This overcomes the seeming independence of the first stage, then returns to that stage, now in the new context. Though not taking the form of linear argument, this process would demand a set of links that would do multiple duty, and it should be traversed from a beginning and return again to that beginning. To intercept only a part of this movement would be to take as independent something that should not stand on its own. To leave the first links behind would be to miss an aspect of how the larger unit exists. To lose the cyclic or spiral movement in a cloud of links would be to diffuse the investigation into comments that presuppose too much independence in the individual moments of the discourse.

Efforts to avoid these problems might demand that individual lexias be very large, which would reintroduce linear texts, or that new forms and uses of links be found. But can the box-and-arrow structure of lexias and links carry a progress of thought that, while it is neither argumentative nor linear, does demand mutual movement of this kind?

It is easy to add qualifications to what you find in a hypertext, but the model that dominates hypertext's mechanism is that of independent bits of information linked to one another. Yet, the fluid discourse that shows that philosophy is not all linear argument also demands more kinds of structure than arbitrarily multiplied links. Connection and linkage are not the same as dialectical relations or mutual constitution. Hypertext's granularity makes it difficult to show two units co-constituting each other. We need a new nonargumentative form for a set of links, above the level of the individual lexia and short of the entire hypertext network. The possibility of new philosophical writing depends in large measure on the creation of such intermediate forms of movement and linkage that make more than argumentative moves.

Of course, in an interactive hypertext such intermediate forms would remain porous and interruptible. They would be at most one set of paths. (If a form is unable to be framed, is it still a form?) Putting the issue this way reminds us that problems about the multiple and porous boundaries of forms have long been debated in the philosophy of art and literature, in which theorists have had to deal with reuse dominating or covering original use (as in reference to and quotation from obscure originals) or in which original unities are dispersed into new artistic forms and genres.

Does this then mean that hypertext might be best thought about not by means of images of great systems but with Derrida's deconstruction, which is an errant descendant of Hegel's dialectic that glories in incomplete wholes and interrupted necessities? Deconstruction emphasizes the lack of totality and closure in any form. The line tends to become encrusted with its preconditions and with meta-comments and amplifications. Suppose it dissolved into them? Imagine a text that became nothing but footnotes and marginalia referring to one another. (It sometimes seems that contemporary deconstructive texts aspire to this status.) This text would say many things at once without granting primacy to any of them. Could this text still be philosophy?

In any case, deconstructive alarms should have been going off during the earlier discussion. I deliberately used the word *supplement*—and *essence, unity, necessary boundaries, fixed identity, full presence, excess:* these are all fighting words nowadays. I am not here interested in what is sometimes called deconstruction but is really an attempt to eliminate any notion of essence and identity. Rather, what interests me is the maneuver of allowing essences, identities, boundaries (and argumentative lines and definite claims) while showing how the claimed essences or unities break their own closure. They function, but they function as effects in a space they cannot dominate.

Hypertext looks like a natural for the attempt to show that any presumed overall structure, narrative or philosophical, argumentative or dialectical, works within a larger field that it does not control. Hypertext's endless possibilities for recombination and reuse should facilitate the creation of texts in which the narrative or philosophical line is self-consciously reinscribed within, yet does not dominate, the space of the text.

In his book *Hypertext,* George P. Landow has shown many parallels between contemporary literary theory and hypertext technology. He is particularly concerned with the overall effect of hypertext as a medium; he argues that it will question the unity of the text, the roles of reader and author, and the power relations of education and access to information. He concedes that "the enumerating linear rhetoric of 'first, second, third' so well suited to print will continue to appear within individual blocks of text," but he argues that the whole will not be structured in a linear fashion. Landow's examples from classroom experience show how a more active hypertext creates pressure on textual unity and traditional roles.[7]

It might seem that Derrida's experiments with parallel columns of text, marginalia, and footnotes that bite the text that feeds them could be read as print substitutes for hypertext, but most of Derrida's deconstructive performances happen in linear text that is made to exceed its own strictures without typographical gymnastics. There are indeed texts with distorted linearity, for instance the book *Glas* or the essay "Tympan," but something is going on in these texts that could not be duplicated in hypertext links. Derrida's typographical maneuvers depend on simultaneous visual access to the related elements. It is important in those texts that the references across the parallel columns be contingent, dependent on how the eye jumps and reads, rather than frozen in the discrete predetermined links of a hypertext. It is the contingency of juxtaposition, rather than the definite link, that helps demonstrate the fecundity of signs and lack of closure Derrida is concerned to show.[8]

Indeed, in some ways hypertext does not question the unity of the text deeply enough. It might seem to a deconstructive eye that hypertext remains too much a system of linked presences rather than a play of presence and absence. Even if it is growing and cannot be summarized in a glance, it exists as a totality of nodes and links, a vast structure that could in principle be made present. This statement is not quite accurate, however. Although there is a totality to be found in the computer records, the "form" of the hypertext is not in the enumeration of nodes and links but in their more complex relations. Pointing to the set of pages in a book or the letters on a page does not tell you whether the book is a novel or a repair manual, or whether the letters are an introduction, a narration, or enact some other intermediate part of a larger book-form. Listing the totality of nodes and links in a hypertext does not tell you what they are doing.

The fact that links are possible challenges the closure of any piece of text. Still, the very endlessness of possible links means that none of them need question the integrity of the individual lexia in the way that deconstructive operations conducted on site might do. Links lack the contingent fecundity of immediate juxtaposition and the self-referentiality of clever textual turns. The links do not necessarily bring off the fragile slippage of a signification that denies its own attempted closure. Hypertext links can change a lexia's relations and its role within a whole or context but they do not make it reflect on or exceed its own unity. One could presumably compose the individual lexias so that they did this self-questioning or self-transgressing, but then what would the hypertext mechanism add to the deconstructive endeavor? It remains to be seen whether hypertext can put enough deconstructive pressure on the individual lexia. There is the danger that the hypertext could become a mass of comments and links in which no single link could gather enough force or distinctiveness to make deconstructive maneuvers. By their very multitude the links would allow individual lexias too much atomistic sufficiency. This returns us to the issue of intermediate form.

We need to understand better the ways in which links and paths can enact forms and figures (intermediate between the lexia and the whole document) that bring pressure to bear on the "internal" being of the individual lexias. We need to understand how to write the individual lexias so that they are more clearly permeable to this influence.[9]

We might also ask whether a hypertext web might expand too far to maintain the pressure on textual unity and authorial roles. A map that is too detailed becomes another nature to be explored. An expanding hypertext web would contain so many kinds of paths that it could not be classifiable as belonging to a single genre, such as philosophy or fiction. Those regions of the web that were genre-similar would be inscribed into a textual space that was not controlled by the rules of their genre. It is an exciting possibility. But as the web became larger it might, like a library, appear only as a background for unified works in various genres. We are concerned here not with such a global library but with the philosophical reading room (even if its walls are porous). An analogous problem emerges there as well. A multiply created philosophical hypertext web (or region of a web) could get large enough that it would resemble a collection of philosophical journal articles responding to one another, or the threads of discussion carried on Internet electronic-mail lists. But then the hypertext might become only a presentation medium for a collection of linear texts. This argument again points to the importance of new intermediate forms other than argument and counter-argument.

I keep stressing the need for new intermediate forms because we must avoid the temptation of seeing hypertext either as a collection of atomistic information units or as an infinite play of signifiers. It is true that hypertext's writing space cannot be restricted by any intermediate forms that might be enacted within it. This lack of restrictability can lead to viewing the hypertext web as itself that general economy that lies behind and within any limited text or economy. This temptation is fueled by dreams of a universal hypertext network. But no matter how extensive, a hypertext web remains an artifact with defined components and links. The unlimited economy or general text cannot be made present, for the act of making present is the creation of a limited economy. The general economy can be indicated only indirectly, because although it is a condition of the possibility of any defined signifier or network, it does not exist in the usual sense as an encounterable signifier or network. Some writers who have been inspired by deconstruction want to liberate us from limitations by instituting the general economy in writing or in community, and they seek institutions or ways of writing that will do the job. But I take deconstruction to be as much about the impossibility of such instauration as about the impossibility of a completely closed text. Nonetheless, a hypertext web can in its way be a strong symbol of the unlimited fecundity of signs, of the varied individuation of texts and entities, and of the endlessness of redescription and reincorporation.

So, after passing by Hegel and Derrida, what can we say about possible new forms of philosophical writing? In our (post)modern world we are gradually trying to create social and political forms that have neither atomic indivisible units nor totalizing structures. These forms, temporary and permeable as they may be, still provide space that we are painfully learning to inhabit without demanding fixity and closure. If there is to be a philosophical writing in hypertext, it needs such forms. The forms will take advantage of the nonlinear characteristics of the hypertext medium. We do not yet know what these forms will be, but they will be in the links.

Putting the matter this way misleads, because it still suggests a neat hierarchy of forms. In a written text, the letters of the alphabet are distinct and relatively stable; attempts to show the play of unity and disunity in a text do not (normally) need to question the identity of the letters that compose it. The form of the text is in the paragraphs and sections. So, too, the form of the hypertext will be in the links and paths, not the individual units. This may be true, but the analogy of letters is far from exact. In printed books (as opposed to illuminated manuscripts) there is little feedback (except some aesthetic judgment) between the overall form of an essay or book and the form of the letters of which it is composed. In a hypertext, the individual units, being themselves already quite complex, could be so influenced by feedback from the larger forms that it would be difficult to speak of a hierarchy of levels. This interplay is one reason it may be better to speak of new figures of discourse rather than new forms. "The task that confronts us as writers in the new medium is precisely to discover effective new figures."[10]

One could object that hypertext makes closed works impossible, so we should not worry about their forms and figures, as if they could be viewed as closed wholes. But this also is misleading. Hypertext does make totally closed works impossible. New links can move in and reuse pieces of my writing, but whatever form I gave my writing remains available. It cannot dominate the hypertext space and it cannot claim to totalize the meaning and role of the individual lexias, but it remains followable. Otherwise the hypertext would have no structure. Were this the case, the text would resemble a modern society that at times seems to have no intermediate structures between the individual and the global state or economy, and the text would be similarly oppressive. Intermediate figuration creates open space.

One could also object that my attempt to find a new form of philosophical writing is misguided, for the old genres will not be able to maintain their boundaries in hypertext. But boundaries are not erased by hypertext; they are made permeable. Form and genre lose their presumed absoluteness in hyperspace, but they do not dissolve into atomized text or bland mixtures. Rather, they stand in tension with other uses and other partial wholes. We have to learn from Hegel and Derrida that the choice is not between rigid boundaries and total flux.

I have been asking about philosophical hypertext works that are not libraries of articles or threads of discussion and argument. The latter are legitimate and straightforward uses of hypertext in philosophy, but they do not address the question I have been pursuing, which is whether there can be nonlinear philosophical works that may include argumentative lines as part of a different texture that takes advantage of the peculiar potentials of the hypertext medium.

Such new forms may come about through what appears to be a more disjointed style of writing, one that is less architectural than linear text. Architecture has traditionally implied hierarchical structure. Designing a traditional building involves intricate adjustments of part to part, so that the building will stand successfully, but also so that it will have a unified effect and the many demands of the program will be harmoniously accommodated. Adjustments to the height of the windows or the width of a room cause compensating changes elsewhere in the structure. Writing texts with an architecture also involves intricate adjustments of part to part. Changes made in one place ripple through the whole structure, so that the whole has a conclusion, a unity of effect and tone, and so that any disunity is purposive and functional.

One could design a building against architecture, perhaps with parts that became relatively independent, that could change without causing balancing changes in other parts. Text could be written like that, with parts that remained outside of other parts, in an assemblage that did not demand balanced unity, wherein changes in one place did not necessarily demand changes elsewhere. Because of its modular nature hypertext will tend to this kind of writing.

But a building made of fragments still has to be carefully designed; random assemblages soon lose their ability to hold our interest. So, too, hypertext needs some form and figure more than simple addition. Flipping the channels on cable television can produce exciting juxtapositions, but only for a while. Active reading becomes passive titillation. Later it becomes noise. We need forms of hypertext writing that are neither standard linear hierarchical unities nor the cloying shocks of simple juxtaposition.

Would such a writing still be philosophy? To some extent such a question is unanswerable, since the criteria for what counts as philosophy evolve over time. But recalling the earlier discussion of Socrates and the arguments about argument, one can perhaps require that to be called philosophy the writing maintain something of the Socratic watchfulness over itself and the abstract or conceptual structures it employs, and that it be responsible in the claims it makes.

Can a philosophical hypertext make claims? Since there would be no one ending point to which it all comes, there might not be one set of propositions that are the focal point of the text. There are many readings with their endings determined in part by the reader. A reading may end with the reader feeling that a claim has been made on her. But does a claim have to be the demand to affirm a proposition?

In a single-author work certain propositions might run through the text the way themes run through a song, so that the reader must encounter them. The author could structure the text so that the reader constantly returned to certain claims, but this structuring would not necessarily make these claims "the" conclusion. Reading a philosophical text might gradually reveal an intricate abstract structure, just as hypertext fiction can gradually reveal a plot, a situation, or a set of characters even if not read in a unique linear fashion. The revealed abstract structure could take the form of one or more arguments, a network of concepts, or a conceptual landscape.

This form of structure would become difficult, however, in the case of interactive or cooperative hypertext. Multiple authors might work by argument and counter-argument focused on a set of claims, but they might not: they might work by forming and re-forming the text. They could create multiple paths and multiple structures without necessarily focusing on any single set of propositions or without revealing any one landscape. In such cases no particular propositional claims or abstract structures would remain central, yet the multiple and interacting structures would not be simply diverse from one another and could still form one work, albeit with a new kind of unity doing a new kind of work. Of course, what I have just described as possible in the case of interactive hypertext is also possible in the case of a single author.

What kind of work could such hypertexts accomplish? A text can still make a claim on you even if it does not support a particular proposition or present a particular abstract structure of argument. The text could claim your acknowledgment (for example, that this question or option is live, that this is who you are, that this is where we live, that these are connected, that there are more possibilities here than you thought, or that something you wanted to do or say is impossible), or make connections (giving "takes" on a subject, evoking atmosphere, exploring a landscape). Is a net of connections a claim? A suit to try on? A terrain to explore? Claims need not be single propositions within argumentative lines. They can be demonstrated in more ways than by argument. I can demonstrate a machine, a technique, a concept, by showing it in action. Exploration can claim territory, making us acknowledge that more lies beyond that horizon or convincing us that there is no gold in those particular hills. These acknowledgments we may report to ourselves with a proposition, but the text may not focus on stating or supporting that proposition.

It is significant that, even after centuries, dispute continues about what claims are made by the most classic of philosophy texts. The enduring significance of the works of Plato, Aristotle, Kant, and Hegel does not rest on our ability to locate their claims definitively but on the works' having opened up new territory for thought. Questions outlast the answers with which they first came, and hypertext is very good for asking questions.

We have some examples of new philosophical forms. From the last century, we have Friedrich Nietzsche's books of aphorisms and Sören Kierkegaard's multiple voices and mixed genres. Among more recent writers, Stanley Cavell's finely crafted yet digressive essays can suggest new kinds of path. The movement of his writing derives from J. L. Austin's tentative essays and from Ludwig Wittgenstein, who spoke of his own writing as criss-crossing a landscape.[11]

Nietzsche may seem to be appearing rather late in this discussion, since his works proclaimed a new mode of fragmentary, questioning philosophy, but it is too easy to draw the wrong lessons from Nietzsche. It was useful first to visit Hegel and raise issues about how one lexia might qualify another and about how concepts may depend on one another in ways that are different from standard hypertext relations. It was useful to see Derrida point to both the instability and the inevitability of form. We needed to consider the problem of intermediate forms and figures. These keep us from seeing in Nietzsche and reproducing in hypertext only an accumulation of titillating fragments.

Hypertext philosophy needs to discover ways to enact complex interactions that are neither flashy juxtapositions nor simple connections of topic and comment. The new writing might seek fluidity and reuse, rather than foundations and definitive position. It might provide paths that bring us to read a given lexia more than once. "The form of the text is rhythmic, looping on itself in patterns and layers that gradually accrete meaning, just as the passage of time and events in one's lifetime."[12]

Such forms and figures would acknowledge their own temporality. Stuart Moulthrop has spoken of "an approach to structure as fundamentally transitional or contingent." The difficulty in all this is to have the hypertext web embody something of the Socratic critical watchfulness over what and how we speak.[13]

I asked near the beginning of this essay, "What is thinking if not linear?" What can "thinking" mean if it does not mean providing beginnings, middles, and ends of the line? Perhaps we have the start of an answer in these new figures that are neither arbitrary nor in complete control. To let the local statements and areas of statement be what they are, without demanding that they be fixed in a real or ideal totality. Let the lexia be in an intermediate locality that belongs to shifting regions. Let the particular "motion" of that "identity" be, while critically acknowledging its limits and its connections, creating a discourse that enacts its responsibility for itself in new figures.

Cavell remarks about Coleridge's *Bibliographia Literaria*:

> To say that this book is composed without digression means accordingly that if it has some end, the approach to it is followed in as straightforward a path as the terrain permits. This suggests that the end is, or requires, continuous self-interruption. But then this will be a way of drawing the consequence of philosophy's self-description as a discourse bearing endless responsibility for itself. And this could be further interpreted as a matter of endless responsiveness to itself—which might look to be exactly irresponsible.[14]

Martin Heidegger entitled one of his collections of essays *Woodpaths* (*Holzwege*). The title referred, he said, to fragmentary paths found in the forest, leading nowhere, not converging, but opening up the dark woods in one another's neighborhood. That plurality of paths seems an appropriate image for the paths we may write in hypertexts, and for thought as seeking what is to be said, with neither atomistic disintegration nor final unity.

NOTES

I would like to thank Mary Hunter, Michael Joyce, and James Parakilas for their insightful comments on earlier versions of this essay. A much longer version, in hypertext, more elaborated and more digressive, is available in a set of essays on hypertext and philosophy (*Hypertext, Argument, Philosophy: Socrates in the Labyrinth* [Cambridge, Mass.: Eastgate Systems, 1994]).

1. Is this larger work structured overall as a linear argument? Jürgen Habermas would suggest that such work is structured as a conversation in which argument is always possible, and needed, but this is not the same as saying that the process is structured as a linear argument. The achievement of consensus (communal will-formation) comes through dialogue and rational argument, but the kinds of judgment it involves encompass more than argument; there are other speech acts involved, and values other than truth, values that have their certifications in other ways than argument. But in hypertext do these other values become difficult to work with since the author and voice become diffused?

2. Robert Coover, "The End of Books," *New York Times Book Review*, June 21, 1992, pp. 1, 23–25.

3. Immanuel Kant, *Critique of Pure Reason* (New York: St. Martin, 1929), B 741ff.

4. Arguments cause problems if hypertext is thought about in terms of units of factual information. For instance, consider John Slatin's statement ("Reading Hypertext: Order and Coherence in a New Medium," in *Hypertext and Literary Studies*, ed. Paul Delany and George P. Landow [Cambridge: MIT Press, 1991], 162):

> There is no set answer to the question, how big should a node be? just as there is no set answer to the question, how long is a paragraph? Like the paragraph, the hypertext node is a way of structuring attention, and its boundaries, like those of the paragraph, are somewhat arbitrary. A node may contain a single paragraph; it may contain many; it may contain something else entirely. Jeff Conklin offers criteria for guidance in determining node size. To what extent, he asks, is the information in question so tightly bound together that (a) you always want to view it together; (b) you never want to take it apart; and (c) you rarely even want to reference parts of it outside of the context of the rest. In other words, a node is an integrated and self-sufficient unit; its size will be a function of the complexity of the integration.

The cited criteria are too oriented to pieces of information that can exist on their own and be considered independently. Arguments must both be viewed as units and be taken apart, in order to see and evaluate their force.

5. G. W. F. Hegel, *Science of Logic* (New York: Humanities Press, 1969), book 1, pp. 212–17, "The employment of numerical distinctions for expressing philosophical notions."

6. Peter Whalley, "Models of Hypertext Structure and Learning," in *Designing Hypermedia for Learning*, ed. David Jonassen and Heinz Mandl (Berlin: Springer, 1990), 63–64.

7. George P. Landow, *Hypertext: The Convergence of Contemporary Critical Theory and Technology* (Baltimore: Johns Hopkins University Press, 1992), 56.

8. Derrida's multiple typography and Nelson's cut-up book format are not as similar as might appear. Derrida is out to have texts jam up against one another in a way that comments on and demonstrates the unlimited production of meaning. Nelson rightly describes his books as being in "magazine" format, a typographically jumbled collection of related short texts with a much more traditional and cooperative task to do.

9. Landow makes an important point in this regard, when he shows that it is crucial for Barthes and Derrida that texts be dividable into relatively stable, quotable, and graftable parts (*Hypertext,* 8).

10. Jay David Bolter, "The Shapes of WOE," *Writing on the Edge* 2 (Spring 1991): 91.

11. Rand J. Spiro remarks, "The metaphor [of the criss-crossed landscape] derives from Wittgenstein, who, in his preface to *Philosophical Investigations,* despaired that all of his attempts to weld his complex ideas into a conventionally unified exposition, to force his ideas into any single direction, crippled those ideas. Rather than reducing the complexity of his ideas for purposes of expositional elegance and (spurious) theoretical parsimony, he opted instead to write a different kind of book. He would treat the philosophical topics that were his subject as forming a complex landscape, and he would sketch those topics as sites within the landscape. He would then arrange these sketches of local regions of the landscape to form a kind of album. The sequences of the 'album' would represent different traversals of the (conceptual) landscape. So, in order to assure that the complex landscape would not be over-simplified, he would endeavor to criss-cross it in many directions; that is, the same sketches of specific issues (or cases) would reappear in different contexts, analyzed from different perspectives" (Rand J. Spiro, Bertram C. Bruce, William F. Brewer, eds. *Theoretical Issues in Reading Comprehension: Perspectives from Cognitive Psychology, Linguistics, Artificial Intelligence, and Education* [Hillsdale, N.J.: Lawrence Erlbaum, 1980], 170). I thank Michael Joyce for bringing this quotation to my attention.

12. Carolyn Guyer and Martha Petry, "Notes for Izme Pass Expose," *Writing on the Edge* 2 (Spring 1991): 82ff.

13. The cited phrase is from "Polymers, Paranoia, and the Rhetoric of Hypertext," *Writing on the Edge* 2 (Spring 1991): 158. Moulthrop is speaking of a possible rhetoric for open-ended "constructive" hypertext. The distinction between exploratory and constructive hypertexts was made by Michael Joyce in "Siren Shapes: Exploratory and Constructive Hypertexts," *Academic Computing*

3 (1988): 10–14, 37–42. Joyce speaks of structure that would be "a version of what [it is] becoming, a structure for what does not yet exist." Such structures would contain "an inexhaustible latency of other orders" (Moulthrop, 157). Or they might involve what Bolter calls "a new concept of structure. In place of a closed and unitary structure, they must learn to conceive of their text as a structure or possible structures. The writer must practice a kind of second-order writing, creating coherent lines for the reader to discover without closing off the possibilities prematurely or arbitrarily" (quoted by Moulthrop, 105). Moulthrop also says that "a rhetoric for constructive hypertext . . . would presumably be founded not on coherence and order but on instability and 'chaos,' an understanding of structure not as an imposition from without but as spontaneous development from within" (155, with reference to Prigogine and Stengers). However, this emphasis on emergence and novelty does not fit quite consistently with Moulthrop's parallel emphasis on structures being already active: "The structures we do see always imply structures—and unstructurings or restructurings—that are not yet apparent. Thus, in contemplating constructive hypertext we might well find ourselves in the grip of a certain 'puritan reflex of seeking other orders behind the visible, also known as paranoia' " (156; the internal quotation is from Pynchon's *Gravity's Rainbow*).

14. Stanley Cavell, *In Quest of the Ordinary: Lines of Skepticism and Romanticism* (Chicago: University of Chicago Press, 1988), 42.

The Miranda Warnings:
An Experiment in Hyperrhetoric

Gregory L. Ulmer

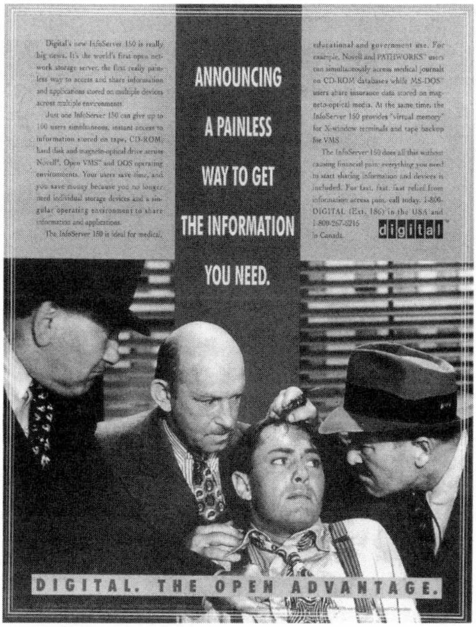

(1) (1)

Truth in the third degree. "This ain't no samba school, Mack!" from *Chronicle of Higher Education,* June 1992.

Part 1

1

I've been thinking about that ad Digital placed in the *Chronicle,* announcing a painless way to get the information I need. My plan is to send it to Landow as my essay, but he wants to know where are the other forty-nine pages? They're in the gap, the gap created in the ad between "computing" and "the third degree." It is an assignment for a class in hyperrhetoric; an article "from concentrate," like Florida orange juice. He persuaded me to fill in the gaps myself, as a sample, which is the only value it has. What does this ad know (is it typical in its way of knowing)? The method is from Richard Foreman, "How to write a play (in which i [*sic*] am really telling myself how, but if you are the right one i am telling you how, too)":

> Make a kind of beauty that isn't an ALTERNATIVE to a certain environment (beauty, adventure, romance, dream, drama all take you out of your real world and into their own in the hope you'll return refreshed, wiser, more compassionate, etc.) but rather make GAPS in the non-beautiful, or look carefully at the structure of the non-beautiful, whatever it is (and remember that structure is always a combination of the THING and the PERCEIVING of it) and see where there are small points, gaps, unarticulated or un-mapped places within it (the non-beautiful) which un-mapped places must be the very places where beauty CAN be planted.[1]

He could be describing an inventio for an electronic rhetoric—the places of invention, storing the means of argument and the commonplaces of the cultural code. Almost any ad will do for the assignment, to give me the experience of reasoning with memory rather than logic, since they all tend to be designed by the bureaucrats of surrealism, the talented copywriters of PR. The task is to fill in the gaps, constructing the two series evoked by the juxtaposed semantic fields. The assignment is to find the point of CONDUCTION (electronic inference) where the two series cross, forming a circuit.

"It is true that a language is a code which pairs phonetic and semantic representations of sentences. However, there is a gap between the semantic representations of sentences and the thoughts actually communicated by utterances. This gap is filled not by more coding, but by inference."[2] Inference does not communicate messages, it orients me in a certain direction by means of evocation. One does not try to "communicate" in hyperrhetoric (any more than one tries to sing in outlining). To the deduction and induction of the natural sciences, and the abduction of the cultural sciences, hyperrhetoric adds conduction, bringing together writing and intuition (including the "unconscious").

There is no "central processor" in hyperrhetoric, no set of rules, but a distributed memory, a memory triggered by a cue that spreads through the encyclopedia, the library, the data base (connectionism suggests that the hardware itself should be designed to support the spread of memory through an associational network). I am learning to write with this remembering, outside of my head, working a prosthesis, but it doesn't matter what the hardware is, since I have introjected hypermedia (that is the experiment).

2

There is something I want to research using this inventio, working the library like a data base, something triggered by the Digital ad—a feeling, an intuition, difficult to name. Or rather, I can name it easily enough in one domain of the popcycle (the circulation of signs through the four educational discourse institutions of our culture—discipline, school, family, entertainment). The discipline name of my feeling is "justice," or perhaps "injustice."

Grammatology produces the discipline context for the feeling in Eric Havelock's study of the invention of conceptual thinking by the Greeks. Analytical thinking in general, and philosophy in particular, emerged in the process of thinking about a specific experience—justice—within the new alphabetic apparatus. Justice was the first concept, the first practice, to pass from the oral mode of representation (dramatized as an event, performed as the actions of a hero) to a literate mode (abstract definition couched in a logical syntax).

> Hesiod weaves together the two justices of the *Iliad* and *Odyssey* to compose his own story of justice. He does it by making *dike* and *hubris,* instead of Agamemnon and Achilles and Odysseus, the subjects and objects of his discourse. Whereas it would be an easy matter for oral memory to recollect what Agamemnon or Achilles did or what happened to them . . . the names of *dike* and *hubris* and related terms were buried deep in the oral matrix. To rely on oral memory not only to recollect but to collect what happened to them would be beyond existing capacity. But place the language of the story visibly before the eye, so that the flow is arrestable and the words become fixed shapes, and the process of selection and collection can begin.[3]

What Hesiod discovered in the epics was a "field" of meaning that he called *dike.* "The Greek dike and its correlatives perform a diversity of symbolic functions, which Hesiod is endeavoring to assemble into his 'field of meaning.' The field had to be prepared for the later growth of a conceptual tree, to the definition and description of which Plato was to devote his most famous treatise" (231). Hesiod builds "his own semi-connected discourse out of disconnected bits and pieces contained in oral discourse, either some pieces in which the term *dike* happened for whatever reason to occur, or others in which incidents occurred that he felt were appropriate to connect with the word. His decision is compositional (rather than ideological), or perhaps we should say re-compositional."[4]

An important link between Hesiod and Plato is Solon, whose law code is more abstract than Hesiod's poetry, though it still treats only the specifics of legal situations. "Solon can earn the title, as far as the record goes, of the first statesman on the European scene, through his program of impartial protection for rich and poor, noble and commoner, powerful and powerless. He describes in a famous passage how he 'stood with my strong shield cast round both parties'" (Havelock, *Greek Concept of Justice*, 254–55). The unifying move by Solon—justice as due process protection for all—is completed by Plato, with the invention of conceptual thinking, moving away from dramatization of an event fully into the creation of an abstract topic, in which narrative turns into logic, persons into generalized entities or classes with properties and attributes, in which "to do" is replaced by "to be."

My assignment is to repeat Hesiod's experiment, formally and conceptually. Such is the project of grammatology as discipline, discovering and inventing the shift from a print apparatus to an electronic one (a matrix-joining technology, institutional practices, and subject formation). The experiment involves three registers, following the example of Hesiod. In the same way that alphabetic literacy made conceptual thinking possible, electronic literacy requires another means for arranging diverse particulars into classes and sets. The new arrangement has to be invented out of the old one, involving a new form and a new style of reasoning. The process of invention cannot occur in general, but, as in the passage from the oral to the alphabetic, must evolve in terms of a specific action and topic.

The feeling I want to research has something to do with justice, in a sense that remains to be discovered. Perhaps it is not so much the invention of justice itself that concerns me but the invention of philosophy, of conceptual thinking, of the form of the treatise, composed of propositions, arguments, definitions, and proofs, arranged in a logical syntax. What needs to be invented (what my experiment addresses) is not so much, or not only, a thought adequate to the continuing demands of injustice, but an electronic supplement for philosophy.

My assignment works with an analogy: electronic classification is to the concept what Hesiod's dike is to Homer's heroes. *Justice* is the name of an alphabetic category which is as inappropriate or inadequate for the operations of electronic literacy as *Achilles* was for alphabetic reasoning. In the same way that *dike* replaced *Agamemnon* in Hesiod, so must (something—I am trying to remember this name) replace *justice* in my experiment (so called because of its intuitive, prelusive, fragmentary nature). Since hyperrhetoric has yet to be invented, it may be too soon to attempt an electronic equivalent of *The Republic*.

3

There are at least three orders, three times, three "methods," involved: the order of discovery (finding the name for the electronic slot); the order of teaching (giving an assignment to a class designed to reproduce the discovery as a skill); the order of representation (this text). My ambition is to perform all three at once. Reference: *Mind Over Machine*, motivated by an attempt to understand why Stuart Dreyfus trusted his feelings about how to buy a new car, rather than an algorithm, a "formal car replacement model": "hunches and intuitions, and even systematic illusions, are the very core of expert decision-making."[5] It is the "commonsense-knowledge problem":

> For a network to be intelligent it must be able to generalize; given sufficient examples of inputs associated with one particular output, it should associate further inputs of the same type with that same output. The question arises, however: What counts as the same type? . . . (All the "continue this sequence" questions found on intelligence tests really have more than one possible answer, but most humans share a sense of what is simple and reasonable and therefore acceptable). (xiii)

The issue, the challenge to artificial intelligence, and to teaching as well, is how to simulate expertise, the way experts, "after years of experience, are able to respond intuitively to situations in a way that defies logic and surprises and awes even the experts themselves" (xiv).

The Digital ad invites me to "continue this sequence." My experiment is to appropriate the quotidian intuitive understanding evoked by the ad, to put that quotidian intuition into this prosthesis, and to write a disciplinary intuition. I can do it on paper or on screen (it is a style of reasoning capable of integrating the cognition of all three types of apparatus: oral, print, electronic). Stuart Dreyfus did not trust the decision-making algorithm proposed by computer engineers. The problem is that the intuitive judgments he fell back on are equally limited in their own way, as untrustworthy and confining as the decision trees used in expert programs. As Seymour Papert noted in his own efforts to join intuitive to formal practices in his invention of "turtle geometry," we need to go beyond the opposition between knowing how and knowing that, by learning how to "debug" our intuitions.[6]

In grammatological terms, the opposition between rule-driven symbolic processing and intuition guided by cultural experience is the oral custom described by Havelock in his study of justice. The Dreyfi want a cooperative relationship between analysis and intuition (in grammatological terms, between literacy and orality). And what makes such an "oralysis" possible is precisely the electronic dimension, whose cognitive style (dream work forming compromises between primary and secondary process thought) may be grasped by analogy with psychoanalysis. In any case, what Freud was trying to show about the psyche with all his variety of models, all the optical devices, magic slates and the like (a device able to combine multiple inputs into one system) is readily displayed in the computer.[7] "Intuition must not be confused with irrational conformity," the Dreyfi note, "the reenactment of childhood trauma, and all the other unconscious and noninferential means by which human beings come to decisions. Those all resist explanation in terms of facts and inferences" (29). They might as well have said that unconscious matters resist explanation in terms of literacy.

The Dreyfi do not deny that part of judgment involves the unconscious, but only that they cannot talk about that part. The task and opportunity of the electronic apparatus is to learn how to teach unconscious reasoning (putting students in contact with the premises of their judgments) by bringing the previous two cognitive apparatuses into a cooperative relationship. Hence this experiment in moving through the popcycle, learning how to write an intuition, that is, how to bring the different discourses of the popcycle into contact with one another for purposes of mutual support and correction. It addresses the dilemma of human culture, in which insights and prejudices are made of the same stuff.

4

The Dreyfi propose that intuition-writing be thought of as a knowing-how rather than a knowing-that, in the style of acquiring a skill rather than solving a problem, a proposal that provides a useful point of departure.

> No evidence suggests that we recognize whole situations by applying rules relating salient elements. A boxer seems to begin an attack, not by combining by rule various facts about his body position and that of his opponent, but when the whole visual scene in front of him and sensations within him trigger behavior which was successful in an earlier similar situation. We call the ability to intuitively respond to patterns without decomposing them into component features "holistic discrimination and association." (28)

To write an intuition (involving a hybrid of concept and habit formation) is not to recognize a pattern but to make one. And this pattern formation will function in electronic thinking the way concepts functioned in literacy, determining how particulars are gathered into sets for classification and categorization. I want to try to write the pattern that might evoke the thought of justice emerging in a postliterate society, but the experiment could be conducted in terms of any other concept as well.

My project to "continue the sequence" suggested by the Digital ad begins, then, by adopting a particular skill as a model or relay for my pattern. The practice I adopt is not one of those noted by the Dreyfi (riding a bicycle, driving a car, boxing), but one presented by Papert, since his idea extends the promise of the Digital ad from painless acquisition of information to painless education.

> I believe that the computer presence will enable us to so modify the learning environment outside the classrooms that much if not all the knowledge schools presently try to teach with such pain and expense and such limited success will be learned, as the child learns to talk, painless, successfully, and without organized instruction. This obviously implies that schools as we know them today will have no place in the future. (Papert, 9)

The pedagogy of *Mindstorms* is to create a connection "between personal activity and the creation of formal knowledge" (59), or, in terms of the popcycle, between the discourses of the family and of entertainment on the personal (private) side, and school and discipline on the formal (public) side. "Our strategy is to make visible even to children the fact that learning a physical skill has much in common with building a scientific theory" (96); to learn "to transfer habits of exploration from personal lives to the formal domain of scientific theory construction" (117).

One of the analogies Papert suggests for this transfer is that of dance. Learning a new dance step (working with a process—dancing—that is already familiar to most people in the culture) may be mapped onto the unfamiliar (the theoretical material). "The educator as anthropologist must work to understand which cultural materials are relevant to intellectual development. Then he or she needs to understand which trends are taking place in the culture. Meaningful intervention must take the form of working with these trends" (32). The discipline problem that concerns me is the grammatological question of electronic writing, which constitutes the "unknown" in my experiment (alluded to in the Digital ad only indirectly, or negatively). My task as educator is to find an on-going trend that may be brought into an explanatory relationship with my unknown. Papert provides a profound insight into the pedagogy, which I want to explore.

> Juggling and writing an essay seem to have little in common if one looks at the product. But the processes of learning both skills have much in common. By creating an intellectual environment in which the emphasis is on process we give

> people with different skills and interests something to talk about. By developing expressive languages for talking about process and by recasting old knowledge in these new languages we can hope to make transparent the barriers separating disciplines. In the schools math is math and history is history and juggling is outside the intellectual pale. Time will tell whether schools can adapt themselves. What is more important is understanding the recasting of knowledge into new forms (184).

Papert offers an analogy for the new school institution that is the next crucial step in the series coordinating the passage from the old paradigm of inquiry (represented in the ad as a scene from an interrogation using the method of "the third degree") to the new, whose nature is in no way indicated, other than to suggest that it is electronic and painless. The model for electronic schooling is the Brazilian samba school. "At the core of the famous carnival in Rio de Janeiro is a twelve-hour-long procession of song, dance, and street theater. One troop of players after another presents its piece. Usually the piece is a dramatization through music and dance of a historical event or folk tale" (178). Each troop represents a social club that may have thousands of members of all ages and skills, who work together as a kind of community during the year preparing for carnival. "In this book we have considered how mathematics might be learned in settings that resemble the Brazilian samba school, in settings that are real, socially cohesive, and where experts and novices are all learning" (179).

The kind of writing I want to learn, or that I am inventing—hyperrhetoric—is like dancing the samba. The methodology, rather, is to use the semantic domain of the samba as one half of a figure, whose other half must come from the other domain of the ad, in order to produce a field within which to evoke the emerging thought of justice. The sequence has started, the memory is spreading, beginning with the domain of computing, passing through the Dreyfi to Papert, to the analogy of the samba.

Hyperrhetoric, in short, is a serial form of composition, whose characteristics have been described by Gilles Deleuze: "First, the terms of each series are in perpetual relative displacement in relation to those of the other. . . . Second, this disequilibrium must itself be oriented: one of the two series—the one determined as signifying, presents an excess over the other."[8] Finally, the most important feature is the existence of a paradoxical case shared by both series without being reducible to either one.

> What are the characteristics of this paradoxical entity? It circulates without end in both series and, for this reason, assures their communication. It is a two-sided

> entity, equally present in the signifying and the signified series. It is the mirror. Thus, it is at once word and thing, name and object, sense and denotatus, expression and designation. It guarantees, therefore, the convergence of the two series which it traverses, but precisely on the condition that it makes them endlessly diverge. . . . As Lacan says, it fails to observe its place. It also fails to observe its own identity, resemblance, equilibrium, and origin. . . . They are strictly simultaneous in relation to the entity by means of which they communicate. They are simultaneous without ever being equal, since the entity has two sides, one of which is always absent from the other. . . . For that which is in excess in the case is nothing but an extremely mobile empty place; and that which is lacking in another case is a rapidly moving object, an occupant without a place, always supernumerary and displaced. (41)

My experiment takes this serial strategy as a guide for the invention of hyperrhetoric.

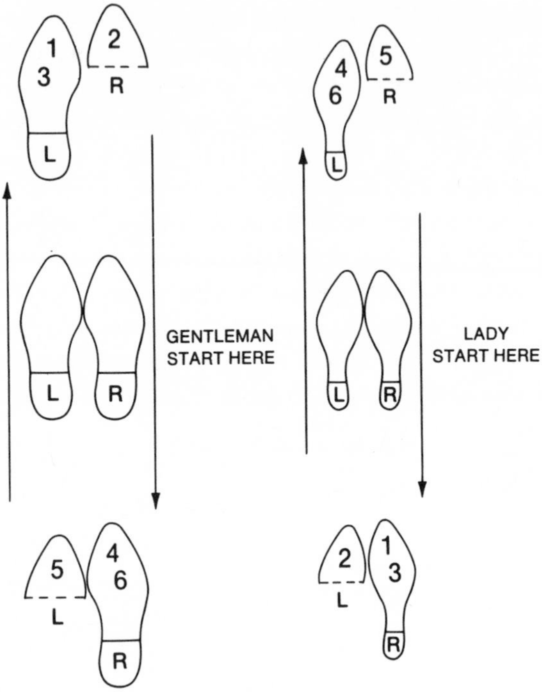

The steps of method. "Samba Basic," from *The Fred Astaire Dance Book*, ed. John Monte (New York: Simon & Schuster, 1978).

Part 2

5

How to get the information I need? I have two metaphors now, two scenarios: in the scenario of literacy, finding out something, doing research, learning the truth, is like giving somebody the third degree. In the electronic scenario, learning the truth is like dancing the samba with someone. But the latter scenario is new, untested, while the former has a history going back more than two millennia. Even if the product is different, the process of constructing the new scenario might be the same, might follow the same laws of formation as its predecessor, whose nature it might be worth reviewing.

Page duBois has written a history of the metaphor associating torture with the search for truth in the alphabetic apparatus. Her focus is the Greek term *basanos*. "It means first of all the touchstone used to test gold for purity; the Greeks extended its meaning to denote a test or trial to determine whether something or someone is real or genuine. It then comes to mean also inquiry by torture, 'the question.' "[9] The semantic field of basanos spread by metaphor from the Greek legal system into philosophy, gathering a set of practices and values: of an ordeal demonstrating fidelity, of silence under torture as a virtue (Spartan hardness), of interrogation as figurative "basanizing" ("You give this slave of mine the third degree [basanize]"—Aristophanes, *The Frogs*) (30). The migration of the term into philosophy concerns the Greek idea of truth as something hidden, buried, a secret, a secret at first associated with the slave's body, and then with a woman's body, as in the tradition of the Delphic oracle, or the associations with the earth as feminine, penetrated by the heroes' visits to the underworld.

"Although all this imagery is witty and playful, as often in Plato's texts the joke has its sinister side," duBois notes, referring to *The Sophist;* "logic and dialectic are police arts. Philosophy becomes a method of arrest and discipline; philosophical argument is a dividing, a splitting, a fracturing of the logical body, a process that resembles torture" (113). In the scenes of interrogation performed in the dialogues, the violence is displaced from the body to the abstract arguments of the adversary.

> Only relations of force and labor, the coercion through questioning to arrive at the truth, the pushing of the young philosopher to the realm of the metaphysical, the power of the master, can enable the achievement of truth, of the philosophical life. We have for centuries idealized this description of truth seeking. . . . But why should we construct our model of discovery as an allegory of force and pain? (122)

The photograph in the Digital ad, depicting a scene of the third degree, is a metonym for this allegory of truth.

6

In the same way that oral practices were carried over metaphorically into literacy (truth as ordeal), so too are certain literate practices guiding electronic development. The Turing test, for example, falls within the field of basanos. It is no wonder that Turing's intelligence test might operate within the tradition of truth as a secret, to be found out by police methods, considering his achievement as the leader of a team that cracked the code of the German Enigma machine during World War II. The Enigma machine put messages into code, using "electrical wirings to perform automatically a series of alphabetical substitutions."[10]

Turing's cryptanalysis treated the problem of decipherment as a mechanization of a detective's abductive guesses. As a process, the approach offers some lessons for the creation of a semantic field, like that constructed by Hesiod for dike. It is a lesson in how to recognize, and to construct, a pattern. Since the military messages Turing was decoding often consisted of stereotyped commands, it was possible, using intuition, to guess a specific word at its exact location in the scrambled string of letters. The goal was to discover the initial setting of the three (and later, four or more) rotors in the machine that scrambled the letters. The decipherment technique was to look for patterns of regularity in the message traffic. "Sometimes it would happen that first and fourth letters would actually be the same—or the second and the fifth. This phenomenon was, for no apparent reason, called 'a female.' Thus, supposing that *TUITUI* were indeed enciphered as *RYNFYP*, that repeated *Y* would be 'a female.' This fact would then give a small piece of information about the state of the rotors" (173).

Turing's biographer does not link the mystery of this naming to the way the metaphor of "female" was mechanized, when the work with patterns made use of perforated sheets. "These were simply tables of all the core-positions, in which instead of printing has 'a female' or 'has no female,' there would either be a hole punched, or not" (174). The procedure was to pile the tables of core positions on top of each other, "staggered in a manner corresponding to the observed relative positions of the females. A 'matching' of the pattern would then show up as a place where light passed through all the sheets." The set of perforated sheets was called a "Bombe." Which came first, the name "female" or the perforation?

As for the Turing test itself—the "Imitation Game"—its exact nature is sometimes forgotten. "If a person failed to distinguish between a man imitating a woman (via teletype) and a computer imitating a man imitating a woman, then the machine succeeded in the Imitation Game."[11] Turing "imagined a game in which an interrogator would have to decide on the basis of written replies alone which of two people in another room was a man and which a woman. The man was to deceive the interrogator, and the woman to convince the interrogator, so they would alike be making claims such as 'I am the woman, don't listen to him!'" (Hodges, 415).

In a BBC television program on the topic of intelligent machines, featuring Alan Turing, most of the questions were couched in the form of gags (like the jocular-Mandarin style of Plato's dialogues), as Turing explained in a letter to his mother. What kind of questions could be asked of the machine? "'Anything,' said Alan, 'and the questions don't really have to be questions, any more than the questions in a law court are really questions. You know the sort of thing, "I put it to you that you are only pretending to be a man," would be quite in order'" (450).

Papert and the Dreyfi recommended adopting a practical skill as the model for constructing a theory. I have to keep in mind, however, that police interrogation is itself a skill, according to the handbooks used to teach it. Thinking of the jocular tone used for "putting the question" in philosophy, I was especially intrigued by one such handbook that began by quoting Groucho Marx: "There's one way to find out if a man is honest—ask him."

> It is appropriate that this book on interview and interrogation begin with a quotation from a comedian. Comedians are perceptive individuals who can see humor and truth in people, two things that sometimes are one and the same. We, as interrogators, are attempting to be as perceptive as comedians—looking for the truth in people. In the following chapters, we are going to follow Groucho Marx's advice and ask suspects whether or not they are telling the truth. The suspects' truthfulness can be evaluated by their verbal and physical behavior as well as by their attitudes toward the interrogator and the investigation.[12]

The modern art of interrogation has been drastically affected by the heirs of Solon on the Supreme Court of the United States, during the activist period of Chief Justice Earl Warren. I am thinking of the famous Miranda decision, which, in our context, has as many implications for philosophers as for policemen.

> Simply described, Miranda could be said to be warnings to a suspect administered during a custodial interrogation. For Miranda to be applicable to an interrogation, it must meet two criteria. First, the setting must be custodial in nature. The court has defined custodial to mean that the suspect's freedom of action has been curtailed in some significant way. Second, the individual conducting the interrogation must be a law enforcement officer. Should a custody situation arise, the suspect must be advised of the following: his right to an attorney, his right against self-incrimination, and his right to remain silent. If a suspect is taken into custody by police and questioned without advising him of his Miranda rights, his responses cannot be used in evidence against him to establish his guilt. (36)

This 1966 ruling was one of the most controversial ever handed down by the Court. This notoriety may account for the fact that the ritual scene of reading a suspect his or her rights has become in recent decades one of the most common scenes in television drama. It is a formula that is to television what "wine-dark sea" is to the ancient epic. The point to be stressed about this ritual scene is that it usually shows the police delivering the warnings in the manner of the third degree, that is, with violence. A prototype for such scenes might be the one in a film called *Nails,* starring Dennis Hopper as the cop. At the mid-point of the plot, Hopper confronts a Hispanic drug dealer in a parking garage, arrests him, and proceeds to beat the man brutally, including a kick to the groin, while shouting the Miranda warnings.

This scene conveys the extraordinary anger felt in certain parts of the society over the perceived "injustice" of Miranda, seeming to protect criminals at the expense of victims. The original Miranda was an indigent Mexican, "a seriously disturbed individual with pronounced sexual fantasies," who, after two hours of questioning without benefit of counsel, confessed to abducting and raping a white teenage woman.[13] The issue was not Miranda's guilt but how that guilt had been established. Nixon used the issue in the law and order theme of his 1968 presidential campaign, and the judges he subsequently appointed to the Court put a stop to the extension of the Miranda shield to ever more categories of cases.[14]

A detail in the police handbook provides a glimpse of how the electronic apparatus is affecting the methodology of interrogation. The authors warn the trainees to avoid performing scenarios made familiar by the media, such as the "good cop/bad cop" routine. "The exposure this technique has received in television and movies and its having been used in an unprofessional manner has made it largely ineffective against suspects. Additionally, depending on the role of the hard interrogator, it may verge on intimidation and coercion, which could render a suspect's statement unusable" (Zulawski and Wicklander, 2). The handbook adds that, because of television, people expect interviewers to take notes. To be credible, therefore, one should at least have the props of writing available, unless the situation becomes accusatory, in which case such props should be hidden, so as not to remind the suspects that what is said could be used against them (28). Another handbook avoids such terms as *trickery* and *bluffing,* "because of the old mystery story concept of the detective creating a false situation which would entrap the suspect into a dramatic admission of guilt. Such a conception could cause a false impression of this practice as a mainstay of the interrogative art."[15]

It is worth noting in this context that the pilot for the *Kojak* series (which ran on CBS from 1973 to 1978) was based on one of the four cases grouped under the Miranda decision—the Wylie-Hoffert murders. In that case, a black teenager being questioned on an unrelated crime incriminated himself by confessing to the slash murders of two women in Manhattan in 1963. In the film, fictionalized as *The Marcus-*

Nelson Murders, Tele Savalas plays a hard-boiled detective who fights to keep the teenager from being wrongly convicted, thus putting the tough guy on the side of due process.

8

The constitutional question concerns the Fifth Amendment right to protection from self-incrimination. The majority opinion in the Miranda decision, authored by Chief Justice Warren, first invokes the need for protection from "torture": "From extensive factual studies undertaken in the early 1930s, including the famous Wickersham Report, it is clear that police violence and the 'third degree' flourished at that time. In a series of cases decided by this Court long after these studies, the police resorted to physical brutality—beatings, hanging, whipping—and to sustained and protracted questioning incommunicado in order to extort confessions" (Cushman, 176).

The even more important aspect of the opinion, however, extends the definition of "the third degree" to cover psychological violence, citing police handbooks as evidence of prejudicial practices.

> A valuable source of information about present police practices may be found in various police manuals and texts which document procedures employed with success in the past, and which recommend various other effective tactics. . . . The setting prescribed by the manuals and observed in practice becomes clear: To be alone with the subject is essential to prevent distraction and to deprive him of any outside support. The aura of confidence in his guilt undermines his will to resist. He merely confirms the preconceived story the police seek to have him describe. Patience and persistence, at times relentless questioning, are employed. . . . It is important to keep the subject off balance, for example, by trading on his insecurity about himself or his surroundings. The police then persuade, trick, or cajole him out of exercising his constitutional rights. (176)

The crucial point for hyperrhetoric, looking for an alternative to the third degree, in all its forms and styles, as the figure of research, is the definition of interrogation provided by the Court, to clarify the application of Miranda.

> Fourteen years after Miranda, the Court adopted a broad definition of this key word. Interrogation, the Court declared unanimously in Rhode Island v. Innis, means more than just the direct questioning of a suspect by police. It includes other "techniques of persuasion," such as staged lineups, intended to evoke statements from a suspect. Indeed, said the Court, interrogation occurs any time police use words or actions "that they should have known were reasonably likely to elicit an incriminating response" from a suspect. (Witt, 207)

In short, Miranda makes rhetoric unconstitutional, at least when it comes to interrogation.

9

The name *Alan Turing* appears in both series—on both sides of the gap articulating two ways of getting the information I need, painful and painless. Turing is a theorist of the computer, whose famous imitation game (one of the legends of computer lore) continues the tradition of the third degree. Thus, the two series set in motion by the Digital ad have already crossed, the two series embodied in two scenes, showing the performance of two skills: police interrogation and dancing the samba (posed as the possible figure for an electronic approach to inquiry).

Returning to the samba series now produces the word/thing I needed to label the set coming into formation in this experiment: "Miranda." "Miranda" is the switch word, the "paradoxical entity" conducting information in a short circuit between the two series. The method of conduction, that is, gathers heterogeneous entities, coordinating the parallel series by means of a pun, forming a "puncept."[16] Researching the vehicle of Papert's analogy, I read a book on Brazilian music that noted the important role of Carmen Miranda in introducing the samba into American popular culture.

> The 1940s saw the first export of samba, as songs like Ary Barroso's marvelous "Brazil" reached North America. Ary's tunes were featured in Walt Disney films and covered in other Hollywood productions by a playful, exotic young woman who wore colorful faced skirts, heaps of jewelry, and a veritable orchard atop her head. Her name was Carmen Miranda, and she sang catchy sambas and marchas by many great Brazilian composers in a string of American feature films. . . . For better or worse, she would symbolize Brazil to the world for decades and become a cultural icon in North America and Europe, a symbol of fun and extravagance.[17]

"Carmen Miranda" is a metonym for "samba" in the entertainment discourse of my American popcycle, which qualifies her to serve as guide to this new relationship to information, replacing the search for truth.

It is the question Plato addressed in the *Cratylus*—the problem of the motivation of meanings; the relation of the material of language and discourse to the materiality of nature and culture. Is the Miranda decision well-named? The case synthesizes four separate trials, each with its own name. The puncept is based on this tuning of discourse to culture, using these lucky finds as a point of departure for further elaboration and development. Why was *Miranda* the name attached to the "shield" protecting the ignorant, or, more significantly, the illiterate (in the cases before the court), confirming the precedent established in the first Scottsboro case? A suspect needs "the guiding hand of counsel at every step in the proceedings against him. Without it, though he be not guilty, he faces the danger of conviction because he does not know how to establish his innocence. If that be true of men of intelligence, how much more true is it of the ignorant and illiterate, or those of feeble intellect" (Witt, 205).

In the electronic apparatus, organizing an era of secondary illiteracy, personification returns to our thinking, with entertainment stars and public celebrities replacing the gods and goddesses of orality. The Miranda decision intervenes in the history of justice, shielding the illiterate from the third degree, and, by extension, shielding everyone from self-incrimination at the hands of rhetoric. That Carmen Miranda might personify this event, opening a passage between literacy and the electronic, exploits the same punning procedure that has directed the invention of justice from the beginning. "The most flagrant of all puns is the one used to indicate that retributive justice has divine status. Dike is, as it were, defended as the daughter of Zeus on the basis of her verbal derivation from him (di-ke: di-os); the pun was 'invented' by Hesiod, improved on by Aeschylus in the Seven" (Havelock, *Greek Concept of Justice*, 294). What Havelock says of Dike as goddess applies to Carmen Miranda as well: "This piece of ingenuity, however bizarre, probably indicates an awareness that she has been placed on Olympus by an act of poetic imagination which needs support."

10

Carmen Miranda's "real" name was Marie do Carmo Miranda da Cunha, and she was born near Lisbon in 1909.[18] In her infancy her parents moved to Rio de Janeiro, where she was educated in a convent. She had to take an assumed name, to hide her career as a samba singer from her family, especially from her father, "who believed entertainers were vile creatures of the lowest social status."[19] The code of her pseudonym is not very difficult to break. Her choice nonetheless evokes a further motivation, recalling an important name in the history of Latin American independence, second perhaps only to that of Simon Bolivar himself. Francisco Miranda, the Venezuelan general known as "the great precursor," was an adventurer committed to the fight for liberty against tyranny, first by serving in the war of American Independence and then in the French revolutionary army. His name is one of those inscribed on the Arc de Triomphe.[20] He was the leader of the first attempt at independence by a South American state. The rebellion failed, partly because of problems with Miranda's leadership, but also because of bad luck. Many of the towns under his control, including Caracas, "were destroyed by one of the worst earthquakes in history" (26 March 1812), which caused heavy loss of life among Miranda's troops (77). Whatever General Miranda's shortcomings might have been, no one doubted that his life was devoted to the cause of freedom.

Miranda, then, is synonymous with *samba*; or rather, it is a metaphor as well as a metonym for *samba*, in that the "meaning" of samba music is precisely "freedom." The most famous samba of all is "Aquarela do Brasil," by Ary Barroso, known internationally simply as "Brazil." It is the opening number of *The Gang's All Here* (1943), perhaps Carmen Miranda's best film, directed by Busby Berkeley.

> Brazil, Brazil
> For me, for me
> Oh! These murmuring fountains
> Where I quench my thirst
> And where the moon comes to play.

In Terry Gilliam's *Brazil* (1985) "the song represented a vision of beauty and freedom to the protagonist, trapped in a futuristic, totalitarian society" (McGowan and Pessanha, 35).

Not that it is possible or even desirable to try to translate *samba* into a concept. Indeed, its resistance to conceptuality is precisely what recommends samba as the model for a new method. "It is common for Cariocas to say, rather ironically, that everything ends up in samba. If things go wrong there's always samba to lift peoples' spirits. Samba is many things: solace, celebration, escape and abandon, plus philosophy, culture, and tradition" (28). The effects of samba are summed up in the word *saudade* ("longing or yearning for something or someone"). "It's a certain poignance, a soulfulness, coming from what Brazilians call *saudade*—a kind of bittersweet longing, which means, in a way, 'glad to be feeling.' (We have no word in English for this concept)" (Paul Winter, in McGowan and Pessanha, 9). Reflecting its origins in the oral traditions of Afro-Brazilians, samba "was an important form of expression for the Carioca lower classes in the early twentieth century. Samba became a voice for those who had been silenced by their socioeconomic status, and a source of self-affirmation in society" (32).

"Miranda" moves between the two series, two styles of memory and freedom in the Digital ad, defensive on one side (the right to silence) and affirming on the other (overcoming enforced silence).

11

To organize the series generated by the gap between the two paradigms of inquiry, I need to construct a mnemonic scene, a "secondary elaboration" of the dispersed items of information into a coherent pattern. The point of departure for this scene is the Turing test, the imitation game, with Carmen Miranda playing the part of the woman. To begin with, I memorize her look, or enter it into the data base.

> Her costume was a combination of native Bahian dress and a designer's nightmare. With bare legs and midriff, she wore sweeping half-open skirts and tons of colorful costume jewelry. She introduced the turban to the American scene, and topped it with the fruits of her native Brazil. This exaggerated Latin spectacle appeared atop five-inch platform shoes, which she claimed to have invented herself. "They come about because I like big men," the five-foot-two-inch star explained. "When I dance with big men I can't see over their shoulders. Maybe they flirt with other girl. So I tell shoemaker to build up my shoes." (Woll, 114)

As for her hats, she was discovered working in a department store where she modeled and "created" hats. Why the tropical fruit on the hats? Perhaps, Katz suggests, it was a (mocking) homage to her father, an importer and exporter running a "prosperous wholesale fruit business."

They called her "The Brazilian Bombshell," reminding me that she is the "Bombe," the "female" (the fragment of information) of the perforated sheets used to break the Enigma machine. "She differed from every movie musical star that Hollywood had yet discovered. Of her debut (singing 'Sous Samerican Why'), a critic wrote, 'Her face is too heavy to be beautiful, her figure is nothing to write home about, and she sings in a foreign language. Yet she is the biggest theatrical sensation of the year'" (115). She died suddenly of a heart attack, at 46 (in 1953), after a demanding number on a segment of the Jimmy Durante television show (Katz, 813).

The key to her ability to function as the personification of the name replacing *dike* in the electronic apparatus is her status as an archetype, a sign that has separated from the historical person of the 1940s and from the Hollywood musicals and Brazilian recordings, to live on in popular culture as a myth. "She inspired legions of Carmen imitators (actor Mickey Rooney was one of the first—in the 1941 film *Babes on Broadway*), and decades later she is still a popular 'character' for costume parties" (McGowan and Pessanha, 12–13).

This aspect of Carmen Miranda—her imitability—is what makes

her so important to the experiment. Giving her the woman's part in the imitation game complicates Turing's test considerably. The fact is that the films of the 1940s reflected the confusion of sex and gender roles in society necessitated by the circumstances of the war, with women taking over from men the jobs vacated by the need for soldiers. It has been observed that film noir (based on hard-boiled detective fiction) reflected the same confusions about gender and sexual identity that marked the musicals. There was much bitterness in the transvestite comedy of the wartime musicals, with one exception:

> Carmen Miranda became the most easily imitated musical star by men and women alike. In such films as *Down Argentine Way, Babes on Broadway,* and *Winged Victory,* both males and females attempted Miranda impressions. The Brazilian's outlandish garb made her an easy mark for her followers. . . . The men in the musicals did not react by attempting to reinforce their traditional roles. Rather, they became confused and disoriented, often turning to transvestite humor as a form of revenge. (Woll, 102)

The qualities that motivated some encyclopedias to disparagingly refer to Carmen as a "kitsch" figure also, no doubt, account for her "camp" status. Her availability for female impersonation evokes the camp sensibility associated with homosexuals. "While camp is now often a joke or pose among gays, it is not without serious value, because it originated as a Masonic gesture by which homosexuals could make themselves known to each other during periods when homosexuality was not avowable. Besides being a signal, camp was and remains the way in which homosexuals and other groups of people with double lives can find a lingua franca."[21]

Associating Carmen with drag queens also evokes their female counterpart. "Outside New York, 'dyke' and 'fag hag' have not entered journalistic vocabulary as unpejoratively as 'gay' or 'camp.' . . . Yet these strident syllables perfectly equate the type of woman whose behaviour is exaggerated to appeal, not to lovers, but to male homosexuals" (11). The punning initiated by Hesiod continues macaronically, then, extending the field of justice, of dike, to dyke (an off-rhyme, of course). The slang meaning of *fruit* in this context allows Carmen's hats to serve as a rebus for this same mnemonic extension of meaning.

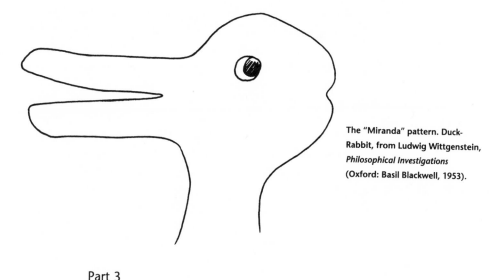

The "Miranda" pattern. Duck-Rabbit, from Ludwig Wittgenstein, *Philosophical Investigations* (Oxford: Basil Blackwell, 1953).

Part 3

12

The role of the man in my Turing test is played by Ludwig Wittgenstein. There are several reasons for this casting, not the least being that, as Turing's biographer observed, Wittgenstein's work was the closest to expressing the questions that most interested Turing. Wittgenstein, moreover, loved American hard-boiled detective fiction. "The ethos of the hard-boiled detective coincides with Wittgenstein's own: they both decry the importance of the 'science of logic,' exemplified in the one case by *Principia Mathematica* and in the other by Sherlock Holmes."[22]

These adventurer heroes were masters of using the third degree on behalf of truth, as in the case of Three-Gun Terry (a creation of Carroll John Daly), the first of many such private eyes: "My life is my own, and the opinions of others don't interest me; so don't form any, or keep them to yourself. If you want to sneer at my tactics, why go ahead; but do it behind the pages—you'll find that healthier. . . . I'm in the center of a triangle; between the crook and the police and the victim."[23] Thugs have kidnapped a woman and are going to torture her to get some information they need. Until Terry Mack intervenes.

> So I push the door very softly, and this Joe waits behind it, all smiles, I guess. Then I suddenly up with my foot and give that door a kick—a real healthy kick. That's the only way to enter a room what you got your doubts on. Bang! Crash! You could hear his head connect with that door in one heavy thud. After that there was nothing to it. I had my flash out and my gun on him, and the door closed and

locked before he knew what had happened. It was five minutes before he recovered enough to speak. (59)

Wittgenstein used phrases from pulp sleuths in his conversation and he sometimes used passages from the pulps as points of departure for his classes dealing with "sense data and private experience": "When he quoted from literature, it was not from the great philosophical works, not from the philosophical journal *Mind,* but from Street & Smith's *Detective Story Magazine*" (Monk, 355). Despite his interest in the perspective of "ordinary life," a friend said of him that "if you had committed a murder, Wittgenstein would be the best man to consult, but that for more ordinary anxieties and fears he could be dangerous" (459).

It is hard to imagine any person who could be more different from Carmen Miranda, more opposed to her sensual style or what she represents, than Ludwig Wittgenstein. He hated ornament of any kind. His rooms were furnished in the simplest possible way, lacking even books (the only visible reading material was a stack of *Detective Story* magazines) (443). His dress was always the same (a kind of uniform that someone said resembled that of a boy scout), and he declared that he didn't care what he ate, as long as it was "always the same." He inherited immense wealth but gave it all away (while Carmen, in her "gold digger" persona, stated that she knew ten English words: men men men men men and monee monee monee monee monee).

Here is the test, then, the imitation game, which at first sight appears so simple—to tell the difference, exclusively by means of teletype, between Carmen Miranda and Ludwig Wittgenstein.

13

The purpose of my experiment is not to play the imitation game straight, nor to leave the Turing test intact, but to devise a replacement for it, based on something having to do with the samba as the metaphor for an electronic relationship to information. The form for my experiment will not be a scene of interrogation but a musical comedy, to take advantage of the plot structure of musicals, organized around a romance in which the two partners in the couple-to-be begin in a state of diametrical opposition, in a dualism that is harmonized through the course of a courtship.[24] The intent of my musical is not to confirm the myth of marriage but to find a point of contact between two models of information access, represented in the characters of Wittgenstein and Miranda. She has to teach him how to samba. "The basis of the dance is a controlled springy knee action, called the 'Samba Pulse.' Integrated with this up-down movement of the legs is a swaying motion of the upper body—the 'pendulum styling.' The effect of this styling is that of a controlled rocking motion, one partner swaying back as the other sways forward in unison."[25]

The affair has a good chance of success, considering that Wittgenstein's favorite actress was Carmen Miranda (along with Betty Hutton). Another favorable factor for my purposes is that "Wittgenstein," perhaps for the same reasons as in the case of "Miranda" (an extremity of manner that lends itself to stereotyping) is starting to separate from his historical and textual place and to become available as a myth. Bruce Duffy novelized Wittgenstein's early years as a student of Russell and Moore in *The World As I Found It.*[26] Terry Eagleton, in *Saints and Scholars,* adapted the philosopher to a political fiction: "This novel is not entirely fantasy. Nikolai Bakhtin, elder brother of the celebrated Russian critic Mikhail Bakhtin, was indeed a close friend of Ludwig Wittgenstein, the foremost English-language philosopher of the century. Wittgenstein did indeed live for a while in a cottage on the west coast of Ireland, although at a later time than suggested here."[27] And now there is the film by Derek Jarman.

I need only a few scenes, such as one with Wittgenstein rushing to the cinema after one of his classes, as he often did, sitting in the front row, leaning forward, in order to cleanse himself of the disgust he felt when he "said too much." The film is *The Gang's All Here,* opening with the famous samba, "Brazil," which ends with Carmen and the other dancers teaching members of the audience how to dance. In my experiment, Carmen gets Ludwig out on the dance floor (abolishing the difference between screen and auditorium, as in Woody Allen's *The Purple Rose of Cairo*). What is at stake is not the literal dance but the figurative one, changing our cultural style of turning information into knowledge.

Carmen's chances of success with Ludwig are good, considering that he has already changed his mind once. His *Tractatus Logico-Philosophicus* is perhaps the book that marks the closure, if not the end, of the methodology of truth by interrogation in the Western tradition. "It is an important thesis of Wittgenstein that all propositions are truth-functions of elementary propositions and can be built up from them in the following way: Suppose all elementary propositions were given. Each of these could be either true or false. Therefore a proposition containing three elementary propositions p, q, r could have a truth-function T,T,F, or T,F,T, and there would be eight such possible truth-functions."[28] This study completed the line of thinking initiated when Wittgenstein first read Russell and Whitehead's *Principia,* whose method of true-or-false logic was shown to have practical application to the design of electrical circuits in Shannon's 1937 thesis, "Symbolic Analysis of Relay and Switching Circuits."[29]

The later Wittgenstein turned against his early work, the whole notion of truth tables, and the two-valued logic of the *Principia*. Is it too late for computer hardware to follow Wittgenstein's change of heart? Does the fact that electronic switches have only two choices limit the future of truth in an electronic apparatus? What made Wittgenstein change his mind? The famous anecdote about this shift could provide a second scene, in which Wittgenstein insists to his Italian friend, Piero Sraffa, "that a proposition and that which it describes must have the same logical form. To this idea, Sraffa made a Neapolitan gesture of brushing his chin with his fingertips, asking: 'What is the logical form of that?'" (Monk, 261).

> The major use of the chin flick is as a disinterest signal, and the French name for it—*la barbe*—gives the clue as to its origins. It is a symbolic beard-flick, the gesturer flipping his real or imaginary beard upwards and forwards at his companion. As a simple insult, this means "I point my masculinity at you," and is associated with verbal messages such as "buzz off, shut up, get lost, don't bother me." But it is also frequently used as a special kind of insult implying boredom. In this context it may be taking its origins from the suggestion that "you are so boring that my beard has grown long listening to you."[30]

Sraffa's gesture means, perhaps: Shut up! Invoke your philosophical Miranda rights! But Wittgenstein (no Neapolitan) sees it with his unconscious.

14

Freed from the confines of "truth" in my experiment, Wittgenstein abandons not the idea of logical space but only the restriction of that notion to the aesthetics of realism. In this musical Turing test, he revises the representation of concepts along the same lines opened up by Einstein in physics, Gertrude Stein in literature, and Picasso in painting, opening a third possible extrapolation from his work, distinct from both symbolic logic and ordinary language philosophy. This third way is anchored historically in the coincidence of dates, locating the publication of the *Tractatus* (1921) in the same decade as the invention of both the hard-boiled detective story in America ("Three-Gun Terry," in *The Black Mask*, 1923) and the samba school in Brazil (1928).

"Technically, samba has a 2/4 meter with its heaviest accent on the second beat, a stanza-and-refrain structure, and many interlocking, syncopated lines in the melody and accompaniment" (McGowan and Pessanha, 30). The first song officially registered and recorded as a samba was released in 1917, about the time Wittgenstein, despite serving at the front in the Austrian army, started a final draft of the *Tractatus*. Question: which of these texts contains the line, "The commandant of fun told me on the phone to dance with joy"?

The part of the "picture theory" serving as the point of departure for this revised methodology may be seen in this item in *Prototractatus*: "A gramophone record, the musical idea, the written notes, and the sound-waves, all stand to one another in the same internal relation of depicting that holds between language and the world. They are all constructed according to a common logical pattern."[31] Wittgenstein, in any case, possessed a fine ear for music, even if his tastes were confined to the classics (not counting American musical films). He learned to play the clarinet in his thirties, and in my musical he replaces Benny Goodman, playing and singing "Paducah" (from *The Gang's All Here*).

He was committed, in his later work, to the idea that understanding philosophy was the same sort of experience as understanding a joke, or music, in which understanding was produced without benefit of concepts. "What is required for understanding here is not the discovery of facts, nor the drawing of logically valid inferences from accepted premises—nor, still less, the construction of theories—but, rather, the right point of view (from which to 'see' the joke, to hear the expression in the music or to see your way out of the philosophical fog)" (Monk, 530).

This "getting a joke" as the aspect from which to revise conceptual thinking is in fact the common ground on which the Wittgenstein-Miranda affair will be played out. Wittgenstein was noted for lapsing into the telling of weak sorts of jokes when around women, and his favorite hard-boiled author was Norbert Davis, the distinguishing feature of whose stories was their sense of humor (he created the team of Doan and Carstairs—Doan with the look of a bumpkin but a style crossing Sam Spade and Groucho Marx, and Carstairs, an enormous Great Dane with contempt for his master). The factor mediating the shift from the third degree to the samba as the metaphor of method is Wittgenstein's sense of humor. Carmen Miranda appealed to him, no doubt, because she was herself a great comedian, with a style based partly on her malapropisms and other hashings of English and on an expressive face and a mouth with an unforgettable curling lip.

Carmen asks Ludwig to dance, then, introducing him to the gesture from which samba derives its name. "The word 'samba' appears to come from Angola, where the Kimbundu term "semba" refers to the umbigada navel-touching 'invitation to the dance' that was originally part of many African circle dances" (McGowan and Pessanha, 28). She touches his navel and says, "Eet rrrimes weeth trooth table." Ludwig (who has quite an accent of his own) is stunned, experiencing an insight at least as strong as the one triggered by the Neapolitan chin flick.

15

The key to the electronic methodology is the recognition and formation of pattern. "Curious though it sounds, proofs in pure mathematics are analogous to the explanations offered in Freudian psychoanalysis. And perhaps the clue to Wittgenstein's shift in concerns, from mathematics to psychology, lies in his finding Freud's 'patterns' more interesting than the 'pictures' of mathematicians. It would, one suspects, have been something of relief for Wittgenstein to have been able to place the events of his own life into some kind of pattern" (Monk, 442).

In my experiment, this pattern is shown, if not told, as if in a style choreographed by Busby Berkeley. "The Fox film of 1943, *The Gang's All Here,* could be seen as the pinnacle of both the sexual and the abstract urges in his work. The former reaches its apotheosis in 'The lady with the tutti-frutti hat' [featuring Carmen Miranda], where gargantuan bananas carried by chorines plunge rhythmically into strawberry centered patterns made by other girls; the latter in 'the polka dot polka' where the designs, at one point viewed through a kaleidoscope, are no longer erotic, or even human, but momentarily attain total abstraction in a rush of changing patterns akin to the abstract experimental cinema associated with figures like Len Lye and Norman McLaren."[32]

In the dance, Carmen would use the connection between her hats and her father's fruit business to help Ludwig find the pattern organizing his own life, ordering the discourses of his popcycle around the figure of the duck/rabbit. Wittgenstein told several close friends about a childhood memory "which obviously had a great significance for him. In the lavatory of his home, some plaster had fallen from the wall, and he always saw this pattern as a duck, but it frightened him; it had the appearance for him of those monsters that Bosch painted in his *Temptation of St Anthony*" (Monk, 451). Ludwig was a virtuoso whistler, able to "whistle whole movements of symphonies, his showpiece being Brahms's St Anthony Variations" (443). Wittgenstein's biographer, however, makes no comment about this link between the discourses of his subject's family and discipline.

In his last term at Cambridge, Wittgenstein came across an ambiguous figure of a duck/rabbit in Joseph Jastrow's *Fact and Fable in Psycholo-*

gy, which he introduced into his lectures on "seeing-as," or aspect-seeing, influenced by Kohler's *Gestalt Psychology* (508). "Suppose I show it to a child. It says 'It's a duck' and then suddenly 'Oh, it's a rabbit.' So it recognises it as a rabbit. . . . The experience only comes at the moment of change from duck to rabbit and back. In between, the aspect is as it were dispositional" (Wittgenstein, in Monk, 507). In my experiment, Wittgenstein comes to recognize that this sense of relief, this feeling of anxiety reduction that accompanied transforming a Bosch-like duck into anything else, such as a rabbit, was the motivating feeling guiding all of his work. He is able to go on (in my musical comedy) to generalize this insight, demonstrating how some basic feeling, or the creation of a specific emotional mood, informs the acts of judgment guiding all styles of analytical reasoning. "Of central importance to his whole later work is the idea that there is a kind of seeing that is also a kind of thinking: the seeing of connections. We see a connection in the same sense that we see an aspect, or a Gestalt" (537). That this theme is one switch point for crossing the gap between the two sides of the Digital ad is signaled and retained mnemonically in the term *miranda,* a participle of the Spanish verb *mirar* (to look, gaze, glance, look at; to respect, appreciate; notice; to think, consider, meditate). The feeling associated with this miranda, that names and motivates the new elaboration of justice in the coming electronic era, is *saudade.* What is it that replaces the concept as the basic category of thought? Not an idea (a visual shape, as in the beginnings of literacy), but a word-thing evoking a feeling. Mood.

16

My experiment is to make a pattern, which I call a miranda—that is the name for this specific pattern, and perhaps for the method of gathering diverse items into a set in electronic reasoning. My prototype miranda has a duck/rabbit pattern, a switch rhythm, an oscillating paradox having to do with silence. In one aspect, the scene gives me the famous ending of Wittgenstein's *Tractatus*:

> The correct method in philosophy would really be the following: to say nothing except what can be said, i.e. propositions of natural science. . . . My propositions serve as elucidations in the following way: anyone who understands me eventually recognizes them as nonsensical, when he has used them—as steps—to climb up beyond them. (He must, so to speak, throw away the ladder after he has climbed up it.) He must transcend these propositions, and then he will see the world aright. What we cannot speak about we must pass over in silence.[33]

In its other aspect, the scene shows the samba, identified as giving voice to all those condemned to silence by the oppressions of race and class (the samba being the discursive "other" of the proposition). Still, there is something of climbing a ladder in both styles: "If you have mastered cakewalking in place," reads one description of the man's part in samba dancing, "swinging your legs under and over each other as if you were climbing an invisible spiral staircase, and pulling up to a sharp halt after sliding sideways very fast with your feet, you are ready to time your performances."[34]

In preparing a field in which an electronically evolving thought of justice might emerge (with miranda replacing dike), I compose a scene that might show more than it is able to tell, something about the place of popular culture in the popcycle. The setting is still the same—a cinema, showing Busby Berkeley's *The Gang's All Here*. Ludwig is already in the theater. Alan Turing makes his way there as well. "Except for those with eyes to see through the stylised heterosexuality of Fred Astaire and Busby Berkeley, the times favored ever more rigid models of 'masculine' and 'feminine'" (Hodges, 127). Busby Berkeley is camp, here, serving as a Masonic sign, recalling the status of truth as a secret in the era of the third degree.

There is a kind of *mise en abyme* at work, a miniaturization linking the back-stage musical (and the courtship between opposite types) to the back-story of the cinema as institution, suggesting that the structure of the musical—and all binary dualisms, from Wittgenstein's truth tables and the team of Astaire and Rogers to the switches of computer hardware—are inadequate to the physicality or materiality of existence. The historical context is the conspiracy of silence confronting homosexuals in the era of Wittgenstein and Turing. "This stretch between the urinal and the cinema was where the male homosexual eye was focused—perhaps the same block as trodden by Ludwig Wittgenstein in 1908, such unofficial institutions lasting as long as the respectable kind. Here straggled a motley convoy of souls, and amidst them the odd independent sailing, like Alan Turing" (Hodges, 428).

This life out of bounds bore a family resemblance to that celebrated in the lyrics of many sambas, treating "the lifestyle of the malandro, a type of hustler or layabout that was a romantic bohemian ideal for some in Rio in the thirties and forties. These malandros made their living exploiting women, playing small confidence tricks, gambling. They liked to dress fine" (McGowan and Pessanha, 33). And here the two series show their common origins in the same historical moment of gender relations. Three-Gun Terry, despite temptations, would have nothing to do with women, while the early sambistas sang, "may God keep me away from today's women. They despise a man just because of the night life" (31).

17

The event in question is the suicide of Alan Turing in 1954 (not long after Carmen Miranda's fatal dance on the Jimmy Durante show). His family hired an investigator, perhaps a hard-boiled type, to check into this death. That would be the alphabetic style of cognition, trying to find the truth of it. But what does the miranda pattern show? The facts are the same in both epistemes—that Turing cooperated with the police while refusing to be blackmailed by his lover. It is an interrogation scene—the police questioning Turing, who told them everything.

What does the interrogator's manual say, by way of instructions? Why does anyone confess? "The emotional 'Achilles' heel' of the human personality is insecurity. Insecurity exists in all human personalities in varying degrees. . . . Insecurity normal to any personality is a pliant or moveable tool. Correctly adjusted and used, insecurity can produce a condition of oral catharsis that exceeds the potent intestinal effects of castor oil" (Royal and Schutt, 135). And what is the source of greatest insecurity? Perhaps it is the question noted by Jacques Lacan in his study of the psychotic Judge Schreber, the question that founds human identity: "What am I, A MAN OR A WOMAN?"[35] For his crime, in lieu of jail, Turing was given court-ordered treatment with estrogen, rendering him impotent and producing breasts (Hodges, 473–74).

I begin to understand how incredibly difficult the Turing test is. Could it be a joke, left for future designers as a switch point from the third degree into some other model of truth? No one can pass the exam with any confidence. Hodges considers the original imitation game—posed as this attempt to tell the difference between a man and a woman—to be a "red herring, and one of the few passages of the paper ["Computing Machinery and Intelligence"] that was not expressed with perfect lucidity. The whole point of this game was that a successful imitation of a woman's responses by a man would not prove anything. Gender depended on facts which were not reducible to sequences of symbols. In contrast, he wished to argue that such an imitation principle did apply to 'thinking' or 'intelligence'" (Hodges, 415).

What might appear to be a red herring in the aspect of the hard-boiled approach to truth as a secret could be the main clue in samba thinking, showing without benefit of concept a feeling of "miranda." If selfhood puts each subject to the Turing test, perhaps self, truth, and the third degree are all dissolved in samba cognition. In miranda formation, unconscious premises of judgment are included, along with intuition and analysis, to produce conductive inferences.

Hodges wondered why Turing did not remain silent when confronted by the interrogators. There were no Miranda rights to protect him from self-incrimination, from the laws against his sexuality, not in England, and not yet in America, either, in 1954. The biography cites the concluding line of the *Tractatus* as the ending for Turing's story. But it could have added a line from the Miranda warnings, authored by Earl Warren: "The warning of the right to remain silent must be accompanied by the explanation that anything said can and will be used against the individual in court. . . . This warning may serve to make the individual more acutely aware that he is faced with a phase of the adversary system—that he is not in the presence of persons acting solely in his interest" (Cushman, 178).

What about schooling as an adversary system? In the new era of "justice" becoming "miranda," perhaps every institution will have its own Miranda warnings. Meanwhile, hyperrhetoric practices writing with the rabbit/duck of the unconscious (oscillating between the right to remain silent and the need to confess) leading toward a learning that touches the dream navel, setting the symbolic order dancing.

Warning. "After Justice," from Jerry Dantzic, *The Official Miranda Manual* (New York: Amphoto, 1966).

NOTES

1. Richard Foreman, "How to Write a Play" *PAJ* 1 (1976): 84.

2. Dan Sperber and Deirdre Wilson, *Relevance: Communication and Cognition* (Cambridge: Harvard University Press, 1986), 9.

3. Eric A. Havelock, *The Greek Concept of Justice: From Its Shadow in Homer to Its Substance in Plato* (Cambridge: Harvard University Press, 1978), 228.

4. Eric A. Havelock, *The Muse Learns to Write: Reflections on Orality and Literacy from Antiquity to the Present* (New Haven: Yale University Press, 1986), 102.

5. Hubert L. Dreyfus and Stuart E. Dreyfus, *Mind Over Machine: The Power of Human Intuition and Expertise in the Era of the Computer* (New York: Free Press, 1986), 10.

6. Seymour Papert, *Mindstorms: Children, Computers, and Powerful Ideas* (New York: Basic Books, 1980), 144.

7. Matthew Hugh Erdelyi, *Psychoanalysis: Freud's Cognitive Psychology* (New York: W. H. Freeman, 1985), 124.

8. Gilles Deleuze, *The Logic of Sense*, trans. Mark Lester (New York: Columbia University Press, 1990), 40.

9. Page duBois, *Torture and Truth* (New York: Routledge, 1991), 7.

10. Andrew Hodges, *Alan Turing: The Enigma* (New York: Simon & Schuster, 1983), 166.

11. Roger C. Schank, *Explanation Patterns: Understanding Mechanically and Creatively* (Hillsdale, N.J.: Lawrence Erlbaum, 1986), 1–2.

12. David E. Zulawski and Douglas E. Wicklander, *Practical Aspects of Interview and Interrogation* (New York: Elsevier, 1992), 1.

13. Robert F. Cushman, *Cases in Civil Liberties,* 2nd ed. (Englewood Cliffs: Prentice-Hall, 1976), 177.

14. Elder Witt, *The Supreme Court and Individual Rights,* 2nd ed. (Washington, D.C.: Congressional Quarterly, 1988), 200.

15. Robert F. Royal and Steven R. Schutt, *The Gentle Art of Interviewing and Interrogation: A Professional Manual and Guide* (Englewood Cliffs: Prentice-Hall, 1976), 146.

16. Gregory L. Ulmer, "The Puncept in Grammatology," in *On Puns*, ed. Jonathan Culler (London: Basil Blackwell, 1988).

17. Chris McGowan and Ricardo Pessanha, *The Brazilian Sound: Samba, Bossa Nova, and the Popular Music of Brazil* (New York: Watson-Guptill, 1991), 12.

18. Ephraim Katz, *The Film Encyclopedia* (New York: Perigee, 1979), 813.

19. Allen L. Woll, *The Hollywood Musical Goes to War* (Chicago: Nelson-Hall, 1983), 114.

20. J. B. Trend, *Bolivar and the Independence of Spanish America* (New York: Harper and Row, 1968), 54.

21. Philip Core, *Camp: The Lie that Tells the Truth* (New York: Delilah Books, 1984), 9.

22. Ray Monk, *Ludwig Wittgenstein: The Duty of Genius* (New York: Free Press, 1990), 423.

23. Carroll John Daly, "Three-Gun Terry," in *The "Black Mask" Boys: Masters in the Hard-Boiled School of Detective Fiction,* ed. William F. Nolan (New York: Morrow, 1985), 43.

24. Rick Altman, *The American Film Musical* (Bloomington: Indiana University Press, 1987).

25. John Monte, ed. *The Fred Astaire Dance Book* (New York: Simon & Schuster, 1978), 143.

26. Bruce Duffy, *The World As I Found It* (New York: Ticknor & Fields, 1987).

27. Terry Eagleton, *Saints and Scholars* (London: Verso, 1987).

28. Frank N. Magill, ed., *Masterpieces of World Philosophy* (New York: Harper, 1961), 833.

29. Charles Eames and Ray Eames, *A Computer Perspective: Background to the Computer Age* (Cambridge: Harvard University Press, 1990), 121.

30. Desmond Morris, et al. *Gestures: Their Origins and Distribution* (New York: Stein & Day, 1979), 170.

31. Ludwig Wittgenstein, *Prototractatus,* trans. D. F. Pears and B. F. McGuinness (Ithaca: Cornell University Press, 1971), 87.

32. Bruce Babington and Peter William Evans, *Blue Skies and Silver Linings: Aspects of the Hollywood Musical* (Manchester: Manchester University Press, 1985), 54.

33. Ludwig Wittgenstein, *Tractatus Logico-Philosophicus,* trans. D. F. Pears and B. G. McGuinness (New York: Routledge, 1961), 151.

34. Alma Guillermoprieto, *Samba* (New York: Vintage, 1990), 98.

35. Jacques Lacan, *Le seminaire, livre III: Les psychoses, 1955–1956* (Paris: Seuil, 1981).

WORKS CITED

Altman, Rick. *The American Film Musical.* Bloomington: Indiana University Press, 1987.

Babington, Bruce, and Peter William Evans. *Blue Skies and Silver Linings: Aspects of the Hollywood Musical.* Manchester: Manchester University Press, 1985.

Core, Philip. *Camp: The Lie That Tells the Truth.* New York: Delilah Books, 1984.

Cushman, Robert F. *Cases in Civil Liberties.* 2nd ed. Englewood Cliffs, N.J.: Prentice-Hall, 1976.

Daly, Carroll John. "Three-Gun Terry." In *The "Black Mask" Boys: Masters in the Hard-Boiled School of Detective Fiction.* Ed. William F. Nolan. New York: Morrow, 1985.

Deleuze, Gilles. *The Logic of Sense.* Trans. Mark Lester. New York: Columbia University Press, 1990.

Dreyfus, Hubert L., and Stuart E. Dreyfus. *Mind over Machine: The Power of Human Intuition and Expertise in the Era of the Computer.* New York: Free Press, 1986.

duBois, Page. *Torture and Truth.* New York: Routledge, 1991.

Duffy, Bruce. *The World As I Found It.* New York: Ticknor & Fields, 1987.

Eagleton, Terry. *Saints and Scholars.* London: Verso, 1987.

Eames, Charles, and Ray Eames. *A Computer Perspective: Background to the Computer Age.* Cambridge: Harvard University Press, 1990.

Erdelyi, Matthew Hugh. *Psychoanalysis: Freud's Cognitive Psychology.* New York: W. H. Freeman, 1985.

Foreman, Richard. "How to Write a Play." *PAJ* 1 (1976): 84–92.

Guillermoprieto, Alma. *Samba*. New York: Vintage, 1990.

Havelock, Eric A. *The Greek Concept of Justice: From Its Shadow in Homer to Its Substance in Plato*. Cambridge: Harvard University Press, 1978.

———. *The Muse Learns to Write: Reflections on Orality and Literacy from Antiquity to the Present*. New Haven: Yale University Press, 1986.

Hodges, Andrew. *Alan Turing: The Enigma*. New York: Simon & Schuster, 1983.

Katz, Ephraim. *The Film Encyclopedia*. New York: Perigee, 1979.

Lacan, Jacques. *Le seminaire, livre III: Les psychoses, 1955–1956*. Paris: Seuil, 1981.

Magill, Frank N., ed. *Masterpieces of World Philosophy*. New York: Harper, 1961.

McGowan, Chris, and Ricardo Pessanha. *The Brazilian Sound: Samba, Bossa Nova, and the Popular Music of Brazil*. New York: Watson-Guptill, 1991.

Monk, Ray. *Ludwig Wittgenstein: The Duty of Genius*. New York: Free Press, 1990.

Monte, John, ed. *The Fred Astaire Dance Book*. New York: Simon & Schuster, 1978.

Morris, Desmond, et al. *Gestures: Their Origins and Distribution*. New York: Stein & Day, 1979.

Papert, Seymour. *Mindstorms: Children, Computers, and Powerful Ideas*. New York: Basic Books, 1980.

Royal, Robert F., and Steven R. Schutt. *The Gentle Art of Interviewing and Interrogation: A Professional Manual and Guide*. Englewood Cliffs, N.J.: Prentice-Hall, 1976.

Schank, Roger C. *Explanation Patterns: Understanding Mechanically and Creatively*. Hillsdale, N.J.: Lawrence Erlbaum, 1986.

Sperber, Dan, and Deirdre Wilson. *Relevance: Communication and Cognition*. Cambridge: Harvard University Press, 1986.

Trend, J. B. *Bolivar and the Independence of Spanish America*. New York: Harper & Row, 1968.

Ulmer, Gregory L. "The Puncept in Grammatology." In *On Pun*. Ed. Jonathan Culler. London: Basil Blackwell, 1988.

Witt, Elder. *The Supreme Court and Individual Rights*. 2nd ed. Washington, D.C.: Congressional Quarterly, 1988.

Wittgenstein, Ludwig. *Prototractatus*. Trans. D. F. Pears and B. F. McGuinness. Ithaca: Cornell University Press, 1971.

———. *Tractatus Logico-Philosophicus*. Trans. D. F. Pears and B. G. McGuinness. New York: Routledge, 1961.

Woll, Allen L. *The Hollywood Musical Goes to War*. Chicago: Nelson-Hall, 1983.

Zulawski, David E., and Douglas E. Wicklander. *Practical Aspects of Interview and Interrogation*. New York: Elsevier, 1992.

CONTRIBUTORS

Espen J. Aarseth is currently research fellow, funded by the Norwegian Research Council, in "cultural informatics" at the Humanities Computing Section at the University of Bergen. He is working on a doctoral dissertation on nonlinear literature and has published several articles in Norwegian and English on topics such as science fiction, digital culture, cyborgs, computer-generated literature, critique of "virtual reality," Internet, and postindustrial culture. He also authored the file conversion utility Paradigma for Macintosh.

J. Yellowlees Douglas is director of the Program in Professional Writing at Lehman College, City University of New York. She is the author of numerous articles on interpretive, aesthetic, and pedagogical issues involving hypertext and hypermedia, as well as the hypertext fiction "I Have Said Nothing" (Eastgate Systems, 1994) and *Print Pathways and Interactive Labyrinths: How Hypertext Narratives Affect the Act of Reading*, forthcoming from Johns Hopkins University Press.

Charles Ess is professor of philosophy and religion at Drury College. He received an EDUCOM award for his work with Intermedia, an advanced hypertext system developed at the Institute for Research in Information and Scholarship, and he helped test the Perseus multimedia project. He has received awards for outstanding teaching and has published in the areas of computer science and the history of philosophy.

Terence Harpold is completing his Ph.D. in comparative literature at the University of Pennsylvania. A working hypertext designer, he has published and lectured on the psychoanalytic interpretation of hypertextual form and visual interface design. One of his current projects is a book-length study of narrative closure in digital media.

David Kolb is the Charles A. Dana Professor of Philosophy at Bates College. His work has centered on questions about modernity and postmodernity and our changing relation to historical traditions and forms of life and writing. His books include *The Critique of Pure Modernity: Hegel, Heidegger, and After* (1986) and *Postmodern Sophistications: Philosophy, Architecture, and Tradition* (1990). Eastgate Systems has recently published his philosophical web *Socrates in the Labyrinth.*

George P. Landow, professor of English and art history at Brown University, was part of the team that developed Intermedia, an advanced hypertext system, at the Institute for Research in Information and Scholarship. His books include studies of nineteenth- and twentieth-century nonfiction, Pre-Raphaelite painting, Victorian biblical interpretation, and aesthetic theory, as well as hypertext and other forms of digital textuality. He is the author of *Hypertext: The Convergence of Contemporary Critical Theory and Technology* (1992), and his publications in electronic form include *The Dickens Web* and the *In Memoriam* web (both 1992) and *Hypertext in Hypertext* (1994).

Gunnar Liestøl, who holds the position of researcher in the Department of Media and Communication at the University of Oslo, teaches hypermedia theory and practice and studies verbal and visual narrative and their relationships to new interactive technologies. His theoretical work has led to the design and development of hypermedia systems, including the Interactive Kon-Tiki Museum. He has published on hypertext and hypermedia in several books and journals and on the Internet. He has been a visiting scholar at Stanford University and visiting lecturer at the University of Zimbabwe.

Stuart Moulthrop is associate professor in the Department of English and Publications Design at the University of Baltimore. He is the author of *Victory Garden,* a hypertext fiction, as well as numerous articles and reviews on hypermedia and on contemporary culture.

Mireille Rosello, associate professor of French at the University of Michigan, has created prototypes of multilingual hypertext versions of Roland Barthes's *Le Plaisir du Texte* in both HyperCard and Intermedia.

Martin E. Rosenberg has taught rhetoric, English literature, and critical theory at the University of Kentucky, University of Eastern Kentucky, and Texas A&M University. He has written numerous articles on the interrelations of science, technology, and literature and is the author of an educational hypertext, RHIZOME.

Gregory L. Ulmer, professor of English and media studies at the University of Florida, Gainesville, is the author of *Heuretics: The Logic of Invention* (1994), *Teletheory* (1989), and *Applied Grammatology* (1985). His current projects include a hypermedia version of his mystory, "Derrida at the Little Bighorn," and the design of an electronic monument.

ACKNOWLEDGMENTS

Once again, I owe a debt of thanks to the people at the Johns Hopkins University Press, particularly to its editor-in-chief Eric Halpern, who had the vision to see the point of a book about computer hypertext and literary theory when editors at other presses told me to take my work to a publisher of scientific texts. Glen Burris and the staff of production and design have once again created a brilliant design while Anne Whitmore has done her best to unify a passel of writings by a group of diverse and often stubborn authors.

I owe a great deal to my student research assistants over the years—Robert Arellano, Melissa Culross, Shoshana M. Landow, Ho Lin, Jane Park, W. Glasgow Phillips, David Stevenson, Gary Weissman, Gene Yu, and Marc Zbyszynski—and I would like to thank Serena Hennigan, Shelley Jackson, and Marc Zbyszynski for helping me read proof of *Hyper/Text/Theory*.

Brown University's Institute for Research in Information and Scholarship (IRIS), which shut its doors on June 30, 1994, is responsible in many ways for this volume, as it was for *Hypertext: The Convergence of Contemporary Critical Theory and Technology* and *Hypertext in Hypertext*. I have to thank William S. Shipp, Martin J. Michel, and Norman Meyrowitz, the institute's first directors, for making me part of the Intermedia project; and I must also thank Rosemarie Antoni, whose efficiency and understanding made all our work possible. Most of all I would like to thank my colleague, collaborator, and friend Paul Kahn, who headed IRIS in its last years, for his invaluable encouragement and support.

This volume is dedicated to the memory of the late James H. Coombs, who contributed so much to humanities computing at Brown and to the Intermedia system.

Library of Congress Cataloging-in-Publication Data

Hyper/text/theory / edited by George P. Landow.

p. cm.

Includes index.

ISBN 0-8018-4837-7 (alk. paper). — ISBN 0-8018-4838-5 (pbk. : alk. paper)

1. Criticism. 2. Criticism, Textual—Data processing.
3. Hypertext systems. I. Landow, George P.

PN81.H96 1995

801'.95—dc20 94-15363